FORCED MIGRATION, HUMAN RIGHTS AND SECURITY

The international protection regime for refugees and other forced migrants seems increasingly at risk as measures designed to enhance security—of borders, of people, of institutions and of national identity—encroach upon human rights. This timely edited collection responds to some of the contemporary challenges faced by the international protection regime, with a particular focus on the human rights of those displaced. The book begins by assessing the impact of anti-terrorism laws on refugee status, both at the international and domestic levels, before turning to examine the effects which offshore immigration control mechanisms and extra-territorial processing have on asylum seekers' access to territory and entitlements (both procedural and substantive). It considers the particular needs and rights of children as forced migrants, but also as children; the role of human rights law in protecting religious minorities in the context of debates about national identity; the approaches of refugee decision-makers in assessing the credibility of evidence; and the scope for an international judicial commission to provide consistent interpretative guidance on refugee law, so as to overcome (or at least diminish) the currently diverse and sometimes conflicting approaches of national courts. The last part of the book examines the status of people who benefit from 'complementary protection'—such as those who cannot be removed from a country because they face a risk of torture or cruel, inhuman or degrading treatment or punishment—and the potential for the broader concept of the 'responsibility to protect' to address gaps in the international protection regime.

Volume 17: Studies in International Law

Studies in International Law

Volume 1: Between Light and Shadow: The World Bank, the International Monetary Fund and International Human Rights Law
Mac Darrow

Volume 2: Toxics and Transnational Law: International and European Regulation of Toxic Substances as Legal Symbolism
Marc Pallemaerts

Volume 3: The Chapter VII Powers of the United Nations Security Council
Erika de Wet

Volume 4: Enforcing International Law Norms against Terrorism
Edited by Andrea Bianchi

Volume 5: The Permanent International Criminal Court
Edited by Dominic McGoldrick, Peter Rowe and Eric Donnelly

Volume 6: Regional Organisations and the Development of Collective Security
Ademola Abas

Volume 7: Islamic State Practices, International Law and the Threat from Terrorism: A Critique of the 'Clash of Civilizations' in the New World Order
Javaid Rehman

Volume 8: Predictablity and Flexibility in the Law of Maritime Delimitation
Yoshifumi Tanaka

Volume 9: Biotechnology and International Law
Edited by Francesco Francioni and Tullio Scovazzi

Volume 10: The Development of Human Rights Law by the Judges of the International Court of Justice
Shiv Bedi

Volume 11: The Environmental Accountability of the World Bank to Third Party Non-State Actors
Alix Gowlland-Gualtieri

Volume 12: Transnational Corporations and Human Rights
Edited by Olivier De Schutter

Volume 13: Biotechnologies and International Human Rights
Edited by Francesco Francioni

Volume 14: Human Security and International Law
Barbara von Tigerstrom

Volume 15: The Arms Trade and International Law
Zeray Yihdego

Volume 16: The Use of Nuclear Weapons and the Protection of the Environment during International Armed Conflict
Erik Koppe

Forced Migration, Human Rights and Security

Edited by
Jane McAdam

•HART•
PUBLISHING
OXFORD AND PORTLAND, OREGON
2008

Published in North America (US and Canada) by
Hart Publishing
c/o International Specialized Book Services
920 NE 58th Avenue, Suite 300
Portland, OR 97213-3786
USA
Tel: +1-503-287-3093 or toll-free: (1)-800-944-6190
Fax: +1 503 280 8832
E-mail: orders@isbs.com
Website: www.isbs.com

Hart Publishing, 16C Worcester Place, Oxford, OX1 2JW
Telephone: +44 (0)1865 517530 Fax: +44(0)1865 510710
E-mail: mail@hartpub.co.uk
Website: http://www.hartpub.co.uk

British Library Cataloguing in Publication Data
Data Available

ISBN: 978-1-84113-770-4

Typeset by Compuscript Ltd, Shannon
Printed and bound in Great Britain by
TJ International Ltd, Padstow, Cornwall

Contents

Editor's Note

The chapters in this book are based on papers presented at a conference held by the Faculty of Law, University of Sydney at NSW Parliament House on 22 November 2005, called 'Moving On: Forced Migration and Human Rights'. Owing to some technical obstacles, it was not possible to publish the papers until now. All authors have endeavoured to update their chapters to reflect the law as at June 2007, but any instances where this was not possible have been noted.

JM

List of Contributors

Joyce Chia (BA (Hons), LLB (Hons) (*Melb*)) is currently undertaking a PhD in the Faculty of Law at University College London, in the field of comparative immigration law. She has previously worked as a research associate at the Federal Court of Australia and at the Victorian Court of Appeal. She has also completed a Bachelor of Arts, with Honours in English (Literature) and with a minor in Political Studies.

Mary Crock (BA (Hons) LLB (Hons) PhD (*Melb*)) has worked in the area of immigration and refugee law since 1985. She is a Professor of Public Law and Associate Dean (Postgraduate Research) at the Faculty of Law, University of Sydney; chief examiner in immigration law in the various specialist accreditation programmes across Australia; and Editor of the *Immigration Review* (LexisNexis Butterworths). She has served in executive positions for the Law Council of Australia and the Refugee Council of Australia, and worked as adviser to the Australian Senate and as a consultant to the Human Rights and Equal Opportunity Commission. She is the author of many books and articles on immigration and refugee law, including *Seeking Asylum Alone: A Comparative Study,* with Jacqueline Bhabha (Sydney, Themis Press, 2007); *Seeking Asylum Alone: A Study of Australian Law, Policy and Practice regarding Unaccompanied and Separated Children* (Sydney, Themis Press, 2006), and *Future Seekers II: Refugees and Irregular Migration in Australia,* with Ben Saul and Azadeh Dastyari (Sydney, Federation Press, 2006). Professor Crock teaches migration law, refugee law and related subjects for both the undergraduate and postgraduate law programmes at the University of Sydney. She has held a number of research grants, including an Australian Research Council Discovery Grant on 'The Impact of Migrants on Public Law in Australia: An Historical and Cultural Study', and an Australian Research Council Linkage Grant on 'Seeking Asylum Alone: The Treatment of Separated and Trafficked Children in Need of Refugee Protection in Australia'.

Erika Feller is the Assistant High Commissioner for Protection, one of the four top management positions with the United Nations High Commissioner for Refugees ('UNHCR'). Her responsibilities include oversight of age, gender and diversity mainstreaming and accountability in UNHCR programs. She is an honours law graduate, with an additional degree in the humanities (specialising in psychology). Her professional career has had a predominantly international law focus, including 14 years and three international postings with the Australian Diplomatic Service, followed by 20 years of progressively more senior appointments with the UN, mainly in the area of international human rights and refugee law. Ms Feller has served for UNHCR in Geneva, but also as the Representative in Malaysia, Singapore and Brunei. Concurrently with this position, she was appointed Regional Co-ordinator for Status Determination under the Comprehensive Plan of Action to resolve the Indo-Chinese refugee problem. Ms Feller was the initiator and manager of the 2001–02 Global Consultations on International Protection, which generated the Agenda for Protection, the internationally endorsed global 'road map' on protection policy for the years ahead. She has run refugee camps and undertaken protection oversight missions to a large majority of the major refugee emergencies of recent years, such as in West Africa, Darfur, Chad, the Caucusus, the Balkans, Colombia and Timor. On a number of occasions she has been UNHCR's chief negotiator of protection agreements with governments, as well as multilateral arrangements with agency partners. Internally, she has served on key management boards and has been responsible for initiatives that have brought significant changes to how UNHCR fulfils its protection responsibilities. She is an academically acknowledged authority on refugee law, has published widely in journals, and is a co-Editor of *Refugee Protection in International Law: UNHCR's Global Consultations on International Protection*, with Volker Türk and Frances Nicholson (Cambridge, Cambridge University Press, 2003).

Arthur Glass (BA, LLB, PhD (*Sydney*)) is an Associate Professor and the Co-ordinator of Postgraduate Education in the Faculty of Law at the University of New South Wales in Sydney. He teaches and publishes in the areas of legal theory, constitutional law and immigration law. He is a part-time member of a number of tribunals, including the Migration Review Tribunal, and is an Editor of *Australian Immigration Law*.

Guy S Goodwin-Gill (MA, DPhil (*Oxon*)) is a Senior Research Fellow of All Souls College and Professor of International Refugee Law at the University of Oxford. He was formerly Professor of Asylum Law at the University of Amsterdam, and served as a Legal Adviser in the Office of the United Nations High Commissioner for Refugees ('UNHCR') in various countries from 1976–88. Since 1997, he has been President of the Refugee Legal Centre (a UK non-governmental organisation). He is the Founding Editor of the *International Journal of Refugee Law* (Oxford University Press) and was Editor-in-Chief from 1989–2001. Professor Goodwin-Gill has written extensively on refugees, migration, elections and child soldiers. Recent publications include *The Refugee in International Law*, 3rd edn, with Jane McAdam (Oxford, Oxford University Press, 2007); *Free and Fair Elections*, 2nd edn (Geneva, Inter-Parliamentary Union, 2006); *Basic Documents on Human Rights*, 5th edn with Ian Brownlie (Oxford, Oxford

University Press, 2006); 'Migrant Rights and "Managed Migration"', in V Chetail (ed), *Mondialisation, migration et droits de l'homme: le droit international en question/Globalization, Migration and Human Rights: International Law under Review* (vol 2, Brussels, Bruylant, 2007); 'State Responsibility and the "Good Faith" Obligation in International Law', in M Fitzmaurice and D Sarooshi (eds), *Issues of State Responsibility before International Judicial Institutions* (Oxford, Hart Publishing, 2004); and 'Refugees and Responsibility in the Twenty-First Century: More Lessons from the South Pacific' (2003) 12 *Pacific Rim Law and Policy Journal* 23. Professor Goodwin-Gill is a barrister and practises from Blackstone Chambers in London. He has represented UNHCR on a number of occasions, including in the House of Lords in *R (European Roma Rights Centre and Others) v Immigration Officer at Prague Airport* [2004] UKHL 55, [2005] 2 AC 1, and in the Court of Appeal in *R (on the Application of Al Rawi and Others) v Secretary of State for Foreign and Commonwealth Affairs* [2006] EWCA Civ 1279.

Rodger Haines QC is a lecturer in Immigration and Refugee Law at the Faculty of Law, University of Auckland, and has co-taught papers in Comparative Asylum Law with Professor James C Hathaway at the University of Michigan Law School, Ann Arbor. He is also the Deputy Chairperson of the New Zealand Refugee Status Appeals Authority, to which he was appointed when it was formed in 1991, and has written many of the Authority's principal decisions. Mr Haines, who earned his Bachelor of Arts and Law degrees at the University of Auckland, has been practising refugee law since 1983 and was appointed Queen's Counsel in May 1999. He also practises in the areas of administrative, immigration, citizenship, customs and extradition law. He has presented many papers at conferences around the world, and participated in the first, second and third colloquia on Challenges in International Law, convened by the Programme in Refugee and Asylum Law, University of Michigan Law School (on the internal protection alternative, causation, and well-founded fear respectively). He is the author of the paper 'Gender-Related Persecution', commissioned by the United Nations High Commissioner for Refugees as part of the Global Consultations on International Protection in the lead up to the 50th anniversary of the 1951 Convention relating to the Status of Refugees. Mr Haines publishes a web database on New Zealand refugee law known as *New Zealand Refugee Law (RefNZ)*, which contains a wealth of information on New Zealand refugee jurisprudence.

Susan Kneebone (PhD (*Monash*), DipEd (*Melb*), MA (*Hong Kong*), LLB (*Adelaide*)) is a Professor at the Faculty of Law, Monash University Clayton and a Deputy Director of the Castan Centre for Human Rights Law. She teaches Forced Migration and Human Rights, International Refugee Law, and Citizenship and Migration Law. Professor Kneebone has twice been a

Senior Visiting Research Fellow at the Refugee Studies Centre in Oxford, and has also been a Visiting Scholar at the Centre for International Studies at the University of Montreal. She has published widely on refugee law and has also made submissions to the Australian Senate and other inquiries into associated issues. Professor Kneebone is the editor of *The Refugees Convention 50 Years On: Globalisation and International Law* (Aldershot, Ashgate, 2003), and *New Regionalism and Asylum Seekers: Challenges Ahead*, with F Rawlings-Sanaei (Oxford/New York, Berghahn Books, 2007). She currently holds an Australian Research Council Discovery Grant on 'The Asylum Seeker in the Legal System: A Comparative and Theoretical Study', and an Australian Research Council Linkage Grant on 'Australia's Response to Trafficking in Women: Towards a Model for Regulation of Forced Migration in the Asia-Pacific Region'.

Penelope Mathew (BA, LLB (*Melb*), LLM, JSD (*Columbia*)) teaches International Law, International Law of Human Rights, and Feminist and Critical Legal Theory in the Faculty of Law at the Australian National University. She has been the assistant Director of Teaching and Learning since 2003. Since July 2006, Dr Mathew has been on leave from the ANU in order to work as the Human Rights Legal and Policy Adviser to the Australian Capital Territory's Human Rights Commission. Prior to her appointment at the ANU, Dr Mathew taught law at the University of Melbourne Law School (1990–2000). While at the University of Melbourne, Dr Mathew served for several years as the Law School's liaison officer for indigenous Australian law students. Dr Mathew's research interests are in international law, human rights law and refugee law, and she has published widely in the areas of refugee law and international human rights law, including as an author of *International Law: Cases and Materials*, with Don Anton and Wayne Morgan (Melbourne, Oxford University Press, 2005). Dr Mathew has worked with and for refugees in many capacities, including with non-government organisations such as the Refugee Advice and Casework Service, the Jesuit Refugee Service and the Lawyers' Committee for Human Rights as an academic consultant, researcher and/or caseworker. She has conducted training sessions for Australian refugee status decision-makers and was one of the academic members of the advanced refugee law workshop organised by the International Association of Refugee Law Judges in Auckland, New Zealand, in 2002. She has also provided academic opinions to lawyers working on refugee cases before Australian courts and to the United Nations High Commissioner for Refugees ('UNHCR') concerning the Australian legislation underpinning the 'Pacific Solution', and she gave evidence to the Australian Senate's Legal and Constitutional Committee concerning the Migration Amendment (Designated Unauthorised Arrivals) Bill 2006. Dr Mathew participated in the third expert panel on refugee law organised by UNHCR as part of the Global Consultations on International Protection during 2001. She is a member of the Editorial Board of the *Australian Yearbook of International Law.*

Jane McAdam (BA (Hons), LLB (Hons) (*Sydney*), DPhil (*Oxon*)) is a Senior Lecturer in the Faculty of Law at the University of New South Wales in Sydney. She is also the Director of International Law Programs, the Director of International Moots, and the Director of the International Law project on 'Climate Change "Refugees"' at the Gilbert + Tobin Centre for Public Law. She previously taught at the University of Sydney and at Lincoln College, University of Oxford. Her books include *Complementary Protection in International Refugee Law* (Oxford, Oxford University Press, 2007) and *The Refugee in International Law*, 3rd edn, with Guy S Goodwin-Gill (Oxford, Oxford University Press, 2007). Dr McAdam is the Associate Rapporteur of the Convention Refugee Status and Subsidiary Protection Working Party for the International Association of Refugee Law Judges; a Member of the Executive Committee of the International Law Association (Australian Branch); and Vice-President of the Management Committee of the Refugee Advice and Casework Service in Sydney. She has worked on a variety of projects with the United Nations High Commissioner for Refugees, the European Union, the Czech–Helsinki Committee, Amnesty International, the Refugee Council of Australia, and the Refugee Studies Centre at the University of Oxford (for whom she still tutors), and has given evidence before Australian Senate Committees on refugee-related matters. Dr McAdam is on the Editorial Board of the *Australian International Law Journal*, is the former General Editor of the *Oxford University Commonwealth Law Journal*, and is a former member of the Editorial Board of the *Sydney Law Review*. She teaches a range of postgraduate and undergraduate subjects in the areas of public international law and forced migration.

Justice Anthony M North was educated at Melbourne University (BA, LLB (Hons)) and the University of London (LLM). He joined the Victorian Bar in 1976 and was appointed a Queen's Counsel in 1989. In 1995, he was appointed a Justice of the Federal Court of Australia. In 1998, His Honour was the first instance judge in *Maritime Union of Australia v Patrick Stevedores No 1 Pty Ltd* (1998) 77 FCR 456, which was the most publicised labour dispute in recent Australian history and involved the mass sacking of workers on the wharves. In 2001, His Honour determined the most celebrated recent refugee law case in Australia. He upheld a claim for habeas corpus in favour of 400 asylum seekers held on board the *MV Tampa*. His Honour has a special interest in refugee law, and has served as President of the International Association of Refugee Law Judges since 2005.

Dr Ben Saul (BA (Hons), LLB (Hons) (*Sydney*), DPhil (*Oxon*)) is Director of the Sydney Centre for International Law, Co-ordinator of the Master of International Law Program, a Senior Lecturer and a barrister (including in the International Criminal Tribunal for the Former Yugoslavia). He specialises in public international law, particularly anti-terrorism law, humanitarian law, international criminal law and human rights law. Dr Saul has published widely in international law journals and his recent book, *Defining Terrorism in International Law* (Oxford, Oxford University Press, 2006), is the first scholarly work on the subject. He has taught law at the University of New South Wales, the University of Oxford and in Cambodia, and is Editor-in-Chief of the *Australian International Law Journal*. Dr Saul is a member of the International Law Association's International Committee for the Compensation of Victims of War and the management committees of the International Law Association (Australian Branch), the Refugee Advice and Casework Service, Australian Lawyers for Human Rights, and Sydney PEN. Internationally, he has been a legal expert for the United Nations Committee on the Inalienable Rights of the Palestinian People, and has monitored election violence in Sri Lanka for the International Commission of Jurists, assisted a member of the UN Human Rights Committee in Geneva and conducted field research on internal displacement in Sudan. He has been heavily involved in public interest litigation, including on challenges to the Israeli security barrier in the Occupied Territories, HIV/AIDS drug pricing in South Africa, mass human rights violations in Peru, the expansion of immigration detention in Britain, the treatment of Guantanamo Bay detainee David Hicks, war crimes against journalists in East Timor (the Balibo inquest), and the trial of the 'Pine Gap Four'.

Savitri Taylor (BCom, LLB (Hons) (*Melb*), PhD (*Melb*)) is a Senior Lecturer in the Law School at La Trobe University in Melbourne. Her primary areas of research interest are international human rights and refugee law and Australian immigration law and policy. Her work has been published in Australian and international journals across a range of disciplines, including law, international relations and social policy. Recent publications include 'From Border Control to Migration Management: The Case for a Paradigm Change in the Western Response to Transborder Population Movement' in C Jones-Finer (ed), *Migration, Immigration and Social Policy* (Oxford, Blackwell Publishing, 2006); 'Australia and Stateless Palestinians' (2006) 23 *Refuge* 106; 'Protection Elsewhere/Nowhere' (2006) 18 *International Journal of Refugee Law* 283; and 'Immigration Detention Reforms: A Small Gain in Human Rights' (2006) 13 *Agenda* 49. She is currently working on a research project funded by an Australian Research Council Linkage Grant, entitled 'The Impact on the Human Rights of Asylum Seekers and Host Communities of Australia's Border Control Co-operation with Indonesia and Papua New Guinea'. Dr Taylor is a member of the Management Committee of the Refugee and Immigration Legal Centre Inc.

1

Forced Migration: Refugees, Rights and Security

GUY S GOODWIN-GILL

I. REFUGEES AND SECURITY

ON 14 SEPTEMBER 2005, the United Nations Security Council adopted one of its now frequent resolutions on terrorism.[1] Once again, it strongly condemned all such acts, whatever their motivation, and, in language promoted by the then British Prime Minister, Mr Blair, it equally condemned incitement and repudiated what it called the 'justification' or 'glorification' of terrorist acts.[2] Closer examination, however, reveals a somewhat more nuanced picture.

In the operative paragraphs, the Security Council calls on all States to adopt the measures necessary and appropriate to prohibit and prevent incitement to commit terrorist acts, to co-operate with a view to strengthening the security of international borders and preventing those guilty of incitement from entering their territory, and to 'deny safe haven' to anyone with respect to whom there is 'credible and relevant information giving serious reasons for considering that they have been guilty of such conduct'. These exact words are relevant, because they recall the terms of Article 1F of the 1951 Convention relating to the Status of

[1] United Nations Security Council ('UNSC') Res 1624 (14 September 2005).

[2] Shortly after the adoption of the above Security Council Resolution, further legislation was enacted in the United Kingdom. The Terrorism Act 2006 (UK) provides, under the rubric of 'encouragement of terrorism', that a person commits an offence if he or she makes 'statements that are likely to be understood by members of the public as indirectly encouraging the commission or preparation of acts of terrorism'. Such statements include every statement which: '(a) glorifies the commission or preparation (whether in the past, in the future or generally) of such acts or offences; and (b) is a statement from which those members of the public could reasonably be expected to infer that what is being glorified is being glorified as conduct that should be emulated by them in existing circumstances': s 1(3).

Refugees[3]—the so-called exclusion provisions—but also because of the particular challenge which these words pose to traditional assumptions about due process and its content.

Significantly, however, and in terms which many governments tend not to mention, the Security Council also insists that States' measures to combat terrorism should be 'in accordance with their obligations under international law', and that *any* such measures should comply with *all* their obligations, in particular under international human rights law, refugee law and humanitarian law. In this, the Security Council continues a tradition going back to 1999,[4] and in which it has followed the lead established earlier by the General Assembly.[5]

Equally, however, both the Security Council and the General Assembly have maintained a worrying and not clearly explicable interest in refugees and asylum seekers as, apparently, likely or suspected terrorists.[6] It is almost a truism that the terrorist, any more than the criminal, will not usually seek admission to a country by going through the detailed examination, photographing, finger-printing and other verification procedures which are now a regular part of the asylum process; it is also the case that recognised refugees have rarely, if ever, been found among those guilty of terrorism or incitement.

Such inconvenient facts are commonly ignored by legislative zealots, for whom rights and security tend to have only one, self-regarding dimension. In a forced migration context, however, the lawful interests of both refugees and States are at issue; the art lies not in balancing one against the other, so much as ensuring that the *common* goal of protection is guaranteed.

In what follows, I am talking about 'security' in the standard dictionary sense, to mean 'being protected from or not exposed to danger', and 'the safety or safeguarding of (the interests of) a state'.[7] The concept is

[3] Convention relating to the Status of Refugees (adopted 28 July 1951, entered into force 22 April 1954) 189 UNTS 137. These and other human rights instruments cited below are collected in I Brownlie and GS Goodwin-Gill, *Basic Documents on Human Rights*, 5th edn (Oxford, Oxford University Press, 2006). The text of the 1951 Convention can also be found in GS Goodwin-Gill and J McAdam, *The Refugee in International Law*, 3rd edn (Oxford, Oxford University Press, 2007) 569, and on the companion website <http://www.oup.com/uk/refugeelaw>.

[4] In the Preamble to UNSC Res 1269 (19 October 1999), the Security Council emphasised the necessity for effective international co-operation on the basis of the principles of the UN Charter, international law, and respect for international humanitarian law and human rights.

[5] Already in 1996, the General Assembly had stressed 'the importance of full compliance by States with their obligations' under the 1951 Convention/1967 Protocol, including the principle of *non-refoulement*: see Declaration to Supplement the 1994 Declaration on Measures to Eliminate International Terrorism, annexed to United Nations General Assembly ('UNGA') Res 51/210, 'Measures to Eliminate International Terrorism' (17 December 1996) Preamble and para 3.

[6] On asylum and refugee status, see the 1994 Declaration on Measures to Eliminate International Terrorism, para 5(f), annexed to UNGA Res 49/60 (9 December 1994); UNSC Res 1269 (19 October 1999) para 4; and further below.

[7] *Oxford English Dictionary*, 2nd edn (Oxford, Oxford University Press, 1989).

sufficiently broad to cover not just the territorial, military or political interests of the State, but also the conditions of 'human security', including the protection of human rights. Terrorism threatens both individual and State security, and I use 'terrorism' here to include such threats,[8] but not to exclude other senses of a threat to security.

II. REFUGEES, PROTECTION AND SECURITY

I begin with the premise that the refugee is entitled to protection, and specifically to the benefit of the principle of *non-refoulement*; he or she is also, of course, entitled to the protection of his or her human rights, irrespective of status or recognition, and to *security*, considered as a shorthand description of the human right to life, liberty and security of the person. The State, as a sovereign entity, also has rights as a subject of international law. It has a right to political independence and territorial integrity; the right to ensure the security of its population; and the right, within the limits of international law, to regulate its domestic affairs, including the admission to its territory of non-citizens.

The refugee who arrives in search of asylum is not obviously a threat to security, absent particular circumstances, but in drafting the various treaties covering the field, States have never been blind to the need to protect essential interests, whether generally, in relation to human rights, or specifically, in relation to the refugee or asylum seeker. For example, when the General Assembly adopted the Universal Declaration of Human Rights ('UDHR') in 1948,[9] States recognised that the exercise of rights can only be considered in context and with due regard to the rights of others and of the community.[10] They were sensitive also to the potential dangers facing a State or system of government committed to the protection of human rights, agreeing in Article 30 that

> [n]othing in this Declaration may be interpreted as implying for any State, group or person any right to engage in any activity or to perform any act aimed at the destruction of any of the rights and freedoms set forth herein.

[8] For a thorough evaluation of the definitional challenges, see B Saul, *Defining Terrorism in International Law* (Oxford, Oxford University Press, 2006).

[9] Universal Declaration of Human Rights (adopted 10 December 1948) UNGA Res 217A (III).

[10] See Art 29: '1. Everyone has duties to the community in which alone the free and full development of his personality is possible. 2. In the exercise of his rights and freedoms, everyone shall be subject only to such limitations as are determined by law solely for the purpose of securing due recognition and respect for the rights and freedoms of others and of meeting the just requirements of morality, public order and the general welfare in a democratic society. 3. These rights and freedoms may in no case be exercised contrary to the purposes and principles of the United Nations'.

And when it came to the right to seek and to enjoy asylum, Article 14(2) provided expressly that it

> may not be invoked in the case of prosecutions genuinely arising from non-political crimes or from acts contrary to the purposes and principles of the United Nations.

Just two years later, States drafting the European Convention on Human Rights ('ECHR') also included general limitations on certain fundamental liberties (respect for private and family life, freedom of thought, conscience and religion, freedom of expression, and freedom of assembly and association: Articles 8–11).[11] They likewise endorsed a mechanism of derogation in time of emergency (Article 15), but within limitations, subject to procedural requirements, and ultimately under the supervisory jurisdiction of the European Court of Human Rights. In addition, following the lead of the UDHR, the ECHR prohibits abuse of rights (any activity or ... act aimed at the destruction of any of the rights and freedoms ... or at their limitation to a greater extent than is provided for: see Article 17; also Article 18).

In the refugee field, the final terms of the 1951 Convention equally reflect States' concern to ensure that the protection of refugees should not compromise essential security interests. Article 1, which defines a refugee, expressly excludes any person with respect to whom there are serious grounds for considering that he or she has committed a war crime, a serious non-political crime, or acts contrary to the purposes and principles of the United Nations (Article 1F). Moreover, while the 1950 Ad hoc Committee on Statelessness and Related Problems, which prepared the draft text, had initially proposed that no exceptions whatsoever should be permitted to the fundamental principle of *non-refoulement*, a year later, States were of a different view. Article 33 now provides that the benefit of *non-refoulement* (the prohibition of return of a refugee to territories where he or she may be persecuted) may not

> be claimed by a refugee whom there are reasonable grounds for regarding as a danger to the security of the country in which he is, or who, having been convicted by a final judgment of a particularly serious crime, constitutes a danger to the community of that country (Article 33(2)).

Apart from the potentially dangerous individual, States have also long been apprehensive that large numbers of refugees might pose a threat to security, for example, because of their national or other characteristics. At the Conference of Plenipotentiaries in 1951, a number of States suggested that such an event might qualify their obligation of *non-refoulement*, at

[11] Convention for the Protection of Human Rights and Fundamental Freedoms (European Convention on Human Rights, as amended) (4 November 1950) ETS No 5.

least if there were no organised and effective international support and assistance measures in place.[12] In recent years, another perspective on mass movements in search of asylum has emerged, and the Security Council has interpreted large-scale refugee and internal displacements as juridical facts relevant to the exercise of its powers under Chapter VII of the UN Charter, that is, as likely to disturb international peace and security.[13]

Developments here once seemed likely to benefit the refugee—finally *political* steps might be taken to deal with the causes of displacement, for example, by way of mediating conflict, peace-making, and so forth; while *institutional* measures would be initiated to ensure prompt action by UN agencies to deal with outflows.[14] The experience of Bosnia and Kosovo, however, shows that much remains to be done, before the *prevention* of flight can be effectively combined with a *solution* for root causes.

What was not anticipated in the brave new post-Cold War world of displacement, was that the individual refugee would become the focus for a different type of attention, linking him or her so determinedly to the threat of terrorism. So, while the Security Council's October 1999 general resolution on international terrorism sets out its unequivocal condemnation of all terrorist acts, whatever their motivation,[15] it also calls on States to take 'appropriate steps' to deny safe haven to those who plan, finance or commit terrorist acts, and to

> take appropriate measures, in conformity with the relevant provisions of national and international law, including international standards of human rights, before granting refugee status, for the purpose of ensuring that the asylum-seeker has not participated in terrorist acts ....

[12] For discussion at the 1951 Conference of Plenipotentiaries, see UN Doc A/CONF.2/SR.16, 6, 11; A/CONF.2/SR.35, 21; and for comment, see Goodwin-Gill and McAdam (n 3 above) 206–32.

[13] Under Art 24 of the UN Charter, Member States confer on the Security Council 'primary responsibility for the maintenance of international peace and security', and agree that in carrying out its duties under this responsibility the Security Council acts on their behalf. In fulfilling its duties, the Security Council in turn 'shall act in accordance with the Purposes and Principles of the United Nations', and Member States correspondingly 'agree to accept and carry out the decisions of the Security Council in accordance with the ... Charter' (Art 25). Art 39 provides that the Security Council shall determine the existence of any threat to the peace, breach of the peace, or act of aggression and shall make recommendations, or decide what measures shall be taken, including the use of force, to maintain or restore international peace and security. Chapter VII of the Charter effectively confers a considerable, and double, discretionary competence on the Security Council, first, to determine whether there exists a threat to international peace and security (thereby establishing its jurisdiction to act), and thereafter to decide what shall be done about it, even to the point of authorising the use or threat of force.

[14] For examples of (mostly) Chapter VII references to displacement as a relevant factor in the assessment of threats to international peace and security, see UNSC Res 688 (5 April 1991) (Iraq); UNSC Res 841 (16 June 1993) (Haiti); UNSC Res 1247 (18 June 1999) (Bosnia and Herzegovina); UNSC Res 1199 (23 September 1998) and UNSC Res 1239 (14 May 1999) (Kosovo).

[15] UNSC Res 1269 (19 October 1999).

Two years later and following the events of 11 September 2001, the Security Council, now acting under Chapter VII of the Charter, unanimously adopted a comprehensive agenda for 'all States' in Resolution 1373.[16] To a significant extent, the language of this agenda is not exhortatory, but mandatory: the Security Council decides that 'all States *shall*' do what is required to achieve the identified ends.[17] In other matters, some margin of appreciation is allowed, and the Security Council simply *calls* upon States to take 'appropriate measures' to ensure, for example, that asylum seekers have not 'planned, facilitated or participated in ... terrorist acts', to 'ensure ... that refugee status is not abused by the perpetrators, organizers or facilitators of terrorist acts', and 'that claims of political motivation are not recognized as grounds for refusing requests for the extradition of alleged terrorists'.[18] Resolution 1373 further *declares* that

> Acts, methods and practices of terrorism are *contrary to the purposes and principles of the United Nations* and that knowingly financing, planning and inciting terrorist acts are *also contrary to the purposes and principles of the United Nations* (emphasis added).[19]

However, the position here adopted on the international protection of refugees is problematic. The measures which States are now required to take and the Security Council's executive pronouncement on the meaning of terms (specifically, what is contrary to the purposes and principles of the United Nations) will clearly have an impact on the substantive content of international protection, and also on the procedural entitlements hitherto recognised as essential to a fair regime and the effective implementation of international obligations. In short, those aspects of the rule of law that require procedural standards of justice and the separation of executive and judicial functions are at risk.

III. REFUGEES AND NATIONAL SECURITY

The manner in which certain States have taken up the Security Council's call confirms these reservations and shows that the requirements of international law are not always adequately implemented at the local level, and that the proclaimed interests of governments in the treatment of refugees and asylum seekers can and often do diverge, objectively speaking, from the interests of States. Indeed, it is arguable that the tenor of the Security Council's approach to refugees and asylum seekers has served to

[16] UNSC Res 1373 (28 September 2001).
[17] *Ibid*, paras 1, 2.
[18] *Ibid*, paras 3(f) and (g).
[19] *Ibid*, para 5; see also UNSC Res 1377 (12 November 2001).

compound national measures which already seriously compromise their security, and impact negatively on the international regime of refugee protection.

In this sense, the already restrictive, hostile and generally repressive measures which States were already taking towards refugees and asylum seekers—such as mandatory detention, denial of support, denial of access to procedures, to legal advice and representation and to appeals, and government-to-government agreements on removals—have been given spurious justification by the terrorism agenda. For some States, (or rather, for some governments), that has been the opportunity to introduce yet more stringent laws and policies, often in the aftermath of a terrorist incident, but also generally under a carefully constructed cloud of fear.

The events of 11 September 2001 were thus followed in many States by new measures targeting foreign nationals, with a view to controlling more rigorously their entry, reviewing their status in the country, evaluating their in-country activities, prosecuting those alleged to have committed offences, detaining them at the discretion of the executive, and removing those said to be a risk to security. Not surprisingly, the introduction or assertion of exceptional powers has resulted in many instances of abuse. In the United States, for example, the Justice Department detained and refused to name or reveal the whereabouts of some 1200 non-citizens, sought to conduct deportation hearings in secret, and in many cases denied access to legal representation.[20]

The detention and interrogation camp established by the United States in Cuba is just another extreme example. An amicus brief from 175 Members of both UK Houses of Parliament in the US case of *Rasul v Bush* pointed out that 'the need for independent judicial examination of the factual and legal bases justifying the indefinite detention without trial of the detainees in Guantanamo' is underscored by the secrecy surrounding their arrest, surrender, and even apparent kidnapping, their detention without charge, their denial of access to legal counsel of their choice, and the denial of opportunity to challenge the legality of their detention before an impartial tribunal.[21] Moreover, their legal situation and presumption of innocence have been seriously undermined by prejudicial executive statements and by unofficial leaks of so-called confidential documents allegedly

[20] S Akram and K Johnson, 'Race, Civil Rights, and Immigration Law After September 11, 2001: The Targeting of Arabs and Muslims' (2002) 58 *New York University Annual Survey of American Law* 295.

[21] Available, together with briefs submitted by other amici, at <www.jenner.com/gitmo> (accessed 6 June 2007), in relation to *Rasul v Bush* 542 US 466 (2004).

attesting to the involvement in terrorist activities of those who remain in detention.[22] As Lord Steyn put it in his 2003 FA Mann lecture,

> [t]he purpose of holding the prisoners at Guantanamo Bay was and is to put them beyond the rule of law, beyond the protection of any courts, and at the mercy of the victors.[23]

The UK Government, despite some 30 years of anti-terrorist legislation on the statute books, has also claimed the need for new powers. Alone among the 43 Member States of the Council of Europe, in December 2001 it lodged a Declaration, since withdrawn, claiming that a 'public emergency' within the meaning of Article 15(1) of the ECHR existed in the United Kingdom. This, it was said, necessitated derogation from the provisions of Article 5(1)(f) of the ECHR, which otherwise imposes certain limitations on detention with a view to deportation.[24] The legislation which followed, the Anti-Terrorism, Crime and Security Act 2001, empowered the Secretary of State to 'certify' a suspected international terrorist,[25] as a first step towards restrictions on liberty, namely, detention and deportation or removal.[26]

Although nominally directed against terrorists, these measures have also had a direct impact on the rights of refugees and asylum seekers.

[22] D Rennie, 'Guantanamo Four Are Too Dangerous to Be Free, Says US' *Daily Telegraph* (8 March 2004) <http://www.telegraph.co.uk/news/main.jhtml?xml=/news/2004/03/08/wguan08.xml&sSheet=/news/2004/03/08/ixnewstop.html> (accessed 25 June 2007).

[23] J Steyn, 'Guantanamo Bay: The Legal Black Hole' (2004) 53 *International and Comparative Law Quarterly* 1 at 8.

[24] The Declaration invoked UNSC Resolutions 1368 and 1373, in particular, relying on the determination of a threat to international peace and security and requiring 'all States to take measures to prevent the commission of terrorist attacks, including by denying safe haven to those who finance, plan, support or commit terrorist attacks'. The derogation was withdrawn with effect from 14 March 2005, on which date the extended powers of arrest and detention under the Anti-Terrorism, Crime and Security Act 2001 (UK) ceased to operate: <http://conventions.coe.int> (accessed 7 June 2007).

[25] This power could be exercised 'if the Secretary of State reasonably ... (a) believes that the person's presence in the United Kingdom is a risk to national security, and (b) suspects that the person is a terrorist': s 21(1). Section 21 of the Anti-Terrorism, Crime and Security Act 2001 was designed to cover those who could not be convicted of offences under the Terrorism Act 2000 (UK), so that by definition the standard of proof for determining who is a terrorist must be lower than the criminal standard: Lord Rooker, in answer to Lord Morris of Aberavon, *Hansard*, HL Debate 629, col 464 (29 November 2001). Following successful challenges in the courts, ss 21–32 of the 2001 Act were repealed by s 16 of the Prevention of Terrorism Act 2005 (UK), which also introduced a system of 'derogating' and 'non-derogating' control orders: see, in particular, ss 1–7.

[26] Under the Anti-Terrorism, Crime and Security Act 2001, a 'suspected terrorist' could appeal against certification, but only to the Special Immigration Appeals Commission ('SIAC'), established in 1997 following a ruling by the European Court of Human Rights (in *Chahal v United Kingdom* (1996) 23 EHRR 413) that the then-existing procedure for appeals against removal in security cases failed to comply with the ECHR. SIAC was required to cancel the certificate if it considered that there were no reasonable grounds for the relevant belief or suspicion, or if it should not have been issued for some other reason (such as procedural irregularity): Anti-Terrorism, Crime and Security Act 2001 (UK) s 25. See now the Prevention of Terrorism Act 2005 (UK) ss 10, 11.

Contrary to established practice and to the principle of individual determination, section 33 of the 2001 Act allowed the Secretary of State, in an asylum appeal that came before the Special Immigration Appeals Commission, to certify that the 1951 Convention did not apply; that is, that the appellant was not entitled to the protection of *non-refoulement* because Article 1F or Article 33(2) applied, and that the removal of the appellant from the United Kingdom would be conducive to the public good.[27] Moreover, section 34 lays down a contentious construction of Convention provisions, to require that no account be taken of the *gravity* of the events or fear which may be relevant to an individual's claim to refugee status, or of any threat to his or her life or freedom. The so-called proportionality test (under which decision-makers weigh matters of risk and degree of harm) has thus been jettisoned.[28]

The legislation adopted in the United Kingdom reflects a level of enthusiasm clearly inspired by the UN Security Council. In many respects, however, it goes beyond what was required, and has been framed in disregard, not only of important qualifications in fact recognised by the Security Council itself, but also of the rule of law, considered as a legal principle having normative implications for the content of legislation. The United Kingdom now has a Human Rights Act, however, and the government's various measures were duly subject to appeal and review. Not surprisingly, given the terms of the legislation and the manner in which it was applied, the law was found to be incompatible and the government to have acted unlawfully.

The case of *A v Secretary of State for the Home Department*—the Belmarsh detainees case—involved 12 or so foreign citizens whom the Secretary of State had ordered to be detained under Part 4 of the 2001 Act. They were detained indefinitely, as none could be deported because each faced a real risk of treatment prohibited by Article 3 of the ECHR (that is, torture or inhuman or degrading treatment) in their home countries. In December 2004, the House of Lords declared that Part 4 was incompatible with the detainees' human rights, in that it unlawfully discriminated against those detained on the basis of their nationality.[29]

The government could hardly be described as having responded in a rights-oriented way. A number of senior ministers sought to blame the courts for the failings of the legislation, even as the declaration of derogation to the ECHR was withdrawn and a new system of so-called

[27] This process of 'certification' has been continued by s 55 of the Immigration, Asylum and Nationality Act 2006 (UK).

[28] Lord Rooker, *Hansard*, HL Debate 629, col 1253 (11 December 2001). See now also the Nationality, Immigration and Asylum Act 2002 (UK) s 72(8); and further, Goodwin-Gill and McAdam (n 3 above) 180–84, 234–4.

[29] *A v Secretary of State for the Home Department* [2004] UKHL 56, [2005] 2 AC 68.

'control orders' was introduced in the Terrorism Act 2006. The issue of discrimination was not addressed directly, and the government did not seek to clear the way to prosecute those alleged to be involved in 'terrorist activities'. On the contrary, it announced renewed efforts to secure so-called diplomatic assurances which, it claimed, would 'provide sufficient safeguards to allow return' to countries where there would otherwise be a risk of torture.[30]

Such assurances are necessarily controversial,[31] and the emerging practice remains of serious concern, not only substantively, but also as another example of government-to-government, executive-to-executive, extra-legal, non-democratic and non-accountable arrangements in actual or potential violation of established rights. In the United Kingdom, the legality and effectiveness of such arrangements have already come up before the Special Immigration Appeals Commission,[32] and are likely to be examined in the higher courts. Among others, the Committee against Torture, the Council of Europe Commissioner for Human Rights and the UN Independent Expert on the Protection of Human Rights and Fundamental Freedoms while Countering Terrorism have indicated their serious doubts about a practice that may be built on any number of assurances, but is rarely founded in guarantees.[33]

[30] See, among others, the printed case submitted by the government to the House of Lords in the case of *A and Others v Secretary of State for the Home Department*, Case for the Secretary of State (13 September 2004) 10 n 2; Mr Charles Clarke, Secretary of State for the Home Department, *Hansard*, HC Debate, col 307 (26 January 2005).

[31] See, among others, the 'Memorandum of Understanding between the Government of the United Kingdom of Great Britain and Northern Ireland and the Government of the Hashemite Kingdom of Jordan regulating the Provision of Undertakings in Respect of Specified Persons Prior to Deportation': (2005) 44 *International Legal Materials* 1511.

[32] In three of five cases determined between January–May 2007, SIAC found that return to Algeria would not violate the individuals' human rights: *Z v Secretary of State for the Home Department* [2007] UKSIAC 37/2005; *W v Secretary of State for the Home Department* [2007] UKSIAC 34/2005; and *U v Secretary of State for the Home Department* [2007] UKSIAC 323/2005. In one case, now on appeal, it held that return to Jordan was also permissible: *Omar Othman (aka Abu Qatada) v Secretary of State for the Home Department* [2007] UKSIAC 15/2005. In the fifth case, it allowed the appeal against return to Libya: *DD v Secretary of State for the Home Department* [2007] UKSIAC 42/2005.

[33] Committee against Torture, 'Conclusions and Recommendations: Fourth Periodic Report of the United Kingdom of Great Britain and Northern Ireland' UN Doc CAT/C/CR/33/3 (10 December 2004) ss 4(d), 5(I); Report by Mr Alvaro Gil-Robles, Commissioner for Human Rights, on His Visit to Sweden (21–24 April 2004) Council of Europe, CommDH (2004) 13 (8 July 2004); UN Commission on Human Rights, 'Report of the Independent Expert on the Protection of Human Rights and Fundamental Freedoms while Countering Terrorism' UN Doc E/CN.4/2005/103 (7 February 2005) para 56. In *Omar Othman* (see n 32 above), SIAC, while ruling in favour of return, nevertheless noted that there were 'no specific sanctions for breaches' of the UK–Jordan memorandum of understanding, which was 'certainly not legally enforceable', that there were 'certain weaknesses' in the monitoring provisions, and no guarantee of access: paras 507, 510, 511. See also Amnesty International, 'United Kingdom: Deportations to Algeria at All Costs', AI Index Eur 45/001/2007 (26 February 2007).

For example, in the case of *Agiza v Sweden*, involving an instance of so-called rendition in December 2001 by members of the US Central Intelligence Agency, acting with the co-operation of Swedish authorities, the Committee against Torture found that the Swedish government knew or ought to have known that torture was practised in Egypt, and that 'security detainees' were especially at risk.[34] The government argued that it had obtained assurances from the Egyptian authorities that torture would not be used, but in the view of the Committee, assurances without any 'enforcement' mechanism provided no protection against that risk.[35]

IV. REFUGEES AND THE RULE OF LAW

Nothing in the resolutions adopted by the Security Council or any other competent UN body has qualified the primacy of the principles of legality and the rule of law.[36] The Security Council's 2003 Declaration on terrorism thus emphasises that 'terrorism can only be defeated, in accordance with the Charter of the United Nations and international law, by a sustained comprehensive approach …'. Moreover,

> States must ensure that any measure taken to combat terrorism comply with all their obligations under international law, and should adopt such measures in accordance with international law, in particular, international human rights, refugee, and humanitarian law.[37]

[34] *Agiza v Sweden* Communication No 233/2003 (20 May 2005) UN Doc CAT/C/34/D/233/2003. See also *Youssef v Home Office* [2004] EWHC 1884 (QB), in which the then British Prime Minister is shown attempting, unsuccessfully, to overrule both Home Office and Foreign Office advice against removal to Egypt.

[35] Some suggestion of possible minimum standards in such return cases is given in the judgment of the Supreme Court of Canada in *Suresh v Minister of Citizenship and Immigration* [2002] SCR 3, 2002 SCC 1 paras 123–5; they include due process, evidence, review, reasons and other procedural protections.

[36] Cf Kofi Annan: 'Our responses to terrorism, as well as our efforts to thwart it and prevent it, should uphold the human rights that terrorists aim to destroy. Respect for human rights, fundamental freedoms and the rule of law are essential tools in the effort to combat terrorism—not privileges to be sacrificed at a time of tension': Meeting of the Security Council's Counter-Terrorism Committee with International, Regional and Sub-Regional Organizations (6 March 2003); Sergio Vieira de Mello (late UN High Commissioner for Human Rights): 'the best—the only—strategy to isolate and defeat terrorism is by respecting human rights, fostering social justice, enhancing democracy and upholding the rule of law': Counter-Terrorism Committee (October 2002).

[37] UNSC Res 1624 (n 1 above); and Declaration on the Issue of Combating Terrorism, Preamble, annexed to UNSC Res 1456 (20 January 2003). See also UNSC Res 1373 (28 September 2001) paras 3(f) and (g), calls upon all States to take appropriate measures 'in conformity with the relevant provisions of national and international law, including international standards of human rights' before granting refugee status; and to ensure, 'in conformity with international law', that refugee status is not abused.

The General Assembly has adopted a similar position,[38] and its continuing commitment to the rule of law is particularly well illustrated in the Global Counter-Terrorism Strategy, annexed to Resolution 60/288 and adopted without a vote on 8 September 2006. Here, compliance with 'human rights law, refugee law and international humanitarian law' is seen as an essential feature of international co-operation and preventive measures.[39] Member States resolve, in accordance with their obligations under international law, to deny safe haven and to bring to justice those involved in terrorism and related activities;[40] to ensure the apprehension and prosecution or extradition of the perpetrators, 'in accordance with the relevant provisions of national and international law, in particular human rights law, refugee law and international humanitarian law'[41] and to ensure, before granting asylum, that asylum seekers have not engaged in terrorist activities, and that refugee status thereafter is not used for terrorist and related activities.[42]

Chapter IV of the Global Strategy specifically emphasises respect for human rights and the rule of law in the fight against terrorism. Member States resolve 'to consider becoming parties without delay to the core international instruments on human rights law, refugee law and international humanitarian law', as well as implementing them and accepting the competence of international and regional human rights monitoring bodies.[43] Earlier in the same session, in the now regular resolution on the protection of human rights while combatting terrorism,[44] the General Assembly stressed the entitlement of everyone, without distinction of any kind, to *all* the rights and freedoms recognised in the UDHR, not excluding therefore the right

[38] See the Declaration to Supplement the 1994 Declaration on Measures to Eliminate International Terrorism (n 5 above) Preamble. The Commission on Human Rights has likewise reaffirmed that 'all measures to counter terrorism must be in strict conformity with international law, including international human rights standards and obligations': Commission on Human Rights Res 2003/37, 'Human Rights and Terrorism' (23 April 2003) Preamble and para 8; also, Commission on Human Rights Res 2003/68, 'Protection of Human Rights and Fundamental Freedoms while Countering Terrorism' (25 April 2003) Preamble and para 3.

[39] UNGA Res 60/288, 'The United Nations Global Counter-Terrorism Strategy' (20 September 2006) Annex 'Plan of Action' para 3.

[40] *Ibid*, Annex pt II ('Measures to Prevent and Combat Terrorism') para 2.

[41] *Ibid*, para 3.

[42] *Ibid*, para 7.

[43] Above n 39, Annex pt IV ('Measures to Ensure Respect for Human Rights for All and the Rule of Law as the Fundamental Basis of the Fight against Terrorism') paras 1–3. See also UNGA Res 61/40, 'Measures to Eliminate International Terrorism' (adopted without a vote, 4 December 2006) Preamble.

[44] UNGA Res 60/158, 'Protection of Human Rights and Fundamental Freedoms while Countering Terrorism' (adopted without a vote, 16 December 2005). In more recent resolutions, the General Assembly appears to be conscious of the fact that human rights violations

to seek and to enjoy asylum from persecution.[45] It also reaffirmed the obligation of States to respect non-derogable rights, and urged States

> to fully respect non-refoulement obligations under international refugee and human rights law and, at the same time, to review, with full respect for these obligations and other legal safeguards, the validity of a refugee status decision in an individual case if credible and relevant evidence comes to light that indicates that the person in question has committed any criminal acts, including terrorist acts, falling under the exclusion clauses under international refugee law.[46]

In 2006, the General Assembly further urged States to 'ensure due process guarantees', consistently with the UDHR, the International Covenant on Civil and Political Rights ('ICCPR'), and the 1949 Geneva Conventions.[47]

Fundamental human rights, including the prohibition of torture and the principle of *non-refoulement*, are matters of international obligation, owed to the international community as a whole.[48] The primary responsibility for the protection of human rights falls upon governments,[49] and the challenges lie in the space between obligation and implementation. Here, the State may enjoy a margin of appreciation; for example, some choice in the selection of methods of implementation appropriate to national legal and

and breaches of international refugee law and international humanitarian law have indeed occurred in the context of the fight against terrorism; see the Preambles to UNGA Res 60/158 and 61/171. For examples of measures tending to such violations, see 'Report of the Special Rapporteur on the Promotion and Protection of Human Rights and Fundamental Freedoms while Countering Terrorism, Martin Scheinin' UN Doc A/HRC/26 (29 January 2007) paras 34, 38–55 (profiling and race); and'Report of the High Commissioner for Human Rights on the Promotion and Protection of Human Rights and Fundamental Freedoms while Countering Terrorism' UN Doc A/HRC/88 (9 March 2007) paras 8–16 (*non-refoulement*); 17–22 (procedural obligations).

[45] UNGA Res 60/158 (n 44 above) final preambular para.

[46] *Ibid*, para 5; reiterated in UNGA Res 61/171 (adopted without a vote, 19 December 2006) para 6.

[47] UNGA Res 61/171 (n 46 above) para 7, referring to the International Covenant on Civil and Political Rights (adopted 16 Dec 1966, entered into force 23 March 1976) 999 UNTS 171; Geneva Convention I for the Amelioration of the Condition of the Wounded and Sick in Armed Forces in the Field (adopted 12 August 1949, entered into force 21 Oct 1950) 75 UNTS 31; Geneva Convention II for the Amelioration of the Condition of Wounded, Sick and Shipwrecked Members of Armed Forces at Sea (adopted 12 August 1949, entered into force 21 Oct 1950) 75 UNTS 85; Geneva Convention III relative to the Treatment of Prisoners of War (adopted 12 August 1949, entered into force 21 Oct 1950) 75 UNTS 135; and Geneva Convention IV relative to the Protection of Civilian Persons in Time of War (adopted 12 August 1949, entered into force 21 Oct 1950) 75 UNTS 287.

[48] *Barcelona Traction Case (Belgium v Spain)* [1970] ICJ Rep 3, para 34: 'the principles and rules concerning the basic rights of the human person'.

[49] World Conference on Human Rights, Vienna Declaration and Programme of Action 1993, UN Doc A/CONF.157/23 (12 July 1993) s I, para 1.

constitutional traditions.[50] In respect of certain exceptional powers, which might include derogating from international obligations, the State (as the 'primary decision-maker') may also benefit, depending on the nature of the obligations themselves, from a measure of respectful consideration of its on-the-spot judgements.

The context of protection and application of human rights, however, though it contains elements of appreciation, remains a legal context in which no State, as a matter of law, is ultimately the sole judge of its actions. This proposition is usefully illustrated by a summary look at the most extreme of situations, namely, the defence of necessity in general international law. 'Necessity' may preclude wrongfulness, but only in exceptional circumstances.[51] In its judgment in *Gabčíkovo-Nagymoros*, the International Court of Justice looked at then draft Article 25 of the International Law Commission's articles on State responsibility. It noted that the exceptional character of the defence of necessity is clear from its negative formulation: 'Necessity may not be invoked'. The court held further that 'necessity' can only be invoked under certain strictly defined conditions. These must be cumulatively satisfied, and the State concerned is not the sole judge of whether the conditions have been met.[52]

These conditions are that an *essential interest* of the State be subject to a *grave and imminent peril*, that the response chosen be the *only means* available, that the response *not seriously impair an essential interest* of the other party or of *the international community as a whole*, and that the responding State shall not have contributed to the state of necessity. 'Those conditions', said the court, 'reflect customary international law'.[53]

Thus, while the essential interests of the State may include its own and its population's security, the threat occasioned by a grave and imminent peril must be objectively established and not merely apprehended. The response of the State will not be permissible, however, if other lawful means are available, even if more costly and less convenient. As the International Court of Justice has emphasised elsewhere, the concept

[50] See ICCPR (n 47 above) Art 2(1).

[51] See now International Law Commission, 'Articles on the Responsibility of States for Internationally Wrongful Acts', annexed to UNGA Res 56/83 (12 December 2001) Art 25: 'Necessity may not be invoked by a State as a ground for precluding the wrongfulness of an act not in conformity with an international obligation of that State unless the act: (a) Is the only way for the State to safeguard an essential interest against a grave and imminent peril; and (b) Does not seriously impair an essential interest of the State or States towards which the obligation exists, or of the international community as a whole …'.

[52] *Gabčíkovo-Nagymoros Project (Hungary v Slovakia)* [1997] ICJ Rep 7, paras 51–2.

[53] *Ibid*.

of necessity implies and permits only what is strictly necessary for the purpose.[54]

The obligations under international human rights and refugee law being clear, what then does the system of international law require? In principle, it requires the good faith implementation by the State of its international obligations. In the arena of national security, in which history only too often confirms a tendency to executive excess, the principle of good faith, concretely implemented, is an essential buttress against the abuse of rights; it requires that rights be exercised compatibly with a State's other obligations, whether arising from treaties or the general law.[55]

Wherever the actions of a State, taken in pursuit of a lawful aim such as protecting the security of its people, run the risk of undermining a particular treaty or of infringing the internationally protected rights of those affected, then the principle of good faith 'conditions' the legality of those actions. In particular, it requires the State to provide objective justification for the course of conduct chosen and to show its consistency with international law.[56] It must therefore show why other alternatives, such as the prosecution of suspected offenders, cannot be employed, and it must permit its judgement on the facts and the law to be subject to independent and impartial judicial review; it is no answer to claim that the evidence alleged to justify detention, or obtained as a result of prolonged interrogation and detention, would be inadmissible in the regular judicial process, for that is a circumstance created by the State itself.

Terrorism threatens democracy, it is said, and a society premised on recognition of the inherent dignity and worth of the individual human

[54] In *Military and Paramilitary Activities in and against Nicaragua (Nicaragua v United States)* [1986] ICJ Rep 14 and the *Case Concerning Oil Platforms (Iran v United States)* [2003] ICJ Rep 161, the International Court of Justice considered the lawfulness of measures taken, inter alia, to protect the 'essential security interests' of one of the parties. It held that the measures taken 'must not merely be such as *tend* to protect' those interests (emphasis added), but must be necessary for that purpose; and 'whether a given measure is "necessary" is not purely a question for the subjective judgement of the party ... and may thus be assessed by the Court': *Case Concerning Oil Platforms*, para 43.

[55] Bin Cheng, *General Principles of Law as applied by International Courts and Tribunals* (London, Stevens and Son, 1953) 121, 131; Goodwin-Gill and McAdam (n 3 above) 387–90; GS Goodwin-Gill, 'State Responsibility and the "Good Faith" Obligation in International Law' in M Fitzmaurice and D Sarooshi (eds), *Issues of State Responsibility before International Judicial Institutions* (Oxford, Hart Publishing, 2004). The requirement of 'consistency' or 'compatibility' is well established, and applicable in times of emergency as much as in normal times. Art 15 of the ECHR provides a clear statement of the principle: 'In time of war or other public emergency threatening the life of the nation any High Contracting Party may take measures derogating from its obligations under this Convention to the extent strictly required by the exigencies of the situation, *provided that such measures are not inconsistent with its other obligations under international law*' (emphasis added). See also the written case submitted by the United Nations High Commissioner for Refugees to the House of Lords: '*R (ex parte European Roma Rights Centre et al) v Immigration Officer at Prague Airport and Another (UNHCR Intervening)*' (2005) 17 *International Journal of Refugee Law* 427.

[56] Cf *Former King of Greece v Greece* (2001) 33 EHRR 21, para 98 (ECtHR).

being. The threat is the greater, I would submit, where democracy reacts in repressive ways that are themselves incompatible with fundamental values, including the rule of law. In times of crisis, constitutional principles and the regular supervisory role of national courts and other checks and balances implicit in a democratic and accountable State may be frustrated or impeded by executive and legislative excesses. The rules and principles of international law may then be called upon to delineate the margins within which power is to be exercised, if it is to remain within the rule of law.

Lord Steyn, in his FA Mann lecture, quotes Aharon Barak, the President of the Supreme Court of Israel, who has noted that the fate of democracy confronted with the terrorist is that

> not all means are acceptable to it, and not all methods employed by its enemies are open to it. Sometimes, a democracy must fight with one hand tied behind its back. Nonetheless, it has the upper hand. Preserving the rule of law and recognition of individual liberties constitute an important component of its understanding of security. At the end of the day, they strengthen its spirit and strength and allow it to overcome its difficulties.[57]

In working towards this goal, the separation between executive and judiciary must be maintained, together with the guarantees that flow from the checks and balances accepted in liberal democratic States. International human rights law and national charters have irrevocably changed the nature of the rule of law, considered as a principle which imposes effective limitations on power at both executive and legislative levels.[58] In meeting the challenges of global terrorism, it may be entirely realistic to expect that the precautionary measures we demand of government should turn on risk assessments that look to the future, are not exclusively based on known or verifiable facts, and are necessarily more fluid than those which have only to determine what happened in the past.

The regular courts are an essential check and balance in a society of accountable government. States are obliged to ensure that anti-terrorist measures are 'in conformity with the relevant provisions of national and international law, including international standards of human rights'.[59] The legislation and practice of a number of States suggest strongly that

[57] A Barak, 'A Judge on Judging: The Role of a Supreme Court in a Democracy' (2002) 116 *Harvard Law Review* 16 at 148, cited in Steyn (n 23 above) 15.

[58] '[I]t is a principle of institutional morality. As such it guides all forms of law making and law enforcement. In particular, it suggests that legal certainty and procedural protections are ... at least fundamental requirements of good governance': J Jowell, 'The Rule of Law Today' in J Jowell and D Oliver (eds), *The Changing Constitution*, 5th edn (Oxford, Oxford University Press, 2000) 19.

[59] UNSC Res 1269 (19 October 1999) para 4; UNSC Res 1373 (28 September 2001) para 3(f), see also para 3(g).

these obligations have not been integrated sufficiently or at all. It remains for the courts, drawing, among others, on the authority of international human rights and international humanitarian law, to insist on compliance with reviewable standards of justification. The art is to translate the rhetoric of human rights protection in time of emergency[60] into a working reality that is commensurate with human dignity, compatible with international obligations and consistent with the rule of law.[61]

[60] Cf Preamble and Art 1(2) of the European Council Framework Decision on Terrorism, discussed in S Peers, 'EU Responses to Terrorism' (2003) 52 *International and Comparative Law Quarterly* 227.

[61] Or as Susan Mendus puts it, '[t]he real trick lies in showing how we can do both simultaneously: how in the political world we may act against evil without becoming tyrannical, and how in the philosophical realm we may accommodate difference without denying that some differences are manifestations of evil': 'Human Rights in Political Theory' (1995) 43 (Spec Issue) *Political Studies* 10.

2

Resolution 1373—A Call to Pre-empt Asylum Seekers? (or 'Osama, the Asylum Seeker')

PENELOPE MATHEW*

I. INTRODUCTION

IN THIS CHAPTER, I explore some effects of counter-terrorism on refugee law and practice. One stimulant for this line of inquiry is the easy association of asylum seekers with terrorists by politicians and the media. It was only a matter of time before someone came up with a headline like 'Osama, the asylum seeker'.[1] After all, what else would he be, given that he could not be located in Afghanistan?

The refugee and the terrorist are quintessential outsiders, and one becomes the whipping boy for the other. The terrorist is perceived to pose fundamental challenges to the State-bound system of international law, while the refugee is an inconvenient problem because he or she also falls outside the State system. Lacking protection from the State of nationality

* The law in this chapter is up-to-date as at June 2006, when the author took leave from her university post in order to be the Human Rights Legal and Policy Adviser to the Human Rights Commission of the Australian Capital Territory. This paper forms part of a research project funded by the Australian Research Council as a large discovery grant, 'Terrorism and the Non-State Actor after September 11: The Role of Law in the Search for Security". My co-chief investigators are Andrew Byrnes, Simon Bronitt, Russell Hogg, Miriam Gani and Mark Nolan. My thanks go to Dr Gabriele Porretto and Dr Mark Nolan for reading and commenting on the conference papers that led to this article, and to Professor Simon Bronitt and my husband, Don Anton, for reading and commenting on the penultimate draft. I would also like to thank three former or current students at the ANU for their assistance. First, I gratefully acknowledge Nick Kelly and Will Bateman, for their indefatigable effort sifting through the reports of the Counter-Terrorism Committee, and extra thanks are due to Nick for reading through the paper for me. I would also like to thank Elinor Jean for her valuable assistance in footnoting the paper. And to all three, thank you for your senses of humour. Any errors remain my own.

[1] See D McGrory, 'The Day When Bin Laden Applied for Asylum—in Britain' *The Times* (29 September 2005). In fact, while it appears that bin Laden was interested in immigrating to England, he did not make a formal application and was banned by the Home Secretary.

or origin, the refugee is granted surrogate protection by international law and this, of course, cuts across the sovereign power to control immigration. In practice, protection is often given most grudgingly, and the asylum seeker who has not yet had refugee status determined is frequently regarded with suspicion. The heightened sense of a terrorist threat since 11 September 2001 has simply raised the level of suspicion.

Generally speaking, there is in fact a huge gulf between the terrorist and the refugee. Terrorism is not a legal term of art, but a political label. Refugee status, on the other hand, is legally defined. Consequently, terrorists attempting to seek refugee status on the basis of their terrorist acts may be told that they flee prosecution rather than persecution.[2] If they did have a claim to meet the 'inclusive aspects' of the refugee definition contained in Article 1A(2) of the Refugee Convention,[3] then in many cases, they would fall within the exclusion clauses in Article 1F of the Convention. In the rare case where a refugee commits terrorist acts after admission to the country of refuge, he or she can be prosecuted, and in the most serious cases, the Refugee Convention permits the 'dangerous' refugee to be expelled,[4] even to the place of persecution[5]—although general human rights law grants further protection from return.

Nevertheless, because of the largely unfounded fear of abusive asylum seekers, strange connections are made to terrorism. In Australia, unfortunately, the conditions became ripe for that connection as the terrible events of 9/11 occurred just after round one of the *Tampa* litigation.[6] In an

[2] UNHCR, 'Guidelines on International Protection: Application of the Exclusion Clauses: Article 1F of the 1951 Convention relating to the Status of Refugees' UN Doc HCR/GIP/03/05 (4 September 2003) ('UNHCR's Guidelines') para 25.

[3] Art 1A(2) of the Convention relating to the Status of Refugees (adopted 28 July 1951, entered into force 22 April 1954) 189 UNTS 137, as altered by the 1967 Protocol relating to the Status of Refugees (adopted 31 January 1967, entered into force 4 October 1967) 606 UNTS 267 (together 'Refugee Convention'), defines a 'refugee' as anyone who 'owing to well-founded fear of being persecuted for reasons of race, religion, nationality, membership of a particular social group or political opinion, is outside the country of his nationality and is unable, or owing to such fear, is unwilling to avail himself of the protection of that country; or who, not having a nationality and being outside the country of his former habitual residence … is unable or, owing to such fear, is unwilling to return to it'.

[4] Refugee Convention (n 3 above) Art 32.

[5] *Ibid*, Art 33.

[6] The *Tampa* was a Norwegian freighter that picked up 433 asylum seekers when their Indonesian fishing vessel sank. The asylum seekers were denied entry to the Australian territory of Christmas Island, and the 'Pacific Solution', involving the transfer of asylum seekers from Australia to Nauru and Papua New Guinea, was developed instead. See P Mathew, 'Australian Refugee Protection in the Wake of the Tampa' (2002) 96 *American Journal of International Law* 661. Attempts to secure entry of the asylum seekers into Australia through litigation in the Federal Court were eventually unsuccessful: *Ruddock v Vadarlis* [2001] FCA 1329, (2001) 110 FCR 491. The response from the public and the media was generally favourable to the government's position—that none of the asylum seekers would set foot in Australia—and it is widely believed that the Howard government won another term of government on the basis of its hard-line stance.

interview with the Australian Minister for Defence, morning radio host Derryn Hinch suggested that while most Afghan boat people would be fleeing the Taliban, 'you have to think of the possibility that some of those males could be bin Laden appointees and could be terrorists'.[7] Mr Reith, who was then the Minister, said, 'Derryn, look I don't know that. We don't know that'. Mr Reith went on to comment that unlawful entry 'can be a pipeline for terrorists to come in and use your country as a staging post for terrorist activities'.[8]

Because of linkages like these, the terrorist may be having some impact on refugee law and related concepts, breathing new life into older techniques for denying asylum.[9] In addition, the heightened sense of a terrorist threat has given governments new vigour in pursuing discredited methods for ridding themselves of persons thought to have participated in terrorism, at the expense of human rights values.

A recent example of the latter is the United Kingdom's move to deport those 'fomenting, justifying or glorifying terrorism',[10] even if there is a risk of torture in the place to which the person is removed, on the basis of diplomatic assurances that torture will not occur.[11] The difficulty with this strategy, as acknowledged by then Prime Minister, Tony Blair, is the prohibition on *refoulement* or return to a place of torture, contained in Article 3 of the European Convention on Human Rights ('ECHR'),[12] and the ruling on that provision by the European Court of Human Rights in the case of *Chahal v United Kingdom*.[13] In that case, the court affirmed that, unlike the Refugee Convention's qualified prohibition of *refoulement*, Article 3 of the ECHR is absolute. The court rejected the idea that a balance had to be struck between the rights of the individual and the national security interests of the State, along with the idea that diplomatic assurances provided a basis for return given (in that case) the continued persecution of Sikhs in India. Return to a place of torture is simply impermissible.

[7] Minister for Defence and Parliamentary Secretary interview with Derryn Hinch, Radio 3AK (13 September 2001) <http://www.minister.defence.gov.au/ReithSpeechtpl.cfm?CurrentId=999> (accessed 21 June 2007).

[8] *Ibid.*

[9] See G Gilbert, 'Current Issues in the Application of the Exclusion Clauses' in E Feller, V Türk and F Nicholson (eds), *Refugee Protection in International Law: UNHCR's Global Consultations on International Protection* (Cambridge, Cambridge University Press, 2003) 429.

[10] See the grounds for deportation and exclusion announced by the Home Secretary, 'Tackling Terrorism—Behaviours Unacceptable in the UK' (24 August 2005) <http://press.homeoffice.gov.uk/press-releases/Tackling_Terrorism-Behaviours_Un?version=1> (accessed 21 June 2007).

[11] See then Prime Minister, Tony Blair's press conference (5 August 2005) <http://www.number-10.gov.uk/output/page8041.asp> (accessed 21 June 2007).

[12] Convention for the Protection of Human Rights and Fundamental Freedoms (European Convention on Human Rights, as amended) (4 November 1950) ETS No 5.

[13] *Chahal v United Kingdom* (1996) 23 EHRR 413 (ECtHR).

Reading the decisions of the UK and European courts relating to Mr Chahal, one gains the impression of a strong claim of persecution with only minor participation in anything likely to be called 'terrorist'. Mr Chahal had arrived in the United Kingdom unlawfully and gained residence on the basis of an amnesty. Married, with two adult children who both held UK citizenship, he had become actively supportive of the Sikh separatist movement in the Punjab. He was convicted on a charge of assault and affray at a Sikh temple in the United Kingdom,[14] although the conviction was subsequently quashed. When the Home Secretary prepared to deport Mr Chahal on national security grounds, he applied for political asylum. The evidence indicated past persecution on a visit to India, when Mr Chahal had been detained without trial for several weeks, during which time, according to Mr Chahal, he had been tortured. Moreover, reports from Amnesty International indicated that persecutory police action against suspected Sikh separatists was still occurring. Indeed, while the House of Lords found that the Secretary of State's decision was not perverse or irrational,[15] it is clear that all judges were concerned by the evidence. It appears Mr Chahal was deemed undesirable by the executive rather than dangerous or unworthy of protection—the two key concepts that limit the Refugee Convention's protection.

Nevertheless, it is clear that the UK government was angered by the European Court's decision at the time,[16] and it still does not accept the court's reasoning. In a press briefing on 5 August 2005, then Prime Minister, Tony Blair indicated that the law needed to be re-tested, noting that the decision in *Chahal* was made by a majority of 12:7.[17]

[14] See the facts stated in the Court of Appeal's decision, *R v Secretary of State for the Home Department, ex parte Chahal* [1995] 1 All ER 658 (CA) (Staughton LJ).

[15] *Ibid*, 669 (Staughton LJ), 672 (Nolan LJ), 676 (Neill LJ). This decision seems overly generous and deferential to the Secretary of State. The terms of the 'undertaking' were as follows (at 669): 'We have noted your request to have a formal assurance to the effect that, if Mr Chahal were deported to India, he would enjoy the same legal protections as any other Indian citizen, and that he would have no reason to expect to suffer mistreatment of any kind at the hands of the Indian authorities'. Staughton LJ even noted that the undertaking left open the possibility of unauthorised ill-treatment.

[16] Patel writes that the 'greater willingness to interfere with the decisions of national authorities ... provoked a strong reaction in Whitehall. The Home Office reacted to the judgment by saying "the Home Secretary and national authorities are better placed to judge what constitutes a threat to national security"': D Patel, 'Chahal v United Kingdom: *An Analysis*' <http://www.nottingham.ac.uk/law/hrlc/hrnews/feb97/chahal.htm> (accessed 20 March 2006), citing 'The European Court Frees Sikh Held in UK', *The Guardian* (16 November 1996).

[17] 'The origin of the problem under Article 3 is the case called the [*Chahal*] Case which was actually decided in 1996 and what that Court decision said, by a majority of 12 to 7, was that even if someone was a threat to national security, if there was a substantial risk of them being subject to torture when returned to a country then that outweighed the national security consideration, and that was absolute, and in our courts, following that, there has

The United Kingdom has been successful in attracting support for its position on these issues,[18] and in late 2005 was joined by three other governments in an intervention before the European Court of Human Rights in the case of *Ramzy v The Netherlands*,[19] challenging the absolute character of Article 3 of the ECHR. Moreover, the United Kingdom may have played a role in the adoption of some very odd and worrying language concerning refugees and asylum seekers in the early, major resolution on terrorism adopted by the Security Council, Resolution 1373 of 2001. This resolution established the Counter-Terrorism Committee and a system of reporting in relation to the obligations set out in the resolution. The remainder of this chapter will analyse the language of Resolution 1373, attempting to trace its origins (part II below) and to analyse its ramifications in theory and practice. In so doing, I will attempt to demonstrate the impact of that language in light of on-going questions surrounding the exclusion clauses in the 1951 Refugee Convention (part III below). Finally, the chapter examines States' reports to the Counter-Terrorism Committee and shows that the language in Resolution 1373 has tended to encourage a culture of impunity with respect to violations of refugees' rights (part IV below).

II. RESOLUTION 1373 AND ITS DRAFTING HISTORY

In paragraph 3 of Resolution 1373, the Security Council 'calls on' States to

> (f) Take appropriate measures in conformity with the relevant provisions of national and international law, including international standards of human rights, before granting refugee status, for the purpose of ensuring that the asylum seeker has not planned, facilitated or participated in the commission of terrorist acts;
> (g) Ensure, in conformity with international law, that refugee status is not abused by the perpetrators, organizers or facilitators of terrorist acts, and that claims of political motivation are not recognized as grounds for refusing requests for the extradition of alleged terrorists.[20]

been this problem with deporting people who are a threat to our national security. Now in respect of British courts we can retest it and, if necessary, we can amend the Human Rights Act and that covers the British courts' interpretation of the law. There is then, of course, the possibility that there is an appeal to the European Court. Now that is where we have also got to deal with that issue as well':Tony Blair (n 11 above).

[18] See, eg United Nations Security Council ('UNSC') Res 1624 (2005) para 1. This resolution was sponsored by the UK: 5261st Meeting of the UNSC, UN Doc S/PV.5261 (14 September 2005).

[19] See 'Observations of the Governments of Lithuania, Portugal, Slovakia and the United Kingdom Intervening in Application No. 25424/05 Ramzy v The Netherlands' <http://www.icj.org/IMG/pdf/UK_observations_Ramzy_case.pdf> (accessed 20 June 2007). A number of non-governmental human rights organisations have also intervened: eg <http://www.icj.org/IMG/pdf/Ramzy_Amicus_ICJ_and_others.pdf>;<http://www.icj.org/IMG/pdf/Ramzy_intervention_Justice.pdf> (accessed 20 June 2007).

[20] UNSC Res 1373 (2001).

In addition, paragraph 5 of Resolution 1373 'declares' that

> acts, methods, and practices of terrorism are contrary to the purposes and principles of the United Nations and that knowingly financing, planning and inciting terrorist acts are also contrary to the purposes and principles of the United Nations.[21]

Most refugee lawyers' reaction to this language would be a mixture of resignation—as the denigration of asylum seekers has been going on for over a decade—and incomprehension—given the lack of evidence to suggest that refugee status is likely to be abused by terrorists. Perhaps there was some concern that Al Qaida members would flee to countries neighbouring Afghanistan and seek refuge. However, this concern is not revealed on the face of the public record. It is now known that none of the 19 hijackers who carried out the attacks of September 11 were asylum seekers, and there would have been no reason to assume otherwise at the time.

Undoubtedly, States take a different view from most refugee lawyers, especially if they have been unable to remove excluded asylum seekers suspected of terrorism because of the obligation of *non-refoulement* attaching to the prohibition on torture. A number of the 'Belmarsh detainees' in the United Kingdom had claimed asylum or been granted refugee status.[22] But how significant or relevant is this? When the detainees challenged their detention under section 23 of the Anti-Terrorism, Crime and Security Act 2001, the House of Lords rightly dismissed the question of immigration status as a distraction. The true question was not whether a particular response—indefinite incarceration—might be a consequence of a person's immigration status, but whether the response was required by the threat it supposedly met.[23] Indefinite detention as a result of discrimination between citizens and non-citizens was not permissible according to the House of Lords, and some of the judges commented that deportation was equally unlikely to counter the terrorist threat effectively.[24]

[21] *Ibid*, para 5.

[22] See 'Who Are the Terror Detainees?' BBC News (11 March 2005) <http://news.bbc.co.uk/1/hi/uk/4101751.stm> (accessed 29 June 2007). The detainees were incarcerated pursuant to s 23 of the Anti-Terrorism, Crime and Security Act 2001 (UK) in Belmarsh prison. They successfully challenged their detention before the House of Lords: *A v Secretary of State for the Home Department* [2004] UKHL 56, [2005] 2 AC 68 ('*Belmarsh case*').

[23] Concerning the mischaracterisation of the case as an immigration matter, see the *Belmarsh case* (n 22 above) para 103 (Lord Hope): 'it would be a serious error ... to regard this case as about the right to control immigration'; and para 171 (Lord Rodger): 'the critical factor is not the suspects' immigration status but the threat that they are suspected of posing to the life of the nation'.

[24] See the *Belmarsh case* (n 22 above) para 43 (Lord Bingham) approving the appellants' 'central complaint' that 'the choice of an immigration measure to address a security

For our purposes here, some relevant questions are as follows. If there are in fact examples of refugees or asylum seekers who have been involved in terrorism, do these examples justify highlighting the issue in Resolution 1373? On what basis have allegations of terrorist connections been made against refugees and asylum seekers—for example, did the United Kingdom have good grounds to suspect the Belmarsh detainees of terrorism, or was the 'intelligence' flawed?[25] Finally, should exclusion from refugee status necessarily translate into *refoulement*? (This, it should be said, is not actually a result specifically asked for in Resolution 1373, but it is clearly one that the United Kingdom wishes to pursue.)

It is not known whether these sorts of questions were asked by the Security Council, as the formal public meeting at which Resolution 1373 was adopted lasted five minutes and there was no debate, so there is no legislative history or *travaux préparatoires* for the resolution.[26] However, it is readily apparent that the language is similar to that of the General Assembly's Declaration to Supplement the 1994 Declaration on Measures to Eliminate International Terrorism. That Declaration (hereafter referred to as the 'General Assembly's Supplementary Declaration on Terrorism') provides that

> States should take appropriate measures in conformity with the relevant provisions of national and international law, including international standards of human rights, before granting refugee status, for the purpose of ensuring that the asylum-seeker has not participated in terrorist acts, considering in this regard relevant information as to whether the asylum-seeker is subject to investigation for or is charged with or has been convicted of offences connected with terrorism and, after granting refugee status, for the purpose of ensuring that that status is not used for the purpose of preparing or organizing terrorist acts intended to be committed against other States or their citizens.[27]

problem had the inevitable result of failing adequately to address that problem (by allowing non-UK suspected terrorists to leave the country with impunity and leaving British suspected terrorists at large)'; para 230 (Baroness Hale): '[w]hat sense does it make to consider a person such a threat to the life of the nation that he must be locked up without trial, but allow him to leave, as has happened, for France where he was released almost immediately?'.

25 R Verkaik, 'Revealed: Flawed Intelligence Exposes the Scandal of Belmarsh Detainees' *The Independent* (6 January 2005) <http://news.independent.co.uk/uk/legal/article18035.ece> (accessed 29 June 2007).

26 See S Talmon, 'The Security Council as World Legislature' (2005) 99 *American Journal of International Law* 175 at 187.

27 Declaration to Supplement the 1994 Declaration on Measures to Eliminate International Terrorism, annexed to United Nations General Assembly ('UNGA') Res 51/210, 'Measures to Eliminate International Terrorism' (17 December 1996) para 3.

The General Assembly's Supplementary Declaration on Terrorism also contains language similar to paragraph 5 of Resolution 1373, relating to the principles and purposes of the United Nations.[28]

There is a legislative history for the General Assembly's Supplementary Declaration on Terrorism, and it may shed some light on the reasons for including similar language in Resolution 1373. The General Assembly's Supplementary Declaration on Terrorism was adopted without a vote by both the General Assembly and, prior to the Assembly's deliberations, the Sixth Committee (the legal committee). In the Sixth Committee, the first draft of the resolution appeared on 22 November 1996 after informal consultations.[29] It appears to have begun life as a proposal by the United Kingdom.[30]

As explained by the UK representative, the proposal had two main aims. The first

> was to make it clear that those who financed, planned and incited terrorist deeds were acting contrary to the purposes and principles of the United Nations and therefore could not claim protection under the 1951 Convention relating to the Status of Refugees.[31]

The United Kingdom's proposal contained an explicit reference to Article 1F of the Refugee Convention. Article 1F, known as the exclusion clause, provides that

> [t]he provisions of this Convention shall not apply to any person with respect to whom there are serious reasons for considering that:
>
> (a) He has committed a crime against peace, a war crime, or a crime against humanity, as defined in the international instruments drawn up to make provision in respect of such crimes;
> (b) He has committed a serious non-political crime outside the country of refuge prior to his admission to that country as a refugee;
> (c) He has been guilty of acts contrary to the purposes and principles of the United Nations.

It is clear that although the United Kingdom did not think its proposal amounted to an amendment of Article 1F(c), it did hope that the resolution, if adopted, would be relevant to interpretation of the Refugee Convention. The interesting question is, what did the United Kingdom hope to gain by putting all terrorist offences within Article 1F(c)?

[28] *Ibid*, para 2.

[29] See Sixth Committee, 'Measures to Eliminate International Terrorism' UN Doc A/51/631 (1996) para 5.

[30] 'Further Declaration in Implementation of the 1994 Declaration on Measures to Eliminate International Terrorism', Statement of Ms Wilmhurst (UK) to the Sixth Committee, 10th meeting (30 October 1996) UN Doc A/C.6/51/SR.10 (1996) para 18ff. The present author has not been able to locate a copy of the proposal itself.

[31] *Ibid*, para 19.

One may speculate that the United Kingdom may have hoped to clearly place terrorist crimes within Article 1F(c) because Article 1F(a) might not cover all cases of terrorism, while Article 1F(b) only deals with 'non-political' crimes and does not adopt a definition of what is or is not political. Indeed, the *second* aim of the United Kingdom's proposal was 'to encourage further cooperation among States in bringing terrorists to justice'.[32] In that connection States were 'to consider limiting the political offence exception in its application to terrorist acts'.[33]

The UK representative also indicated that the United Kingdom was concerned that the asylum process could be invoked by persons who should not be able to benefit from refugee status at the end of the day. In so doing, particular reference was made to the fact that Articles 32 and 33(2) of the Refugee Convention apply *after* admission to the State of refuge, and, indeed, after the national grant of refugee status.[34]

At this point, it is helpful to set out Articles 32 and 33 in full.

Article 32. – Expulsion

1. The Contracting States shall not expel a refugee lawfully in their territory save on grounds of national security or public order.
2. The expulsion of such a refugee shall be only in pursuance of a decision reached in accordance with due process of law. Except where compelling reasons of national security otherwise require, the refugee shall be allowed to submit evidence to clear himself, and to appeal to and be represented for the purpose before competent authority or a person or persons specially designated by the competent authority.
3. The Contracting States shall allow such a refugee a reasonable period within which to seek legal admission into another country. The Contracting States reserve the right to apply during that period such internal measures as they may deem necessary.

Article 33. – Prohibition of expulsion or return ('refoulement')

1. No Contracting State shall expel or return ('refouler') a refugee in any manner whatsoever to the frontiers of territories where his life or freedom would be threatened on account of his race, religion, nationality, membership of a particular social group or political opinion.
2. The benefit of the present provision may not, however, be claimed by a refugee whom there are reasonable grounds for regarding as a danger to the security of the country in which he is, or who, having been convicted by a final judgement of a particularly serious crime, constitutes a danger to the community of that country.

[32] *Ibid*, para 23.
[33] *Ibid.*
[34] *Ibid*, paras 19 and 20.

The United Kingdom's representative to the Sixth Committee commented that these provisions

> allowed States to expel a refugee in cases where the refugee was a threat to national security or public order or where the refugee had been convicted of a particularly serious crime and thus constituted a danger to the community. Those articles, however, applied to persons who had already been granted refugee status. In the United Kingdom currently, once a person had claimed asylum, he or she might be entitled to remain in the country until the claim had been determined and legal appeals had been exhausted, a process that could take years. The purpose of the draft declaration was to emphasize that the process of seeking asylum might not be available to those participating in or actively supporting terrorism.[35]

Clearly, the United Kingdom wanted to ensure that asylum seekers could be excluded if they committed terrorist acts prior to or while waiting for a determination of refugee status, regardless of where the crime was committed. The United Kingdom's proposal may have been driven by recent litigation, as it was introduced around the same time as the *Chahal* decision and a couple of other decisions which had raised difficulties concerning application of the Refugee Convention to suspected terrorists.[36]

Given the United Kingdom's concerns, one can certainly see why there would be a preference for Article 1F(c) over Article 1F(b), given that the latter refers to someone 'admitted to [the country of refuge] as a refugee' and to crimes committed *outside* the country of refuge and *prior to* that entry. One can also see why the United Kingdom would not wish to rely on the provisions concerning dangerous refugees. These clauses seem to require a determination that someone is a refugee, in the sense that the person meets the inclusive elements of the definition set out in Article 1A(2), followed by a determination that the person falls within the categories described in Article 32 or 33(2), and a decision to lift the protections normally accorded to a refugee.[37] It is possible that the United Kingdom was endorsing a position whereby terrorist acts would provide a basis for

[35] *Ibid*.

[36] The language was first used in a General Assembly resolution of 17 December 1996, discussed above (see the text to n 27 above), and the UK proposal which led to the adoption of the language was introduced into the Assembly's Sixth Committee on 30 October 1996. The *Chahal* decision was handed down on 15 November 1996. Kapferer discusses a couple of earlier decisions in which the Immigration Appeals Tribunal (replaced by the Asylum and Immigration Tribunal) had held that it was wrong simply to use the label 'terrorism'—a term not used by the Refugee Convention—to exclude people: S Kapferer, 'Exclusion Clauses in Europe—A Comparative Overview of State Practice in France, Belgium and the United Kingdom' (2000) 12 (Spec Issue) *International Journal of Refugee Law* 195 at 204.

[37] The UK is not alone. As Gilbert states, '[i]n other parts of Europe, rather than use Article 33(2), with its higher demands, States would prefer to use Article 1F where a refugee commits a terrorist act in the country of refuge': Gilbert (n 9 above) 458.

exclusion without consideration as to whether the asylum seeker would otherwise fall within the definition of a refugee.[38]

The United Kingdom's stated endgame was to prosecute or extradite those asylum seekers who abused the asylum process or refugee status.[39] However, both the reaction to the European Court's decision in the *Chahal* case, and the later experience of the Belmarsh detainees, suggest that the United Kingdom also wishes to rid itself of 'undesirables'—persons against whom there is insufficient evidence for a conviction—perhaps because it is thought best to pre-empt terrorist threats. If so, one can see why the United Kingdom would move to categorise the polymorph 'terrorism' as being against the purposes and principles of the United Nations.

At the end of the day, the UK proposal met with opposition and was modified. The express reference to Article 1F(c) of the Refugee Convention was deleted.[40] It is apparent that some States took a narrow view of the exclusion clause Article 1F(c) of the Refugee Convention, namely that it is only applicable to persons high in the echelons of the State, as it is the State which is responsible for acting in accordance with the United Nation's principles and purposes.[41]

This is not a completely uncontested understanding of the provision. Goodwin-Gill and McAdam point out that the context—particularly the Constitution of the International Refugee Organization—may lead to a different interpretation and that the jurisprudence in some cases has developed in a different direction.[42] Interestingly, the Constitution of the

[38] As argued by Hathaway and Harvey, '[t]he attraction of Article 1(F) is that, in contrast to Article 33(2), it authorizes a State to forego its usual responsibility to assess refugee status. For States committed to barring the entry of potentially violent non-citizens to the greatest extent legally possible, it presents an administratively "least bad option". Reliance on Article 1(F) does not sanction automatic denials of entry, but it does allow the adjudication of safety issues as a preliminary matter and according to a lower standard of proof': JC Hathaway and CJ Harvey, 'Framing Refugee Protection in the New World Disorder' (2001) 34 *Cornell International Law Journal* 257 at 260. Indeed, the present position in the UK is that exclusion can occur before inclusion. See *Gurung v Secretary of State for the Home Department* [2003] INLR 133, paras 64–5; and s 33 of the Anti-Terrorism, Crime and Security Act 2001 (UK) which permits the Home Secretary to certify that an asylum seeker is not entitled to the protection of the Convention. (This provision was not repealed by the Prevention of Terrorism Act 2005 (UK)).

[39] The UK delegate said that '[t]he situation that the draft declaration was intended to address was one in which individuals escaped from one State and established themselves in another State in order to plan, fund or incite terrorist acts to be carried out in their home State or elsewhere. Thus, para 3 provided that States must also take their own measures to ensure that refugees in their territory did not prepare or organize terrorist acts abroad. In that connection, her Government had recently undertaken a study of its criminal-law [sic] provisions in the light of proposals to extend the jurisdiction of the courts to cover acts of conspiracy and incitement in the United Kingdom aimed at the perpetration of serious offences in other countries': UK Declaration (n 30 above) para 22.

[40] See the statement of the Netherlands in explanation of its vote in the General Assembly, 11th plenary meeting (26 September 1996) UN Doc A/51/PV.88 (1996) 29.

[41] See, eg Hathaway and Harvey (n 38 above) 266.

[42] GS Goodwin-Gill and J McAdam, *The Refugee in International Law*, 3rd edn (Oxford, Oxford University Press, 2007) 186–9.

International Refugee Organization provided for the exclusion of, among other persons, those who *have participated in any terrorist organization*.[43] In policy terms, this position might be justified by the argument that as the point of the exclusion clauses is to deny safe haven to persecutors, it has to be acknowledged that there are non-State agents of persecution.[44] One might also draw support from Article 29(3) of the Universal Declaration of Human Rights, which provides that the rights and freedoms set out in that instrument 'may in no case be exercised contrary to the purposes and principles of the United Nations'.[45]

Nevertheless, during the debate concerning the General Assembly's Supplementary Declaration on Terrorism, several States indicated their disapproval of focusing on non-State actors as violators of human rights.[46] Moreover, it is clear that some States were only able to join in the consensus concerning the resolution because they understood the Declaration not to alter the interpretation of the Refugee Convention.[47] This understanding, as noted by the New Zealand delegate,[48] is reflected in the preamble to the Declaration.[49] It is generally consistent with what UNHCR's Guidelines now say on the issue, too.[50]

[43] Constitution of the International Refugee Organization (1946) Annex One, Pt II, Art 6. For an example of a case concerning arguments relating to a non-State actor participating in acts against the purposes and principles of the United Nations, see the Canadian Supreme Court case of *Pushpanathan v Canada (Minister of Citizenship and Immigration)* [1998] 1 SCR 982.

[44] E Kwakwa, 'Article 1F(c): Acts Contrary to the Purposes and Principles of the United Nations' (2000) 12 (Spec Issue) *International Journal of Refugee Law* 79 at 86.

[45] UNGA Res 217A (III) (10 December 1948). Art 14(2) of the Universal Declaration includes similar language, but the argument could be raised that this applies only to persons high in the State apparatus, whereas Art 29(3) appears to be a quite general provision.

[46] Statement of Norway to the Sixth Committee, 10th meeting (30 October 1996) UN Doc A/C.6/51/SR.50 (1996) para 27; Statement of Liechtenstein to the General Assembly, 11th plenary meeting (26 September 1996) UN Doc A/51/PV.88 (1996) 28.

[47] For example, the Netherlands (n 40 above) and Liechtenstein (n 46 above) 28. See also the statement of Switzerland in the Sixth Committee after the UK's introduction of the proposal: UN Doc A/C.6/51/SR.10 (1996) para 97.

[48] UN Doc A/C.6/51/SR.50 (1996) para 29.

[49] Preambular paras 6 and 7 of the Declaration state that 'the Convention relating to the Status of Refugees, done at Geneva on 28 July 1951, does not provide a basis for the protection of perpetrators of terrorist acts, and notes in this context articles 1, 2, 32 and 33 of the Convention, and emphasizing in this regard the need for States parties to ensure the proper application of the Convention' and '[s]tressing the importance of full compliance by States with their obligations under the provisions of the 1951 Convention and the 1967 Protocol relating to the Status of Refugees, including the principle of *non-refoulement* of refugees to places where their life or freedom would be threatened on account of their race, religion, nationality, membership in a particular social group or political opinion, and affirming that the present Declaration does not affect the protection afforded under the terms of the Convention and Protocol and other provisions of international law'.

[50] 'Given that Articles 1 and 2 of the United Nations Charter essentially set out the fundamental principles States must uphold in their mutual relations, it would appear that in principle only persons who have been in positions of power in a State or State-like entity would appear capable of committing such acts': UNHCR's Guidelines (n 2 above) para 17.

III. THEORETICAL RAMIFICATIONS OF A SHIFT TO ARTICLE 1F(C)

Even though the United Kingdom's proposal was watered down, the language that was adopted is still problematic and capable of taking on a life of its own. To begin with, there is no international consensus on a definition of 'terrorism'.[51] The definitional issue was a constant theme in the debates on the General Assembly's Supplementary Declaration on Terrorism. Predictably polarised views emerged regarding the difference between terrorism, on the one hand, and self-determination or national liberation movements, on the other.[52] This occurred despite some apparent measure of agreement on a definition in the Assembly's earlier Declaration on Measures to Eliminate Terrorism.[53]

The lack of a definition becomes particularly problematic in light of certain features of Article 1F(c) which I have already begun to explore in trying to ascertain what motivated the United Kingdom to put forward its proposal in the first place. The analysis below focuses on four points. The first (addressed in part A) is the fact that exclusion can take place without consideration of inclusion. The second, related question (addressed in part B) is that Article 1F(c) does not require a balance to be struck between the persecution feared and the act on which exclusion is based. The third point (addressed in part C) is that the threshold for invocation of the exclusion clauses is rather low, especially when compared with the provisions concerning dangerous refugees. My analysis of this point includes an examination of the effects of the Security Council's denomination of all terrorism as being against the purposes and principles of the United Nations without supplying a definition of the term 'terrorism'; the low standard of proof—'serious reasons for considering'; and the uncertain level of due process. I will also demonstrate that there may be some extremely worrying consequences for general human rights law, particularly the absolute prohibition on *refoulement* to a place of torture (see part D). I conclude

[51] For a discussion of relevant international instruments, see Gilbert (n 9 above) 441–3. The instruments are often non-binding General Assembly resolutions. The only one of the 13 United Nations terrorism treaties that contains a general definition of 'terrorism' is the widely ratified 1999 Convention for the Suppression of the Financing of Terrorism (adopted 9 December 1999, entered into force 10 April 2002) 2178 UNTS 229, para 2(1)(b) (158 parties as at 10 June 2007). See also B Saul, *Defining Terrorism in International Law* (Oxford, Oxford University Press, 2006).

[52] See, eg statement of Lebanon to the General Assembly, 88th plenary meeting (17 December 1996) UN Doc A/51/PV.88 (1996) 27.

[53] 'Criminal acts intended or calculated to provoke a state of terror in the general public, a group of persons or particular persons for political purposes are in any circumstance unjustifiable, whatever the considerations of a political, philosophical, ideological, racial, ethnic, religious or any other nature that may be invoked to justify them': 1994 Declaration on Measures to Eliminate International Terrorism, annexed to UNGA Res 49/60 (9 December 1994) operative para 3. This definition was 'reiterated' in UNGA Res 58/81, 'Measures to Eliminate International Terrorism' (8 January 2004) para 2.

(in part E) by arguing that together, the factors examined in parts A–C may result in the exclusion of persons on the basis that they are 'undesirable' rather than undeserving of protection or that they pose a clear danger to society. Just as 'preventative detention' is used in an attempt to counter the often ill-defined terrorist threat,[54] the exclusion clauses may now be viewed by some States as an alternative form of pre-emption.[55]

A. Exclusion without Consideration of Inclusion

It is clear that the impetus for the United Kingdom's proposal in the Sixth Committee was that it wished to avoid the prospect of asylum seekers remaining in the United Kingdom when they fall within the exclusion categories of Article 1F.[56] The point of the exclusion clauses, as compared with the provisions on dangerous refugees, is, according to Hathaway and Harvey, that Article 1F permits the State not to consider whether or not a person falls within the inclusive aspects of the definition.[57] The language of the Refugee Convention tends to support that view, as Article 1F simply says the provisions of the Convention 'shall not apply' to persons in relation to whom there are serious grounds for considering that they have committed particular acts, although Article 1F(b) is perhaps phrased so as to suggest otherwise, referring to persons '[admitted] as a refugee'.[58] Gilbert notes the possibility that 'a special case can be made for always determining refugee status before seeing whether article 1F(b) excludes the applicant'.[59]

[54] The UK is not the only State to have adopted preventative detention as a 'response' to terrorism. See, eg Australia's Anti-Terrorism Act (No 2) 2005 (Cth), inserting Division 105 into the Criminal Code Act 1995 (Cth).

[55] The most famous and obvious example is the Bush doctrine of pre-emption, which refers to the pre-emptive use of military force. See *The National Security Strategy of the United States of America* (2002) <http://www.whitehouse.gov/nsc/nss.html> (accessed 20 June 2007). However, the detention imposed in Guantanamo Bay, Belmarsh prison and under Australian provisions introduced in 2005 share the hallmarks of pre-emption.

[56] The UK's present position is that exclusion can occur without considering inclusion: Kapferer (n 36 above) 216.

[57] Hathaway and Harvey (n 38 above).

[58] In the Australian High Court's decision in *Minister for Immigration and Multicultural Affairs v Singh* [2002] HCA 7, (2002) 209 CLR 533, all members of the court said that this provision was not to be read literally: see 539 (Gleeson CJ) 'the reference to "admission … as a refugee" [should be read] as a reference to putative admission as a refugee'; 548 (Gaudron J) '[t]he fact that the person has not, at the relevant time been admitted as a refugee is not to the point if the crime in question was committed before he or she could be so admitted. In such circumstances, the crime was necessarily committed "prior to … admission … as a refugee"'; 557 (McHugh J), concurring with Gleeson CJ; 563 (Kirby J); and 592 (Callinan J).

[59] Gilbert (n 9 above) 466.

UNHCR has taken the view that although there is 'no rigid formula', inclusion should generally be considered before exclusion.[60] In part, this is argued to follow from the 'exceptional nature of Article 1F',[61] and in part from the fact that the 'serious reasons for considering' will generally arise during the determination of a person's claim for asylum. Only if a person were already on a terrorist blacklist or the subject of an indictment or an extradition request would it be likely that exclusion could be contemplated as the first step in the proceedings. Thus, UNHCR's Guidelines provide that exclusion could be considered without reference to inclusion in the following cases:

(i) where there is an indictment by an international criminal tribunal;
(ii) in cases where there is apparent and readily available evidence pointing strongly towards the applicant's involvement in particularly serious crimes, notably in prominent Article 1F(c) cases; and
(iii) at the appeal stage in cases where exclusion is the question at issue.[62]

UNHCR suggests that there should be specialised exclusion units.[63]

Courts in some common law jurisdictions have already taken the view that exclusion may take place before inclusion.[64] It seems likely that the suggested shift to Article 1F in Resolution 1373 will attract States as the exclusion clauses become another pre-emptive measure against potential terrorists. The danger, as with pre-emptive measures generally, is that everyone becomes suspect. As Nyinah argues, conducting exclusion proceedings without consideration of inclusion

> creates a 'presumption of excludability' by promoting the erroneous impression that the exclusion clauses are potentially applicable to all asylum-seekers as a matter of course

and 'elevates exclusion issues to a predominant position which they were never intended to occupy in the status determination process'.[65]

[60] UNHCR's Guidelines (n 2 above) para 31.
[61] *Ibid*.
[62] *Ibid*.
[63] *Ibid*, para 32.
[64] See, eg the Australian High Court's decision in *Singh* (n 58 above), in particular the judgment of Kirby J; and the Canadian Supreme Court's decision in *Pushpanathan* (n 43 above) 999, where the majority commented on the enormous significance of falling within Art 1F as opposed to the provisions on dangerous refugees. For the UK's position, see n 38 above.
[65] MK Nyinah, 'Exclusion under Article 1F: Some Reflections on Context, Principles and Practice' (2000) 12 (Spec Issue) *International Journal of Refugee Law* 295 at 305.

B. Balancing

Another large and related[66] issue is whether exclusion decisions involve balancing the persecution feared against the excludable act or crime. UNHCR advocates balancing, particularly in relation to Article 1F(b):

> The incorporation of a proportionality test when considering exclusion and its consequences provides a useful analytical tool to ensure that the exclusion clauses are applied in a manner consistent with the overriding humanitarian object and purpose of the 1951 Convention. The concept has evolved in particular in relation to Article 1F(b) and represents a fundamental principle of many fields of international law. As with any exception to a human rights guarantee, the exclusion clauses must therefore be applied in a manner proportionate to their objective, so that the gravity of the offence in question is weighed against the consequences of exclusion. Such a proportionality analysis would, however, not normally be required in the case of crimes against peace, crimes against humanity, and acts falling under Article 1F(c), as the acts covered are so heinous. It remains relevant, however, to Article 1F(b) crimes and less serious war crimes under Article 1F(a).[67]

The idea that balancing is required may still be the majority view, as Kälin and Künzli point out.[68] They put forward some interesting arguments concerning discrimination clauses in modern extradition treaties in order to support balancing.[69] They point out that when extradition is sought for extraneous political reasons in relation to a crime that has been committed, 'persons whose extradition is not permissible precisely on account of their being politically persecuted would not be recognized as refugees in asylum procedures!'[70] Persuasive arguments may also be made for balancing in particular cases, such as children.[71] Balancing might also be a way of dealing with people who have expiated their crimes, although some case law rejects balancing on the premise that Article 1F(b) is not solely about fugitives from justice.[72]

Hathaway and Harvey argue that the language of the Refugee Convention does not suggest that balancing is required,[73] that State

[66] As Bliss notes, the idea that a balancing exercise is required lends itself to the idea that exclusion is to be considered only after inclusion: M Bliss, '"Serious Reasons for Considering": Minimum Standards of Procedural Fairness in the Application of the Article 1F Exclusion Clauses' (2000) 12 (Spec Issue) *International Journal of Refugee Law* 92 at 107–8.

[67] UNHCR's Guidelines (n 2 above) para 24.

[68] See W Kälin and J Künzli, 'Article 1F(b): Freedom Fighters, Terrorists, and the Notion of Serious Non-Political Crimes' (2000) 12 (Spec Issue) *International Journal of Refugee Law* 46 at 72.

[69] *Ibid*, 71–4.

[70] *Ibid*, 72. See also Gilbert (n 9 above) 452.

[71] The particular difficulties concerning children are discussed in Gilbert (n 9 above) 473.

[72] See, eg *Zrig v Canada (Minister of Citizenship and Immigration)* 2003 FCA 178, [2003] 3 FC 761 (CA) para 78 (Nadon JA, with Létourneau JA concurring).

[73] Hathaway and Harvey (n 38 above) 311.

practice is trending away from a balancing test,[74] and that it is in fact dangerous to invite States to engage in a balancing exercise.[75] The last argument is the most compelling one, as the language is open to interpretation and State practice may sometimes be dismissed as a violation of the Refugee Convention.[76] As argued by Nyinah,

> [t]he more interesting objections to the balancing test are those which raise such questions as whether one can validly speak of 'degrees of persecution'; whether the seriousness of an Article 1F(b) crime necessarily bears a relationship to the degree of persecution; why exclusion should not apply equally to two persons who commit the same offence even if one of them has a 'stronger' refugee claim; and the lack of clarity regarding its relationship to the proportionality test required for evaluating the 'non-political' element of Article 1F(b).[77]

It is not my purpose to answer these questions. Rather, my point is that governments will seek to avoid asking them on the basis that there is less authority for balancing in relation to Article 1F(c). UNHCR's view, which is that most cases involving terrorism should be dealt with under Article 1F(b)[78] and that balancing is required with respect to that provision, may be ignored on the basis of the Security Council's pronouncement in Resolution 1373 that terrorism is contrary to the United Nation's purposes and principles. Article 1F(c) will be particularly attractive to governments such as the United Kingdom which are inclined to the view

[74] See the discussion of the case law in Hathaway and Harvey (n 38 above) 311–13. For relevant jurisprudence, see the UK Court of Appeal's decision in *T v Secretary of State for the Home Department* [1995] 1 WLR 545, upheld by the House of Lords on appeal and confirmed by s 34 of the Anti-Terrorism, Crime and Security Act 2001 (UK) (a provision that was not affected by the Lords' decision in the *Belmarsh case* (n 22 above); the US Supreme Court's decision in *INS v Aguirre-Aguirre* 526 US 415 (1999) 426 (although, strictly speaking, the court's comments on this point would appear to be obiter, since it deferred to the Board of Immigration Appeal's reading of the statute); the Canadian Federal Court's decision in *Malouf v Canada (Minister of Citizenship and Immigration)* [1995] 1 FC 537; the Australian Federal Court's decision in *NADB of 2001 v Minister for Immigration and Multicultural Affairs* [2002] FCAFC 326, (2002) 126 FCR 453; and the New Zealand Court of Appeal's decision in *S v Refugee Status Appeals Authority* [1998] 2 NZLR 291. For discussion of the case law, see M Zagor, 'Persecutor or Persecuted: Exclusion under Article 1F(a) and (b) of the Refugees Convention' (2000) 23 *University of New South Wales Law Journal* 164 at 186. See also the acknowledgement of the trend in jurisprudence by the Lisbon Expert Roundtable on Exclusion, reproduced in Feller, Türk and Nicholson (n 9 above) 481.

[75] Hathaway and Harvey (n 38 above) 299–310. Arguing for a link between Art 1F(b) and extradition, Hathaway and Harvey state (at 310) that 'UNHCR effectively invites states to impose exclusion for crimes that fail to meet the drafters' basic litmus test of extraditable criminality'.

[76] Hathaway argues in general that State practice should be down-played: JC Hathaway, *The Rights of Refugees under International Law* (Cambridge, Cambridge University Press, 2005) 68–74.

[77] Nyinah (n 65 above) 307.

[78] UNHCR's Guidelines (n 2 above) para 26.

that no amount of persecution can outweigh excludable crimes, and that, conversely, a risk of torture should be outweighed by the threat to national security.[79]

C. Fungible Thresholds

There are a number of other aspects of Article 1F(c) which make the possibility of exclusion a very appealing proposition. States may welcome the possibility of exclusion on the basis of an ill-defined 'terrorist' threat to the nation, a low standard of proof and uncertain levels of due process.

i. The Pull of the Undefined

Both the provisions on dangerous refugees and Article 1F(c) contain terms that are capable of overly broad definitions. The provisions on dangerous refugees refer, among other things, to 'national security'.[80] Meanwhile, Article 1F(c) is acknowledged to be the least determinate of the exclusion clauses. As will be demonstrated, this indeterminacy has been exacerbated by the UN Security Council categorising terrorism as an act contrary to the 'purposes and principles' of the United Nations, without defining 'terrorism' itself.

Article 1F(c) has a further layer of indeterminacy. In addition to the vagaries of the terms it uses, it does not require a specific threat to the country of refuge. This issue was raised in the debates on the General Assembly's Supplementary Declaration on Terrorism in the Sixth Committee, when the UK delegate expressed a concern regarding crimes committed in other States but planned in the United Kingdom.[81] Although Article 33(2) contains no express geographic limitation on where the crime is committed, it does refer to a refugee who is a 'danger to the security of the country in which he is' or to criminals who are 'a danger to the community of that country'. This suggests that in general, the crimes would be committed within the country of refuge.[82] Similarly, although less clear, Article 32 refers to *national* security.[83]

It is, of course, possible that a person could reasonably be viewed as a threat to security if he or she commits crimes, particularly terrorist crimes,

[79] See the intervention in the *Ramzy case* (n 19 above).

[80] For useful discussion of the case law on the concept of security, see Hathaway (n 76 above) 264–6, 345–8.

[81] See n 30 above.

[82] Hathaway and Harvey (n 38 above) 289–90.

[83] As Gilbert notes, the concept of national security is broader than the phrase 'danger to the community of that country': Gilbert (n 9 above) 460.

elsewhere. For example, consider the following words from the Canadian Supreme Court in *Suresh*:

> Whatever the historic validity of insisting on direct proof of specific danger to the deporting country, as matters have evolved, we believe courts may now conclude that the support of terrorism abroad raises a possibility of adverse repercussions on Canada's security.[84]

Moreover, the tendency to redraft national laws to cover inchoate offences related to terrorism, such as conspiracy, arguably means that States may, through the extension of their criminal jurisdiction, exclude refugees who plan terrorist acts, including acts committed abroad. Nevertheless, the lack of a requirement concerning a specific threat in Article 1F(c) means that it has the potential to be used to respond to ill-defined, possibly even illusory, 'threats'.

Article 1F(c) seems concerned with acts affecting the international community as a whole, rather than threats to a particular State. A rigorous interpretation of such a requirement could mean that the threshold for invoking Article 1F(c) is very high. UNHCR's Guidelines state that

> Article 1F(c) is only triggered in extreme circumstances by activity which attacks the very basis of the international community's coexistence. Such an activity must have an international dimension .... In cases involving a terrorist act, a correct application of Article 1F(c) involves an assessment as to the extent to which the act impinges on the international plane—in terms of its gravity, international impact, and implications for international peace and security.[85]

However, the Security Council's approach in Resolution 1373 may loosen and politicise the threshold. The Council has taken a fairly broad-brush approach to the question of the challenge that terrorist acts must pose to the United Nations in order for it to be said that they are acts against its principles and purposes. The Council stated in the Preamble to Resolution 1373 that 'any act of international terrorism, constitute[s] a threat to international peace and security',[86] and then referred to terrorism *simple* in operative paragraphs 3(f) and (g) and 5. Thus, the resolution appears to signal that terrorist acts of a lesser scale than September 11 and which have no cross-border element might result in exclusion. Perhaps this should not surprise us. After 11 September 2001, it is supposed that terrorism everywhere threatens everyone. Locale, and perhaps context, is irrelevant.

[84] *Suresh v Canada (Minister of Citizenship and Immigration)* [2002] 1 SCR 3, 2002 SCC 1, 50–51.

[85] UNHCR's Guidelines (n 2 above) para 17.

[86] UNSC Res 1373 (2001) preambular para 3.

The way in which Resolution 1373 frames the issue suggests that the identity of the terrorist is equally beside the point. Resolution 1373 may work a shift in jurisprudence from the conservative approach to Article 1F(c), which requires the excludable person to be high in the echelons of the State.

Such a shift would make the provision more user-friendly. Terrorists generally work outside the formal framework of the State, although many are State-sponsored. Indeed, given the Security Council's tendency to refer to terrorist acts of any kind, it may be that fairly 'low-level players' may be caught by Article 1F(c) as interpreted by the Security Council, transforming it from a little used provision to a veritable catch-all.

Certainly, it would appear that the reiteration of the traditional interpretation of the Refugee Convention has been 'lost in translation' as the language has migrated to Resolution 1373.[87] On the one hand, paragraphs 3(f) and (g) of Resolution 1373 refer to international law—presumably as it stood at the time the resolution was adopted. Moreover, the later Resolution 1456 provides that

> States must ensure that any measure taken to combat terrorism comply with all their obligations under international law, and should adopt such measures in accordance with international law, in particular international human rights, refugee, and humanitarian law.[88]

On the other hand, in Resolution 1373, the language concerning the purposes and principles of the United Nations and the references to refugees appear shorn of the General Assembly Declaration's preambular references safeguarding the interpretation of the Refugee Convention and, indeed, without any reference to the Assembly's Declaration at all. While the clause concerning human rights and refugee law has been reiterated in a number of Security Council resolutions since Resolution 1373,[89] so

[87] The process of migration began earlier than Resolution 1373. UNSC Res 1269 (1999) picked up some of the General Assembly's language. Para 4 calls upon States to 'take appropriate measures in conformity with the relevant provisions of national and international law, including international standards of human rights, before granting refugee status, for the purpose of ensuring that the asylum-seeker has not participated in terrorist acts'. However, it is notable that while Council resolutions prior to Resolution 1373 link terrorism to international peace and security, they do so in weaker terms and they certainly do not use the language which describes terrorism as being against the principles and purposes of the United Nations. Resolution 1373 marks a quite sharp departure from previous Security Council resolutions.

[88] UNSC Res 1456 (2003) para 6.

[89] This very important paragraph has been repeated in several Security Council resolutions on terrorism since then: see, eg UNSC Res 1566 (2004). It should also be noted that Resolution 1624, in a preambular paragraph, puts the emphasis back on the right to seek asylum, with exclusion as the exception. Preambular para 7 of UNSC Res 1624 (2005) states that the Council recalls 'in addition the right to seek and enjoy asylum reflected in Article 14 of the Universal Declaration and the non-refoulement obligation of States under the Convention Relating to the Status of Refugees adopted on 28 July 1951 … and … that the protections afforded by the Refugees Convention and its Protocol shall not extend to any person with respect to whom there are serious reasons for considering that he has been guilty of acts contrary to the purposes and principles of the United Nations'.

has the paragraph concerning terrorist acts contravening the purposes and principles of the United Nations.[90] One must ask what the use is of declaring terrorist acts to be against the purposes and principles of the United Nations if this declaration is not intended to inform the interpretation of the exclusion clauses of the Refugee Convention, especially when the compromise reached in the General Assembly has not been expressly transferred to the Security Council's resolutions.

Again, perhaps we should not be surprised. The very lack of international consensus on a definition of 'terrorism'[91] stems from the politicisation of the term and its utility in describing any political opponent who engages in violence. As Kälin and Künzli demonstrate, the label 'terrorism' ignores the circumstances in which violence by individuals is specifically authorised, as in the case of illegally occupied territories, or is at least tolerated, as in the case of national liberation movements.[92]

If 'terrorism' were to be clearly and appropriately defined, the push to place it beyond the pale and consequentially for it to provide the basis for exclusion from refugee status would be acceptable, in my view.[93] As it is, however, States may well unfairly exclude asylum seekers on the basis of domestic understandings of terrorism, understandings that may wilfully turn a blind eye to the transnational context on the basis that the terrorist threat is the same no matter what its origins, its aims or who is involved.

ii. A Low Standard of Proof and Uncertain Levels of Due Process

States may be drawn to the low standard of proof referred to in Article 1F. Indeed, there may be a temptation for States to use the exclusion clauses to revoke refugee status,[94] with the result that the person concerned is no longer 'lawfully' within the country and, possibly, that due process is diminished.

[90] See, eg UNSC Res 1624 (2005) preambular para 8. Following straight on from the explicit reference to the Refugee Convention and the exclusion clauses, that paragraph states that the Security Council reaffirms 'that acts, methods, and practices of terrorism are contrary to the purposes and principles of the United Nations and that knowingly financing, planning and inciting terrorist acts are also contrary to the purposes and principles of the United Nations'.

[91] Although the Convention for the Suppression of the Financing of Terrorism (n 51 above) contains a general definition and is widely ratified, the debate has continued in the context of the drafting of a comprehensive treaty against international terrorism.

[92] Kälin and Künzli (n 68 above) 47–63.

[93] See, eg the attempt by the Special Rapporteur on the Promotion and Protection of Human Rights and Fundamental Freedoms while Countering Terrorism, who draws on the approach taken in UNSC Res 1566 (2004) para 3: United Nations Commission on Human Rights, 'Report of the Special Rapporteur on the Promotion and Protection of Human Rights while Countering Terrorism', UN Doc E/CN.4/2006/98 (2005) para 50.

[94] UNHCR has taken the view that it is permissible to revoke refugee status *ex nunc* (literally meaning 'as from now'): UNHCR's Guidelines (n 2 above) paras 5 and 6. The move to use the exclusion clauses to revoke refugee status is highly questionable, but it is beyond the scope of this chapter to analyse this point fully.

Article 1F provides for exclusion where 'there are *serious reasons for considering that*' (emphasis added) the person has committed a crime against peace, a war crime or a crime against humanity (paragraph (a)), or a serious non-political crime outside the country of refuge (paragraph (b)), or has been guilty of acts contrary to the purposes and principles of the United Nations (paragraph (c)). In contrast, Article 33(2) refers to a refugee

> *whom there are reasonable grounds for regarding as a danger to the security of the country* in which he is, *or* who, having been *convicted of a particularly serious crime constitutes a danger* to the community of that country (emphasis added).

The reference to 'reasonable grounds' in Article 33(2) appears lower than 'serious reasons', and some jurisprudence sets a very low threshold.[95] However, the requirement of a conviction (and a conviction of a *particularly* serious crime, not merely a serious one) in the second part of Article 33(2) is clearly a higher threshold than that imposed by Article 1F. Further, whatever 'serious reasons for considering' means, it is not the same as the criminal standard of proof, namely 'beyond reasonable doubt'.[96]

Gilbert argues persuasively that serious reasons to consider someone guilty *approaches* the level of proof for a criminal conviction and that the burden rests upon the excluding State.[97] Similarly, Bliss suggests that the standard of proof for Article 1F should be higher than the civil standard of balance of probabilities, given the 'severe consequences of a decision to exclude, the exceptional nature of exclusion and the general protection purpose of the Convention'.[98]

UNHCR recognises that the criminal standard of proof does not have to be met in relation to Article 1F, but its Guidelines state that 'clear and credible evidence is required'.[99] This seems to indicate that the standard is at least the balance of probabilities, but State practice does not consistently adopt a particularly high standard.[100]

[95] See *In Re A–H–* 23 I & N Dec 774 (2005) 789, where the US Attorney-General determined that 'reasonable grounds for regarding' was 'substantially less stringent than preponderance of the evidence' (balance of probabilities).

[96] See Bliss (n 66 above) 115.

[97] Gilbert (n 9 above) 470.

[98] Bliss (n 66 above) 116. At 120, Bliss gives an illustrative list of the evidence which would constitute 'serious reasons for considering', including:

- — a credible confession by the asylum seeker of involvement in excludable crimes;
- — a verified and legitimate conviction of an excludable crime;
- — an indictment by an international tribunal; and
- — other clear and convincing evidence.

[99] UNHCR's Guidelines (n 2 above) para 35.

[100] See, eg the Australian case of *SZCWP v Minister for Immigration and Multicultural and Indigenous Affairs* [2006] FCAFC 9, para 22: 'The adopted standard, "serious reasons for considering", does not require proof, even on a balance of probabilities. It is sufficient

Related to the question of thresholds is the issue of due process. Immigration decisions are a jealously guarded aspect of State sovereignty, and, in general, the Refugee Convention is silent on refugee status determination procedures, while the exclusion clauses do not mention due process. By contrast, by virtue of Article 32 of the Refugee Convention, all expulsions of refugees *lawfully* in the country are to be 'in pursuance of a decision reached in accordance with due process of law', although the level of due process can be limited when 'compelling reasons of national security … require [otherwise]'. It is expressly provided that, unless the national security clause is invoked,

> the refugee is to be allowed to submit evidence to clear himself, and to appeal to and be represented for the purpose before competent authority or a person or persons specially designated by the competent authority.[101]

Article 33(2) should only be invoked if the protections of Article 32—in particular, due process of law—are adhered to in the case of refugees 'lawfully' within the country.[102] Thus, Gilbert states that

> it is clearly justified to require that determinations with respect to Article 33(2) apply not only the procedural safeguards of Article 32, but do so with heightened care.[103]

A person who has already had refugee status determined and has, as will usually be the case, been granted a lawful immigration status, is expressly owed some level of due process.

if there is "strong evidence of the commission of one of the relevant crimes or acts": see *Dhayakpa v Minister for Immigration and Ethnic Affairs* (1995) 62 FCA 556 at 563 (French J). See also *Ovcharuk v Minister for Immigration and Multicultural Affairs* (1998) 88 FCR 173 at 179 and *Arquita v Minister for Immigration and Multicultural Affairs* (2000) 106 FCR 465 at 476'. See also *SRYYY v Minister for Immigration and Multicultural & Indigenous Affairs* [2005] FCAFC 42, (2005) 147 FCR 1, para 80. For a discussion of the problematic nature of the low standard, see M Zagor, 'No Mean Feat to Walk the Line between Refugees and Criminals' *Sydney Morning Herald* (8 December 2005) <http://www.smh.com.au/news/opinion/walking-the-line-between-refugees-and-criminals/2005/12/07/1133829660319.html> (accessed 20 June 2007). See also *Ramirez v Canada (Minister of Employment and Immigration)* [1992] 2 FC 306 (CCA).

[101] For analysis of the due process protections, see Hathaway (n 76 above) 670–77.

[102] Art 32 is limited to refugees lawfully within the country. Although Hathaway argues that this should include anyone permitted to stay and apply for refugee status, States may not take this view. Contrast Hathaway (n 76 above) 173–85, with *Szoma v Secretary of State for the Department of Work and Pensions* [2005] UKHL 64, [2006] 1 AC 564. Robinson notes that Art 33(2) is to be read subject to Arts 32 and 31, meaning, for example, that before expulsion or return takes place under Art 33(2), the refugee must be given time and facilities to secure admission to a third (non-persecutory) country: N Robinson, *Convention Relating to the Status of Refugees: Its History, Contents and Interpretation* (New York, Institute of Jewish Affairs, World Jewish Congress, 1953) 165. See also P Weis, *The Refugee Convention, 1951, the Travaux Préparatoires Analysed with a Commentary* (Cambridge/New York, Cambridge University Press, 1995) 342. Furthermore, Hathaway notes that '[t]he duties of *non-refoulement* and non-expulsion were never conceived as mutually exclusive; indeed, they were originally proposed as two aspects of a common obligation': Hathaway (n 76 above) 664.

[103] Gilbert (n 9 above) 460–61.

In practice, the textual differences between the exclusion clauses and the provisions on dangerous refugees may not be as important as first appears. The New Zealand case of *Zaoui* demonstrates that recognised refugees may be faced with decision-making that occurs at a political level and which offers relatively minimal due process when national security is at stake.[104] Moreover, although the exclusion clauses do not deal with due process, there is a clear requirement on States to observe some level of due process when invoking the exclusion clauses. Good faith implementation of the Refugee Convention requires a refugee status determination procedure—unless the State concerned is happy to accept all asylum seekers' claims at face value. Good faith also requires due process,[105] and, given the exceptional nature of the exclusion clauses, the consequences of exclusion and the focus on criminal activities, it is clear that due process is particularly important in exclusion proceedings.

UNHCR has spelt out procedural requirements in relation to the exclusion clauses. Its Guidelines provide that the burden generally rests on the State and that the benefit of the doubt principle applies, although a rebuttable presumption of exclusion arises if the asylum seeker has been indicted by an international criminal tribunal.[106] UNHCR also stipulates that 'clear and credible evidence is required',[107] and advocates that exclusion 'should not be based on sensitive evidence that cannot be challenged by the individual concerned',[108] making particular reference to the necessity of establishing procedures that protect due process if the evidence concerned relates to national security. Arguably, then, any anticipated gains on the question of due process flowing from the use of Article 1F as opposed to Article 32 should be illusory, depending on States' acceptance of UNHCR's Guidelines.

Another factor weighing against the use of the exclusion clauses to bypass due process is the procedural protection offered by more general human rights law. Similarly to Article 32 of the Refugee Convention, Article 13 of the International Covenant on Civil and Political Rights ('ICCPR') provides protection from expulsion to aliens *lawfully* in the territory.[109] The ICCPR, like the Refugee Convention, does not grant a right of entry (which is really what exclusion cases are about, even if the person currently has some form of lawful immigration status). However,

[104] *Zaoui v Attorney-General (No 2)* [2006] 1 NZLR 289 (NZSC).
[105] See Bliss (n 66 above) 95.
[106] UNHCR's Guidelines (n 2 above) para 34.
[107] *Ibid*, para 35.
[108] *Ibid*, para 36.
[109] International Covenant on Civil and Political Rights (adopted 16 Dec 1966, entered into force 23 March 1976) 999 UNTS 171.

where implicit obligations of *non-refoulement* are involved, due process guarantees may follow as a result of general provisions concerning remedies, and these remedies will not depend on the immigration status of the subject of the decision-making process.

This point is illustrated by the *Chahal* case. The European Court of Human Rights held unanimously that there had been violations of Article 5(4) of the ECHR—the provision dealing with judicial control of detention—and Article 13—concerning effective remedies for violations. When dealing with Article 13 of the ECHR and its relationship with the prohibition on torture in Article 3 of that instrument, the court commented on the procedure before the Home Office's advisory panel (a procedure which has since been changed to some degree) as follows:[110]

> [T]he Court notes that in the proceedings before the advisory panel the applicant was not entitled, inter alia, to legal representation, that he was only given an outline of the grounds for the notice of intention to deport, that the panel had no power of decision and that its advice to the Home Secretary was not binding and was not disclosed. In these circumstances, the advisory panel could not be considered to offer sufficient procedural safeguards for the purposes of article 13.[111]

Nevertheless, the fact that the prospect of procedurally unfair decision-making may be a legal mirage will not necessarily deter States from attempting to get away with it, especially if there is an apparent legal lacuna or aperture to be exploited.

D. Erosion of the Absolute Guarantee of *Non-Refoulement* to a Place of Torture

In addition to offering a higher level of due process, as discussed above, human rights law offers an absolute guarantee against *refoulement* in cases involving return to torture or related forms of treatment or loss of life.[112]

[110] See the description of the Special Advocate procedure in House of Commons Constitutional Affairs Committee, *The Operation of the Special Immigration Appeals Commission (SIAC) and the Use of Special Advocates* Vol 1 (London, The Stationery Office, 2005) para 44ff.

[111] *Chahal v United Kingdom* (n 13 above) para 154. The views and Concluding Observations of the Human Rights Committee and the Committee against Torture also evince a concern that a person facing return to torture or death has had due process. See also *Zaoui* (n 104 above).

[112] See Human Rights Committee, 'General Comment No 20' UN Doc HRI/GEN/1/Rev.7 (12 May 2004) para 9; Human Rights Committee, 'General Comment 31 on Article 2 of the Covenant: The Nature of the General Legal Obligation Imposed on States Parties to the Covenant' (29 March 2004) UN Doc CCPR/C/21/Rev.1/Add.13 (26 May 2004) para 12; and J McAdam, *Complementary Protection in International Refugee Law* (Oxford, Oxford University Press, 2007).

Accordingly, as mentioned in part I above, the United Kingdom is campaigning to read down Article 3 of the ECHR so that its reach is consonant with the Refugee Convention.

The intervening governments in the *Ramzy case* argue that the European Court of Human Rights should read down the absolute prohibition on torture and the related *non-refoulement* obligation so that it is no longer absolute, but is consonant with the narrower obligation of *non-refoulement* set out in the Refugee Convention. The governments point out that *non-refoulement* has been read into Article 3 of the ECHR, whereas the Refugee Convention expressly denies refugee status to persons who act contrary to the principles and the purposes of the United Nations.[113] They argue that

> [i]n those circumstances, it is difficult to see how those who negotiated and agreed upon both Conventions can have intended that that position under the 1951 Convention should effectively be reversed by interpretation of article 3 of the Convention.[114]

Thus, the intervening governments contend that a dynamic interpretation of provisions which do not expressly forbid or permit *refoulement* should be pulled back to the notion of 'unworthiness' adopted by the framers of the Refugee Convention in 1951. This argumentative strategy is required because the intervening governments would otherwise have to accept that the absolute prohibition on *refoulement* to torture effectively trumps, or at least supplements, the more limited prohibition on *non-refoulement* in the Refugee Convention. Article 5 of the Refugee Convention contains a savings clause for more generous rights protected by other instruments, and it is widely accepted that the prohibition on torture is a norm of *jus cogens* permitting no derogation.[115]

The intervening governments' strategy is flawed. Given the object and purpose of all human rights treaties—the protection of the *inherent* and *universal* rights of the individual—the idea that any person is *unworthy* of rights protection is to be treated with suspicion. Rights are not dependent on notions of desert, as all human beings are treated as equally deserving of rights protection. *Limitations* are imposed for reasons such as the protection of others, while complete *derogation* is permitted only in the face of exceptional circumstances, and then only temporarily.[116] The one

[113] See 'Observations' in the *Ramzy case* (n 19 above) paras 8–9.3.

[114] See *Ibid*, para 9.3.

[115] Treaties covering different subject matter may come into conflict, leaving States to choose whether to violate one treaty in order to comply with another. In the case of a 'choice' between a limited norm and an absolute one, both norms can, of course, be complied with and the *jus cogens* nature of one norm simply strengthens the duty to comply with it.

[116] See, eg the general limitations clause in Art 4 of the International Covenant on Economic, Social and Cultural Rights (adopted 16 December 1966, entered into force 3 January 1976) 993 UNTS 3, and the derogation clause in Art 4 of the ICCPR.

area in which the general human rights instruments might be said to have departed from this understanding of rights is in relation to the death penalty, and this is only because State practice demanded that the international community tolerate the death penalty while moving towards its abolition.[117] Therefore, the idea of *unworthiness* leading to exclusion requires further thought. Saul simply states that 'the denial of protection in refugee law to persons because they are "unworthy" is outdated given developments in modern human rights law'.[118]

It may be that there are valid reasons to deem persons unworthy of protection *as refugees*, and the rights *that pertain to refugees* in particular, even though the fact that human rights are due to all persons within a State's territory and jurisdiction serves to limit the practical impact of denial of refugee status.[119] One reason would be to preserve commitment to the fundamental principle of *non-refoulement* of refugees, which is, after all, a moral principle. Underlying the principle of *non-refoulement* is the desire not to become complicit in persecution. Complicity in persecution would also follow from granting protection to a person who was him- or herself a persecutor (as some war criminals would be, for example). Equally, to grant protection to a mere fugitive from justice (one of the persons encompassed by Article 1F(b)) degrades the concept of protection from persecution by equating persecution with prosecution, and it may also make the

[117] The compromise is encapsulated in Art 6 of the ICCPR (n 109 above):

> '2. In countries which have not abolished the death penalty, sentence of death may be imposed only for the most serious crimes in accordance with the law in force at the time of the commission of the crime and not contrary to the provisions of the present Covenant and to the Convention on the Prevention and Punishment of the Crime of Genocide. This penalty can only be carried out pursuant to a final judgement rendered by a competent court'.
>
> '6. Nothing in this article shall be invoked to delay or to prevent the abolition of capital punishment by any State Party to the present Covenant'.

However, note the recent comments of the Human Rights Committee in *Judge v Canada*, Comm No 829/1998, UN Doc CCPR/C/78/D/829/1998 (5 August 2003) para 10.4: 'For countries that have abolished the death penalty, there is an obligation not to expose a person to the real risk of its application. Thus, they may not remove, either by deportation or extradition, individuals from their jurisdiction if it may be reasonably anticipated that they will be sentenced to death, without ensuring that the death sentence would not be carried out'. In the European Union, 'subsidiary protection' may be granted if a person faces a real risk of being exposed to the death penalty or execution if returned to his or her country of origin: Council Directive 2004/83/EC of 29 April 2004 on Minimum Standards for the Qualification and Status of Third Country Nationals or Stateless Persons as Refugees or as Persons Who Otherwise Need International Protection and the Content of the Protection Granted [2004] OJ L304/12, Art 15(a).

[118] B Saul, 'Exclusion of Suspected Terrorists from Asylum: Trends in International and European Refugee Law' Institute for International Integration Studies, Discussion Paper No 6 (July 2004) 11.

[119] For a detailed analysis of the way in which the Refugee Convention grants rights protection over and above that owed under general human rights law, see Hathaway (n 76 above).

State of refuge an accomplice in serious wrong-doing.[120] The fact that the moral principle of *non-refoulement* cuts across the face of the State's sovereign power to control immigration may, insofar as refugee status imposes positive obligations on States, underscore the need for an exception in the cases mentioned above.

However, the consequence of 'exclusion' is not *necessarily* return to a place of persecution, and there may still be negative obligations in the cases of those persons deemed unworthy of refugee status. Article 1F(b) is designed in part to permit extradition for those who flee prosecution rather than persecution,[121] and therefore, surely, to ensure prosecution, rather than persecution. Furthermore, the practical necessity of *refoulement* is diminishing with the willingness of some States to exercise universal jurisdiction and the establishment of the International Criminal Court.[122] Meanwhile, Article 33(2) is clearly framed as a last resort in order to protect States of refuge. With the passage of time, the international community has accepted that in some cases—particularly that of torture—return can never be justified, as it too involves complicity in something which is simply unacceptable.

To counter this fundamental insight, the governments intervening in the *Ramzy case* make some interesting arguments about the degree of possible risk to the community involved and the requisite standard of proof for criminal prosecution, as compared to the degree of possible risk of torture for someone to be returned in cases involving terrorism.[123] However, the reasons asserted as to why national prosecutions are not sufficient to protect the community are generally weak:

> An individual concerned in terrorism may take great care not to commit any criminal offences until the time comes for him to strike or provide material assistance to his cause;
>
> Any criminal offences he commits may be only tangentially related to his terrorist intentions (eg petty theft or fraud), and the sentence imposed must be appropriate for the crime rather than based upon a preventative principle to safeguard the public against a quite different activity and risk, namely terrorist action;
>
> Even if criminal offences are committed, there may be insuperable impediments in the way of the authorities in the Contracting State being able to rely upon secret intelligence information in criminal proceedings in order to secure a conviction (eg it may be impossible to rely upon evidence from an informant, where the disclosure of that evidence would necessarily reveal the informant's identify and place him at serious risk of harm or murder); and

[120] Nyinah (n 65 above) 296–7.

[121] See the discussion in Hathaway and Harvey (n 38 above) 276 about the references to extradition treaties in the *travaux préparatoires*.

[122] See the discussion in Gilbert (n 9 above) 430.

[123] See 'Observations' in the *Ramzy case* (n 19 above) paras 17–26.

> The evidence available to the authorities may amply indicate that the individual in question does pose a serious risk to national security through involvement in terrorism, without enabling them to establish that he has engaged in such activity to the level of proof beyond reasonable doubt, sufficient to secure a criminal conviction.[124]

In light of these submissions, it appears that the 'evidence' of a terrorist 'threat' justifying returning someone to a place where there are 'substantial grounds for believing that he would be in danger of being subject to torture'[125] could be slight indeed. Moreover, the arguments concerning 'intelligence' are outweighed by the likelihood that a criminal accused will suffer inequality of arms with the prosecution when 'national security' is invoked and that ensuing convictions will be unfair.

Perhaps because the intervening governments recognise that they are in fact arguing for violations of human rights, the submission sets up its argument as a balancing act between the rights of citizens, on the one hand, and aliens on the other,[126] as well as attempting to assert a hierarchy of rights with the right to life at the top, and so-called negative rights or inaction by governments prevailing over positive rights or duties of non-complicity on the part of governments.[127] In other words, a complete subversion of the ideas fundamental to human rights—universality, indivisibility, interdependence and inter-relatedness—is being attempted.

It is not the first time that this sort of argument has been run.[128] There is a real danger that the Security Council's emphasis on denial of refugee status to terrorists may become a stalking horse for the erosion of the absolute protection against return to a place of torture currently guaranteed by general human rights law.

E. A Pre-emptive Short Cut for Getting Rid of 'Undesirables'

The above analysis has shown that using Article 1F(c) to respond to asylum seekers allegedly involved in terrorism has a number of attractions for States. It is possible to avoid consideration of the inclusive aspects of the refugee definition on the basis of low evidentiary thresholds and for States

[124] *Ibid*, para 14.

[125] Convention against Torture and Other Cruel, Inhuman or Degrading Treatment or Punishment (adopted 10 December 1984, entered into force 26 June 1987) 1465 UNTS 85, Art 3.

[126] 'Observations' in the *Ramzy case* (n 19 above) para 5, as compared with para 8.

[127] *Ibid*, para 10.

[128] Similar arguments were mounted in the key Canadian case of *Suresh* (n 84 above) (although the arguments there concerned the Canadian Charter of Rights and Freedoms, Pt I of the Constitution Act 1982, being Schedule B to the Canada Act 1982 (UK)), and the court did not rule out deportation to face torture in 'exceptional circumstances': [2002] 1 SCR 3, 2002 SCC 1, 46.

to capitalise on the lack of clarity in the Refugee Convention concerning due process. There is also little authority requiring 'balancing' in the case of Article 1F(c). Thus, the move to characterise 'terrorism' as an act against the principles and purposes of the United Nations, without providing a definition of 'terrorism', may encourage States to rely on their own characterisations of someone as a terrorist and avoid particularly hard scrutiny of exclusion decisions. In particular, I would argue that States may move to exclude those whom they regard as undesirable—for example, because they espouse extreme views, a ground for exclusion that is nowhere to be found in the Refugee Convention[129]—in a vain attempt to pre-empt terrorism.

This stance may work unfairly against some persons who should not be excluded,[130] and, of course, it may prove impractical. Despite its efforts to secure diplomatic guarantees and to rewrite the law relating to the prohibition on torture, the United Kingdom may not always be able to secure the deportation of Belmarsh detainees such as Abu Qatada. Moreover, to impose measures of immigration control on persons who are 'undesirable' because, for example, they are extremists, may simply be a distraction. Of course, some speech amounts to incitement to violence and hate speech is prohibited by international human rights law.[131] However, it is surely a mistake to think that one can truly counter these views by simply removing one of their protagonists through deportation. This is particularly true if the racism and intolerance of citizens against minority groups goes unchecked, thereby assisting in perpetuating and creating grievances. Unfortunately, a review of States' reports to the Counter-Terrorism Committee indicates that many States are succumbing to the temptation of punishing outsiders in order to look as though obligations to combat terrorism have been observed.

[129] For an illustration in the different context of Art 1F(b) and drug-smuggling, see *Ovcharuk v Minister for Immigration and Multicultural Affairs* (1998) 88 FCR 173. In this case, the Australian Federal Court applied Art 1F(b) to a conviction for an *extraterritorial Australian* offence, which involved an absurdly literal approach to the terms 'serious reasons for considering'. The basis for this approach was the argument that Art 1F exists to protect countries of refuge, a rationale that is arguably unsound. Contrast Hathaway and Harvey (n 38 above) with 'Summary Conclusions: Exclusion from Refugee Status' (Expert Roundtable, Lisbon, 3–4 May 2001) in Feller, Türk and Nicholson (n 9 above) 479. More importantly, perhaps, in the face of the Administrative Appeals Tribunal's finding that 'Ovcharuk has *genuine concerns for his safety* from the drug underworld in Russia because of his *role in assisting the investigation of drug importation into Australia*' (emphasis added), one senses that Ovcharuk was being dispensed with as an undesirable, rather than as a person unworthy of protection from the harm he feared *or* as a danger to the Australian community. See *Ovcharuk v Minister for Immigration and Multicultural Affairs* (1997) 50 ALD 618 (AAT) 622.

[130] See Sloan's analysis of the Canadian jurisprudence prior to *Pushpanathan*, in which Art 1F(c) had become a fertile playground for the exclusion of persons deemed undesirable on the basis of minor criminal activities: J Sloan, 'The Application of Article 1F of the 1951 Convention in Canada and the United States' (2000) 12 (Spec Issue) *International Journal of Refugee Law* 222 at 246.

[131] See, eg ICCPR (n 109 above) Art 20.

IV. RESOLUTION 1373 IN PRACTICE—FROM PRE-EMPTION TO REFRAMING REFUGEE RIGHTS VIOLATIONS AS COUNTER-TERRORISM

One way of measuring the impact of Resolution 1373 so far is to examine States' reports to the Counter-Terrorism Committee. There are, in fact, numerous difficulties in relying on such reports for an accurate picture. Reading the reports is tedious, as many of them have not been well translated and sometimes do not describe the legal situation well, nor do they give real practical detail as to how the laws are implemented. Nevertheless, preliminary research on States' reports to the Counter-Terrorism Committee shows that Resolution 1373 may indeed be having an adverse effect on refugee law and practice. Many of the practices adopted may be seen as 'pre-emptive'—for example, closure of borders, denial of political rights and detention. It also appears that rights violations—often ones that were occurring prior to September 11—are being recast as counter-terrorism.

There is some evidence of a trend towards reliance on Article 1F(c) in cases involving suspected terrorists. Finland, after express reference to Article 1F(c), noted that

> [t]he UN General Assembly, in the Declaration to Supplement the 1994 Declaration on Measures to Eliminate International Terrorism ... has confirmed that acts of terrorism, knowingly financing, planning or inciting terrorist acts, are contrary to the purposes and principles of the United Nations. Finland interprets the Convention accordingly.[132]

Similarly, Bulgaria relies on Article 1F(c) of the Convention in order to exclude terrorism, stating that terrorist acts 'undoubtedly' are contrary to the purposes and principles of the United Nations.[133] This may result in unfairness to refugee applicants, as I have endeavoured to show above.

A number of other States appear to be taking too broad an approach to the issue of exclusion, in indicating that national security or public order are sufficient grounds to exclude a refugee, thus confusing exclusion with the provisions on dangerous refugees. According to Angola's description of its laws, 'refugee status may not be conceded' when 'the person in question has committed serious crimes against the independence and sovereignty of the republic of Angola'.[134] (It should be noted that Angola

[132] *First Report of Finland* UN Doc S/2001/1251 (28 December 2001) para 10.

[133] *First Report of Bulgaria* UN Doc S/2001/1273 (27 December 2001) para 10.

[134] *Fourth Report of Angola* UN Doc S/2003/1210 (29 December 2003) 18. Art 2(a) of Law No 8/1990 of 26 May 1990, Law on Refugee Status, does indeed provide for exclusion from refugee status ('refugee status shall not be granted') on this basis: see *Refworld* database <http://www.unhcr.org/cgi-bin/texis/vtx/home/opendoc.htm?tbl=RSDLEGAL&page=research&id=3ae6b4df8> (accessed 20 June 2007).

has a very broad 'declaration' that should surely be considered an invalid reservation. Angola declared

> that the provisions of the Convention shall be applicable in Angola provided that they are not contrary to or incompatible with the constitutional and legal provisions in force in the People's Republic of Angola.[135]

Similarly to Angola, Austria stated that exclusion from refugee status applied not only when the conditions for Article 1F were met, but

> also if aliens constitute a danger to the security of the Republic for significant reasons or if they have been sentenced on the basis of a final conviction by an Austrian court for a very serious crime, and if they constitute a danger to the public because of this criminal act.[136]

Austria went on to report that asylum could be 'lost if such circumstances occur afterwards'.[137] This suggests that instead of benefiting from the protections of Article 32, for example, the refugee is stripped of refugee status. Perusal of Article 14 of Austria's 1997 Asylum Law confirms that this is the case. Armenia also reported that Article 6 of its Law on Refugees permits denial of refugee status where the applicant 'could endanger national security',[138] although the provision seems to track Article 1F of the Refugee Convention fairly closely and does not expressly refer to national security.[139] Benin reported that under its law, asylum seekers are 'granted asylum only on condition that they do not, or do not intend to, engage in activities which are incompatible with their status',[140] and that refugee

[135] See the declarations and reservations available at the United Nations Treaty Series database <http://untreaty.un.org/ENGLISH/bible/englishinternetbible/partI/chapterV/treaty2.asp> (accessed 15 June 2007). Angola has also exempted itself from the ICJ clause in relation to disputes concerning the interpretation of the Protocol <http://untreaty.un.org/ENGLISH/bible/englishinternetbible/partI/chapterV/treaty5.asp> (accessed 29 June 2007).

[136] *First Report of Austria* UN Doc S/2001/1242 (26 December 2001) para 9. Art 13(2) of the 1997 Asylum Law clearly provides that 'asylum shall be denied' in these circumstances. See the unofficial consolidation of the Asylum Law on the *Refworld* database <http://www.unhcr.org/cgi-bin/texis/vtx/home/opendoc.pdf?tbl=RSDLEGAL&id=3ae6b50c0> (accessed 29 June 2007).

[137] *Ibid.*

[138] *First Report of Armenia* UN Doc S/2002/162 (12 February 2002) 5. Armenia has no reservations to the Refugee Convention.

[139] See the unofficial translation of the Law on Refugees of the Republic of Armenia, adopted 3 March 1999, as amended in 2001, 2002 and 2004, available on the *Refworld* database <http://www.unhcr.org/cgi-bin/texis/vtx/home/opendoc.pdf?tbl=RSDLEGAL&id=3ae6b5180> (accessed 29 June 2007).

[140] *First Report of Benin* UN Doc S/2002/435 (17 April 2002) 5. The 1975 Law on the Status of Refugees says nothing of such conditions, so the conditions must be imposed through regulation or some other instrument. See Ordonnance no 75-41 du 16 juillet 1975 portant status des réfugiés, on the *Refworld* database <http://www.unhcr.org/cgi-bin/texis/vtx/home/opendoc.htm?tbl=RSDLEGAL&page=research&id=3ae6b4d544> (accessed 29 June 2007).

status has been withdrawn in a number of cases on this basis. Refugee status has also been refused to persons who did not meet character and moral standards.[141]

The reports also show a distressing tendency to laud actions that are frankly inconsistent with refugee and human rights law, clearly showing the dangers of the 'unwarranted linkage between refugees and terrorists'[142] made by the Security Council, and the General Assembly before it. In a few cases, we see States touting the fact that they never grant asylum or refugee status as best practice in counter-terrorism. The worst example of this is Sri Lanka, which reported to the Counter-Terrorism Committee that 'Sri Lanka, as a matter of policy, does not grant asylum'.[143] This is not surprising, given what Sri Lanka had to say in the Sixth Committee debates on the General Assembly's Supplementary Declaration on Terrorism:

> One of the principal causes of the continuance of terrorist movements was the sustenance they received from hard-core supporters and sympathizers resident abroad who exploited rights granted under the 1951 Convention relating to the Status of Refugees.[144]

Similarly, Micronesia, which is not party to the Refugee Convention or its Protocol, reported that

> Federated States of Micronese law does not allow 'refugee' status. Any individual arriving in the Federated States of Micronesia seeking refugee status must immediately depart, or risk detention while efforts are made to certify their status through the United Nations. Additionally, legislation more clearly defining this will shortly be drafted and presented to the Federated States of Micronesia Congress for action.[145]

It also stated that

> [s]ince 11 September, the FSM has denied entry to a number of foreign nationals who were from regions known to harbour terrorism.[146]

141 *First Report of Benin* (n 140 above).

142 See the statement by the UNHCR representative before the Sixth Committee, 40th meeting (9 December 1996) UN Doc A/C.6/51/SR.40, para 71.

143 *First Report of Sri Lanka* UN Doc S/2001/1282 (27 December 2001) 6.

144 The statement continued: 'The extreme laxity in enforcing the provisions concerning conditions of entry had led to enormous problems both for the countries that had indiscriminately admitted such persons and for their countries of nationality. It was therefore necessary to re-examine the whole question of the granting of refugee status and, even after an asylum seeker was admitted to a State, to maintain strict surveillance of his subsequent activities. The conditions for expulsion from the admitting State or return to the country of origin also needed to be considered in the light of both the current and potential danger arising from his continued state in the receiving State as well as from the State in which he had sought refuge': UN Doc A/C.6/51/SR.11 (1996) para 10.

145 *First Report of Micronesia* UN Doc S/2002/531 (7 May 2002) 8.

146 *Ibid*, 5.

Meanwhile, some States parties to the Refugee Convention indicated that it was perfectly acceptable to close the border in order to prevent the arrival of refugees. In the Chinese report to the Counter-Terrorism Committee, China said that

> [f]ollowing the events of 11 September 2001, China promptly closed its border with Afghanistan and intensified controls along its borders with Pakistan and neighbouring countries in the region.[147]

Similarly, Iran said that

> [i]mmediately after the tragic terrorist attacks of 11 September and the ensuing military operation against the Taliban, the Islamic Republic of Iran closed its borders with Afghanistan to prevent entry to the Islamic Republic of Iran of individuals suspected of involvement in acts of terrorism.[148]

Of course, it is highly likely that the Security Council *was* concerned with the potential escape of Al Qaida members from Afghanistan. But while this is a reasonable concern, Resolution 1373 only talks about ensuring that asylum seekers have not participated in terrorist acts and that refugees do not abuse their status, rather than denying refugee status to those who have not so participated and will not be abusive. Both States are party to the Refugee Convention, and while a refugee has to have crossed an international border, UNHCR has exhorted States to comply with the principle of non-rejection at the frontier in cases of mass influx.[149]

Of course, there are particularly difficult issues involved with situations of mass influx of refugees. It has been argued that in some situations, derogation from certain rights should be permitted pursuant to a formal, supervised process similar to the process of derogation under human rights instruments,[150] and even that in some circumstances closure of borders might be permitted.[151] However, in the cases of both China and Iran referred to above, it is not the problem of mass influx that is said to drive the closure of the border. Rather, the closure of the border is cited as a way of keeping terrorists out, at the expense of those needing protection. What is really required—and again, this is difficult—is an attempt to separate out armed elements of a mass influx and later to screen out terrorists, war criminals and other like people in

[147] *First Report of China* UN Doc S/2001/1270 (27 December 2001) 13.

[148] *First Report of Iran* UN Doc S/2001/1332 (31 December 2001) 4.

[149] Executive Committee Conclusion No 22 (XXXII), 'Protection of Asylum-Seekers in Situations of Large-Scale Influx' (1981).

[150] J-F Durieux and J McAdam, '*Non-Refoulement* through Time: The Case for a Derogation Clause to the Refugee Convention in Mass Influx Emergencies' (2004) 16 *International Journal of Refugee Law* 4.

[151] Hathaway (n 76 above) 359–63.

line with the exclusion clauses.[152] It seems that there is a very easy slippage occurring in these frontline States whereby refugees themselves are seen as the threat to international peace and security.[153] In other words, closure of the border is a pre-emptive measure that takes no account of protection obligations.

Still other reports suggest that restricting refugees' rights may be acceptable given the context of terrorism. For example, take the restrictions on political activities imposed by Senegal, which is party both to the Refugee Convention and the 1967 Protocol as well as the African Union's 1969 Convention Governing the Specific Aspects of the Refugee Problem in Africa ('OAU Convention').[154] In its report, Senegal states that

> [t]he Senegalese laws on political asylum prohibit refugees admitted to Senegal from engaging in any kind of political activity. They would thus lose their refugee status if they participated in terrorist groups or acts, and they could be liable to prosecution, like any other resident in Senegalese territory.[155]

This is not apparent when one reads Senegal's 1968 Law on the Status of Refugees, although some other instrument may be relevant.[156] In any event, it would not be permissible for Senegal to take such an approach. Apart from Article 2 of the Refugee Convention which imposes duties on refugees to abide by the laws of the country, including those concerning 'public order', there is nothing in the Convention that could justify a blanket restriction on

[152] Nyinah (n 65 above) 313–14. See also C Beyani, 'International Legal Criteria for the Separation of Members of Armed Forces, Armed Bands and Militia from Refugees in the Territories of Host States' (2000) 12 (Spec Issue) *International Journal of Refugee Law* 251.

[153] It is not the first time a Security Council resolution may have encouraged this perception. In UNSC Res 688 (1991), which was prompted by the attacks on Kurds and ensuing flight into the mountainous border region, the Council referred in preambular para 3 to 'the repression of the Iraqi civilian population in many parts of Iraq, including most recently in Kurdish populated areas, which led to a massive flow of refugees towards and across international frontiers and to cross-border incursions, which threaten international peace and security in the region'. The resolution went on to state that the Council 'condemns the repression of the Iraqi civilian population in many parts of Iraq, including most recently in Kurdish populated areas, the consequences of which threaten international peace and security in the region' (operative para 1). In this case, the Council may be excused for looking for a cross-border element in order to pronounce an internal situation as constituting a threat to international peace and security given the early phase of the Council's revival and a certain tentativeness about declaring internal situations in and of themselves to constitute a threat to international peace and security.

[154] Organization of African Unity Convention Governing the Specific Aspects of Refugee Problems in Africa (adopted 10 September 1969, entered into force 20 June 1974) 1001 UNTS 45.

[155] *First Report of Senegal* UN Doc S/2002/51 (14 January 2002) 9.

[156] See Loi No 68-27 du 24 juillet 1968 modifiée portent statut des réfugiés, available on the *Refworld* database <http://www.unhcr.org/home/RSDLEGAL/3ae6b5038.html> (accessed 29 June 2007).

'political activity' of refugees in particular,[157] let alone loss of refugee status.[158] The OAU Convention is more particular and does allow States significant lee-way to prohibit political activities by refugees.[159] However, it seems difficult to justify a complete ban on political activities of refugees within Senegal on the basis of the relevant provision. It cannot simply be assumed that all refugees' political activities are an 'attack' on the State, or that they would cause tension between Member States of the African Union, which is what is required by the OAU Convention. Moreover, Senegal is a party to the ICCPR, to which it has no reservations, and that instrument contains a number of articles that protect 'political activity'.[160]

Similarly to Senegal, Angola reported that according to its law, a refugee cannot 'be involved in … Angolan political life'.[161] Article 6 of the Law on Refugee Status[162] provides that refugees must 'not interfere in Angolan politics'—a phrase which seems to be interpreted extremely broadly in Angola's report to the Counter-Terrorism Committee. It should be noted here that although, as mentioned previously, Angola has an overly broad reservation to the Refugee Convention, it is party to the ICCPR and maintains no reservations to that treaty.

Lebanon[163] and Libya made similar statements[164] to those of Angola and Senegal. Neither Libya nor Lebanon is party to the Refugee Convention, however Libya is party to the OAU Convention. Moreover, both States are party to the ICCPR and neither maintains relevant reservations.

In other States, the language of 'terrorism' may work to stretch the boundaries of offences by excluding asylum seekers who are members of 'terrorist organisations'. For example, the United States reported that '[t]errorists are ineligible … for asylum and refugee status'.[165] Further,

[157] Hathaway (n 76 above) 100–01 notes that the framers agreed that any laws applicable to foreigners generally in relation to political activity would apply.

[158] It should be noted that Senegal has no reservations to the Convention or the Protocol.

[159] Art 3 of the OAU Convention (n 154 above) is entitled 'Prohibition of Subversive Activities' and provides:

> '1. Every refugee has duties to the country in which he finds himself, which require in particular that he conform with its laws and regulations as well as with measures taken for the maintenance of public order. He shall also abstain from any subversive activities against any Member State of the OAU.
>
> 2. Signatory States undertake to prohibit refugees residing in their respective territories from attacking any State member of the OAU, by any activity likely to cause tension between Member States, and in particular by use of arms, through the press, or by radio'.

[160] ICCPR (n 109 above) Arts 19–22. Another relevant article, Art 25, is restricted to citizens.

[161] *Fourth Report of Angola* UN Doc S/2003/1210 (29 December 2003) 18.

[162] See n 134 above.

[163] 'As stipulated in the Law promulgated on 10 July 1962, Lebanese laws on political asylum prohibit refugees admitted to Lebanon from engaging in any political activity whatever': *First Report of Lebanon* UN Doc S/2001/1201 (13 December 2001) 8.

[164] 'It is … established practice in Libya that whoever is granted the right of refuge is forbidden to engage in any political activity': *ibid*, 14.

[165] *First Report of the United States* UN Doc S/2001/1220 (21 December 2001) 15.

> [t]he law excludes from asylum any person who has engaged or may engage in terrorist activity, who incites terrorist activity, or who is a *knowing member of a terrorist organization*. Representatives of a terrorist organization, or of certain groups whose endorsement of terrorism undermines U.S. counterterrorism efforts are also barred from asylum.[166]

Section 212(a)(3)(B) of the US Immigration and Nationality Act,[167] which was enacted prior to the events of 11 September 2001 and subsequently strengthened by the Patriot Act, excludes such people from any kind of US visa,[168] and several of the categories, including knowing membership of certain terrorist organisations, are cross-referenced in section 208 of the Act, the provision which deals with asylum.[169] Similarly, the United Kingdom's report referred to provisions of the Anti-Terrorism, Crime and Security Act 2001 permitting the Secretary of State for the Home Department to 'certify that a person with *terrorist connections* should not be entitled to the protection of the 1951 Convention' (emphasis added).[170]

Although there is jurisprudence which acknowledges the possibility of complicity in violent actions through membership of the organisation that commits them,[171] the phrase used in the US statute—'knowing member of a terrorist organization'—leaves too much lee-way to bypass accepted concepts of individual responsibility, especially given the ill-defined nature of the 'terrorist' label. The phrase used in the UK legislation—'person with terrorist connections'—is even more fungible. UNHCR takes a more nuanced approach, stating that

> [t]he fact that a person was at some point a senior member of a repressive government or a member of an organization involved in unlawful violence does not in itself entail individual liability for excludable acts.[172]

UNHCR's Guidelines do raise a *rebuttable presumption*, however, in cases of voluntary membership where 'the purposes, activities and methods of some groups are of a particularly violent nature'.[173]

166 *Ibid*, 24.

167 USC Title 8 §1182(a)(3)(B).

168 USC Title 8 §1158(b)(2)(A)(v). In addition, see the provisions concerning removal: USC Title 8, ch 12, sub-ch V.

169 But see the contrary analysis in R Germain, 'Rushing to Judgment: The Unintended Consequences of the USA Patriot Act for Bona Fide Refugees' (2002) 16 *Georgetown Immigration Law Journal* 505 at 509.

170 *First Report of the United Kingdom* UN Doc S/2001/1232 (24 December 2001) 9. See s 33 of the Anti-Terrorism, Crime and Security Act 2001. While ss 21–32 of that Act have been repealed by the Prevention of Terrorism Act 2005, which permits 'control orders' to be placed on foreigners and UK citizens, s 33 is still on foot.

171 See, eg *Zrig v Canada (Minister of Citizenship and Immigration)* (n 72 above).

172 UNHCR's Guidelines (n 2 above) para 19.

173 *Ibid*, para 34.

In these two States, the United States and the United Kingdom, mandatory and prolonged detention has also been permitted in the case of terror suspects.[174] The United Kingdom, in its first report to the Counter-Terrorism Committee, referred to the provisions of the Anti-Terrorism, Crime and Security Act 2001, which had introduced indefinite incarceration for persons who could not be removed, and the derogation from the ECHR which that had entailed.[175]

The United Kingdom was questioned on this aspect of its legislation by the Counter-Terrorism Committee. This shows that human rights aspects of the legislation are sometimes touched on by the Counter-Terrorism Committee, however, examples are rare indeed.[176] The Special Rapporteur on the Promotion and Protection of Human Rights and Fundamental Freedoms while Countering Terrorism mentions only two cases in which he thought that the Counter-Terrorism Committee was promoting 'best practice' in counter-terrorism, in the sense of promoting compliance with human rights.[177]

The exchange between the Counter-Terrorism Committee and the United Kingdom over the indefinite incarceration of persons who cannot be deported is a particularly puzzling example of the Counter-Terrorism Committee's forays into an issue that has made world headlines and which appears to have been a driving force for the United Kingdom over the last 10 years—ever since the *Chahal* decision[178]:

> Q. The report states that where removal is not a realistic possibility, the Anti-Terrorism and Security Act [sic] provides for indefinite detention of such persons in the UK. Does this mean indefinite detention in prison?
> A. Yes. Because of the limited nature of the derogation from Article 5 ECHR, which underpins the power to detain indefinitely, the power is only exercised when detention is a measure strictly required by the exigencies of the public emergency threatening the life of the nation.[179]

The 'exchange' went no further.

Since the date of the United Kingdom's report, the House of Lords determined in the *Belmarsh case* that indefinite imprisonment of

[174] For the relevant provisions in the United States, see USC Title 8 §1226a.

[175] Since the House of Lords' decision in the *Belmarsh case* (n 22 above), the approach has had to change from one that focuses on non-nationals to one that permits the imposition of 'control orders' on both nationals and foreigners alike. See the Prevention of Terrorism Act 2005.

[176] Another example is when Belgium was asked: 'How would a person be treated if he or she were charged with a terrorist crime to which the death penalty applies in the country where it was committed?': *Second Report of Belgium* UN Doc S/2003/526 (30 April 2003) 9.

[177] See 'Report of the Special Rapporteur' (n 93 above) para 58.

[178] *Chahal v United Kingdom* (n 13 above).

[179] *Second Report of the United Kingdom* UN Doc S/2002/787 (19 July 2002) 6.

non-nationals when nationals are not so detained is not strictly required by the exigencies of the public emergency, because it is discriminatory,[180] and the relevant provisions of the Anti-Terrorism, Crime and Security Act 2001 have been repealed.[181]

Without public analysis of the reports by the Counter-Terrorism Committee,[182] one gets the sense from an exchange such as the above that the Committee's heart is not really in the few human rights questions that it has asked. This is hardly surprising. The only references to human rights in Resolution 1373 are those that appear in the paragraphs that single out asylum seekers as possible terrorists. The early approach of the Committee, as described by its first Chair, Sir Jeremy Greenstock—the gist of which still appears in the section on human rights on the Counter-Terrorism Committee's website—was that it is up to other parts of the United Nations system to monitor counter-terrorism efforts and their compliance with human rights:

> [T]he Counter-Terrorism Committee is mandated to monitor the implementation of Resolution 1373 (2001). Monitoring performance against other international conventions, including human rights law, is outside the scope of the Counter-Terrorism Committee's mandate. But we will remain aware of the interaction with human rights concerns, and we will keep ourselves briefed as appropriate. It is, of course, open to other organizations to study States' reports and take up their content in other forums.[183]

While the language of Resolution 1456 is now contained in letters from the Chair of the Counter-Terrorism Committee to States,[184] the 'further guidance' on human rights issues suggested by the Office of the High Commissioner on Human Rights was not expressly adopted by the Counter-Terrorism Committee.[185] The organisation chart of the

[180] *Belmarsh case* (n 22 above).

[181] See Prevention of Terrorism Act 2005 (UK) s 16.

[182] In a briefing of the Security Council on 21 February 2006, the Chair of the Counter-Terrorism Committee told the Council that the backlog of reports had now been cleared and referred to 'timely analysis' of the reports with a view to engaging in dialogue with States: 5375th Meeting of the UNSC, UN Doc S/PV.5375 (2006) 2–3. However, unlike the human rights treaty body reporting system, there are no Concluding Observations on States' reports. This may be because the Counter-Terrorism Committee does not view itself as an arbiter in the same way as the human rights treaty bodies.

[183] UN Doc S/PV.4453 (2002) 5.

[184] CA Ward, 'Building Capacity to Combat International Terrorism: The Role of the United Nations Security Council' (2003) 8 *Journal of Conflict and Security Law* 289 at 298.

[185] See the proposals for 'further guidance' for the submission of reports pursuant to para 6 of UNSC Res 1373 (2001) (intended to supplement the Chairman's note on 'Guidance' of 26 October 2001) in the annex to *Human Rights: A Uniting Framework* UN Doc E/CN.4/2002/18 (2002). For the 'note on guidance' from the Chair of the Counter-Terrorism Committee that goes out to States, see <http://www.un.org/Docs/sc/committees/1373/guide.htm> (accessed 20 June 2007).

Counter-Terrorism Committee[186] shows that a 'human rights, humanitarian, asylum law officer' has been appointed to the Counter-Terrorism Committee Executive Directorate ('CTED'). However, the CTED was only established by the Council in April 2004 and was declared operational in December 2005. The more explicit mandate to have dialogue with Member States on human rights compliance conferred by Resolution 1624[187]—which of course was not adopted until 14 September 2005—is also very late in the peace.

On the whole, perusal of the State reports to the Counter-Terrorism Committee tends to show that States have been emboldened to frame violations of refugee law as counter-terrorist action. This conforms to the trend identified by Human Rights Watch in relation to general human rights in the early phase of reporting,[188] and the more recent appraisal of around 640 reports offered by the Special Rapporteur on the Promotion and Protection of Human Rights and Fundamental Freedoms while Countering Terrorism, Martin Scheinin. Despite the mandate concerning human rights compliance conferred on the Counter-Terrorism Committee by Resolution 1456 and Resolution 1624, Professor Scheinin stated that he

> remain[ed] concerned that the message that States receive from the consideration of their reports by the Counter-Terrorism Committee has not always been sufficiently clear in respect of the duty to respect human rights while countering terrorism. In some instances, States may even have understood the Counter-Terrorism Committee as promoting measures of counter-terrorism irrespective of their adverse consequences for human rights.[189]

V. CONCLUSION

This chapter has shown that the UN Security Council has set in train a process to counter terrorism with far-reaching implications for asylum seekers. The Council is implicitly suggesting a shift to Article 1F(c) in

[186] See <http://www.un.org/sc/ctc/documents/CTEDorgchart.pdf> (accessed 20 June 2007).

[187] UNSC Res 1624 (2005). See particularly para 4 (reiterating the obligation on Member States to comply with human rights in their counter-terrorism efforts) and para 6 (which directs the CTC to include in its dialogue with Member States their efforts to implement Resolution 1624).

[188] Human Rights Watch, 'Hear No Evil, See No Evil: The UN Security Council's Approach to Human Rights Violations in the Global Counter-Terrorism Effort' Briefing Paper (10 August 2004) <http://www.hrw.org/backgrounder/un/2004/un0804/> (accessed 1 June 2007).

[189] 'Report of the Special Rapporteur' (n 93 above) para 63.

order to deal with claims involving suspected terrorists. This could have a number of adverse effects. It could exclude from protection persons who are in fact 'worthy' of protection, without considering their claims to refugee status and without due process. Exclusion may occur on the basis of a low threshold 'serious reasons for considering', while the absence of a definition of 'terrorism' encourages States to adopt their own definitions and to move away from accepted notions of individual responsibility. Meanwhile, the mere mention of terrorism and asylum seekers in the same breath encourages guilt by association of a different kind—that is, asylum seekers are presumed to be terrorists. This provides a new legitimating force for *non-entrée* and rights-violative measures. In addition, there could be serious ramifications for general human rights law prohibitions on *refoulement* to a place of torture.

It is extremely concerning that in the new 'legislative' phase of the UN Security Council,[190] the Council should be acting with so little real regard for the principles and purposes of the Charter,[191] in the name of defeating a non-State actor responsible for violating the same. We have been spared any possibility of debate concerning Resolution 1373's potential to trump human rights obligations pursuant to Article 103 of the United Nations Charter by the adoption of Resolution 1456,[192] and it is worth reiterating that the language concerning asylum seekers is generally hortatory rather than mandatory. However, it may be that the Security Council has effectively created a great deal more work for the already over-burdened United Nations human rights system by unleashing a spirit of impunity for rights violations in the name of counter-terrorism.

Moreover, while the call for States to move to exclude terrorists and to ensure that extradition can take place is relatively uncontroversial, the short answer to the idea that refugee status is something that may be abused by terrorists is that terrorism is just a criminal act. It follows that terrorism has to be countered in the same way as other criminal acts,

[190] For a prescient analysis of the Security Council's capacity to enact 'secondary legislation', see C Tomuschat, *Obligations Arising for States against Their Will* (The Hague, Recueil des Cours, vol IV/1993) para 344ff. Concerning Resolution 1373 in particular, see JE Alvarez, 'The UN's "War" On Terrorism' (2003) 31 *International Journal of Legal Information* 238 at 241.

[191] Art 24(2) of the United Nations Charter provides that 'in discharging these duties the Security Council shall act in accordance with the Purposes and Principles of the United Nations'.

[192] A Clapham, 'Terrorism, National Measures and International Supervision' in A Bianchi (ed), *Enforcing International Norms Against Terrorism* (Oxford, Hart Publishing, 2004) 294. A full discussion concerning the potential for review of the Security Council's use of its powers under Chapter VII is beyond the scope of this chapter.

whether by nationals or foreigners—namely prosecution, whether or not via extradition—as recognised in paragraph 2(e) of Resolution 1373. What is concerning about paragraphs 3(f) and (g) of the resolution is that they 'name' asylum seekers as potential terrorists, insinuating that the problem comes from 'outside', indeed from a generally vulnerable group of outsiders who require protection.

Resolution 1373 may thus encourage a focus on immigration control mechanisms as part of the solution to terrorism. This is a mirage. We may well not want violent people among us, but the fact has to be faced that it is not only 'outsiders' who commit terrorist crimes. Furthermore, a sovereignty-based border control approach is probably going to be of limited effect in a globalised world. Deportation, as some of the Law Lords commented in the *Belmarsh case*, is no solution.[193] Neither is pouring the wine of deterrence into the new bottle of counter-terrorism. Yet, one sees fascinating traces of the traditional tough approach to illegal immigration—'we don't want to be a soft touch or we'll attract more'[194]—raised in the new context of national security, and the accompanying secrecy shrouding some of the 'evidence'.

That traditional deterrence argument seems even more misguided in this new context, for the same old reasons, including probable ineffectiveness. The impact of deterrence measures on illegal immigration is difficult to measure and the evidence is easily manipulated.[195] It is questionable how any of it translates to terrorist activities.

In Resolution 1373, the Security Council adopted language that appears to have been fashioned in large part by one State's perception of a problem

[193] See n 24 above.

[194] *Belmarsh case* (n 22 above) para 128 (Lord Hoffman), inferring that 'the problem which was thought to be in need of being addressed in the case of foreign nationals immediately, and was capable of being so addressed, was the perception in some countries that the United Kingdom was a safe option. This was because it could encourage terrorists to travel to this country'.

[195] To take perhaps the greatest deterrence mechanism ever adopted (certainly relative to the size of the 'problem', it is a 'great' effort), the Australian government touts the Pacific Strategy as a success given the few boats that have arrived since its inception. However, it should be noted that the first round of 'border protection' legislation was introduced in 1999 in response to an *increase* in asylum seekers that had somehow occurred, despite Australia's mandatory detention policy for illegal arrivals—the harshest such regime in the western world. The analysis of push versus pull factors is equally problematic. If one looks at the statistics that drove Australia's first border control legislation, we see that the asylum claimants were from Iraq and Afghanistan, which were at the time among the highest refugee-producing countries in the world. This suggests that push factors, not pull factors, were to blame for the increase. See further P Mathew, 'Safe for Whom? The Safe Third Country Concept Finds a Home in Australia' in S Kneebone (ed), *The Refugees Convention 50 Years On: Globalisation and International Law* (Aldershot, Ashgate Publishing, 2003).

with refugee law. In so doing, the Council has given new impetus and its imprimatur to arguments concerning immigration that have always been highly contentious, and will now be dressed in the language of national security and secrecy. Perhaps we will one day be told that 'intelligence' indicates that 'whole villages' of terrorists are packing up and leaving for western shores.[196]

[196] See the question put by television interviewer Kerry O'Brien to Phillip Ruddock, then Australian Minister for Immigration (*7.30 Report*, 15 November 1999): 'Is it true that you've been told that whole villages are actually getting ready to pack and come?' (Transcript: <http://www.abc.net.au/7.30/stories/s66377.htm> (accessed 29 June 2007)). Mr Ruddock subsequently became Australia's Attorney-General and therefore played a lead role in Australia's adoption of anti-terrorist legislation.

3

National Security and Non-Refoulement *in New Zealand: Commentary on* Zaoui v Attorney-General (No 2)

RODGER HAINES QC*

I. INTRODUCTION

AS IS WELL known, the *non-refoulement* obligation in Article 33 of the 1951 Convention relating to the Status of Refugees and the 1967 Protocol relating to the Status of Refugees is not absolute.[1] Expulsion and return to a risk of being persecuted is permitted where there are reasonable grounds for regarding the refugee as a danger to the security of the country in which he or she is, or where the refugee, having been convicted by a final judgment of a particularly serious crime, constitutes a danger to the community of that country.[2]

New Zealand is a party to both the Refugee Convention and the Protocol.[3] In recent times, the Minister of Immigration and his officials have been required to address difficult expulsion cases which have

* The opinions expressed in this paper are the personal views of the author.

[1] Convention relating to the Status of Refugees (adopted 28 July 1951, entered into force 22 April 1954) 189 UNTS 137; Protocol relating to the Status of Refugees (adopted 31 January 1967, entered into force 4 October 1967) 606 UNTS 267 (together 'Refugee Convention').

[2] Refugee Convention (n 1 above) Art 33.

[3] New Zealand acceded to the Refugee Convention on 30 June 1960 and, subject to a reservation concerning Art 24(2), it entered into force for New Zealand on 28 September 1960: Ministry of Foreign Affairs and Trade, *New Zealand Consolidated Treaty List as at 31 December 1996 Part I (Multilateral Treaties)* (Wellington, Ministry of Foreign Affairs and Trade, May 1997) 183. New Zealand acceded to the Protocol on 6 August 1973 and it entered into force for New Zealand on the same day: Ministry of Foreign Affairs and Trade, *New Zealand Consolidated Treaty List as at 31 December 1996 Part I (Multilateral Treaties)* (Wellington, Ministry of Foreign Affairs and Trade, May 1997) 244.

brought into focus both the 'security' and 'danger to the community' exceptions to the *non-refoulement* obligation in Article 33. Those cases include:

(a) An Algerian national, recognised as a refugee by the Refugee Status Appeals Authority, but in respect of whom the Director of Security issued a security risk certificate under Part 4A of the Immigration Act 1987.[4]

(b) An Iraqi resettlement refugee originally sentenced to nine years in prison for the rape of two Auckland women and for assault with intent to rape a third. Two months after he was released, he attacked his fourth victim.[5] On the latest charges, he was found guilty of sexual violation by rape, detaining a woman without her consent with intent to have sexual intercourse, and assault, and was sentenced to preventive detention, the court ordering that he serve at least seven years of the preventive detention sentence. An appeal to the Court of Appeal against both conviction and sentence was unsuccessful, that court noting:

> The gravity of Mr Al Baiiaty's offending was at a high level. It involved a brutal and sustained attack upon a young woman, with a degree of premeditation. As to public protection, Mr Al Baiiaty clearly poses a serious risk to the community. He has been assessed as presenting a high risk of re-offending and has not addressed the causes of his offending. Nor does he appear prepared to do so in the future. Further, he continues to deny the offending against this complainant.[6]

The then Minister of Immigration, with specific reference to Article 33(2) of the Refugee Convention, called for a report on the deportation issues raised by the case, acknowledging that no precedent existed for such action in New Zealand.[7]

(c) Two Iranian nationals convicted on drug smuggling charges and presently serving sentences of imprisonment of seven-and-a-half years and nine years respectively, had both, prior to their convictions, been recognised as refugees.[8] In this regard it has been reported that Iranian criminals in New Zealand have become a

[4] *Zaoui v Attorney-General (No 2)* [2006] 1 NZLR 289 (NZSC).

[5] New Zealand Press Association, 'Refugee Rapist Attacks for Fourth Time' *NZ Herald* (18 November 2004) A5.

[6] *R v Al Baiiaty* (NZCA120/05, 17 October 2005, Glazebrook, Ronald Young and Doogue JJ); see also New Zealand Press Association, 'Iraqi Refugee Loses Rape Appeal' *NZ Herald* (18 October 2005) A7.

[7] A Gregory, 'Rapist Faces Expulsion from NZ' *NZ Herald* (19 November 2004) A4.

[8] B Taylor, 'Immigration Offers No Answers on Jailed Man' *NZ Herald* (19 November 2005) A10.

> major problem for drug enforcement authorities, one report alleging that 42 per cent of the 35 kilograms of imported crystal methamphetamine seized in the 12 months prior to March 2005 was due to a loose association known by Customs and Police as the 'Iranian network'.[9]

It is in the context of these difficult cases that both the executive and the courts are now accumulating experience in the application of Article 33(2). To date, the provision has never been invoked.[10]

The explicitly limited obligation to which States parties have bound themselves under the Refugee Convention can be contrasted with other treaty obligations assumed by New Zealand, particularly Article 3 of the 1984 Convention against Torture and Other Cruel, Inhuman or Degrading Treatment or Punishment ('CAT'), which contains a discrete *non-refoulement* obligation:

1. No State Party shall expel, return ('refouler') or extradite a person to another State where there are substantial grounds for believing that he would be in danger of being subjected to torture.
2. For the purpose of determining whether there are such grounds, the competent authorities shall take into account all relevant considerations including, where applicable, the existence in the State concerned of a consistent pattern of gross, flagrant or mass violations of human rights.[11]

The *non-refoulement* obligation under this treaty is not explicitly qualified by the 'security' and 'danger to community' exceptions found in Article 33 of the Refugee Convention. Nor does the CAT, unlike the Refugee Convention, explicitly exclude a person with respect to whom there are serious reasons for considering that he or she has committed a crime against peace, a war crime, a crime against humanity or a serious non-political crime, or that he or she has been guilty of acts contrary to the purposes and principles of the United Nations.[12] The issue is whether qualifications and exceptions of this nature can be implied.

[9] F Barber, 'Ice Age: The Iranian Meth Smugglers' *North & South* (December 2005) 52.

[10] P Taylor, 'Jailed Iranians Face Deportation' *NZ Herald* (10 December 2005) A16.

[11] Convention against Torture and Other Cruel, Inhuman or Degrading Treatment or Punishment (adopted 10 December 1984, entered into force 26 June 1987) 1465 UNTS 85, Art 3. New Zealand signed the Convention against Torture on 14 January 1986 and it entered into force for New Zealand on 9 January 1990: *New Zealand Consolidated Treaty List* (n 3 above) 324–5. On ratification, New Zealand made a reservation regarding the awarding of compensation to torture victims referred to in Art 14, made declarations, pursuant to Arts 21(1) and 22(1) respectively, recognising the competence of the Committee against Torture, and lodged objections to a declaration and reservations made respectively by two countries.

[12] See the Refugee Convention (n 1 above) Art 1F.

Also of potential relevance are Articles 6 and 7 of the 1966 International Covenant on Civil and Political Rights ('ICCPR'), which safeguard the right to life and the right not to be subjected to torture or to cruel, inhuman or degrading treatment or punishment.[13] Neither of these provisions explicitly applies in the expulsion or *refoulement* context. Whether such application can be implied is a substantive issue.[14] The articles provide:

> **Article 6**
> 1. Every human being has the inherent right to life. This right shall be protected by law. No one shall be arbitrarily deprived of his life.
>
> ...
>
> **Article 7**
> No one shall be subjected to torture or to cruel, inhuman or degrading treatment or punishment. In particular, no one shall be subjected without his pre-consent to medical or scientific experimentation.

The recent judgment of the Supreme Court of New Zealand in *Zaoui v Attorney-General (No 2)* potentially advances New Zealand domestic law on these forms of protection, sometimes referred to as complementary or subsidiary protection.[15] The qualifier 'potentially' is necessary because the issue did not arise on the facts, was not apparently the subject of argument and the judgment does not address the question whether the

[13] International Covenant on Civil and Political Rights (adopted 16 Dec 1966, entered into force 23 March 1976) 999 UNTS 171. New Zealand ratified the ICCPR on 28 December 1978 and it entered into force for New Zealand on 28 March 1979: *New Zealand Consolidated Treaty List* (n 3 above) 242. Arts 6 and 7 of the ICCPR have domestic analogues in the form of ss 8 and 9 of the New Zealand Bill of Rights Act 1990. For a commentary on these provisions in the extradition, deportation and removal contexts, see A Butler and P Butler, *The New Zealand Bill of Rights Act: A Commentary* (Wellington, LexisNexis, 2005) para 9.5.

[14] The Human Rights Committee has incrementally, and with some controversy, arrived at an 'absolutist' interpretation of these two provisions: see the analysis in M Nowak, *UN Covenant on Civil and Political Rights: CCPR Commentary*, 2nd edn (Kiel, NP Engel, 2005) 150–53, 185–8. He even suggests (at 150) that the prohibition of *refoulement* in principle might be applicable to all ICCPR rights. Reference might also be made to the Human Rights Committee, 'General Comment 20: Replaces General Comment 7 concerning Prohibition of Torture and Cruel Treatment or Punishment' (10 March 1992) para 9: 'In the view of the Committee, States parties must not expose individuals to the danger of torture or cruel, inhuman or degrading treatment or punishment upon return to another country by way of their extradition, expulsion or refoulement. States parties should indicate in their reports what measures they have adopted to that end'.

[15] Zaoui (n 4 above). According to J McAdam, *Complementary Protection in International Refugee Law* (Oxford, Oxford University Press, 2007) 2–3 (footnote omitted), complementary protection 'denotes protection granted to individuals on the basis of a legal obligation other than the principal refugee treaty. In contemporary practice, it describes the engagement of States' legal protection obligations that are complementary to those assumed under the 1951 Refugee Convention (as supplemented by its 1967 Protocol), whether derived from treaty or customary international law. Importantly, it stems from legal obligations preventing return to serious harm, rather than from compassionate reasons or practical obstacles to removal'. Although it implies the granting of a legal status, there is inconsistent State practice on its content, especially when it comes to people who would be excluded under Art 1F of the Refugee Convention.

interests of the State and its citizens are to be taken into account in expulsion decisions. On the face of the obiter dicta, New Zealand is bound not to expel an individual no matter how grave a threat that person poses to the security of the nation and no matter how grave a danger he or she poses to the community. The particular right of the individual would seem to trump all other interests, as well as the human rights of the individuals who comprise the community.

Zaoui must be understood within the New Zealand statutory context for determining refugee status. The statutory provisions are briefly outlined below.

II. THE STATUTORY CONTEXT

A. Domestic Incorporation of the Refugee Convention

The New Zealand refugee determination system was first given a formal structure in 1991.[16] Since then, both the Refugee Status Branch of the New Zealand Immigration Service at first instance and the Refugee Status Appeals Authority on appeal have accumulated substantial experience in the application of the inclusion and exclusion provisions of the refugee definition set out in Article 1 of the Refugee Convention. However, neither body presently has jurisdiction to make *refoulement* determinations under Article 33(2) or complementary protection decisions under the CAT and the ICCPR. Such determinations are made by the Minister of Immigration.

The New Zealand refugee status determination procedures were placed on a statutory footing by the Immigration Amendment Act 1999 which inserted a new Part 6A into the Immigration Act 1987 ('Act'). The effect of the new sections 129C and 129D was that for the purposes of determining refugee status, refugee status officers (at first instance) and the Refugee Status Appeals Authority (on appeal) must act in a manner consistent with New Zealand's obligations under the Refugee Convention:

129C. Refugee status to be determined under this Part—

(1) Every person in New Zealand who seeks to be recognised as a refugee in New Zealand under the Refugee Convention is to have that claim determined in accordance with this Part.

[16] That structure was given by informal Terms of Reference promulgated pursuant to the prerogative. Following adverse judicial comment in *Butler v Attorney-General* [1999] NZAR 205 (NZCA) 218–20 and *S v Refugee Status Appeals Authority* [1998] 2 NZLR 291 (NZCA) 294, the system was given a statutory footing in 1999: Immigration Amendment Act 1999, s 1(3). The new Part 6A of the Immigration Act 1987 came into force on 1 October 1999. These provisions are to be read with the Immigration (Refugee Processing) Regulations 1999 (SR 1999/285). The context of the statutory amendments is reviewed in R Haines, 'International Law and Refugees in New Zealand' [1999] *New Zealand Law Review* 119.

(2) Every question as to whether a person in New Zealand should continue to be recognised as a refugee in New Zealand under the Refugee Convention is to be determined in accordance with this Part.

129D. Refugee Convention to apply—

(1) In carrying out their functions under this Part, refugee status officers and the Refugee Status Appeals Authority are to act in a manner that is consistent with New Zealand's obligations under the Refugee Convention.

(2) The text of the Refugee Convention is set out in the Sixth Schedule.

In practical terms this means that *within* the refugee determination context, the Refugee Convention has been domesticated.

Outside the refugee determination context, however, incorporation has been limited to Articles 32 and 33 of the Refugee Convention. Section 129X of the Act provides:

(1) No person who has been recognised as a refugee in New Zealand or is a refugee status claimant may be removed or deported from New Zealand under this Act, unless the provisions of Article 32.1 or Article 33.2 of the Refugee Convention allow the removal or deportation.

(2) In carrying out their functions under this Act in relation to a refugee or a refugee status claimant, immigration officers must have regard to the provisions of this Part and of the Refugee Convention.

In the context of refugees, security and deportation, section 114C(6)(a) of the Act provides:

(6) The relevant refugee deportation security criteria are a combination of any 1 or more of the criteria listed in subsection (4)[17] as relevant deportation security criteria, taken together with either or both of the following criteria:

(a) That there are reasonable grounds for regarding the person as a danger to the security of New Zealand, in terms of Article 33.2 of the Refugee Convention;

(b) That the person is a danger to the community of New Zealand, having been convicted by a final judgment of a particularly serious crime, in terms of Article 33.2 of the Refugee Convention.

In *Attorney-General v Refugee Council of New Zealand Inc*, McGrath J, while describing the 1999 provisions as giving the Refugee Convention

[17] The criteria listed in sub-s (4) are: (a) that the person constitutes a threat to national security in terms of s 72; and (b) any of the criteria set out in s 73(1) (which relates to suspected terrorists).

legislative effect and incorporating it into New Zealand's domestic law, nevertheless drew attention to the fact that section 129X(1) makes a distinction between direct and indirect implementation:

> [I]t is not surprising that in incorporating the Refugee Convention into New Zealand legislation Parliament used a formula giving some but not all of its provisions the force of law. The expression of a duty under domestic law as being to have regard to a Treaty duty can reflect a perception that the international obligation is an inappropriate standard in itself for more direct implementation.[18]

B. National Security and Terrorists

In the past 40 years, New Zealand has had only two statutes regulating immigration: the Immigration Act 1964 and (23 years later) the Immigration Act 1987. The latter statute is now two decades old.[19]

The first substantive statutory provisions addressing national security in the immigration context were introduced by the Immigration Amendment Act 1978, section 7. Under the (then) new Part 4 the Minister of Immigration was given new powers to deal with national security and terrorism cases:

(a) In national security cases, the Governor-General, by Order in Council, had power to order a person to leave New Zealand where the Minister of Immigration certified that the continued presence in New Zealand of that person constituted a threat to national security.
(b) The Minister could order a person to leave New Zealand where there was reason to believe that the individual was a terrorist, had engaged in an act of terrorism or would engage in any act of terrorism.

[18] *Attorney-General v Refugee Council of New Zealand Inc* [2003] 2 NZLR 577 (NZCA) para 103. Compare *de Guzman v Canada (Minister of Citizenship and Immigration)* (2005) 262 DLR (4th) 13 (FC:CA) discussing the Immigration and Refugee Protection Act 2001 (Canada) s 3(3)(f) and J Brunnée and SJ Toope, 'A Hesitant Embrace: *Baker* and the Application of International Law by Canadian Courts' in D Dyzenhaus (ed), *The Unity of Public Law* (Oxford, Hart Publishing, 2004).

[19] However, in April 2006 the Minister of Immigration launched a comprehensive review of the legislation: Department of Labour, 'Immigration Act Review: Discussion Paper' (April 2006). Excluded from the review were the statutory provisions in Part 4A of the Act relating to special procedures in cases involving security concerns. Following public consultation, the Cabinet in November 2006 reached a number of decisions published as the 'Immigration Act Review: Summary of Cabinet Decisions' (November 2006). On 5 December 2006 the Minister of Immigration announced that instructions had been given for a new Immigration Bill to be drafted for introduction into Parliament in April 2007: Hon David Cunliffe, 'Comprehensive Immigration Law Closer' (Media Statement, 5 December 2006). However, as at 25 June 2007 no such legislation had been introduced.

These 1978 provisions were largely brought forward into Part 3 of the Immigration Act 1987 by sections 72 and 73 respectively.

National security cases are clearly envisaged as being at the most serious end of the scale, removal being preconditioned by no less than an Order in Council. Section 72 of the Act provides:

> **72. Persons threatening national security—**
> Where the Minister certifies that the continued presence in New Zealand of any person named in the certificate constitutes a threat to national security, the Governor-General may, by Order in Council, order the deportation from New Zealand of that person.

In the two cases in which section 72 has been used, deportation has been summary.[20]

By contrast, suspected terrorists have a statutory right of appeal to the High Court against the making of a deportation order.[21] That appeal right, conferred by section 81 of the Act, envisages a de novo review by the High Court on both the facts and the law. Section 81(3) provides:

> On any appeal under this section, the High Court may confirm or quash the deportation order, as it thinks fit.

These statutory provisions address removal after entry to New Zealand has occurred. To prevent entry in the first place to New Zealand of persons who are threats to national security or suspected terrorists, sections 7(1)(e), (f), (g), (h) and (i) of the Act prescribe that such persons are not eligible for a permit, and they may be detained and summarily expelled on arrival in New Zealand pursuant to section 128. This 'turnaround' power has lately been surrounded by safeguards where a claim to refugee status is made.[22]

C. The Use of Classified Security Information in Expulsion Cases

Only belatedly has the New Zealand Parliament addressed in any detailed way the use of classified security information in cases involving security

[20] Section 72 has reportedly been used only twice in the past 19 years. The first time was in 1991, when an alleged USSR spy was deported. The second was in May 2006, when a Yemeni national alleged to be directly associated with persons responsible for the terrorist attacks in the United States on 11 September 2001 was deported. See G Cumming, 'Pilot with 9/11 Links Found in NZ' *Weekend Herald* (10 June 2006) 1; and Hon David Cunliffe, 'NZ Deports Man for Security Reasons' (Media Statement, 10 June 2006). The Immigration Act 1987 does not define 'national security', but there is a definition of 'security' in s 2 of the New Zealand Security Intelligence Service Act 1969.

[21] The term 'act of terrorism' is defined in s 2(1) of the Immigration Act 1987, while the terms 'terrorist act' and 'terrorist bombing' are defined in ss 5(1) and 7(1) of the Terrorism Suppression Act 2002 respectively.

[22] See ss 128A, 128AA–128AD and 128B of the Act. These provisions are complex and an analysis lies outside the scope of this paper. Some of the provisions are examined in *Attorney-General v Refugee Council of New Zealand Inc* [2003] 2 NZLR 577 (NZCA).

concerns. Section 35 of the Immigration Amendment Act 1999 introduced a new Part 4A into the 1987 Act, setting out an elaborate mechanism for the use of classified security information. These new procedures were described in the following terms in *Zaoui v Attorney-General (No 2)*:

> In brief, the process established by the new part is that the Director of Security has the power to provide the Minister with a security risk certificate if satisfied the grounds are made out; the Minister has the power to make a preliminary decision to rely on the certificate; the person affected may then seek a review of the Director's decision to make the certificate by the Inspector-General of Intelligence and Security (acting under his own statute as well as under Part 4A); the Inspector-General on review decides whether or not the certificate was properly made; if the review application fails, the person then has the right to appeal to the Court of Appeal on a point of law; the Minister has the power within three days to decide to rely on a confirmed or non-challenged certificate; if the Minister does so decide the immigration process resumes with the immediate prospect of the person being removed from New Zealand.[23]

The provisions are silent as to whether the review conducted by the Inspector-General is confined to the decision to provide a security risk certificate, or whether the function of the Inspector-General is also to inquire into the broader human rights issues raised by the particular case. It was this issue which was addressed by the Supreme Court of New Zealand in *Zaoui.*

III. THE ISSUES BEFORE THE SUPREME COURT IN *ZAOUI v ATTORNEY-GENERAL (NO 2)*

A. The Function of the Inspector-General

The first substantive issue addressed by the Supreme Court was the statutory function of the Inspector-General of Intelligence and Security. Addressing the statutory silence as to whether the Inspector-General is required to inquire into human rights issues, the Supreme Court held that in carrying out his function under Part 4A of the Immigration Act 1987, the Inspector-General is concerned only to determine whether the relevant security criteria are satisfied:[24] for example, whether the person constitutes a threat to national security (section 72) or whether there are reasonable grounds for regarding the person a danger to the security of New Zealand in terms of Article 33(2) of the Refugee Convention. The Inspector-General is not required by the Act to determine whether the individual in question is subject to a threat which would or might prevent his or her removal from New Zealand.

[23] *Zaoui* (n 4 above) para 9.
[24] *Ibid*, para 73.

B. The Proportionality Issue

In arriving at this conclusion, the Supreme Court addressed the requirements of Article 33(2) and, in particular, whether Article 33(2) contains an element of 'proportionality' or weighing and balancing. The Court of Appeal had held that the Inspector-General was required to assess the possible consequences to the refugee of deportation or removal and to weigh those consequences against the extent of the danger to the security of New Zealand. The Supreme Court framed the issue in the following terms:

> Accordingly, we consider (a) whether the national security limit placed by article 33.2 on the bar on deportation stated in para (1) sets a single standard which, if satisfied, operates by itself as an exception to the bar or (b) whether it requires or permits consideration of the dangers to the individual by reference to the human rights law beyond the express terms of article 33.2, and whether, as a result, it incorporates some element of proportionality or balancing. We consider this question in the first place in terms of the position under international law and in particular under article 33.2, leaving until the next part of these reasons the role under the Immigration Act of the various decision makers, especially the Inspector-General of Security. We are able to do this because article 33.2 is directly incorporated into the law of New Zealand by s 114C(6)(a).[25]

In reversing the Court of Appeal on this point and holding that Article 33(2) requires no proportionality or weighing and balancing, the Supreme Court had regard to the following:

(a) Article 33 is in two distinct parts. Each part is distinct and,

> [a]ccording to their ordinary meaning, the two provisions operate in sequence. They are not related in any proportionate or balancing way. The second, if satisfied in its own terms, defeats the prohibition in the first.[26]

(b) This sequential reading is reinforced by

> a consideration of what the proportionality or sliding scale proposition would require. The decision-maker would have to measure against one another two matters which are very difficult to relate: the level of threat to the life or liberty of an individual, on the one side, and, on the other, the level of reasonably perceived danger to the security of the State.[27]

(c) The sequential reading is supported by the operation of the exclusion clause in article 1F(b).[28] The Supreme Court approved the

[25] *Ibid*, para 22.
[26] *Ibid*, para 25.
[27] *Ibid*, para 27.
[28] *Ibid*, para 29.

decision in *S v Refugee Status Appeals Authority*,[29] in which the Court of Appeal considered and rejected an argument that the gravity of the crime is to be weighed against the gravity of the possible persecution. The court in that case stated:

> It directs attention to the commission of a serious crime, nothing more, nothing less. The seriousness of a crime bears no relationship to and is not governed by matters extraneous to the offending. There is nothing in art 1F to justify reading into its provisions restrictive or qualifying words such as those which would be necessary to require a balancing exercise of the kind suggested.[30]

(d) State pract ice did not support the principle of proportionality, nor did the drafting history of the legislation.[31]

The conclusion arrived at by the Supreme Court in *Zaoui* as to the meaning of Article 33(2) was in the following terms:

> We accordingly conclude that the judgment or assessment to be made under article 33.2 is to be made in its own terms, by reference to danger to the security, in this case, of New Zealand, and without any balancing or weighing or proportional reference to the matter dealt with in article 33.1, the threat, were Mr Zaoui to be expelled or returned, to his life or freedom on the proscribed grounds or the more specific rights protected by the New Zealand Bill of Rights Act 1990 read with the International Covenant on Civil and Political Rights and the Convention against Torture and other Cruel, Inhuman or Degrading Treatment or Punishment. Paragraph (2) of article 33 of the Refugee Convention states a single standard.[32]

C. The Test for 'Reasonable Grounds for Regarding as a Danger to Security'

A related interpretation issue addressed by the Supreme Court was the meaning of the phrase: 'a refugee whom there are reasonable grounds for regarding as a danger to the security of the country in which he is' in Article 33(2) of the Refugee Convention.

After emphasising that the wording and drafting history of Article 33 and its very subject matter indicated that the executive has a broad power

[29] *S v Refugee Status Appeals Authority* (n 16 above) 297.
[30] *Ibid.*
[31] *Zaoui* (n 4 above) para 34.
[32] *Ibid*, para 42.

of appreciation of the relevant facts and considerations, the Supreme Court advanced the following interpretation:

> To come within Article 33(2) the person in question must be thought on reasonable grounds to pose a serious threat to the security of New Zealand; the threat must be based on objectively reasonable grounds and the threatened harm must be substantial.[33]

This, the court noted, was essentially the test stated by the Supreme Court of Canada in *Suresh v Canada (Minister of Citizenship and Immigration)*.[34]

D. Whether Article 33(2) has been Amended by Later Human Rights Instruments

Among the arguments advanced before the Supreme Court was the submission that Article 33(2) of the Refugee Convention had been amended by Article 3(1) of the CAT and by Articles 6(1) and 7 of the ICCPR, and that the exceptions to the *non-refoulement* obligation permitted by Article 33(2) of the Refugee Convention were overridden in cases where torture was threatened. The Supreme Court did not accept that Articles 30(3) and (4) (on successive treaties relating to the same subject matter) of the 1969 Vienna Convention on the Law of Treaties applied. In the court's view, Article 33(2) of the Refugee Convention had not been *amended by* the later ICCPR and CAT provisions.[35] Rather, they had to be applied in a *successive* way. In any event, only Article 33(2) of the Refugee Convention had been incorporated into New Zealand law by Part 4A of the Immigration Act 1987.

E. Whether the Prohibition on *Refoulement* to Torture is a Peremptory Norm

A final argument was that the prohibition on *refoulement* to torture has the status of a peremptory norm or *jus cogens*. As to this, the Supreme Court held that while there was overwhelming support for the proposition that the prohibition on torture *itself* is *jus cogens*, there was no support in State practice, judicial decisions or commentaries to which the court was referred for the proposition that the prohibition on *refoulement* to torture has that status.[36]

[33] *Ibid*, paras 44–5.
[34] *Suresh v Canada (Minister of Citizenship and Immigration)* [2002] 1 SCR 3, 2002 SCC 1.
[35] *Zaoui* (n 4 above) para 50.
[36] *Ibid*, para 51. L Yarwood, '*Zaoui* and jus cogens' [2006] *New Zealand Law Journal* 170 points out, however, that the opinion of the Supreme Court (expressed later in the judgment) that threat of torture in the originating State overrides the application of Art 33 of the

F. The Conclusion Reached by the Supreme Court

The overall conclusion reached by the court was expressed in the following terms:

> We accordingly conclude that those applying article 33.2 under Part 4A of the Immigration Act are to apply it in its own terms. In particular, to come within article 33.2, the person in question must be thought on reasonable grounds to pose a serious threat to the security of New Zealand; the threat must be based on objectively reasonable grounds and the threatened harm must be substantial.[37]

IV. COMPLEMENTARY PROTECTION

Having held that it was not the role of the Inspector-General of Intelligence and Security, on a review under Part 4A of the Immigration Act 1987, to assess the possible consequences of the deportation or removal from New Zealand of a recognised refugee, and having further held that Article 33(2) permitted expulsion notwithstanding a risk of being persecuted, the Supreme Court exhausted the issues argued before it. The court nevertheless went on to consider an issue not apparently argued, namely that of complementary protection—that is, protection in circumstances which fall outside the Refugee Convention.[38] Its comments in this regard must therefore be treated as obiter dicta.[39] These dicta presently nevertheless constitute the only New Zealand 'law' on the subject.[40]

The court first examined the international obligations assumed by New Zealand under both the ICCPR and the CAT to determine whether a person, lawfully expellable from New Zealand under the Refugee Convention, was nevertheless protected from return to his or her own country. That is, whether, in certifying to the Governor-General under section 72 of the Immigration Act 1987 that the continued presence in New Zealand of a person constitutes a threat to national security, the Minister of Immigration is duty bound to assess the possible

Refugee Convention implicitly recognises the prohibition on *refoulement* as a *jus cogens* norm, and the court, in its attribution of *jus cogens* status to the *refoulement* prohibition, 'assumed a bold—if inadvertent—stance'.

[37] *Zaoui* (n 4 above) para 52.

[38] See generally McAdam (n 15 above); M-T Gil-Bazo, 'Refugee Status, Subsidiary Protection, and the Right to be Granted Asylum under EC Law', UNHCR *New Issues in Refugee Research* Research Paper No 136 (November 2006).

[39] For the issues canvassed during the argument, see the summary in *Zaoui* (n 4 above) 291–5. Useful reference might also be made to the grounds of appeal recorded in the judgment at paras 13–18.

[40] It is anticipated that the new Immigration Bill will contain complementary protection provisions, but as at 25 June 2007 the intended legislation had not been introduced into Parliament.

consequences of the deportation on the recognised refugee and to refrain from signing a certificate where a potential breach of the ICCPR or the CAT has been established.

A. The Crown Concession

In this regard a significant concession had been made by the Crown. It expressly accepted that it was obliged to act in conformity with New Zealand's obligations under Articles 6(1) and 7 of the ICCPR and Article 3 of the CAT:

> [75] The result of the two rulings we have already made is that it is not for the Inspector-General to address the existence of any threat to Mr Zaoui were the Government to act to remove him from New Zealand. But the Government, through the Solicitor-General, accepts that it is obliged to comply with the relevant international obligations protecting Mr Zaoui from return to threats of torture or the arbitrary taking of life.
>
> [76] ... the Crown accepts in particular that it is obliged to act in conformity with New Zealand's obligations under Articles 6(1) and 7 of the ICCPR and Article 3 of the Convention against Torture.[41]

This brought the Supreme Court to the issue, which it formulated in the following terms:

> The question which remains to be considered is the way in which under New Zealand law those obligations may be met, including the question of who is to meet them, given that it is not the Inspector-General.[42]

B. The Issue of Extraterritoriality

The Supreme Court noted that neither Article 6 nor Article 7 of the ICCPR and their domestic analogues in sections 8 and 9 of the New Zealand Bill of Rights Act 1990 *expressly* applied to actions taken outside New Zealand by other governments in breach of the rights therein stated. But the court drew on the jurisprudence of the European Court of Human Rights, particularly *Soering v United Kingdom*[43] and *Chahal v United Kingdom*,[44] and observed that Articles 6(1) and 7 of the ICCPR (reflected there in Articles 2 and 3 respectively of the European Convention on Human Rights[45]) have long been understood as applying to actions of a State party if that State

[41] *Zaoui* (n 4 above) paras 75–6.
[42] *Ibid*, para 77.
[43] *Soering v United Kingdom* (1989) 11 EHRR 439, paras 90–91 (ECtHR).
[44] *Chahal v United Kingdom* (1996) 23 EHRR 413, paras 73–82 (ECtHR).
[45] Convention for the Protection of Human Rights and Fundamental Freedoms (European Convention on Human Rights, as amended) (4 November 1950) ETS No 5.

proposes to take action, say, by way of deportation or extradition, where substantial grounds have been shown for believing that the person as a consequence faces a real risk of being subjected to torture or the arbitrary taking of life. The focus is not on the responsibility of the State to which the person may be sent. Rather, it is on the obligation of the State considering whether to remove the person to respect the substantive rights in issue.[46]

C. Translation of International Treaty Obligations into Domestic Law

The next logical issue was the effect of this obligation on relevant New Zealand legislation. Addressing the translation of international treaty obligations into New Zealand domestic law, the court referred to the New Zealand Bill of Rights Act 1990, the long title of which states that it is:

> An act—
>
> (a) To affirm, protect, and promote human rights and fundamental freedoms in New Zealand; and
>
> (b) To affirm New Zealand's commitment to the International Covenant on Civil and Political Rights.

Sections 8 and 9 of the New Zealand Bill of Rights Act 1990 address the right to life and security of the person:

> **8. Right not to be deprived of life—**
> No one shall be deprived of life except on such grounds as are established by law and are consistent with the principles of fundamental justice.
>
> **9. Right not to be subjected to torture or cruel treatment—**
> Everyone has the right not to be subjected to torture or to cruel, degrading, or disproportionately severe treatment or punishment.

These provisions mirror, but do not duplicate exactly, the obligations undertaken by New Zealand in Articles 6 and 7 of the ICCPR.

While section 4 of the New Zealand Bill of Rights Act 1990 provides that no enactment is to be held to be impliedly repealed or revoked or to be in any way invalid or ineffective by reason only that the provision is inconsistent with any provision of the Bill of Rights,[47] the court noted that

[46] *Zaoui* (n 4 above) para 79.

[47] The text of s 4 is as follows: 'No court shall, in relation to any enactment (whether passed or made before or after the commencement of this Bill of Rights),— (a) Hold any provision of the enactment to be impliedly repealed or revoked, or to be in any way invalid or ineffective; or (b) Decline to apply any provision of the enactment— by reason only that the provision is inconsistent with any provision of this Bill of Rights'.

section 6 of the Act provides that an interpretation consistent with the Bill of Rights is to be preferred:[48]

> Wherever an enactment can be given a meaning that is consistent with the rights and freedoms contained in this Bill of Rights, that meaning shall be preferred to any other meaning.

In the specific factual context, the court accepted that the power 'to expel on national security grounds' must be given a meaning, if it can be, consistent with the rights and freedoms contained within the New Zealand Bill of Rights Act.[49] In a controversial passage the court concluded that such meaning could indeed be given to section 72 of the Immigration Act 1987, as there was nothing to *prevent* the Minister of Immigration or Cabinet having regard to the obligations under Articles 6(1) and 7 of the ICCPR and Article 3 of the CAT when exercising the power under section 72:

> Section 72 confers powers on the Minister and the Governor-General in Council. The Minister has the power to certify that the continued presence of any person in New Zealand constitutes a threat to national security. There is nothing in the statement of the broad powers conferred on the Minister and in particular the Governor-General in Council to prevent the Minister or Cabinet having regard to the mitigating factors which the Minister or Cabinet might consider indicate that the person should not be deported. The power conferred by s 72 is to be interpreted and exercised consistently with the provisions of ss 8 and 9 of the Bill of Rights and with the closely related international obligations in the Covenant and the Convention against Torture. Because the power can be so interpreted and applied, those provisions, as a matter of law, prevent removal if their terms are satisfied even if the threat to national security is made out in terms of s 72 and article 33.2.[50]

The court then expressed the view that deportation under section 72 of the Act was not possible if there were substantial grounds for believing that, as a result of the deportation, the person would be in danger of being

[48] *Zaoui* (n 4 above) para 90. See further P Rishworth, 'Interpreting Enactments: Sections 4, 5 and 6' in P Rishworth, G Huscroft, S Optican and R Mahoney (eds), *The New Zealand Bill of Rights* (Oxford, Oxford University Press, 2003); and Butler and Butler (n 13 above) 157–96.

[49] *Zaoui* (n 4 above) paras 90–91.

[50] *Ibid*, paras 91–92. The violence done to the language of s 114K(1) of the Immigration Act 1987 in the cause of consistency with international obligations has been noted both by C Geiringer, '*Zaoui* Revisited' [2005] *New Zealand Law Journal* 285 at 288 and by T Dunworth, 'Public International Law' [2006] *New Zealand Law Review* 367 at 376. A mandatory three-day statutory time frame within which the Minister of Immigration must make a final decision whether to rely on the confirmed security risk certificate has been judicially 'overruled'. Dunworth makes two observations. First, in taking this approach the Supreme Court has stretched the presumption of consistency to its extreme. Secondly, an important aspect of the presumption of consistency is that the domestic statute must prevail. Indeed, this is the key to maintaining what is a fragile balance between domestic and international law.

arbitrarily deprived of life or of being subjected to torture or to cruel, inhuman or degrading treatment or punishment:

> It is accordingly our view that the Minister, in deciding whether to certify under s 72 of the Immigration Act 1987 that the continued presence of a person constitutes a threat to national security, and members of the Executive Council, in deciding whether to advise the Governor-General to order deportation under s 72, are not to so decide or advise if they are satisfied that there are substantial grounds for believing that, as a result of the deportation, the person would be in danger of being arbitrarily deprived of life or of being subjected to torture or to cruel, inhuman or degrading treatment or punishment.[51]

In this obiter 'view', on an issue not argued, the Supreme Court has erected an apparently absolute bar to expulsion from New Zealand no matter how grave a threat the individual might be to the security of the nation or to its community.[52]

V. COMMENTARY

The holdings of the New Zealand Supreme Court in relation to Article 33(1) and (2) clearly have a significance beyond New Zealand, relating as they do to an international human rights treaty to which there are presently 147 States parties.[53]

The obiter dicta in relation to complementary protection are, however, of more limited international application, addressing as they do the domestic application in New Zealand of unincorporated treaties. Nevertheless, a few observations can be made.

A. The Incorporation Point

The place of unincorporated international treaties in domestic law is an issue which has proved problematic in several common law jurisdictions, including New Zealand.[54] In the absence of direct incorporation by statute, administrative law has, with varied success, been suggested as an alternative, if indirect, route to incorporation. In Australia, the

[51] *Zaoui* (n 4 above) para 93.

[52] The 'Discussion Paper' published by the Department of Labour (n 19 above) subsequent to the judgment uncritically repeats the Supreme Court view in the context of proposals to set up a formal, statute-based system of complementary protection: para 1094.

[53] As at 1 December 2006: UNHCR, *States Parties to the 1951 Convention relating to the Status of Refugees and the 1967 Protocol* <http://www.unhcr.org/cgi-bin/texis/vtx/protect/opendoc.pdf?tbl=PROTECTION&id=3b73b0d63> (accessed 25 April 2007).

[54] For a notable recent collection of papers discussing *Baker v Canada (Minister of Citizenship and Immigration)* [1999] 2 SCR 817, see Dyzenhaus (n 18 above).

choice made in *Minister for Immigration and Ethnic Affairs v Teoh*[55] was to rely on the concept of legitimate expectation; that is, a person who is the subject of a decision by the executive has a legitimate expectation that the executive will act in conformity with the international obligations to which Australia is a State party. Necessarily, the High Court accepted that that expectation could be displaced by 'statutory or executive indications to the contrary'. Predictably, an 'executive indication of the contrary' was immediately forthcoming from the Federal Government in the form of a *Joint Statement by the Minister for Foreign Affairs, Senator Gareth Evans, and the Attorney-General, Michael Lavarch—International Treaties and the High Court Decision in Teoh*.[56] The High Court itself has indicated that *Teoh* may require re-visiting.[57] Michael Taggart has suggested that the approach taken in *Teoh* was both misconceived and unfortunate.[58]

In New Zealand, one suggested approach has been to treat the unincorporated international obligation not as the source of a legitimate expectation, but as a mandatory relevant consideration to be taken into account by the decision-maker.[59] But it is an approach which, in the context of the Convention on the Rights of the Child,[60] has led to considerable ambiguity, if not indecision, in the Court of Appeal in the cases of *Puli'uvea v Removal Review Authority*,[61] *Puli'uvea v Removal Review Authority*[62] and *Rajan v Minister of Immigration*.[63] A second approach adopted by New Zealand courts to unincorporated international law obligations is to

[55] *Minister for Immigration and Ethnic Affairs v Teoh* (1995) 183 CLR 273 (HCA).

[56] *Joint Statement—International Treaties and the High Court Decision in Teoh* (10 May 1995). The *Joint Statement* contained the following relevant paragraph: 'We now make such a clear and express statement. We state, on behalf of the government, that entering into an international treaty is not reason for raising any expectation that government decision-makers will act in accordance with the treaty if the relevant provisions of that treaty have not been enacted into domestic Australian law. It is not legitimate, for the purpose of applying Australian law, to expect that the provisions of a treaty not incorporated by legislation should be applied by decision-makers. Any expectation that may arise does not provide a ground for review of a decision. This is so both for existing treaties and for future treaties that Australia may join'.

[57] See *Re Minister for Immigration and Multicultural Affairs, ex parte Lam* [2003] HCA 6, (2003) 214 CLR 1, paras 102, 122, 147.

[58] M Taggart, 'Legitimate Expectation and Treaties in the High Court of Australia' (1996) 112 *Law Quarterly Review* 50; see also AM North and P Decle, 'Courts and Immigration Detention: "Once a Jolly Swagman Camped by a Billabong"' (2002) 10 *Australian Journal of Administrative Law* 5.

[59] See *Tavita v Minister of Immigration* [1994] 2 NZLR 257 (NZCA).

[60] Convention on the Rights of the Child (adopted 20 November 1989, entered into force 2 September 1990) 1577 UNTS 3.

[61] *Puli'uvea v Removal Review Authority* (1996) 14 FRNZ 322 (NZCA).

[62] *Puli'uvea v Removal Review Authority* [1996] 3 NZLR 538 (NZCA).

[63] *Rajan v Minister of Immigration* [1996] 3 NZLR 543 (NZCA).

presume, when interpreting legislation, that Parliament did not intend to legislate contrary to those international obligations.[64]

The possibly innovative feature of *Zaoui v Attorney-General (No 2)* is the deployment of the New Zealand Bill of Rights Act 1990 as the route to consistency with international human rights treaty obligations. This was an option available to the Supreme Court only because the Bill of Rights happens to contain domestic analogues to the Article 6 and 7 obligations under the ICCPR. It was through this aperture of domestic human rights legislation, the Supreme Court has suggested, that the ICCPR and CAT obligations enter decision-making under the Immigration Act 1987.[65]

B. Complementary Protection

The implications of the approach in *Zaoui* have yet to be worked out. The decision raises for the first time in New Zealand domestic law, in an acute form, the issue of complementary protection. In the refugee context, this means the protection from *refoulement* of those who are either excluded from the Refugee Convention by Articles 1D, 1E and 1F of the Refugee Convention or those who, having been recognised as refugees, no longer have the protection of the Refugee Convention by virtue of the operation of Article 33(2). In the wider context, it means the protection from *refoulement* of an individual who faces in his or her home country a real risk to his or her life or a danger of being subjected to torture or cruel, inhuman or degrading treatment or punishment.

In its obiter and somewhat abbreviated treatment of the topic, the Supreme Court judgment does not address the hard issues raised by a complementary protection regime of this nature. In particular, it fails to address the point that protection under the Refugee Convention is given only to those who are the victims, or potential victims, of human rights abuses. Those who themselves have abused human rights or who have committed serious non-political crimes are explicitly excluded from the protection regime by Article 1F. Article 33(2) further underlines the fact that the obligation of a State party to protect a genuine refugee is not

[64] See, eg *New Zealand Airline Pilots' Association v Attorney-General* [1997] 3 NZLR 269 (NZCA) and *Sellers v Maritime Safety Inspector* [1999] 2 NZLR 44 (NZCA), neither of which involved a treaty protecting fundamental human rights. For a commentary on these two models and the impact of unincorporated treaty obligations on administrative power, see C Geiringer, '*Tavita* and All That: Confronting the Confusion Surrounding Unincorporated Treaties and Administrative Law' (2004) 21 *New Zealand Universities Law Review* 66.

[65] For an unsuccessful attempt to use the mobility rights of citizen children under s 18 of the New Zealand Bill of Rights Act 1990 to prevent the removal from New Zealand of non-citizen parents, see *Schier v Removal Review Authority* [1998] NZAR 230 (NZHC), not over-ruled on this point in *Schier v Removal Review Authority* [1999] 1 NZLR 703 (NZCA).

an obligation to protect him or her at all costs. The State is entitled to expel a refugee where there are reasonable grounds for regarding that person as a danger to the security of the country or as a danger to the community of that country. According to the view of the Supreme Court, New Zealand now has an obligation to protect from expulsion or return everyone—even those categories of persons previously excluded from the refugee protection regime, namely:

(a) Any person with respect to whom there are serious reasons for considering that:
   (i) He or she has committed a crime against peace, a war crime or a crime against humanity;
   (ii) He or she has committed a serious non-political crime outside the country of refuge;
   (iii) He or she has been guilty of acts contrary to the purpose and principles of the United Nations.
(b) Any person with respect to whom there are reasonable grounds for regarding him or her as a danger to the security of the country;
(c) Any person who, having been convicted by final judgment of a particularly serious crime, constitutes a danger to the community of that country.

In the context of the convicted rapist Al Baiiaty, the outcome of the Supreme Court decision would be that while, as a consequence of his convictions and the serious risk he poses to the community, he is lawfully expellable from New Zealand under the Refugee Convention, he has an absolute and unqualified right to remain living in New Zealand if he is able to establish that in Iraq there is a risk to his life or of his being tortured. This right, being an absolute one, overrides the interests of the female citizens of New Zealand in being kept safe from him.

It is remarkable that consequences or outcomes of this nature are neither referred to nor discussed by the Supreme Court. Instead there is the implicit assertion that no matter how extreme the danger to the security of the country and no matter how grave a danger to the community an individual may be, the risk of that individual being subjected to arbitrary deprivation of life or to torture trumps all other considerations. This is not a proposition which is self-evidently correct.[66]

It is the claimed absolute character of the obligation which is particularly troublesome in this narrow category of cases. Articles 6 and 7 of the ICCPR do not on their face apply in the expulsion and 'return' situations. Their extension to expulsion and return is by judicial interpretation only, the foundational decisions of the European Court of Human Rights in

[66] See also Geiringer (n 50 above) 288.

Soering v United Kingdom and *Chahal v United Kingdom* being of enduring influence. But the characteristically conclusionary language employed by the European Court of Human Rights in those and related cases does not address the issue of how the 'right' of the potential returnee trumps absolutely the rights of the citizens of the sending State, including the right of those citizens to be free from the risk to their lives by the returnee and to be free also from the risk of being tortured or subjected to inhuman or degrading treatment at his or her hands.[67] Once a court steps outside the express terms of a treaty and asserts an implied extension of the magnitude in question, it is necessary for that court to explain why it is not also implied that the rights of citizens and the duty of the State to protect those rights do not equally deserve consideration. This the European Court of Human Rights does not do; nor does the New Zealand Supreme Court in *Zaoui*.

Doubt as to the correctness of the assertion of absolute rights of non-citizens over the rights and interests of citizens and of the State has in recent times begun to emerge from the jurisprudence of the European Court of Human Rights itself in the 'inhuman or degrading treatment' category of cases involving access to medical treatment. The landmark case is *D v United Kingdom*,[68] in which D, while serving a six-year prison sentence for importing a class A drug, was diagnosed as HIV-positive and as suffering from AIDS. The infection had apparently occurred some time before his arrival in the United Kingdom. Returning him to his country of origin, St Kitts, would have resulted in his inevitable death. The European Court concluded that a complaint under Article 3 of the ECHR had been made out because it might be inhuman treatment to send someone to a country where urgently needed medical and social treatment is not available. The court reiterated that Article 3 of the ECHR prohibits in absolute terms return to torture or inhuman or degrading treatment or punishment and that this guarantee applies irrespective of the reprehensible nature of the conduct of the person in question.[69] In this analysis, the rights of the citizens of the host State are subservient to the guarantee of article 3 protection.

Given that since the early 1980s HIV/AIDS has claimed 25 million lives and infected over 60 million persons, and will kill millions more before it is controlled, the implications of *D v United Kingdom* are serious, a point remarked upon by Lord Brown in *N v Secretary of State for the Home Department*.[70] Perhaps for these policy reasons the European

[67] See, for example, *Chahal v United Kingdom* (n 44 above) paras 75–82.
[68] *D v United Kingdom* (1997) 24 EHRR 423 (ECtHR).
[69] *Ibid*, paras 47, 51–3.
[70] *N v Secretary of State for the Home Department* [2005] UKHL 31, [2005] 2 AC 296, para 72. The statistics are taken from the Human Rights Watch Welcome Page on *HIV/AIDS & Human Rights* <http://www.hrw.org/doc/?t=hivaids&document_limit=0,2> (accessed 22 August 2006).

Court has in subsequent cases sought to distinguish its decision in *D v United Kingdom*. The analysis of these cases by the House of Lords in *N v Secretary of State for the Home Department* has revealed that the European (or 'Strasbourg') Court has been at pains to avoid any further extension of the exceptional category of case which *D v United Kingdom* represents.[71] The policy reasons why there must be an implied limitation to the obligations under Article 3 of the ECHR were articulated in the following terms. Lord Nicholls stated:

> But, as the Strasbourg jurisprudence confirms, article 3 cannot be interpreted as requiring contracting states to admit and treat AIDS sufferers from all over the world for the rest of their lives. Nor, by the like token, is article 3 to be interpreted as requiring contracting states to give an extended right to remain to would-be immigrants who have received medical treatment while their applications are being considered. If their applications are refused, the improvement in their medical condition brought about by this interim medical treatment, and the prospect of serious or fatal relapse on expulsion, cannot make expulsion inhuman treatment for the purposes of Article 3.[72]

Lord Hope noted:

> It must be borne in mind too that the effect of any extension would be to widen still further the gap that already exists between the scope of articles 32 and 33 of the Refugee Convention and the reach of article 3 of the Human Rights Convention to which the Strasbourg court referred in *Chahal v United Kingdom* 23 EHRR 413, para 80. It would have the effect of affording all those in the appellant's condition a right of asylum in this country until such time as the standard of medical facilities available in their home countries for the treatment of HIV/AIDS had reached that which is available in Europe. It would risk drawing into the United Kingdom large numbers of people already suffering from HIV in the hope that they too could remain here indefinitely so that they could take the benefit of the medical resources that are available in this country. This would result in a very great and no doubt unquantifiable commitment of resources which it is, to say the least, highly questionable the states parties to the Convention would ever have agreed to.[73]

Significantly, Lord Hope had earlier cited at length from the judgment of Lord Bingham of Cornhill in *Brown v Stott* on the limits to implying obligations into a human rights treaty such as the ECHR:

> In interpreting the Convention, as any other treaty, it is generally to be assumed that the parties have included the terms which they wished to include and on which they were able to agree, omitting other terms which they did not wish to

[71] *N v Secretary of State for the Home Department* (n 70 above) para 48 (Lord Hope, with whom Lord Nicholls, Lord Walker and Baroness Hale agreed).

[72] *Ibid*, para 17 (Lord Nicholls).

[73] *Ibid*, para 53 (Lord Hope).

> include or on which they were not able to agree. Thus particular regard must be had and reliance placed on the express terms of the Convention, which define the rights and freedoms which the contracting parties have undertaken to secure. This does not mean that nothing can be implied into the Convention. The language of the Convention is for the most part so general that some implication of terms is necessary, and the case law of the European court shows that the court has been willing to imply terms into the Convention when it was judged necessary or plainly right to do so. But the process of implication is one to be carried out with caution, if the risk is to be averted that the contracting parties may, by judicial interpretation, become bound by obligations which they did not expressly accept and might not have been willing to accept. As an important constitutional instrument the Convention is to be seen as a 'living tree capable of growth and expansion within its natural limits' (*Edwards v Attorney General for Canada* [1930] AC 124, 136 per Lord Sankey LC), but those limits will often call for very careful consideration.[74]

In the more recent decision of the English Court of Appeal in *ZT v Secretary of State for the Home Department*,[75] a Zimbabwean national diagnosed as being HIV positive and given anti-retroviral treatment (which controlled the disease) had unsuccessfully applied for leave to remain on the basis that to return her to Zimbabwe, where treatment would be difficult or impossible to obtain, would infringe her right under Article 3 of the ECHR as she would be unlikely to survive for more than a year or two, during which time she would be burdened with serious illness. Agreeing that the claim must fail, Sedley LJ commented that if HIV were a rare affliction, readily treatable in the United Kingdom but not treatable except for the fortunate few in many other countries, the courts would have little hesitation in holding removal of sufferers to such countries to be inhuman treatment contrary to Article 3. But it was

> the sheer volume of suffering now reaching these shores that has driven the Home Office, the Immigration Appellate Authority and the courts to find jurisprudential reasons for holding that neither art 3 nor art 8 can ordinarily avail HIV sufferers who face removal.[76]

In a characteristically candid passage, he articulated the policy reasons why the implied extension of Article 3 to medical cases would be unsustainable:

> We have in consequence had to set the bar in both art 3 and art 8 cases unusually high for removal cases. The reasoning of the House in *N v SSHD* accepts, in effect, that the internal logic of the Convention has to give way to the external logic of events when these events are capable of bringing about the collapse of

[74] *Ibid*, para 22 (Lord Hope), referring to *Brown v Stott* [2003] 1 AC 681 (PC) 703.
[75] *ZT v Secretary of State for the Home Department* [2006] INLR 256, [2006] Imm AR 84 (CA).
[76] *Ibid*, para 41.

> the Convention system ... But the underlying message of *N v SSHD* and *Razgar*, and *R (Ullah) v Special Adjudicator; DO v Immigration Appeal Tribunal* [2004] UK HL 26, [2004] 2 AC 323, [2004] INLR 381 too is that the European Convention is neither a surrogate system of asylum nor a fall back for those who have otherwise no right to remain here. It is for particular cases which transcend their class in respects which the Convention recognises. None of this could find any place in an originalist reading of the Convention; but just as the Convention has grown through its jurisprudence to meet new assaults on human rights, it is also having to retrench in places to avoid being overwhelmed by its own logic. If what results are rules rather than law, that may be an unavoidable price to be paid for the maintenance of the Convention system.[77]

Once it is acknowledged that policy considerations have driven the imposition of unexpressed duties on States parties, it becomes more difficult to accept, without compelling justification, why other policy considerations should be excluded in the context of national security and safety of the community cases. The uncritical assumption that *Soering v United Kingdom* and *Chahal v United Kingdom* were correctly decided is pervasive.[78] But as the decisions in *N v Secretary of State for the Home Department* and *ZT v Secretary of State for the Home Department* demonstrate, the 'inhuman or degrading treatment or punishment' cases may force a re-examination of the unexplained ruling that the rights of citizens and of the State to exist in safety and security are irrelevant under Article 3 of the ECHR.

The decision in *N v Secretary of State for the Home Department* was not referred to by the New Zealand Supreme Court in *Zaoui v Attorney-General (No 2)*. The obiter views in *Zaoui* as to the nature and extent of the complementary protection afforded by Articles 6 and 7 of the ICCPR are the more superficial for failing to address the complex policy issues which have driven both the European Court of Human Rights and the House of Lords to acknowledge that, in the words of Sedley LJ,

> the internal logic of the [European] Convention must give way to the external logic of events when those events are capable of bringing about the collapse of the Convention system.

Expressed another way, the assertion that a non-citizen has an absolute and unqualified right to *non-refoulement*, to which the rights of citizens are subjugated, is a contestable proposition and the European Court of

[77] *ZT v Secretary of State for the Home Department* (n 75 above) para 42.

[78] See, eg the discussion of the 'views' of the Human Rights Committee on Arts 7 and 10 of the ICCPR in S Joseph, J Schultz and M Castan, *The International Covenant on Civil and Political Rights: Cases, Materials, and Commentary*, 2nd edn (Oxford, Oxford University Press, 2005) ch 9. Note, however, the challenge to *Chahal v United Kingdom* in 'Observations of the Governments of Lithuania, Portugal, Slovakia and the United Kingdom Intervening in Application No. 25424/05 Ramzy v The Netherlands' <http://www.icj.org/IMG/pdf/UK_observations_Ramzy_case.pdf> (accessed 20 June 2007).

Human Rights and the English courts have already been forced in 'medical care' cases to retreat from absolutism. That retreat is based on policy grounds. This makes it easier to see that the asserted absolute nature of the *non-refoulement* obligation in torture cases is itself the outcome of policy choices by judges and of the judicial selection of factors permissibly taken into account when inferring that obligation out of the language of the ECHR. Hitherto, those policy choices have been unarticulated, if not disguised and unjustifiably narrowed by the exclusion of any consideration relating to the rights of citizens and the duties of the State to protect those citizens.

While Article 3 of the CAT (unlike the ICCPR provisions) does have an explicit *non-refoulement* obligation, it is still necessary for absolutists to assume that this obligation was intended to trump all national security considerations and the safety of the citizens of the State. As to this, it cannot be easily assumed that States parties to the CAT intended to make supreme the interests of the non-citizen, to elevate them over all rights and interests possessed by citizens and to continue to hold them supreme even when the non-citizen threatens the life of the State itself. The language, object and purpose of both the CAT and Articles 6 and 7 of the ICCPR do not compel such interpretation.[79] On the contrary, the exclusion of a narrow category of cases as envisaged in the Refugee Convention will immeasurably strengthen the credibility of the complementary protection regime. The decision of the New Zealand Supreme Court does not address any of these issues.

Additionally, the Supreme Court neither refers to nor addresses section 5 of the New Zealand Bill of Rights Act 1990, which provides:

> Subject to section 4 of this Bill of Rights, the rights and freedoms contained in this Bill of Rights may be subject only to such reasonable limits prescribed by law as can be demonstrably justified in a free and democratic society.[80]

[79] The general rule of interpretation contained in Art 31(1) of the 1969 Vienna Convention on the Law of Treaties (adopted 23 May 1969, entered into force 27 January 1980) 1155 UNTS 331 is that '[a] treaty shall be interpreted in good faith in accordance with the ordinary meaning to be given to the terms of the treaty in their context and in the light of its object and purpose'.

[80] On s 5, see further S Mize, 'Resolving Cases of Conflicting Rights under the New Zealand Bill of Rights Act' (2006) 22 *New Zealand Universities Law Review* 50. Mize concludes that there needs to be a greater thoroughness and consistency in judicial resolutions, and an appreciation of the important role that s 5 has to play in resolving conflicts between rights. The author also addresses the issue whether the interests of hypothetical persons amount to a competing rights claim. In Butler and Butler (n 13 above) 117 it is observed at 6.1.2 that while overseas experience indicates that the assessment of the reasonableness of limits placed on rights is the stuff of most rights disputes, in New Zealand that has not been so much the case. As a result, more than 14 years into the life of the Bill of Rights Act 1990, practitioners, governmental officials and judges still operate with little native New Zealand guidance as to the proper interpretation and application of s 5. This section has been considered tentatively in the context of New Zealand's obligations under the Convention on the Rights of the Child: *Elika v Minister of Immigration* [1996] 1 NZLR 741 (NZHC) 749.

In the result, the Supreme Court obiter dicta do not grapple with the hard issues. Nor do the dicta explain why New Zealand should provide a safe haven for war criminals, genocidaires, suspected terrorists and other criminals. The fact that since 1 October 2000 New Zealand has asserted, pursuant to the International Crimes and International Criminal Court Act 2000, jurisdiction to try genocide, crimes against humanity and war crimes hardly addresses the issue. The difficulties inherent in prosecuting international crimes in New Zealand are seriously under-estimated and the asserted jurisdiction is largely aspirational, if not symbolic. The resources required for the investigation and prosecution of such crimes may help to illustrate the point.[81] The International Criminal Tribunal for the Former Yugoslavia was established by the UN Security Council in May 1993. As at 16 August 2006, the Tribunal had indicted 161 persons, 47 of whom had been found guilty.[82] The Tribunal's regular budget in 1993 was US$276,000. In 2006–07 it was US$276,474,100 and the cumulative allocated budget for the 13 years amounts to US$1,243,157,722.[83] The International Criminal Tribunal for Rwanda has, as at June 2006, handed down only 22 judgments involving 28 accused. 25 of them were convicted and three acquitted.[84] For 2006–07 the budget was US$269,758,400.[85] There are also formidable evidentiary problems in the prosecution of international crimes in New Zealand, not least of which is that it has been held that evidence given in support of a refugee claim cannot be used in subsequent criminal proceedings under the International Crimes and International Criminal Court Act 2000.[86] Yet most often, it is the evidence given by the asylum seeker in

[81] Two experienced prosecutors at the International Criminal Tribunal for the Former Yugoslavia have commented on the fact that even mid-level and low-level perpetrators' trials last in excess of one year. They argue that the common law 'is imperfect generally, and probably ill-suited for war crimes trials': G Nice and P Vallières-Roland, 'Procedural Innovations in War Crimes Trials' in H Abtahi and G Boas (eds), *The Dynamics of International Criminal Justice: Essays in Honour of Sir Richard May* (Leiden, Martinus Nijhoff Publishers, 2006) 155 and 163. See also Human Rights Watch, *Universal Jurisdiction in Europe: The State of the Art* (June 2006).

[82] <http://www.un.org/icty/glance-e/index.htm> (accessed 19 June 2007).

[83] See 'General Information' (updated 7 February 2007) <http://www.un.org/icty/glance-e/index.htm> (accessed 5 June 2007).

[84] International Criminal Tribunal for Rwanda, 'Fact Sheet: Achievements of the ICTR' <http://www.ictr.org> (accessed 5 June 2007).

[85] International Criminal Tribunal for Rwanda, 'General Information' <http://69.94.11.53/ENGLISH/geninfo/index.htm> (accessed 5 June 2007).

[86] *X v Refugee Status Appeals Authority* [2006] NZAR 533 (NZHC). The decision was upheld by the Court of Appeal but on other grounds: *Attorney-General v X* [2007] NZCA 388. The Crown has applied to the Supreme Court for leave to appeal against that decision. The decision in *X v Refugee Status Appeals Authority* has, however, been applied in *Z v Attorney-General* (High Court Auckland, CIV2007-404-330, 30 March 2007, Andrews J).

the course of the refugee claim which is the most direct and 'best' evidence of complicity.[87]

It is also problematic that, having held that the prohibition on *refoulement* to torture does not have the status of *jus cogens*, the Supreme Court does not in this respect explain its view that members of the Executive Council cannot advise the Governor-General to order deportation under section 72 if they are satisfied that there are substantial grounds for believing that, as a result of the deportation, the person would be in danger of being subjected to torture or to cruel, inhuman or degrading treatment or punishment.[88] On one view, the introduction into domestic law of absolute obligations which put at potential risk not only the safety of citizens but also the very existence of the State itself is best left to Parliament.[89] The complexities are underlined by *A v Secretary of State for the Home Department*,[90] where indefinite detention in preference to removal to the prospect of torture or inhuman treatment was successfully challenged. Unanswered is the question how States can protect themselves and their citizens if expulsion is not a lawful alternative.

The Supreme Court judgment in *Zaoui* has potentially wide ramifications. At the most immediate level there is the question of the shape and form of the proposed new procedures for the determination of claims in New Zealand for protection under Article 3 of the CAT and for the determination of complementary protection claims based on the ICCPR.[91] Not without significance in this context is the fact that New Zealand recognises the competence of the Committee against Torture to receive and consider communications from or on behalf of individuals subject to

[87] See, eg *Garate v Refugee Status Appeals Authority* [1998] NZAR 241 (NZHC), where the refugee claimant admitted that he had been involved in the routine torture of prisoners during the Sendero Luminoso insurgency in Peru.

[88] For a commentary on this anomaly, see Yarwood (n 36 above). In this commentary, it is argued that the Supreme Court, in its (de facto) attribution of *jus cogens* status to the *refoulement* prohibition, assumed a bold, if inadvertent, stance. But even if the prohibition of torture (cf *refoulement* to torture) does have the standing of *jus cogens*, this does not automatically override all other rules of international law: *Case concerning Arrest Warrant of 11 April 2000 (Democratic Republic of Congo v Belgium)* [2002] ICJ Rep 3, followed in *Jones v Ministry of the Interior of the Kingdom of Saudi Arabia* [2006] UKHL 26, [2006] 2 WLR 1424 (HL) paras 24 and 48–49. That decision, in turn, has been applied in New Zealand: *Fang v Jiang* (High Court Auckland, CIV2004-404-5843, 21 December 2006, Randerson J).

[89] See also Geiringer (n 50 above) 288.

[90] *A v Secretary of State for the Home Department* [2004] UKHL 56, [2005] 2 AC 68.

[91] The issue was identified in the recent review of the Immigration Act 1987 (NZ): see 'Discussion Paper' (n 19 above) paras 1089–145. In November 2006 the Cabinet determined (inter alia) that new immigration legislation would provide for a single determination procedure incorporating New Zealand's core immigration-related international obligations: see 'Summary of Cabinet Decisions' (n 19 above).

its jurisdiction who claim to be victims of a violation by a State party of the provisions of the CAT. It is also a party to the First Optional Protocol to the ICCPR and thus recognises the right of the Human Rights Committee to receive and consider communications from individuals subject to its jurisdiction who claim to be victims of a violation by New Zealand of any of the rights set forth in the ICCPR.[92] Neither of these two committees has power, however, to issue binding rulings. They can only express 'views'. This is not necessarily a regrettable omission.[93]

Other difficult substantive issues remain. Not only does the Supreme Court decision fail to address how it is that those whom the Refugee Convention identifies as not deserving of international protection should nevertheless be given absolute protection under the ICCPR and the CAT, it does not grapple with the question raised by *Suresh v Canada (Minister of Citizenship and Immigration)*,[94] namely whether lawful expulsion under domestic law can take place notwithstanding a breach or potential breach of the CAT or the ICCPR. Another disappointing aspect of the obiter observations of the Supreme Court is the failure to explain why those who abuse human rights should receive a greater degree of protection of their rights than their victims (or potential victims). There appears to be no awareness that there is a very real question as to why, for example, women in New Zealand should continue to be exposed to what the Court of Appeal has acknowledged to be the 'serious risk' posed by Mr Al Baiiaty. The court does not address how it is that his 'right' not to be exposed to the risk of being tortured trumps the right of New Zealand women not to be exposed to the serious risk that he will again commit

[92] First Optional Protocol to the International Covenant on Civil and Political Rights, United Nations General Assembly Res 2200A (XXI) of 16 December 1966 (entered into force 23 March 1976) 999 UNTS 302. New Zealand acceded to the Protocol on 26 May 1989 and it entered into force for New Zealand on 26 August 1989: *New Zealand Consolidated Treaty List* (n 3 above) 243.

[93] See P Rishworth, 'The Rule of International Law?' in G Huscroft and P Rishworth (eds), *Litigating Rights: Perspectives from Domestic and International Law* (Oxford, Hart Publishing, 2002); S Davidson, 'Intention and Effect: The Legal Status of the Final Views of the Human Rights Committee' in Huscroft and Rishworth (eds), *Litigating Rights*; contrast the views expressed by E Evatt, a former member of the Human Rights Committee, in 'The Impact of International Human Rights on Domestic Law' in Huscroft and Rishworth (eds), *Litigating Rights*. For recent judicial acknowledgement that the Committee Against Torture has no power to bind States, see *Jones* (n 88 above) paras 23, 57. For observations as to the binding effect of decisions of the Committee against Torture, see *Ahani v Canada (Attorney General)* (2002) 208 DLR (4th) 66 (Ont CA) paras 34–40. In this case, even the Federal Court declined to act on an interim request by the Human Rights Committee that the deportation of Ahani be stayed pending determination of his petition to the Committee. For a commentary, see M Coutu and M-H Giroux, 'The Aftermath of 11 September 2001: Liberty vs Security before the Supreme Court of Canada' (2006) 18 *International Journal of Refugee Law* 313 at 329.

[94] *Suresh v Canada (Minister of Citizenship and Immigration)* (n 34 above).

rape in New Zealand.[95] Similar questions arise in relation to those who import illicit and harmful drugs and those who are a danger to the security of the country.

One of the principal reasons why the Refugee Convention contains exclusion clauses as well as exceptions to the *non-refoulement* obligation is that it encourages full and good faith discharge by States parties to the Refugee Convention of their obligations under that treaty. It also encourages support by citizens of the refugee protection regime. Once public faith in that regime evaporates, hostility, xenophobia and racism fill the vacuum and governments look elsewhere for 'solutions' to what is then described as the 'refugee problem'. In short, the Refugee Convention, by protecting only those who both need and deserve the surrogate protection of the international community, maintains its own integrity and credibility. By contrast, there is little apparent credibility to a complementary protection regime that requires a State party to the Refugee Convention, the CAT and the ICCPR to protect, at all costs to the State and its community, those who are a danger to the security of the State and those who are a danger to the community. The challenge which the Supreme Court did not meet in *Zaoui v Attorney-General (No 2)* was to provide a clear, compelling and persuasive basis for the new complementary protection regime it has apparently brought into being.

[95] *Prosecutor v Kunarac* (ICTY Appeals Chamber, Case No IT-96-23 and IT-96-23/1-A, 12 June 2002) para 150 acknowledges that sexual violence necessarily gives rise to severe pain or suffering, whether physical or mental, and in this way justifies its characterisation as an act of torture.

4

Offshore Barriers to Asylum Seeker Movement: The Exercise of Power without Responsibility?

SAVITRI TAYLOR*

I. INTRODUCTION

SINCE 2001 THE number of asylum applications made in western countries generally has been trending downwards.[1] This decline in asylum applications is partly attributable to the fact that western countries are placing ever more formidable barriers in the way of persons trying to make their way to their borders, even with the purpose of requesting asylum.[2] In Australia's case, the downward trend began reversing during 2006,[3] but this was not due to any abatement in Australia's efforts to prevent asylum seeker arrivals. In fact, the territorial border is becoming less and less important as a site of immigration control because most of the real action in that respect is occurring offshore.

For the sake of keeping to a reasonable length, this chapter does not explore all the international legal issues raised by all of the offshore immigration control activities in which Australia and other western States

* This article was first revised for publication in mid-February 2006, and again in early March 2007 to reflect to the greatest extent possible developments in the intervening period. When in doubt, however, readers should assume that this article reflects the state of play in late 2005/early 2006.

[1] UNHCR, 'Asylum Levels and Trends in Industrialized Countries, 2006: Overview of Asylum Applications Lodged in European and Non-European Industrialized Countries in 2006' (23 March 2007) 3–5 <http://www.unhcr.org/statistics> (accessed 8 June 2007).

[2] MJ Gibney, 'Beyond the Bounds of Responsibility: Western States and Measures to Prevent the Arrival of Refugees', Global Commission on International Migration, *Global Migration Perspectives*, No 22 (January 2005) 6. It should be noted that barriers to entry are only part of the explanation for this decline in asylum applications. The other part of the explanation lies in improving world conditions during the period, since the total number of asylum applications across 50 industrialised States halved between 2002 and 2006: UNHCR (n 1 above) para 13.

[3] UNHCR (n 1 above) 10 (Table 1).

engage. Rather, it focuses on whether the interception in overseas airports of individuals who are attempting to travel without valid authorisation to the territory of the intercepting State, engages that State's *non-refoulement* obligations.

II. OFFSHORE BARRIERS TO ASYLUM SEEKER MOVEMENT

A. Visa Requirements

Australia requires all non-citizens travelling to Australia to have authorisation in the form of a visa to do so. Potential asylum seekers are unlikely to be granted visas for travel to Australia. In fact, as a result of the Department of Immigration and Citizenship's ever improving 'risk management' techniques, potential asylum seekers are less and less likely to be granted visas for travel to Australia, as evidenced by the downward trend in the proportion of Visitor Visa-holders making Protection Visa applications over the past few years.[4] Likewise, the proportion of Student Visa-holders making Protection Visa applications is decreasing.[5] While Australia is unique in imposing a *universal* visa requirement on non-citizens, it is by no means the only western country to use visas as a means of forestalling the entry of 'unwelcome' non-citizens, including asylum seekers.

B. Foreign Country Interception of Potential Unauthorised Arrivals

i. The Activities of the Airline Liaison Officer Network

The next barrier to entry upon which Australia relies, in conjunction with its universal visa requirement, is interception prior to arrival of those attempting to travel to Australia without proper authorisation.

[4] 2441 (0.07 per cent) of Visitor Visa-holders applied for Protection Visas in 2005–06, described by the Department as a 'similar result to' 0.06 per cent in 2004–05: Department of Immigration and Multicultural Affairs, *Annual Report 2005–06* (Canberra, Cth of Australia, 2006) 61, 65. However, over a longer period the trend is definitely downward. 0.06 per cent of Visitor Visa-holders applied for Protection Visas in 2004–05, compared to 0.07 per cent in 2003–04, 0.1 per cent in 2002–03 and 0.15 per cent in 2001–02: see Department of Immigration and Multicultural Affairs and Indigenous Affairs, *Annual Report 2004–05* (Canberra, Cth of Australia, 2005) 55; Department of Immigration and Multicultural Affairs and Indigenous Affairs, *Annual Report 2003–04* (Canberra, Cth of Australia, 2004) 24; Department of Immigration and Multicultural Affairs and Indigenous Affairs, *Annual Report 2002–03* (Canberra, Cth of Australia, 2003) 32–33. (The immigration department was renamed the Department of Immigration and Citizenship in early 2007. Given the number of name changes the department has had, for ease of reference, this chapter frequently uses the standard abbreviation of 'Immigration Department' or 'Department of Immigration').

[5] Immigration Department *Annual Report 2005–06* (n 4 above) 79; Immigration Department *Annual Report 2004–05* (n 4 above) 62; Immigration Department *Annual Report 2003–04* (n 4 above) 51; Immigration Department *Annual Report 2002–03* (n 4 above) 36.

Since most unauthorised air arrivals to Australia transit through airports in Asia and the Middle East,[6] one way in which Australia has put its interception strategy into operation is to post Australian Airline Liaison Officers ('ALOs') in those airports which are major gateways to Australia. The main function of Australian ALOs, who are specialist document examiners, is to assist local immigration and airport authorities and airline personnel to identify document fraud by checking documents and providing advice on authenticity.[7] The 'visible presence' of ALOs is also intended to act as a deterrent to 'people smugglers, potential inadmissible passengers and persons of potential security concern'.[8]

According to the Department of Immigration,

> Australia negotiates border security arrangements on a bilateral basis, with such arrangements acknowledging that the presence of Australian ALOs is at the invitation of the host government.[9]

The arrangements are made with the immigration authority of the host government and vary in their level of formality, with the more formal agreements being set out in memoranda of understanding (arrangements of less than treaty status).[10] The matters covered by the arrangements are usually 'limited to operational restrictions imposed by the host government', for example restrictions on the parts of the airport to which ALOs are allowed access.[11] While ALOs 'work closely' with airlines and their assistance is 'warmly received' by airlines, there are apparently

> no formal or informal arrangement[s] between [the Department of Immigration] and individual airlines dealing with the functions of Australian ALOs.[12]

Starting with ALOs in the international airports of Singapore and Bangkok in 1990,[13] Australia managed to increase its ALO network by the end of 2005–06 to 22 ALOs at 16 airports.[14] The airports at which

[6] Department of Immigration and Multicultural Affairs and Indigenous Affairs, *Managing the Border: Immigration Compliance: 2004–05 Edition*' (Canberra, Cth of Australia, 2005) 22.

[7] Department of Immigration and Citizenship, 'Border Control' <http://www.immi.gov.au/managing-australias-borders/border-security/border.htm> (accessed 1 March 2007); Immigration Department *Annual Report 2003–04* (n 4 above) 81.

[8] Letter from P Thurborn (Assistant Secretary, Entry Policy Branch, Immigration Department) to S Taylor (21 September 2005) (copy on file with author).

[9] *Ibid*.

[10] Letter from J Rees (Acting Assistant Secretary, Entry Policy and Procedures Branch, Department) to S Taylor (21 October 2005) (copy on file with author).

[11] *Ibid*. The terms of individual arrangements are, however, confidential.

[12] *Ibid*.

[13] J Bedlington, 'The Hows and Whys of Interception: A State Perspective' (2003) 3 *Revue Juridique Polynésienne (Numéro hors série)* 59 fn 68.

[14] Immigration Department *Annual Report 2005–06* (n 4 above) 125.

ALOs were posted at that date included the international airports in Bangkok (Thailand), Denpasar and Jakarta (Indonesia), Hong Kong and Shanghai (China), Johannesburg (South Africa), Kuala Lumpur (Malaysia), Manila (Philippines), Mumbai (India), Port Moresby (Papua New Guinea), Nadi (Fiji), Seoul (South Korea), Singapore and Taipei (Taiwan).[15] In addition, brief ad hoc postings are undertaken at short notice to places which are expected to be 'of concern'.[16]

While ALOs focus on Australia-bound flights, they also cover 'certain flights that are not directly Australia bound', with the aim of intercepting improperly documented passengers who may be attempting 'to travel to Australia by more circuitous travel routes'.[17] In some airports ALOs co-operate informally with out-posted immigration liaison officers of other countries in order to cover as many flights as possible.[18] In late 2005, the only instance of an on-going formal co-operation arrangement appeared to be the arrangement in place in Bangkok's Don Muang International Airport, pursuant to which ALOs co-operate with the representatives of 11 other countries achieving 'nearly 24/7 coverage of flights'.[19] From time to time, however, ALOs participate in 'short-duration multinational

[15] Immigration Department, Answers to Questions on Notice, Senate Legal and Constitutional References Committee Inquiry into the Administration of the Migration Act 1958 (11 October 2005) 11 <http://www.aph.gov.au/senate/committee/legcon_ctte/migration/qon/07feb-dimia.pdf> (accessed 1 March 2007). The 15th location was most likely the airport in Colombo (Sri Lanka), as an ALO posting there was foreshadowed in the Immigration Department's 'Submission to Joint Standing Committee on Public Accounts and Audit, Inquiry into Development of Aviation Security since the Committee's June 2004 Report 400: Review of Aviation Security in Australia' (2005) 4 <http://www.aph.gov.au/house/committee/jpaa/aviation_security2/subs/sub45.pdf> (accessed 1 March 2007). The author was unable to ascertain the location of the 16th airport. Strangely, an Immigration Department factsheet dated 30 January 2007 referred to ALOs being placed at 11 airports, and provided a listing which did not include Johannesburg, Shanghai, Mumbai or Colombo: see 'Fact Sheet 73: People Smuggling' (revised 30 January 2007) <http://www.immi.gov.au/media/fact-sheets/73smuggling.htm> (accessed 2 March 2007). It seems doubtful that this is a complete listing. For example, in evidence given to a parliamentary committee in November 2006, a Department of Immigration official mentioned the Australian ALO in Mumbai without indicating that the arrangement was to be terminated. In fact, he said: 'We have an airline liaison officer in Mumbai. The Indian government has been very interested in that model, and has again sought to learn from us on the experience that we have had with our LO network across the world': *Official Committee Hansard: Joint Standing Committee on Foreign Affairs, Defence and Trade (Reference: Australia's Relationship with India as an Emerging World Power)* (Canberra, Cth of Australia, 3 November 2006) 67–8 (Mr Fox, Immigration Department).

[16] Immigration Department 'Border Control' (n 7 above); Letter from P Thurborn (n 8 above).

[17] Immigration Department 'Review of Aviation Security' (n 15 above) 5.

[18] N Siegmund (Immigration Department), Evidence to Senate Legal and Constitutional Legislation Committee, *Official Committee Hansard: Senate Legal and Constitutional Legislation Committee (Consideration of Budget Estimates)* (Canberra, Cth of Australia, 28 May 2003) 528. Canada, the US and several European countries also engage in immigration compliance activities beyond their own borders: Gibney (n 2 above) 8.

[19] Letter from P Thurborn (n 8 above).

exercises' targeting irregular movement through particular airports.[20] The immigration control authorities and national airlines of Australia and 18 other mostly western countries[21] are, in fact, members of the International Air Transport Association/Control Authorities Working Group ('IATA/CAWG'), which was formed in 1987 in order to

> develop and pursue a co-operative programme for the facilitation and processing of a growing number of passengers, while ensuring effective action against illegitimate traffic, and to focus on such concepts as risk management, sharing of information and convergence of processes.[22]

In 2005–06, Australia's ALOs assisted in the interception of 'over' 2500 persons with fraudulent documentation, of whom 143 were attempting to board Australia-bound flights.[23] The Department of Immigration's arrangements with host country governments do not specify processes for dealing with asylum claims made by intercepted persons.[24] However, the IATA/CAWG Code of Conduct for Immigration Liaison Officers ('ILOs'), a set of non-binding best practice guidelines by which Australia purports to abide,[25] specifies that if ILOs

> receive requests for asylum, applicants should be directed to the office of the United Nations High Commissioner for Refugees, to the appropriate diplomatic mission(s), or to an appropriate local Non-Governmental Organization (NGO).[26]

[20] Immigration Department 'Border Control' (n 7 above). The terms of agreement under which these exercises are carried out vary from country to country and are confidential.

[21] The other countries are Austria, Belgium, Canada, Denmark, Finland, France, Germany, Italy, Japan, the Netherlands, Norway, Portugal, South Africa, Spain, Sweden, Switzerland, the UK and the US: Bedlington (n 13 above) 58 n 64.

[22] IATA/CAWG Vision Statement, quoted in IATA/CAWG, 'Guidelines on Deportation and Escort' (10 October 1999, reviewed without change May 2003) 1 <http://www.iata.org/WHIP/_Files/WgId_0009/DepGuide03.pdf> (accessed 1 March 2007).

[23] Immigration Department *Annual Report 2005–06* (n 4 above) 142. In 2002–03, Australia's ALOs assisted in the interception of 1256 persons with fraudulent documentation, of whom 288 were attempting to board Australia-bound flights: Immigration Department *Annual Report 2003–04* (n 4 above) 82. In 2003–04, ALOs assisted in the interception of 1613 persons, of whom 223 were attempting to board Australia-bound flights: Immigration Department *Annual Report 2003–04* (n 4 above) 82. In 2004–05, ALOs assisted in the interception of 2543 persons, of whom 179 were attempting to board Australia-bound flights: Immigration Department *Annual Report 2004–05* (n 4 above) 110. The Department's explanation for the downward trend in interceptions of those attempting to board Australia-bound flights with fraudulent documentation is that the ever-increasing likelihood of detection is deterring more and more of those persons who might otherwise have attempted to do so: Immigration Department *Annual Report 2003–04* (n 4 above) 82. The alternate explanation for the statistics, ie declining success in intercepting those using fraudulent documents, is unlikely in light of the fact that the number of persons arriving in Australia who are found to be travelling on fraudulent documentation is also decreasing.

[24] Letter from J Rees (n 10 above).

[25] *Ibid.*

[26] IATA/CAWG, 'A Code of Conduct for Immigration Liaison Officers' (October 2002) Guideline 2.3 <http://www1.iata.org/WHIP/_Files/WgId_0014/ALOconductOct02.pdf> (accessed 6 June 2007).

In response to a query, the Department of Immigration indicated that

> [a] diplomatic mission is 'appropriate' if it is a diplomatic mission of the country to which the person seeks entry. Assuming a person is seeking entry to Australia this will be an Australian diplomatic mission, or a diplomatic mission of another country with authority to act on behalf of Australia. The appropriateness of a non-governmental organisation ('NGO') would depend on whether/what NGOs in a particular country are able to assist persons fleeing persecution. This could include a local NGO appointed by the United Nations High Commissioner for Refugees ('UNHCR') to undertake refugee assessments, or other NGOs with the responsibility of caring for asylum seekers.[27]

While no mention is made in the Code of Conduct for Immigration Liaison Officers of the possibility of referring intercepted asylum applicants to host country asylum authorities, this is what IATA/CAWG member Canada says it does in countries which are party to the Refugee Convention or Protocol, with referrals to UNHCR taking place only in non-party countries.[28] It is, in any event, apparently the case, according to one Department of Immigration official, that

> IATA CAWG has indicated that where ALOs are not able to refer to UNHCR or to the relevant diplomatic mission, they are expected to have other procedures in place to manage asylum claims.[29]

The proof of the pudding is, of course, in the eating. In a letter to the author dated 21 October 2005, the Department of Immigration stated that 'no Australian ALO has interdicted a passenger where the passenger stated that they wished to seek asylum' but conceded that 'it is possible … that passengers interdicted by Australian ALOs have later claimed asylum'.[30] The letter then went on to make the point that

> [t]here is no requirement for host immigration authorities to report such cases to the Department, and as such no data is available on the numbers of either host government officials or airline personnel who have intercepted asylum seekers attempting to travel to Australia.[31]

Notwithstanding the general unavailability of such data, the Department of Immigration indicated in the same letter that it was aware that 11 Afghans attempting to travel from the Middle East to Brisbane with counterfeit Australian visas, who were intercepted in Kuala Lumpur by an

[27] Letter from J Rees (n 10 above).

[28] A Brouwer and J Kumin, 'Interception and Asylum: When Migration Control and Human Rights Collide' (2003) 21(4) *Refuge* 10–11.

[29] Bedlington (n 13 above) 58 fn 66.

[30] Letter from J Rees (n 10 above).

[31] *Ibid.*

Australian ALO after identification by the Advance Passenger Processing system on 1 January 2005, 'claimed asylum after they were detained by Malaysian Immigration Authorities'.[32] The letter added:

> It is our understanding that the UNHCR is currently assisting them with their applications for Global Special Humanitarian visas (subclass 202).[33]

The problem is that, according to a ministerial press release dated 6 January 2005 relating to the same incident, the intercepted individuals were 'returned to the Middle East later that evening [namely 1 January 2005]'.[34]

ii. Advance Passenger Processing ('APP')

In January 2005, Australia completed the phasing-in of Advance Passenger (and crew) Processing by all airlines which have regular flights to Australia.[35] The APP system works as follows. When a passenger checks in at an international airport for any Australia-bound flight, airline personnel must[36] feed certain information about the passenger into the APP system, which automatically checks whether the passenger holds a valid Australian visa or valid Australian or New Zealand passport.[37] Depending on the outcome of the check, the check-in operator is issued with a passenger boarding directive such as 'OK TO BOARD' or 'DO NOT BOARD', upon which the operator is expected to act.[38] An airline's check-in supervisor is allowed to override a 'DO NOT BOARD' directive if the passenger, though not the holder of any of the documents specified above, still qualifies for travel according to published guidelines (such as 'military personnel from certain countries travelling on military orders and military identification').[39] Otherwise, override of a 'DO NOT BOARD'

[32] *Ibid*. Some of the details have been filled in from the following sources: Minister for Immigration and Multicultural Affairs (A Vanstone), 'Australian Border Security Foils Fraudulent Visitors in Kuala Lumpur' (Media Release, 6 January 2005); Immigration Department *Annual Report 2004–05* (n 4 above) 110.

[33] Letter from J Rees (n 10 above).

[34] Media Release (n 32 above). The author sought an explanation for this apparent discrepancy in an email to J Rees dated 29 November 2005, but received no response.

[35] Minister for Immigration and Multicultural Affairs (A Vanstone), 'Screening of All Air Passengers, Crew, Enhances Border Security' (Media Release, 24 January 2005).

[36] Migration Act 1958 (Cth), ss 245I–245N; Migration Regulations 1994 (Cth), reg 3.13A.

[37] Immigration Department 'Border Control' (n 7 above).

[38] Department of Immigration and Multicultural Affairs, *Australia's APP Check-In Guide: An Information Booklet Containing Operating Instructions for Service Providers* (November 2006) <http://www.immi.gov.au/managing-australias-borders/border-security/APP-check-in-htm> (accessed 2 March 2007). The APP system has also been in place since January 2004 for all cruise ships travelling to Australia, and since March 2006 has been progressively implemented in the cargo ship sector: Immigration Department *Annual Report 2005–06* (n 4 above) 135.

[39] *APP Check-in Guide* (n 38 above) 22.

directive is only permitted if 'approval for uplift' is given by Australia's Entry Operations Centre.[40] In the Department of Immigration's own words, '[t]he APP process effectively creates an "offshore" border for Australia at the embarkation point overseas'.[41]

Nowhere in the booklet setting out APP operating instructions for service providers is any mention made of asylum seekers.[42] When asked what would happen if passengers prevented from boarding identified themselves to airlines as asylum seekers, the Department of Immigration responded:

> It is our understanding that, in most cases, airlines would refer such cases to the host country Immigration Authorities. Airline responsibilities in this regard would depend on individual host government requirements.[43]

C. Carrier Sanctions

Australia buttresses its offshore interception strategy through the device of imposing penalties on international carriers (air and sea) if they bring non-citizens into the country without a valid visa.[44] The fear of having their profit margin eroded by such penalties is supposed to encourage carriers to deny passage to Australia to those who are inadequately or irregularly documented. The fact that the number of infringement notices actually served on carriers has been dropping markedly from year to year[45] indicates that sanctions have had their intended effect.[46] That the intended effect is to encourage carriers to deny passage to all inadequately or irregularly documented passengers, *including asylum* seekers, is evidenced by the fact that Australian law and policy makes no provision for non-imposition or refund of penalties in cases where the passenger makes a successful asylum claim upon arrival in Australia.

[40] *Ibid*, 23.

[41] *Managing the Border* (n 6 above) 4.

[42] *APP Check-In Guide* (n 38 above).

[43] Letter from J Rees (n 10 above).

[44] In addition, the Immigration Department has foreshadowed the introduction in 2006–07 of a legislated APP infringements regime, the purpose of which is 'to increase the level of compliance with mandatory APP': Immigration Department *Annual Report 2005–06* (n 4 above) 124.

[45] Immigration Department *Annual Report 2005–06* (n 4 above) 136; Immigration Department *Annual Report 2004–05* (n 4 above) 105; Immigration Department *Annual Report 2003–04* (n 4 above) 79.

[46] Qantas, for example, received 996 infringement notices in 2001–02 and 915 in 2002–03, but by taking further steps to reduce the number of infringements, managed only to garner 149 infringement notices in the first six months of the 2003–04 financial year: O Guerrera, 'Law Breaches Cost Qantas $9.5m' *The Age* (4 March 2004) 10.

Australia is not the only western country to have carrier sanctions in place. In fact, most do.[47] On the other hand, unlike Australia, some countries actually waive the imposition of carrier sanctions in the case of improperly documented passengers who make successful asylum claims.[48] However, it is a moot point whether the availability of such waivers does much to avoid asylum seeker movement being impeded. Airlines are enthusiastic about States' use of liaison officers and APP systems to provide boarding advice because this relieves them of the burden of investing in the human and other resources which would be necessary to identify improperly documented passengers themselves.[49] They are unlikely to voluntarily invest in training or hiring personnel to expertly assess asylum claims made by improperly documented passengers and, even if they did, it would still be impossible for an expert to make an asylum claim assessment in the available processing time at check-in of one minute per passenger.[50] The only viable manner in which airlines could ensure that they did not deny passage to persons with genuine asylum claims would be to accept all claims at face value, but as Bigo points out, 'the limits of sympathy [would be] quickly reached' as the financial penalties for getting it wrong (or, if the destination country is Australia, even for getting it right) mounted up.[51]

D. Bottom Line

In the five-year period from 1998–99 to 2002–03, the total number of persons refused immigration clearance at Australian airports decreased steadily. The Department of Immigration plausibly attributed the steady decrease to an equally steady stepping-up of its foreign country interception activities.[52] The downward trend appeared to be reversing in 2003–04 and 2004–05,[53] but 2005–06 saw a decrease in refusals

[47] Gibney (n 2 above) 7.

[48] Brouwer and Kumin (n 28 above) 10.

[49] W Everson (Air Transport Association of Canada), 'Session III: Reviewing Safeguards Currently in Place and Their Limits', *Interception and Refugee Protection: Bridging the Gap* (Canadian Council for Refugees, International Workshop, Ottawa, 29 May 2003) 16–17.

[50] Scandinavian Airlines System, 'Comments to the Ministry of Foreign Affairs, Department for Migration and Asylum Policies Regarding Department Memorandum on Carriers' Responsibility in the Aliens Act' (2001) 74, quoted in A Sianni, 'Interception Practices in Europe and Their Implications' (2003) 21(4) *Refuge* 28.

[51] D Bigo, 'Criminalisation of "Migrants": The Side Effect of the Will to Control Frontiers and the Sovereignty Illusion' in B Bogusz and others (eds), *Irregular Migration and Human Rights: Theoretical, European and International Perspectives* (Leiden/Boston, Martinus Nijhoff Publishers, 2004) 89.

[52] Department of Immigration and Multicultural and Indigenous Affairs, *Annual Report 2001–02* (Canberra, Cth of Australia, 2002) 55.

[53] 1241 persons were refused immigration clearance at Australian airports in 2003–04 and 1632 were refused in 2004–05: *Managing the Border* (n 6 above) 21.

from 2004–05.[54] The Department of Immigration attributes the 2003–04 and 2004–05 increases to

> a number of factors including sophisticated fraud detection measures, closer scrutiny of some [passenger] profiles and an increase in total passenger arrivals,[55]

rather than a decline in the effectiveness of its offshore interception measures, and the other available evidence seems to support this conclusion.[56]

Turning now to an even more significant set of figures, in the five-year period from 1998–99 to 2002–03, the number of persons who, after being refused immigration clearance at Australian airports, were 'screened in' to Australia's Protection Visa application process kept decreasing.[57] In fact, in the same period that the total number of airport immigration clearance refusals fell by 56 per cent, the number of air arrivals refused immigration clearance who went on to make Protection Visa applications fell by 97 per cent. Although the numbers refused immigration clearance at airports started increasing from 2003–04, in 2003–04 only 23 of those persons refused immigration clearance were screened into the Protection Visa application process, and in 2004–05 only 40 were screened in[58]—in other words, much lower numbers than one would have expected, all else being equal.

One possible explanation for the disparity is that there are simply fewer asylum seekers amongst those who attempt irregular travel to Australia; another is that the Department of Immigration at the Australian end is screening out individuals who really ought to be screened into

[54] There were 1598 persons refused immigration clearance at Australian airports in 2005–06: Immigration Department *Annual Report 2005–06* (n 4 above) 141.

[55] Immigration Department *Annual Report 2003–04* (n 4 above) 81–2; Immigration Department *Annual Report 2004–05* (n 4 above) 30.

[56] In particular, it should be noted that in 2004–05, visa cancellation as a result of an adverse bona fide assessment made upon arrival at an Australian airport accounted for a massive 62 per cent of immigration clearance refusals. As a result of 98 per cent of Australia-bound air passengers being subject to APP in 2004–05, only four per cent of those refused immigration clearance that year were actually undocumented passengers. In 2003–04, when 96 per cent of Australia-bound air passengers were subject to APP, undocumented passengers accounted for seven per cent of immigration clearance refusals at Australian airports: Immigration Department *Annual Report 2004–05* (n 4 above) 30. Comparable figures were not contained in the Immigration Department's *Annual Report 2005–06* (n 4 above).

[57] Screen-ins decreased from 651 in 1998–99 (Department of Immigration and Multicultural Affairs, *Protecting the Border: Immigration Compliance: 2000 Edition* (Canberra, Cth of Australia, 2001) 37) to 366 in 1999–2000 (*Managing the Border* (n 6 above) 25), to 201 in 2000–01, 85 in 2001–02 (Immigration Department *Annual Report 2001–02* (n 52 above) 55) and 21 in 2002–03 (Department of Immigration and Multicultural and Indigenous Affairs, *Managing the Border: Immigration Compliance: 2003–04 Edition* (Canberra, Cth of Australia, 2005) 25).

[58] *Managing the Border* (n 6 above) 25. More recent comparable figures were not available as at 10 June 2007.

the Protection Visa application process; equally possible is that the Department of Immigration's offshore interception measures are increasingly effective in preventing asylum seekers reaching Australia. If the last of these is the correct explanation (or one of them), the question arises whether Australia is responsible for any *refoulement* that may result from asylum seekers being prevented from boarding Australia-bound flights in the airports of third countries.

A State commits an international wrong for which it is responsible if conduct attributable to it constitutes a breach of one of its international obligations.[59] Thus, in order to answer the question whether Australia is responsible for *refoulement* which results from the interception activities taking place in third countries' airports, it is necessary to answer two subsidiary questions: (a) Is any or all of the interception activity taking place in third-country airports attributable to Australia?; and (b) Does interception amount to a breach of *non-refoulement* obligations owed by Australia to the persons intercepted?

III. ATTRIBUTION OF CONDUCT

A. Own State Officials

It is well-established in international law that the conduct of an official of a State, who appears to be acting in his or her official capacity, is attributable to that State, even if, in terms of the State's domestic law, that person is actually acting outside his or her competence.[60] It is irrelevant for the purposes of attribution whether an official's conduct took place within or outside the territory of the State on whose behalf he or she is acting or appears to be acting.[61] Precisely because the actions of its ALOs are unquestionably attributable to Australia, Australia is very keen to emphasise a quite different point and that is the fact that while its ALOs may provide *advice* that a passenger lacks proper documentation, it is in the end up to airlines whether they choose to carry that passenger.[62] Other western States are equally keen to emphasise the same point, namely that it is airline personnel rather than their out-posted immigration officials who make the actual decision to allow a particular passenger to board

[59] International Law Commission ('ILC'), 'Articles on the Responsibility of States for Internationally Wrongful Acts', annexed to UNGA Res 56/83 (12 December 2001) Arts 1 and 2. Most of the provisions are intended to be a codification of existing customary international law rules and for present purposes will be relied upon as representing customary international law (except, of course, where the ILC has indicated that this is not the case).

[60] ILC Articles (n 59 above) Arts 4(1) and 7.

[61] Brouwer and Kumin (n 28 above) 13–14.

[62] Siegmund (n 18 above) 529; Immigration Department 'Border Control' (n 7 above).

or not to board.[63] These States are attempting to rely on the general rule that the conduct of private actors is not normally attributable to the State under international law. However, there are certain circumstances in which the general rule does not apply and attribution is possible.

B. Private Actors

i. Elements of Governmental Authority

According to Article 5 of the International Law Commission's Articles on the Responsibility of States for Internationally Wrongful Acts (which merely codifies the existing customary international law rule),

> [t]he conduct of a person or entity which is not an organ of the State under article 4 but which is empowered by the law of that State to exercise elements of the governmental authority shall be considered an act of the State under international law, provided the person or entity is acting in that capacity in the particular instance.

The rule in Article 5 has developed as a safeguard against States avoiding international responsibility for the consequences of governmental activity by simply 'farming out' the conduct of those activities to the private sector. Of course, the rule pre-supposes a common understanding about what functions are governmental—as opposed to private—functions, and it is questionable whether such an understanding exists at a global level.[64] Notwithstanding this concession, however, the discussion which follows is based on the assumption that at present it is universally accepted that immigration control is a governmental function.

The ILC's commentary on Article 5 in fact lists as an example of private conduct attributable to the State the situation in which airlines have 'delegated to them certain powers in relation to immigration control'.[65] It is not, however, possible to jump from the use of this example to the conclusion that all arrangements which involve airlines playing a role in preventing inadequately documented passengers from travelling to a particular State are necessarily arrangements which result in the conduct of airline personnel being attributable to the State in question under Article 5. In relation to any particular arrangement it is necessary to ask: Is this an arrangement under which the airline is being empowered by the

[63] Brouwer and Kumin (n 28 above) 22 fn 62 (re Canada).

[64] C Chinkin, 'A Critique of the Public/Private Dimension' (1999) 10 *European Journal of International Law* 390.

[65] International Law Commission ('ILC'), 'Draft Articles on Responsibility of States for Internationally Wrongful Acts with Commentaries 2001' (2005) 92 <http://untreaty.un.org/ilc/texts/instruments/english/commentaries/9_6_2001.pdf> (accessed 7 June 2007).

State's internal law to exercise 'elements of [its] governmental authority'? In the Australian case, the Migration Act 1958 obliges airlines to report passenger information to the APP system and refrain from bringing inadequately documented passengers to Australia, and penalties are imposed for failure to comply with either obligation. While the discharge of these obligations by airlines is clearly a functional substitute for an Australian immigration officer refusing entry into Australia to a non-citizen who does not have a valid visa, airlines have not actually been given any power which would otherwise be exercisable only by the Australian government.

ii. Acting on Instructions

Article 8 of the ILC Articles on State Responsibility sets out yet another situation in which the conduct of private actors can be attributed to a State. Unlike Article 5, Article 8 does not require a distinction to be drawn between governmental and private functions. What matters for the purposes of Article 8 is not the nature of the *activity*, but the nature of the *State's involvement* in it. According to Article 8,

> [t]he conduct of a person or group of persons shall be considered an act of a State under international law if the person or group of persons is in fact acting on the instructions of, or under the direction or control of, that State in carrying out the conduct.

Can it be said that an airline is acting on the 'instructions of' Australia in refusing to allow a passenger to board an Australia-bound flight? In the past it would have been necessary to inquire into the circumstances of each case to ascertain whether Australia had, through one of its ALOs or its APP system, actually issued boarding advice in that case. Now that the APP system is fully in place, however, it can be taken as given that in the case of every passenger checking-in for an Australia-bound flight, the airline has been given an 'OK TO BOARD' or 'DO NOT BOARD' directive. Australia would obviously wish to make the argument that an airline is not acting under its instructions simply by choosing to follow the boarding advice it provides through its APP system, since the airline could equally well choose to ignore the boarding advice. It is true that Australia does not have the legal power on foreign soil physically to compel airline personnel to deny boarding to a particular person. However, Australia's boarding 'advice' must be considered in the context of the provisions in Australia's Migration Act 1958, making the carriage into Australia of non-citizens with inadequate documentation an offence. For Australia to argue that airlines have a 'choice' in the matter is for Australia to argue that it regards obedience to its domestic law as optional!

In its commentary on Article 8, the ILC also deals with acts in excess of authority. It states:

> In general a State, in giving lawful instructions to persons who are not its organs, does not assume the risk that the instructions will be carried out in an internationally unlawful way. On the other hand, where persons or groups have committed acts under the effective control of a State the condition for attribution will still be met even if particular instructions may have been ignored. The conduct will have been committed under the control of the State and it will be attributable to the State in accordance with article 8.[66]

However, Australia cannot argue that airlines are acting in excess of instructions if they prevent asylum seekers from boarding. If nothing else, the fact that Australia does not waive the imposition of carrier sanctions in the case of improperly documented passengers who make successful asylum claims makes it clear that asylum seekers are encompassed in a 'DO NOT BOARD' directive.

IV. THE RELEVANCE OF PLACE TO *NON-REFOULEMENT* OBLIGATIONS

Thus far, all that has been established is that the conduct of Australia's ALOs is definitely attributable to Australia, and the conduct of airline personnel in preventing a particular person from boarding an Australia-bound flight is conduct that is probably also attributable to Australia. It still remains to be considered whether the conduct which we have determined is attributable to Australia actually constitutes a breach of any of Australia's obligations under international law.

A. Refugee Convention

147 States,[67] including Australia, are parties to the 1951 Refugee Convention ('Refugee Convention')[68] and/or its 1967 Protocol ('Protocol').[69] The prohibition on *refoulement* is the key provision of the Refugee Convention. Article 33(1) provides that, subject to article 33(2),[70] no State party

[66] ILC Commentary (n 65 above) 108–9.

[67] UNHCR, *States Parties to the 1951 Convention relating to the Status of Refugees and the 1967 Protocol* (as at 1 December 2006) <http://www.unhcr.org/protect/PROTECTION/3b73b0d63.pdf> (accessed 4 June 2007).

[68] Convention relating to the Status of Refugees (adopted 28 July 1951, entered into force 22 April 1954) 189 UNTS 137.

[69] Protocol relating to the Status of Refugees (adopted 31 January 1967, entered into force 4 October 1967) 606 UNTS 267.

[70] According to Art 33(2), the Art 33(1) obligation does not apply in respect of a refugee whom 'there are reasonable grounds for regarding as a danger to the security of the country in which he is, or who, having been convicted by a final judgement of a particularly serious crime, constitutes a danger to the community of that country'.

> shall expel or return ('refouler') a refugee in any manner whatsoever to the frontiers of territories where his life or freedom would be threatened on account of his race, religion, nationality, membership of a particular social group or political opinion.

The phrase 'in any manner whatsoever' has the effect of prohibiting indirect, as well as direct, expulsion or return of the refugee to a persecuting country.[71]

It is well established that the obligation of *non-refoulement* contained in Article 33 of the Refugee Convention applies in respect of any 'refugee'[72] who is physically at or within the territorial borders of a State.[73] Moreover, the obligation of *non-refoulement* applies regardless of a refugee's immigration status. It follows that whenever a State removes non-citizens presenting at its borders without prior authorisation (or unlawfully present in its territory), without giving those persons access to its protection claim determination procedures, it risks breaching its Article 33 obligation towards those who happen to be 'refugees'. Of the countries in which Australia is known to have ALOs posted, mainland China,[74] Fiji, Papua New Guinea, the Philippines, South Africa and South Korea are parties to the Refugee Convention and Protocol,[75] and their own Refugee Convention *non-refoulement* obligation is therefore potentially also engaged by persons intercepted within their territory by Australian agents.

[71] See, eg A Achermann and M Gattiker, 'Safe Third Country: European Developments' (1995) 7 *International Journal of Refugee Law* 26; and United Kingdom Delegation, Geneva, 'Sending Asylum Seekers to Safe Third Countries' (1995) 7 *International Journal of Refugee Law* 119 at 121.

[72] The Refugee Convention, Art 1A(2), as modified by the Protocol, Art I(2), provides that for the purposes of the Convention, the term 'refugee' applies to any person who: 'owing to well-founded fear of being persecuted for reasons of race, religion, nationality, membership of a particular social group or political opinion, is outside the country of his nationality and is unable or, owing to such fear, is unwilling to avail himself of the protection of that country; or who, not having a nationality and being outside the country of his former habitual residence, is unable or, owing to such fear, is unwilling to return to it'. Art 1A(1) of the Convention defines an additional category of refugee, but one which is of little relevance in the present day. It should be noted also that Arts 1D, 1E and 1F of the Refugee Convention provide that the 'provisions of this Convention shall not apply' to certain categories of people (despite the fact that they meet the 'refugee' definition in Art 1A).

[73] GS Goodwin-Gill and J McAdam, *The Refugee in International Law*, 3rd edn (Oxford, Oxford University Press, 2007) 208 at 253–7; M Pallis, 'Obligations of States towards Asylum Seekers at Sea: Interactions and Conflicts between Legal Regimes' (2002) 14 *International Journal of Refugee Law* 343.

[74] Although Hong Kong SAR is part of China, application of the Refugee Convention does not extend to Hong Kong: UNHCR, *Global Report 2004* (Geneva, UNHCR, 2004) 386. Taiwan is a province of China in theory, but not in practice. However, since Taiwan is not a recognised State, it cannot be a party to multilateral treaties.

[75] *States Parties to the 1951 Convention* (n 67 above). The other countries in which Australia has ALOs posted (India, Indonesia, Malaysia, Singapore and Thailand) are not parties to either treaty.

Also relevant for present purposes, however, is the question whether a State's Refugee Convention *non-refoulement* obligation is potentially engaged in relation to asylum seekers who are affected by its extraterritorial activities. The majority of the US Supreme Court in *Sale, Acting Commissioner, Immigration and Naturalization Service v Haitian Centers Council, Inc*[76] gave a negative answer to this question. However, in his dissenting judgment, Blackmun J convincingly rebutted the reasoning of the majority and came to the opposite answer. Likewise, UNHCR, in its amicus brief to the court, took the position (which it continues to take to the present day) that there is no geographical limit on the Article 33 obligation. The Inter-American Commission on Human Rights has agreed with UNHCR's position.[77]

It is not surprising that the position taken by the majority in *Sale* has been rejected by organisations whose mandate is refugee and human rights protection. While historically the principle of *non-refoulement* has tended to be framed as a constraint on a State's treatment of non-citizens at or within its territorial borders, the obvious explanation for this framing is that in the past, States did not attempt to project their power beyond their own territory in the policing of entry by non-citizens into it. However, now that western States are increasingly (in their own words) placing the border 'offshore' for immigration control purposes, the underlying purpose of the *non-refoulement* obligation is in danger of being defeated unless it is interpreted as applying regardless of where the State chooses to exercise powers which previously it exercised at or within the physical line demarcating its territory from the rest of the world.[78]

Notwithstanding the decision in *Sale*, many academic commentators, too, continue to take the position that a State's Refugee Convention *non-refoulement* obligation is engaged at the moment when a person who is in fact a 'refugee' comes within the effective control of an agent of that State, *wherever* in the world this occurs.[79] By contrast, in *R v Immigration Officer*

[76] *Sale, Acting Commissioner, Immigration and Naturalization Service v Haitian Centers Council, Inc*, 509 US 155 (1993).

[77] Inter-American Commission on Human Rights, Haitian Boat People (United States of America) Merits Report No 51/96, Case 10.675 (13 March 1997) paras 156–8.

[78] Executive Committee Standing Committee (18th meeting), 'Interception of Asylum-Seekers and Refugees: The International Framework and Recommendations for a Comprehensive Approach' UN Doc EC/50/SC/CRP.17 (9 June 2000) para 23; A Ataner, 'Refugee Interception and the Outer Limits of Sovereignty' (2004) 3 *Journal of Law and Equality* 7 at 25–6.

[79] See, eg E Lauterpacht and D Bethlehem, 'The Scope and Content of the Principle of *Non-Refoulement*: Opinion' in E Feller, V Türk and F Nicholson (eds), *Refugee Protection in International Law: UNHCR's Global Consultations on International Protection* (Cambridge, Cambridge University Press, 2003) para 67. See, on the other side, N Robinson, *Convention relating to the Status of Refugees: Its History, Contents and Interpretation* (New York, Institute of Jewish Affairs, 1953); A Grahl-Madsen, *The Status of Refugees in International Law* vol 2 (Leiden, AW Sijthoff, 1972) 94; and *The Refugee Convention, 1951: The Travaux Préparatoires*

at Prague Airport, ex parte European Roma Rights Centre[80] two members of the House of Lords agreed with the US Supreme Court that the *non-refoulement* obligation has no extraterritorial application.[81] However, this aspect of their judgments was clearly obiter.

Turning to Australia's position, the Department of Immigration's response to the question whether Australia accepts that its Refugee Convention *non-refoulement* obligation and its other obligations under that instrument are engaged if it intercepts asylum seekers in the territory of third countries is that 'Australia's international obligations are not engaged in these circumstances'.[82]

Notwithstanding that some support exists for Australia's position, the position taken in this chapter is that the Convention's *non-refoulement* obligation at least is extraterritorially binding on States parties. This interpretation of Article 33 accords with the ordinary meaning to be given to the terms of the treaty in their context and in light of the treaty's object and purpose of protecting refugees.[83] While it is true that in the interpretation of treaties it is necessary to take into account, together with the context, '[a]ny subsequent practice in the application of the treaty which establishes the agreement of the parties regarding its interpretation',[84] it is argued that an agreement regarding interpretation which runs counter to a treaty's object and purpose ought not lightly to be inferred from State practice. Otherwise, human rights and humanitarian treaties would quickly be rendered worthless in a world in which few States 'walk their talk' in relation to the subject matter of such treaties.

B. Convention against Torture

144 States,[85] including Australia, are parties to the Convention against Torture and Other Cruel, Inhuman or Degrading Treatment or Punishment ('CAT').[86] Article 3 of the CAT provides that no State party

Analysed, with a Commentary by the Late Paul Weis (New York, Cambridge University Press, 1995) 334–5.

[80] *R v Immigration Officer at Prague Airport, ex parte European Roma Rights Centre* [2004] UKHL 55, [2005] 2 AC 1.

[81] *Ibid*, para 17 (Lord Bingham); para 68 (Lord Hope).

[82] Letter from J Rees (n 10 above).

[83] This is a customary international law principle of treaty interpretation. The principle is also codified in Art 31(1) of the Vienna Convention on the Law of Treaties (adopted 23 May 1969, entered into force 27 January 1980) 1155 UNTS 331 ('VCLT').

[84] VCLT (n 83 above) Art 31(3) (codifying customary international law).

[85] United Nations Treaty Collection, Status of Multilateral Treaties Deposited with the Secretary-General, Convention against Torture <http://untreaty.un.org/ENGLISH/bible/englishinternetbible/partI/chapterIV/treaty14.asp> (accessed 10 June 2007).

[86] Convention against Torture and Other Cruel, Inhuman or Degrading Treatment or Punishment (adopted 10 December 1984, entered into force 26 June 1987) 1465 UNTS 85.

> shall expel, return ('refouler') or extradite a person to another State where there are substantial grounds for believing that he would be in danger of being subjected to torture.

The protection of Article 3 is available to every person and cannot be derogated from under any circumstances. Further, Article 3 encompasses an obligation to refrain from removing a person to a third country in which he or she faces a real risk of being expelled or returned to a country where there are substantial grounds for believing he or she would be subjected to torture.[87] Of the countries in which Australia has ALOs posted, mainland China, Hong Kong, Indonesia, the Philippines, South Africa and South Korea are parties to the CAT, and their CAT *non-refoulement* obligation is potentially engaged, therefore, by persons intercepted within their territory by Australian agents.[88]

Again, however, there is the question of whether *Australia's* CAT *non-refoulement* obligation is engaged in relation to asylum seekers who are affected by its extraterritorial activities. Australia takes the position that it is not.[89] Rather than independently considering the scope of the *non-refoulement* obligation in Article 3 of the CAT, the position taken here will be that given the similarity of wording, it is reasonable to regard the obligation as extraterritorially applicable to the same extent as the Refugee Convention *non-refoulement* obligation.[90]

C. International Covenant on Civil and Political Rights ('ICCPR')

160 States,[91] including Australia, are parties to the ICCPR.[92] Unlike the CAT, the ICCPR does not actually contain an express *non-refoulement* obligation. Nevertheless, according to the United Nations Human Rights Committee General Comment on Article 2 of that instrument, which in this respect reiterates its previous jurisprudence,

> the article 2 obligation requiring that States Parties respect and ensure the Covenant rights for all persons in their territory and all persons under their control entails an obligation not to extradite, deport, expel or otherwise remove

[87] *Mutombo v Switzerland* Communication No 13/1993 (17 April 1994) UN Doc CAT/C/12/D/13/1993 (Committee against Torture).

[88] The other countries in which Australia has ALOs posted (Fiji, India, Malaysia, Papua New Guinea, Singapore, Taiwan and Thailand) are not parties to the CAT: see n 85 above.

[89] Letter from J Rees (n 10 above).

[90] See also R Boed, 'The State of the Right of Asylum in International Law' (1994) 5 *Duke Journal of Comparative and International Law* 1 at 27–8.

[91] United Nations Treaty Collection, Status of Multilateral Treaties Deposited with the Secretary-General, International Covenant on Civil and Political Rights <http://untreaty.un.org/ENGLISH/bible/englishinternetbible/partI/chapterIV/treaty6.asp> (accessed 10 June 2007).

[92] International Covenant on Civil and Political Rights (adopted 16 Dec 1966, entered into force 23 March 1976) 999 UNTS 171.

> a person from their territory, where there are substantial grounds for believing that there is a real risk of irreparable harm, such as that contemplated by articles 6 [right to life] and 7 [right not to be subjected to torture or to cruel, inhuman or degrading treatment or punishment] of the Covenant, either in the country to which removal is to be effected or in any country to which the person may subsequently be removed.[93]

As in the case of the *non-refoulement* obligation in the CAT, the implicit *non-refoulement* obligation in the ICCPR is owed to every person and cannot be derogated from.[94] Article 2(1) requires each State party to the ICCPR

> to respect and to ensure to all individuals within its territory *and* subject to its jurisdiction the rights recognized in the present Covenant (emphasis added).

Of the countries in which Australia has ALOs posted, Hong Kong,[95] India, Indonesia, the Philippines, South Africa, South Korea and Thailand are parties to the ICCPR and their ICCPR *non-refoulement* obligation is potentially engaged, therefore, by persons intercepted within their territory by Australian agents.[96]

Whether Australia's ICCPR *non-refoulement* obligation is engaged in the course of third-country airport interception activities is a question which is far more difficult to answer. Australia takes the position that it is not,[97] and it is certainly the case that the use in Article 2(1) of 'and' instead of 'or' in the description of individuals to whom ICCPR obligations are owed provides some support for this position.[98] However, the view taken by Human Rights Committee is that

> States Parties are required by article 2, paragraph 1, to respect and to ensure the Covenant rights to all persons who may be within their territory and to all persons subject to their jurisdiction. This means that a State party must respect

[93] Human Rights Committee, 'General Comment 31 on Article 2 of the Covenant: The Nature of the General Legal Obligation Imposed on States Parties to the Covenant' (29 March 2004) UN Doc CCPR/C/21/Rev.1/Add.13 (26 May 2004) para 12.

[94] ICCPR (n 92 above) Art 4, which permits derogation from certain ICCPR provisions in the case of a 'public emergency which threatens the life of the nation', does not apply to Arts 6 and 7.

[95] Office of the Ombudsman (Hong Kong), 'The Ombudsman and Protection of Human Rights in Hong Kong' (2001) <http://www.ombudsman.gov.hk/english/09_publications/18_human_right/index.htm> (accessed 2 March 2007). See also ICCPR, note 13 on the UNTS database <http://untreaty.un.org/ENGLISH/bible/englishinternetbible/partI/chapterIV/treaty6.asp> (accessed 6 June 2007).

[96] The other countries in which Australia has ALOs posted (mainland China, Fiji, Malaysia, Papua New Guinea, Singapore and Taiwan) are not parties to the ICCPR: see n 91 above.

[97] Letter from J Rees (n 10 above).

[98] G Noll, J Fagerlund and F Liebaut, *Study on the Feasibility of Processing Asylum Claims outside the EU against the Background of the Common European Asylum System and the Goal of a Common Asylum Procedure: Final Report* (Danish Centre for Human Rights and European Commission, 2002) 41.

> and ensure the rights laid down in the Covenant to anyone within the power or effective control of that State Party, even if not situated within the territory of the State Party.[99]

Unfortunately, the position taken by the Human Rights Committee on the interpretation of Article 2 is not the end of the matter, because as States such as Australia are constantly pointing out, the Committee's views on interpretation are not legally binding on States parties. States which wish to argue against the Human Rights Committee's position are likely to attempt, therefore, to construct legal arguments which apply to Article 2 the reasoning applied by the European Court of Human Rights in *Banković v Belgium*[100] to the interpretation of Article 1 of the European Convention on Human Rights ('ECHR').[101]

Banković was a case arising out of NATO's armed intervention in the Former Republic of Yugoslavia in March 1999, which involved, among other things, the bombing of a television station building in Belgrade. The proceedings were commenced by relatives of persons killed in that particular bombing incident (on their own behalf and on behalf of the deceased) against each of the Member States of NATO, which were also parties to the ECHR. They alleged that those Member States had violated Article 2 (right to life), Article 10 (freedom of expression) and Article 13 (right to an effective remedy) of the ECHR. However, the European Court of Human Rights ruled the application inadmissible on the basis that the applicants were not within the 'jurisdiction' of the States parties, as required by Article 1 of the ECHR:

> The High Contracting Parties shall secure to everyone within their jurisdiction the rights and freedoms defined in section 1 of the Convention.

According to the court, the phrase 'within their jurisdiction' had to be given its 'ordinary meaning', and as to that the court was 'satisfied that, from the standpoint of public international law, the jurisdictional competence of a State is primarily territorial', with the exercise of extraterritorial jurisdiction being allowable only on specific bases 'defined and limited by the sovereign territorial rights of the other relevant States'.[102] The court referred to 'cases involving the activities of its diplomatic or consular agents abroad and on board craft and vessels registered in, or flying the flag of, that State' as examples of bases on which the exercise

[99] Human Rights Committee (n 93 above) para 10.
[100] *Banković v Belgium* (2001) 11 BHRC 435 (ECtHR).
[101] Convention for the Protection of Human Rights and Fundamental Freedoms (European Convention on Human Rights, as amended) (4 November 1950) ETS No 5.
[102] *Banković* (n 100 above) para 59.

of extraterritorial jurisdiction by a State was permissible.[103] It followed, according to the court, that it was

> only in exceptional cases that acts of the Contracting States performed, or producing effects, outside their territories can constitute an exercise of jurisdiction by them within the meaning of Article 1 of the Convention.[104]

Martin Scheinin, a former member of the UN Human Rights Committee, has described this aspect of the court's reasoning in *Banković* as 'particularly problematic'.[105] Scheinin cogently argues that while the court's discussion of the meaning of 'jurisdiction' would have made perfect sense in the context of ascertaining the '*permissibility* of a state exercising jurisdiction beyond its own territory', it was actually irrelevant to the question raised on the facts of *Banković* which related to 'the legal *consequences* of the exercise of authority abroad, be it permissible or not'.[106] More specifically,

> [t]he question posed by the complainants ... was not whether NATO countries were entitled, under public international law, to destroy a television station in Belgrade. The question was whether they had any human rights obligations if they decided to do so. The fact that Yugoslavia perhaps had a sovereign 'territorial right' to demolish its own TV station does not mean that action by other states to the same effect would not trigger off the applicability of human rights law in respect of them.[107]

Moving on from this point, it is important to note that notwithstanding its dubious approach to the interpretation of 'jurisdiction',[108] the court in *Banković* did go on to find, on the basis of previous ECHR jurisprudence, that a State's jurisdiction would be engaged extraterritorially for purposes of Article 1 where that State,

> through the effective control of the relevant territory and its inhabitants abroad as a consequence of military occupation or through the consent, invitation or acquiescence of the Government of that territory, exercises all or some of the public powers normally to be exercised by that Government.[109]

[103] *Ibid*, para 73.

[104] *Ibid*, para 67.

[105] M Scheinin, 'Extraterritorial Effect of the International Covenant on Civil and Political Rights' in F Coomans and MT Kamminga (eds), *Extraterritorial Application of Human Rights Treaties* (Antwerp/Oxford, Intersentia, 2004) 79.

[106] *Ibid*.

[107] *Ibid*, 79–80. See also R Wilde, 'The "Legal Space" or "*Espace Juridique*" of the European Convention on Human Rights: Is it Relevant to Extraterritorial State Action?' (2005) 2 *European Human Rights Law Review* 115.

[108] *Banković* (n 100 above) para 61.

[109] *Ibid*, para 71.

While the latter would qualify as a permissible exercise of jurisdiction, the former usually would not.

Also significant are the 2003 and 2005 judgments of the European Court of Human Rights in *Öcalan v Turkey*. Mr Öcalan, the leader of the Worker's Party of Kurdistan (the PKK), was a man in respect of whom Turkey had issued several arrest warrants. In February 1999, Turkish officials arrested Mr Öcalan at Nairobi airport, detained him, and brought him back to Turkey where he was tried and convicted on various charges. Mr Öcalan made an application to the European Court of Human Rights alleging the violation by Turkey of several provisions of the ECHR. When the proceedings were before the Chamber, Turkey in fact invoked *Banković* in support of the argument that the ECHR did not apply to its actions in Kenya.[110] The response of the court to this argument was as follows:

> In the instant case, the applicant was arrested by members of the Turkish security forces inside an aircraft in the international zone of Nairobi Airport. Directly after he had been handed over by the Kenyan officials to the Turkish officials the applicant was under effective Turkish authority and was therefore brought within the 'jurisdiction' of that State for the purposes of Article 1 of the Convention, even though in this instance Turkey exercised its authority outside its territory. The Court considers that the circumstances of the present case are distinguishable from those in the aforementioned *Banković and Others* case, notably in that the applicant was physically forced to return to Turkey by Turkish officials and was subject to their authority and control following his arrest and return to Turkey.[111]

In other words, the court could be taken as saying that Mr Öcalan came within Turkey's jurisdiction upon its agents acquiring effective control over him and by reason of that control.[112] On appeal, the Turkish government did not raise (and the Grand Chamber did not bother to deal with) *Banković* and the extraterritoriality issue.

Taken together, the jurisprudence relating to Article 1 of the ECHR up to and including the *Öcalan* decision would appear to establish that the 'jurisdiction' of a State party to the ECHR will be engaged extraterritorially whenever that State can be said to exercise effective control over the territory in which the impugned actions took place, *or* effective control over the person who claims to be the victim of those actions, regardless

110 *Öcalan v Turkey* [2003] ECHR 125 (ECtHR) para 84.
111 *Ibid*, para 93.
112 See, eg T Abdel-Monem, 'How Far Do the Lawless Areas of Europe Extend? Extraterritorial Application of the European Convention on Human Rights' (2005) 14 *Journal of Transnational Law and Policy* 195.

of whether such control was acquired in an internationally lawful or unlawful manner.[113] To this extent, therefore, the ECHR jurisprudence on the meaning of 'jurisdiction' can be seen as being in agreement with the ICCPR jurisprudence.[114] The real problem lies in applying this broadly articulated test of jurisdiction to the kind of factual situation involved in third-country airport interceptions.

If it is accepted that 'jurisdiction' under Article 2 of the ICCPR is engaged extraterritorially whenever a State can be said to exercise effective control over the person who claims to be the victim of its actions, the question still remains whether the sort of control exercised over asylum seekers by States engaged in third-country airport interception involves a sufficient degree of control to meet the 'effective control' test. If a State detains an individual, he or she is subject—as completely as it is possible to be—to the power of the detaining State. By contrast, preventing a person from boarding a particular aeroplane is an exercise of State power which curtails that individual's freedom of action in only that one very specific respect. Considered from this perspective, it seems implausible that airport interceptions involve the exercise by the intercepting State of 'effective control' over the person intercepted such as to trigger the jurisdictional provision in the ICCPR. On the other hand, the intercepted individual is subject to the power of the intercepting State in a manner which affects his or her most vital interests,[115] and from that perspective the argument that the effective control test is met seems extremely plausible.

Of course, if the European Court of Human Rights had accepted this approach to the effective control test, the applicants in *Banković* ought to have succeeded in making out jurisdiction. However, in *Banković*, the court found that precision air strikes did not involve a degree of control over either territory or persons that was sufficient to engage Article 1 jurisdiction extraterritorially.[116] It is difficult to see how the court could, consistently with the *Banković* finding, treat third-country airport interceptions as involving 'effective control' sufficient to trigger ECHR jurisdiction. All that can be said in response to this point is that the ICCPR is a different treaty, and its interpretation can, and in this particular case should, follow a different path.

[113] F Coomans and MT Kamminga, 'Comparative Introductory Comments on the Extraterritorial Application of Human Rights Treaties' in Coomans and Kamminga (n 105 above) 3–4.

[114] *Ibid*.

[115] Ataner (n 78 above) 22.

[116] Abdel-Monem (n 112 above) 196.

D. Customary International Law

In addition to the *non-refoulement* obligations imposed by the treaties discussed above, it is almost certainly the case that *non-refoulement* has become a principle of customary international law[117] and is, therefore, binding on all States regardless of whether they are parties to any of the treaties imposing the same or similar obligation. The substantive content of the customary international law obligation is generally thought to more or less mirror the CAT and ICCPR *non-refoulement* obligations in relation to all persons, and, in relation to refugees specifically, additionally to mirror the Refugee Convention *non-refoulement* obligation.[118]

All of the States in which Australia carries out airport interceptions are *at least* bound by the customary international law *non-refoulement* obligation in respect of persons in their territory. In the cases of Malaysia and Singapore, the customary law *non-refoulement* obligation is the only *non-refoulement* obligation binding on them. However, if the treaty-based *non-refoulement* obligations are not extraterritorially binding, the question of whether Australia's customary international law *non-refoulement* obligation is potentially engaged in the course of third-country airport interception activities depends on whether the customary law obligation's mirroring of the treaty-based obligations extends to an incorporation of the jurisdictional limitations of the treaty-based obligations.[119] While the existence and observance of the *non-refoulement* obligation in international and regional treaties is part of the State practice and *opinio juris* relied upon for the proposition that *non-refoulement* has become a principle of customary international law, it is by no means all of it,[120] leaving open the possibility that the customary international law *non-refoulement* obligation does not include the jurisdictional limitations which may apply to the treaty obligations.

While eminent commentators such as Goodwin-Gill and McAdam take the position that a State's customary international law *non-refoulement* obligation is engaged upon an asylum seeker coming within the effective

[117] Cf N Coleman, '*Non-Refoulement* Revised: Renewed Review of the Status of the Principle of *Non-Refoulement* as Customary International Law' (2003) 5 *European Journal of Migration and Law* 23, who questions the correctness of the orthodox position.

[118] Lauterpacht and Bethlehem (n 79 above) para 253; Goodwin-Gill and McAdam (n 73 above) 345–54.

[119] In an article on the extraterritorial application of the ICCPR, McGoldrick queried in passing whether the customary international law human rights obligations of States also have jurisdictional limits, but did not pause to consider the answer: D McGoldrick, 'Extraterritorial Application of the International Covenant on Civil and Political Rights' in Coomans and Kamminga (n 105 above) 42 fn 5.

[120] See Lauterpacht and Bethlehem (n 79 above) paras 201–16 for a detailed justification of this proposition.

control of an agent of that State, wherever in the world this occurs,[121] the unfortunate fact of the matter is that Australia[122] and many other States are not prepared to concede that this position is correct. Canada, for example, takes the view that a State's customary international law *non-refoulement* obligation ceases at the border of another State.[123] According to Canada, '[i]f a state intercepts a person in another country, the *non-refoulement* obligation lies with the other country'.[124]

On the other hand, Canada simultaneously accepts the position that '[t]he intercepting state should ... have guidelines to ensure that a proper referral takes place'.[125] It will be recollected, moreover, that Canada, Australia and the 17 other countries which are members of CAWG purport, in fact, to abide by the IATA/CAWG Code of Conduct for Immigration Liaison Officers which specifies that if immigration liaison officers

> receive requests for asylum, applicants should be directed to the office of the United Nations High Commissioner for Refugees, to the appropriate diplomatic mission(s), or to an appropriate local Non-Governmental Organization (NGO).[126]

There are also efforts being made through International Civil Aviation Organization[127] processes to encourage States to build asylum seeker safeguards into their airport interception measures. Finally, UNHCR's 2003 Executive Committee Conclusion on Protection Safeguards in Interception Measures recommends that

> interception measures be guided by the following considerations in order to ensure the adequate treatment of asylum-seekers and refugees amongst those intercepted
>
> ...
>
> iv. Interception measures should not result in asylum-seekers and refugees being denied access to international protection, or result in those in need of international protection being returned, directly or indirectly, to the frontiers of territories where their life or freedom would be threatened on account of

[121] Goodwin-Gill and McAdam (n 73 above) 244–53; see also Lauterpacht and Bethlehem (n 79 above) paras 218 and 242.

[122] Bedlington (n 13 above) 48–50.

[123] Rapporteur, 'Session IV: Exploring Options for the Future', *Interception and Refugee Protection* (n 49 above) 30.

[124] *Ibid*.

[125] *Ibid*.

[126] IATA/CAWG (n 26 above) Guideline 2.3.

[127] The ICAO's function is to co-ordinate and regulate international air travel. It was established under the Convention on International Civil Aviation (adopted 7 December 1944, entered into force 4 April 1947) 15 UNTS 295, which has 190 States parties, including Australia <http://www.icao.int/icao/en/leb/chicago.pdf> (accessed 10 June 2007).

> a Convention ground, or where the person has other grounds for protection based on international law. Intercepted persons found to be in need of international protection should have access to durable solutions;
>
> ...
>
> viii. All persons, including officials of a State, and employees of a commercial entity, implementing interception measures should receive specialized training, including available means to direct intercepted persons expressing international protection needs to the appropriate authorities in the State where the interception has taken place, or, where appropriate, to UNHCR.[128]

It seems to be the case, therefore, that regardless of whether a State is bound by a *non-refoulement* obligation when carrying out interception activities in the territory of another State, it can at least be said that a procedural obligation on the part of the intercepting State to do something, such as referring protection claims made in the course of interception to a body capable of considering and responding to those claims, has either emerged or is in the process of emerging.

V. WHAT CONSTITUTES *REFOULEMENT?*

R v Immigration Officer at Prague Airport, ex parte European Roma Rights Centre dealt with an interception operation conducted by UK immigration officers at Prague airport, pursuant to which Czech citizens were refused pre-clearance to enter the United Kingdom if their purpose in seeking entry was believed to be for asylum or some other purpose not endorsed by UK immigration law. Carrier sanctions ensured, of course, that those refused pre-clearance would also be denied boarding on to UK-bound flights. The appellants in the case were all Czech citizens of Roma origin who had been refused pre-clearance. They attempted, inter alia, to rely on the United Kingdom's obligations under the ECHR. Lord Bingham of Cornhill expressed the view that even if the assumption were made that the actions of UK immigration officers in Prague constituted an exercise of 'jurisdiction' by the United Kingdom, the facts did not

> disclose any threat to life such as might engage article 2 of the European Convention or any risk of torture or inhuman or degrading treatment or punishment such as might engage article 3,

because those actions left the appellants free to travel to other countries (or even to the United Kingdom 'otherwise than by air from Prague').[129] According to Lord Bingham,

[128] Executive Committee Conclusion No 97 (LIV), 'Protection Safeguards in Interception Measures' (2003).

[129] *European Roma Rights Centre* (n 80 above) para 21.

> [t]he appellants' position [therefore differed] by an order of magnitude from that of the Haitians, whose plight was considered in *Sale*, above, and whose treatment by the United States authorities was understandably held by the Inter-American Commission of Human Rights ... to breach their right to life, liberty and security of their persons as well as the right to asylum protected by article XXVII of the American Declaration of the Rights and Duties of Man.[130]

Although Lord Bingham's argument appears far from reasonable in the context of the facts of the case before the House of Lords, which involved UK immigration officials—at the very least—substantially delaying asylum seekers in their attempt to leave the very country in which they claimed to be at risk of serious human rights violations, it is not an argument which is necessarily unreasonable in the context of transit country interception. Whether the return of the intercepted person to a country in which he or she will be exposed to a risk of a serious human rights violation is a likely consequence of transit country interception will probably depend on all the circumstances of the particular case. However, the only way to ascertain what the likely consequences of a particular interception action are is to undertake some sort of inquiry into the matter. As the philosopher JR Lucas puts it, in discussing individual moral responsibility for the consequences of actions,

> [i]f I choose to act, I thereby take on a special responsibility of care, to consider all the possible consequences of my action, and to make sure that nothing untoward comes of it.[131]

Because of this,

> [w]e hold a man responsible not only for the actually foreseen, but for the reasonably foreseeable consequences of his action, and will not automatically excuse him if he pleads that he did not know that his action would be likely to engender them.[132]

In the offshore immigration control context, intercepting States are effectively treating the State in which interception takes place as a safe third country. Though the 'safe third country' principle has thus far been explicitly invoked by States seeking to remove asylum seekers from their territory to the third country, it must, if logic has anything to do with the matter, be applicable in the extraterritorial context also.

In 1995, UNHCR suggested that State practice established a definition of 'safe' (in the third-country context) which included 'not only

[130] *Ibid*.
[131] JR Lucas, *Responsibility* (Oxford, Oxford University Press, 1993) 54.
[132] *Ibid*, 52.

protection from *refoulement* but also "the absence of violations of other fundamental human rights"'.[133] Whether the meaning of 'safe' extends so far—or even further—has been the subject of much debate.[134] Rather than enter into that debate here, the minimalist version of the safe third country principle will be accepted, namely that a country is safe if it provides protection from *refoulement*.

In determining whether a third country is safe, it is generally accepted that the focus must be on the third country's *actual* practice and not merely on the obligations it has formally undertaken.[135] Thus, for example, if the third country in question has violated a *non-refoulement* obligation in the past in dealing with certain categories of person, it cannot be regarded as 'safe' in relation to those categories.[136] By way of another example, if the third country does not have adequate procedures in place for identifying persons to whom *non-refoulement* obligations are owed, it is likely (albeit unknowingly) to return persons who are, in fact, owed a *non-refoulement* obligation, to a place in violation of that obligation. Such a country cannot be regarded as 'safe'.[137]

If we examine the practice of States in which Australia has posted ALOs, we find that the Philippines, South Africa and South Korea are the only countries which are parties to all relevant treaties, have domestic mechanisms in place for implementing their *non-refoulement* obligations, and additionally host a UNHCR office.[138] Even more to the point, the Philippines does not appear to *refoule* persons in practice.[139] By contrast,

133 UNHCR, 'The Concept of "Protection Elsewhere"' (1995) 7 *International Journal of Refugee Law* 123 at 125, quoting UK Delegation (n 71 above) 120.

134 See discussion in S Taylor, 'Protection Elsewhere/Nowhere' (2006) 18 *International Journal of Refugee Law* 283.

135 UNHCR (n 133 above) 126.

136 Achermann and Gattiker (n 71 above) 26.

137 Erika Feller (Director of the Department of International Protection, UNHCR), Evidence to United Kingdom, House of Lords, European Union Select Committee, Subcommittee F (Social Affairs, Education and Home Affairs) Inquiry into New Approaches to the Asylum Process (22 October 2003) <http://www.publications.parliament.uk/pa/ld/lduncorr/euf2210.pdf> (accessed 2 March 2007); Goodwin-Gill and McAdam (n 73 above) 392–6, 531; UNHCR, 'Note on International Protection' UN Doc A/AC.96/815 (31 August 1993) para 22.

138 US Department of State, 'Country Reports on Human Rights Practices for 2005, Volume I' (2006) 505 <http://internationalrelations.house.gov/archives/109/26464.001.pdf> (accessed 17 June 2007); UNHCR, 'Country Operations Plan 2007: Republic of Korea' <http://www.unhcr.org/home/RSDCOI/44f7f66f2.pdf> (accessed 4 March 2007); UNHCR, 'Regional Operations Plan 2007 covering Indonesia, Brunei Darussalam, the Philippines, Singapore, and Timor-Leste' <http://www.unhcr.org/home/RSDCOI/44f8473a2.pdf> (accessed 4 March 2007).

139 US Department of State, vol I (n 138 above) 966; UNHCR 'Regional Operations Plan' (n 138 above).

South Africa[140] and South Korea[141] have been known to remove asylum seekers without considering their claims adequately or at all, which could, of course, result in *refoulement*.

Fiji and Papua New Guinea are both parties to the Refugee Convention and Protocol. At the time of writing, Papua New Guinea's Migration Act 1978 gave the Minister of Foreign Affairs and Immigration the power to grant refugee status, but there was no legislative framework or established administrative procedure for refugee status determination.[142] Nevertheless, the government of Papua New Guinea does conduct refugee status determinations[143] and the UNHCR office in Port Moresby provides it with technical and financial assistance in this endeavour.[144] At the time of writing, Fiji had passed legislation for the purpose of giving effect to its treaty obligations under the Refugee Convention and Protocol, but related regulations had not yet come into effect.[145] On the other hand, UNHCR's regional office in Canberra has indicated that 'it would offer support and advice to the Fijian officials in the event that they were required to perform RSD.'[146]

In any event, the bottom line is that, in practice, both countries appear to provide protection against *refoulement*.[147]

India and Thailand are parties to the ICCPR and Indonesia is a party to the ICCPR and the CAT. However, neither India nor Indonesia has in place its own legal or administrative system for dealing with asylum seekers.[148] In late 2005, Thailand established Provisional Admissions

140 US Committee for Refugees and Immigrants, *World Refugee Survey* (2006) (South Africa).

141 US Committee for Refugees and Immigrants, *World Refugee Survey* (2004) (South Korea).

142 UNHCR, 'Country Operations Plan 2007: Papua New Guinea' <http://www.unhcr.org/home/RSDCOI/452f50342.pdf> (accessed 4 March 2007). This remains correct as at June 2007.

143 Senate Legal and Constitutional References Committee, *Official Committee Hansard: Migration Amendment (Designated Unauthorised Arrivals) Bill 2006* (26 May 2006) 10 (Mr Wright, UNHCR).

144 Email from UNHCR Regional Office (Australia, New Zealand, Papua New Guinea and the South Pacific) to S Taylor (10 February 2006); UNHCR 'Country Operations Plan' (n 142 above).

145 UNHCR Regional Office (Australia, New Zealand, Papua New Guinea and the South Pacific), 'Regional Asylum Systems, Fiji Country Information' <http://www.unhcr.org.au/fijiqanda.shtml> (accessed 4 March 2007). This is still correct as at June 2007. See the Immigration Act 2003 (Fiji) <http://www.parliament.gov.fj/legislative/bills.aspx?billID=243&viewtype=acts&billnav=bill> (accessed 10 June 2007).

146 Email from UNHCR Regional Office (n 144 above).

147 US Department of State, vol I (n 138 above) 810 (Fiji) and 954 (Papua New Guinea).

148 US Department of State, 'Country Reports 2005, Volume II' (2006) 2155; US Committee for Refugees and Immigrants, *World Refugee Survey* (2006) (India); US Department of State (n 138 above) 831.

Boards to conduct refugee status determination in relation to Burmese nationals seeking admission into camps along the Thai–Burma border, but it has no national procedure for dealing with non-Burmese asylum seekers.[149] On the other hand, all three countries host UNHCR offices, which provide asylum seekers in at least some parts of their territory with access to refugee status determination (which includes determining whether persons who are not Convention refugees fall within UNHCR's wider mandate as having 'other protection needs'[150]) and resettlement.[151] Since there is no evidence that Indonesia has *refouled* anyone,[152] it can probably be treated as a safe country (in the minimalist sense accepted for the purposes of this article). India is probably safe for most asylum seekers, but there have been reports of *refoulement* of Burmese refugees.[153] Thailand has *refouled* dozens of refugees of different nationalities[154] and cannot be regarded as safe.

Mainland China does not have a legal or administrative system in place for giving effect to its *non-refoulement* obligations under the Refugee Convention or the CAT.[155] However, there is a procedure in place in Hong Kong for implementation of the *non-refoulement* obligation under the CAT.[156] Further, there are UNHCR offices in mainland China and Hong Kong which conduct refugee status determination.[157] The problem is that, while, as a general rule, China tolerates the presence in its territory of asylum seekers and refugees pending status determination and resettlement by UNHCR, it *refoules* thousands of North Koreans each year.[158] China is not, therefore, a safe country for North Koreans.

Taiwan is for all practical purposes a separate country from China. However, the internationally endorsed fiction that Taiwan is part of China precludes Taiwan from being a party to the Refugee Convention,

[149] US Department of State, vol I (n 138 above) 1013; UNHCR, *Analysis of Gaps in Refugee Protection Capacity: Thailand* (November 2006) 5.

[150] UNHCR, *Procedural Standards for Refugee Status Determination under UNHCR's Mandate* (Geneva, UNHCR, 2004) Annex 4-2 (RSD Assessment Form).

[151] US Department of State, vol II (n 148 above) 2155; US Committee for Refugees and Immigrants, *World Refugee Survey* (2006) (India); UNHCR 'Regional Operations Plan' (n 138 above); UNHCR (n 149 above) 4.

[152] US Department of State, vol I (n 138 above) 831.

[153] US Department of State, vol II (n 148 above) 2156; US Committee for Refugees and Immigrants, *World Refugee Survey* (2006) (India).

[154] US Committee for Refugees and Immigrants, *World Refugee Survey* (2006) (Thailand); US Department of State, vol I (n 138 above) 1013–14.

[155] US Department of State, vol I (n 138 above) 743.

[156] UNHCR, 'Country Operations Plan 2007: People's Republic of China (covering Mainland China, Hong Kong SAR, Macao SAR and Mongolia)' <http://www.unhcr.org/home/RSDCOI/450e588a2.pdf> (accessed 4 March 2007).

[157] *Ibid.*

[158] US Department of State, vol I (n 138 above) 743; US Committee for Refugees and Immigrants, *World Refugee Survey* (2006) (China).

Protocol, CAT or ICCPR. At the time of writing Taiwan did not have a legal or administrative system in place for dealing with asylum seekers,[159] nor did UNHCR have an operational presence in the country.[160] Whether it is a safe country in practice is difficult to say. The US Department of State describes the Taiwanese authorities as 'reluctant to return to the mainland those who might suffer political persecution', but on the other hand adds that

> they regularly deported to the PRC, under provisions of the Mainland Relations Act, mainlanders who illegally entered the island for what were presumed to be economic reasons.[161]

Malaysia and Singapore are two other countries which are not parties to any relevant treaties and do not have their own legal or administrative system for dealing with asylum seekers.[162] However, UNHCR, through its office in Malaysia and its NGO implementing partner in Singapore, provides asylum seekers in the two countries with access to refugee status determination and resettlement.[163] While UNHCR describes Singapore as having a 'persistently difficult protection environment',[164] there is no evidence of deliberate *refoulement* by its government,[165] so it is probably a safe country in the minimalist sense. By contrast, the Malaysian government has directly or indirectly *refouled* hundreds of people,[166] so not even as a matter of rebuttable presumption can Malaysia be regarded as a safe country.

VI. MULTIPLE ACTORS AND THE ALLOCATION OF RESPONSIBILITY

Thus far in this chapter, one complicating factor in the allocation of responsibility for *refoulement* resulting from foreign country interception

[159] US Department of State, vol I (n 138 above) 788. This situation may have changed by the time of publication as a draft bill providing for refugee protection was approved by the Executive Yuan in January 2007 and was to be referred to the Legislative Yuan for formal enactment: D Kuo, 'Cabinet Passes Draft Refugee Law' *Central News Agency English News* (31 January 2007). It had not changed as at June 2007.

[160] Email from UNHCR Regional Office (n 144 above).

[161] US Department of State, vol I (n 138 above) 788–9.

[162] UNHCR, 'Country Operations Plan 2007: Malaysia' <http://www.unhcr.org/home/RSDCOI/45221ff62.pdf> (accessed 4 March 2007); UNHCR 'Regional Operations Plan' (n 138 above).

[163] UNHCR 'Country Operations Plan' (n 162 above); UNHCR 'Regional Operations Plan' (n 138 above).

[164] UNHCR, 'Country Operations Plan Overview: Country: Indonesia and Singapore, Planning Year: 2006' <http://www.unhcr.org/home/RSDCOI/4337c6732.pdf> (accessed 4 March 2007).

[165] US Department of State, vol I (n 138 above) 989.

[166] US Committee for Refugees and Immigrants, *World Refugee Survey* (2006) (Malaysia); US Department of State, vol I (n 138 above) 905.

of asylum seekers has been ignored, namely the involvement of two or more States in such interception activities. In such situations, must responsibility be allocated *exclusively* to one of the States involved (and if so, which), or is responsibility shared (and if so, how)? Article 16 of the ILC Articles on State Responsibility provides:

> A State which aids or assists another State in the commission of an internationally wrongful act by the latter is internationally responsible for doing so if:
>
> (a) That State does so with knowledge of the circumstances of the internationally wrongful act; and
> (b) The act would be internationally wrongful if committed by that State.[167]

According to Article 16, the wrongful act which the aiding or assisting State is committing is that of 'providing aid or assistance in the commission of an internationally wrongful act'. In other words, the aiding or assisting State is committing a wrong quite distinct from, and lesser than, the wrongful act of the State being aided or assisted.[168]

A commonly cited example of one State aiding or assisting another to commit a wrongful act is that of one State permitting another to use its territory to wage a war of aggression against a third State.[169] At first glance, third-country interception activities might appear to be analogous. In actual fact, they are not. Where third-country interception results in *refoulement*, it is necessarily the case that the territorial State has played an active role. It is the territorial State, not the intercepting State, which takes the final fateful step of expelling the asylum seeker from its territory. The separate actions of the territorial State and the intercepting State contribute to a single harm.

Neither Article 16 nor any other provision of the ILC Articles explicitly articulates the principle of joint and several liability of participants for the consequences of joint action or separate actions contributing to a single harm, though this is a principle applied within most national legal systems. It is possible to argue, however, that because the principle of joint and several liability *is* one which national legal systems appear to have in common, it can be treated as one of the 'general principles of

[167] Both the plain words and the drafting history of Art 16 suggest that it is not a requirement for imposition of responsibility that the State providing aid or assistance has done so with the actual purpose of facilitating the commission of the wrongful act, but merely that it has done so with knowledge that it would be facilitating the commission of the wrongful act: K Nahapetian, 'Confronting State Complicity in International Law' (2002) 7 *UCLA Journal of International and Foreign Affairs* 99 at 126–7.

[168] *Ibid*, 104; I Brownlie, *System of the Law of Nations: State Responsibility (Part 1)* (Oxford, Oxford University Press, 1983) 190–91. If the assisting State plays more than a 'supporting role', it would in fact be a 'co-perpetrator' and would not fall within Art 16: ILC Commentary (n 65 above) 155.

[169] B Graefrath, 'Complicity in the Law of International Responsibility' (1996) 29 *Revue Belge de Droit International* 370 at 372–3.

law' referred to in Article 38(1)(c) of the Statute of the International Court of Justice as a source of international law.[170] The problem, according to Brownlie and the other academic commentators who argue that the principle of joint and several liability ought to be regarded as an international legal principle,[171] is that although a theoretical case can be made for the existence of the principle, there is little evidence of the principle actually being invoked in international relations. This may well be an accurate generalisation, but for present purposes what is significant is that the existence of the concept of indirect *refoulement* must mean that States accept the principle of joint and several liability for *refoulement*. It is well accepted that a country which removes an asylum seeker from its territory to a third country, which in turn removes the asylum seeker to a country in which he or she faces the risk of persecution or other serious human rights violations, has engaged in indirect *refoulement*.[172] The third country has, of course, engaged in direct *refoulement*. The salient point, though, is that each of the countries involved in this scenario is regarded as responsible for the act of *refoulement*.

In the specific context of third-country interception measures, the Executive Committee Conclusion on Protection Safeguards in Interception Measures states that

> [t]he State within whose sovereign territory, or territorial waters, interception takes place has the primary responsibility for addressing any protection needs of intercepted persons.[173]

However, since the Conclusion is not itself legally binding on States, it ought not to be read as overriding the position which would otherwise exist under international law.[174] It is suggested that the Conclusion should instead be read as dealing with responsibility for implementation, rather than responsibility for outcome. In other words, since hard international law has nothing to say about how the tasks involved in identifying persons with protection needs and protecting them are to be distributed among the States involved in interception, the Conclusion specifies that those tasks fall to the lot of the State in whose territory the intercepted person actually is. Of course, 'primary responsibility' is not the same thing as 'sole responsibility'. The Conclusion implicitly accepts that other States involved in interception have at the least default responsibility for addressing the protection needs of intercepted persons.

[170] Brownlie (n 168 above) 189 dealing with joint responsibility for joint action.

[171] See, eg Graefrath (n 169 above); and JE Noyes and BD Smith, 'State Responsibility and the Principle of Joint and Several Liability' (1998) 13 *Yale Journal of International Law* 225.

[172] See Goodwin-Gill and McAdam (n 73 above) 252–3.

[173] Executive Conclusion No 97 (n 128 above) para (a)(i).

[174] Brouwer and Kumin (n 28 above) 18–19.

The question of which State or States have committed an internationally wrongful act if an intercepted person is *refouled* is, however, a different question, and one which is not answered by the Conclusion but by pre-existing international law as discussed above. What this means, in effect, is that, while there is no rule of law precluding the intercepting State from relying on the territorial State to address the protection needs of intercepted persons, the intercepting State bears the risk of miscalculation. If the territorial State ends up *refouling* the intercepted person, the intercepting State's *non-refoulement* obligation is also breached. In other words, the territorial State and intercepting State are jointly and severally liable for the *refoulement*. The implication of this for an intercepting State which wishes to avoid breaching its international legal obligations is that it ought *itself* to consider protection claims made by intercepted persons, and provide protection if necessary, unless it is convinced that the territorial State is both willing and able to do the same for the particular individual concerned.

VII. CONCLUSION

There is evidence to support the inference that the interception of inadequately documented travellers in third-country airports is having the effect of preventing asylum seekers from reaching Australia. This chapter has argued that the actions of Australian officials and airline personnel resulting in asylum seekers being prevented from reaching Australia are attributable to Australia. In order to constitute an international wrong, however, conduct attributable to a State must actually be in breach of that State's international obligations. The greater part of the chapter therefore dealt with the more difficult question whether Australia's third-country airport interception activities constitute a breach of its *non-refoulement* obligations under the Refugee Convention, the CAT, the ICCPR and/or customary international law. It was argued that the better view is that the Refugee Convention, CAT and ICCPR *non-refoulement* obligations are all extraterritorially binding on States parties to those treaties, and are triggered by interception activities by agents of a State party wherever occurring. (It was conceded, however, that, were this not the case, customary international law probably cannot be relied upon to remedy the deficiency.) Further, it was argued that there is at least a procedural obligation on the part of an intercepting State to do something like referring protection claims made in the course of interception to a body capable of considering and responding to those claims.

Even if Australia's *non-refoulement* obligations are applicable extraterritorially, whether *refoulement* is a likely consequence of third-country interception will depend on all the circumstances of the particular case. It was argued that in order to ascertain the likely consequences of a particular interception action, the intercepting State must inquire into the matter in the same way it would were it purporting to invoke the safe third country principle in relation to an asylum seeker presenting at or within its own borders. It was demonstrated that even the most cursory investigations into actual practice lead to the conclusion that many of the countries in which Australia carries out airport interceptions cannot be treated as safe third countries for at least some categories of asylum seekers. The final point made in the chapter was that if *refoulement* actually occurs as a result of third-country interception activities, the territorial State and the intercepting State should be considered jointly and severally responsible for that wrong.

The overall conclusion of this chapter, therefore, is that States are mistaken if they believe that by engaging in offshore interception of asylum seekers they avoid their *non-refoulement* obligations in respect of those asylum seekers. With power goes responsibility, and that is as it should be.

5

The Legal and Ethical Implications of Extraterritorial Processing of Asylum Seekers: The 'Safe Third Country' Concept

SUSAN KNEEBONE*

I. INTRODUCTION

IN EUROPE, THE concept of extraterritorial processing of asylum seekers is on the agenda, particularly as a response to the large numbers of persons seeking to cross the Mediterranean to reach Italy, Greece and Spain, which has escalated in the past few years. The majority of these persons have moved from sub-Saharan Africa and areas of known 'protracted' refugee situations in Africa.[1] It is not known how many of these people are asylum seekers because most are not given a chance to make a protection claim.[2] Instead, many are interdicted and removed (as described below) to prevent them from exercising their right to seek asylum. Extraterritorial processing involves interdiction of persons in flight and removal to a 'safe third country' ('STC') for processing.[3]

The issues examined in this chapter are the legal and ethical implications of extraterritorial processing of asylum seekers. There are three perspectives from which to consider this issue. First, there is that of the

* I thank Dr Matthew Gibney and Professor Stephen Legomsky for their helpful comments and suggestions. Any remaining misconceptions are my own.

[1] J Crisp, 'Forced Displacement in Africa: Dimensions, Difficulties and Policy Directions', UNHCR, *New Issues in Refugee Research*, Research Paper No 126 (July 2006) 11 states that 22 out of 38 protracted refugee situations are in Africa.

[2] A Betts, 'Towards a Mediterranean Solution? Implications for the Region of Origin' (2006) 18 *International Journal of Refugee Law* 652 suggests that 100,000–120,000 migrants cross the Mediterranean illegally each year, the majority of whom come from sub-Saharan Africa.

[3] In this paper I do not consider another option that has been canvassed within the EU, namely intra-EU processing, as this does not involve a 'third country'.

asylum seeker in flight, for whom interdiction and removal means denial of the right to seek asylum in the destination State. Secondly, there is the State's perspective, which is primarily concerned with border control and protecting the interests of its community. Thirdly, there is the global justice perspective, which requires a balance between the interests of asylum seekers (including refugees and other displaced persons) and States. Interestingly, the issue is often framed by States in terms of 'choice': States have the right to choose who will penetrate their borders, but asylum seekers do not have the right to choose a destination. Indeed, it is often suggested that asylum seekers who are attempting to exercise a choice are 'abusing the system'. This assumes that asylum seekers are making rationale choices about destinations, whereas in reality those decisions are the result of complex factors, including transportation routes, often chosen by smugglers in response to *non-entrée* strategies practised by industrialised countries (as discussed below). The important point is that whilst the narratives of asylum seekers are absent from this dialogue, and assumptions are made about their motives, we do know a lot about the motives of States. Governments can make choices about who comes to their countries, but asylum seekers cannot. What justifies this lack of agency on the part of asylum seekers?

The third (global justice) perspective is relevant to answering that question. The global picture of the refugee 'issue' shows two trends. First, there has been a decline in the number of people seeking asylum in industrialised countries.[4] According to the United Nations High Commissioner for Refugees ('UNHCR'), in 2006, at 9.2 million people, the number was at its lowest level for 25 years.[5] But at the same time, the number of people living in protracted refugee situations is static and the number of 'persons of concern' is on the rise, as continuing conflicts in Somalia and Iraq lead to an increase in the number of internally displaced persons ('IDPs').[6] This picture reflects the settlement of conflicts in the Balkan States and in

[4] Between 2001–04 the number of asylum applications to the traditional western industrialised 'receiving' countries dropped 40 per cent on average: UNHCR, 'Asylum Levels and Trends in Industrialized Countries, 2004: Overview of Asylum Applications Lodged in European and Non-European Industrialized Countries in 2004' (1 March 2005) para 9. Subsequently, the numbers have continued to decline, 'albeit at a lower pace': UNHCR, 'Asylum Levels and Trends in Industrialized Countries, 2006: Overview of Asylum Applications Lodged in European and Non-European Industrialized Countries in 2006' (23 March 2007) para 12. (Statistical reports available at <http://www.unhcr.org/statistics>).

[5] UNHCR, *The State of the World's Refugees: Human Displacement in the New Millennium* (Oxford, Oxford University Press, 2006) x. According to UNHCR, *Refugees by Numbers* (2006 edn) the number of refugees is now 8.4 million: see <http://www.unhcr.org> (accessed 29 April 2007).

[6] See generally Crisp (n 1 above). The number of IDPs has risen and the total number of 'persons of concern' is 20.8 million: *Refugees by Numbers* (n 5 above).

Afghanistan, the repatriation of many asylum seekers to their countries of origin, and the failure to solve the conflicts in Africa and Iraq. Many refugees have fled to countries of first asylum as a result of persecution in their countries of origin. There they remain trapped, partly as a result of industrialised States' *non-entrée* strategies. Others (IDPs) remain trapped within the borders of their country of origin.[7] In fact the 'containment' of refugees in, or in regions close to, the country of origin is in the interests of industrialised countries.

The basis upon which the notion of 'choice' by refugees is condemned is when a 'secondary movement' is made from the country of first asylum towards an industrialised State. Here the argument is a variant of the 'flood-gates' argument: States should not be put under pressure to accept people who turn up at the border, partly because it is very difficult to manage large 'flows' of refugees, but also because of the global justice perspective. Because some States are more popular than others, it is argued that granting asylum according to 'choice' can lead to inequities between States. In this context, the actions of States in refusing admission to asylum seekers are justified on the basis that others (such as IDPs and those in countries of first asylum) have greater 'need', and that spontaneous asylum seekers are not entitled to priority merely by their physical presence.

These arguments are very difficult to refute in the absence of empirical evidence, including clear narratives from asylum seekers themselves. However, it may be that States have overstated the case in their favour, that is, of denying asylum seekers the right to seek asylum in the country of 'choice'. António Guterres, the United Nations High Commissioner for Refugees, has outlined three principal contemporary challenges facing international refugee protection:

> The first is rising intolerance. Second, there is the difficulty of protecting refugees within complex migratory flows. And third … the gap between relief and development.[8]

In this speech of 12 October 2005, the High Commissioner commented upon the rising intolerance towards foreigners and the increasing populism in such issues. He said: 'The populist approach confuses everything: security issues, migration and asylum'. It is encouraging to note, as summarised below, that the European Union ('EU') is increasingly turning its attention to development issues through the external dimension of its asylum policy. Extraterritorial processing is but one strand in its

[7] UNHCR has indicated that IDPs, estimated at 25 million, are now the second largest group 'of concern': *The State of the World's Refugees* (n 5 above).

[8] Remarks by Mr António Guterres, UNHCR, on the occasion of the European Council of Ministers of Justice and Home Affairs (Luxembourg, 12 October 2005) <http://www.libertysecurity.org/article522.html> (accessed 27 April 2007).

consideration of approaches to the refugee 'problem'. But the challenge is to tie extraterritorial processing with burden and responsibility sharing. In its Agenda for Protection,[9] UNHCR encourages burden and responsibility sharing, and international collective action in the interests of global justice.

In this chapter I examine the legal justifications put forward by States for extraterritorial processing to demonstrate that they are not based upon the idea of responsibility, but rather on *denial* of State responsibility. I argue that the regime of international protection established by the 1951 Refugee Convention[10] and its 1967 Protocol[11] is premised upon the responsibility of States to respect the institution of asylum.[12] I argue further that if States seek to move away from their core responsibilities, it is incumbent on them to demonstrate clear legal and ethical justifications for their actions. Extraterritorial processing involves an extension of the so-called STC 'concept' or notion which is based on the proposition that the receiving State is not obliged to process an application for asylum. The legal justification for the STC notion is grounded in denying the right to seek asylum in the country of choice. This is based in turn upon an interpretation of the scope of the *non-refoulement* obligation in Article 33 of the 1951 Refugee Convention. I re-examine the legal rationales of the STC notion to demonstrate that these justifications have been overstated in favour of States at the expense of the rights of individuals. This is hardly a surprising conclusion, since the legal justifications stress

[9] In late 2000, UNHCR launched the Global Consultations on International Protection to engage States and others in a dialogue in support of the 50-year-old Refugee Convention. The Agenda for Protection, which arose out of this process, has six inter-related goals, of which the following five are the most relevant to the present discussion:

- strengthening implementation of the 1951 Refugee Convention and 1967 Protocol (see nn 10 and 11 below);
- protecting refugees within broader migration movements;
- sharing burdens and responsibilities more equitably and building capacities to receive and protect refugees;
- addressing security-related concerns more effectively;
- redoubling the search for durable solutions for refugees.

[10] Convention relating to the Status of Refugees (adopted 28 July 1951, entered into force 22 April 1954) 189 UNTS 137.

[11] Protocol relating to the Status of Refugees (adopted 31 January 1967, entered into force 4 October 1967) 606 UNTS 267.

[12] This conclusion is supported by James Hathaway, who argues that the concept of 'STC' was envisaged by the drafters of the Refugee Convention to embody the *responsibility* of States: Comment at the workshop on 'Protection Elsewhere: International Law and the Off-shore Processing and Protection of Refugees' (Melbourne University Law Faculty, 23 February 2007). *The Michigan Guidelines on Protection Elsewhere* (adopted 3 January 2007) are premised upon the principle that STC and 'protection elsewhere' are neither expressly authorised nor expressly prohibited by the Refugee Convention, and that such practices must therefore be conducted with due respect to the rights set out in Arts 2–34 of the Refugee Convention.

the 'territorial–sovereignty nexus' (or the right to exclude strangers). However, it provides a useful link to the ethical implications of extraterritorial processing of asylum seekers. A consideration of the ethical implications reveals a debate which provides useful insights into the contested legal implications of extraterritorial processing. It also encourages burden and responsibility sharing.

To begin, it is important to consider briefly the context in which the proposals for extraterritorial processing are taking place within the EU.

II. EUROPEAN PROPOSALS FOR EXTRATERRITORIAL PROCESSING IN CONTEXT

The tradition of granting asylum is on the wane as a result of restrictive *non-entrée* policies in western industrialised countries. Europe, or its political manifestation, the EU, has long been a leader in developing such policies as part of its programme of harmonisation,[13] and ironically it is beginning now to suffer the consequences. In particular, in curious parallels with the graphic images of Australia's Pacific Strategy, it is seeing large numbers of asylum seekers in leaky boats attempting to enter 'Fortress Europe' through the southern Member States.

In recent years there has been an upsurge in asylum seekers and 'illegal' immigrants entering countries such as Italy and Spain by boat through the Mediterranean. These people largely come from North African countries such as Libya and Morocco and from other nearby Mediterranean countries (such as Albania). The Italian island of Lampedusa in the Mediterranean, close to Libya, has become a particular magnet for boat arrivals since 2003. In 2003, Italy recorded a total of 14,017 'boat people' from North Africa. In 2004 the figure was 12,737,[14] in 2005 it was 22,939, and for the first eight months of 2006 it was 14,567.[15] Initially, the Italian

[13] Member States committed themselves to the progressive establishment of the EU as an 'area of freedom, security and justice' upon signing the Treaty of Amsterdam (Treaty of Amsterdam amending the Treaty on European Union, the Treaties establishing the European Communities and Certain Related Acts on 2 October 1997, [1997] OJ C340/1). The Treaty of Amsterdam, which entered into force on 1 May 1999, reshaped co-operation on justice and home affairs and included measures on asylum and immigration within the realm of EU competence by creating a new Title IV 'Visas, Asylum, Immigration and Other Policies related to Free Movement of Persons' within the EC Treaty (Treaty establishing the European Economic Community (consolidated text) [2002] OJ C325/33). These issues had previously come under the 'inter-governmental' rules laid down in Title VI of the Treaty on European Union [2002] OJ C325/5.

[14] European Commission, *Technical Mission to Libya on Illegal Immigration, 27 November to 6 December 2004: Report*, Doc No 7753/05 (2005) 38.

[15] Communication from the Commission to the Council, 'Reinforcing the Management of the EU's Southern Maritime Borders', COM (2006) 733 final.

government was generous in its reception of these people, but from October 2004 it began to take a tougher stance. Italy and Libya have an arrangement in relation to those who land on Lampedusa. They are returned to Libya by aircraft, where there are established reception camps. From there, people are returned to their countries of origin, often without proper examination of their claims for asylum. Italy has also financed a programme of charter flights for the repatriation of illegal immigrants from Libya to their countries of origin.

Spain, like Italy, has traditionally been a country of emigration. But in recent years, it, too, has become a major destination country as a gateway to the EU and has experimented with a number of different policies, including amnesties. Like Italy, it has begun to practise maritime interdiction and the removal and detention of individuals. This has led to new relations and arrangements between Spain and Morocco, similar to those between Italy and Libya. These arrivals of Mediterranean 'boat people' are driving the push for offshore processing—or a 'Mediterranean Plan'—in that region.[16] In this context, Europe has turned to Australia for inspiration.

The call for offshore or extraterritorial EU processing centres also arises from the expansion of the EU borders (in 2004 and again in 2007) to include 12 new Member States. The surrounding countries of Eastern and Central Europe now form a 'buffer zone' for the EU. As a large proportion of the world's refugees come from countries contiguous to the new EU border, this increases the vulnerability of 'Fortress Europe'.

Since early 2003, the UK government has advocated the adoption of processing centres for refugees outside of the United Kingdom and the EU border. Together with the Netherlands and Denmark, it led the push for extraterritorial processing of asylum seekers in 'transit processing centres'. The German government also put forward a proposal in July 2004 for 'safe zones' or camps to be set up in North Africa. Although this was rejected by EU Member States at the time, there was a renewed call by the German Interior Minister, Schily, for extraterritorial processing centres in late 2005.

In parallel with the development of Australia's Pacific Strategy, the 'crisis' in the Mediterranean is said to be exaggerated or 'manufactured' by politicians in EU Member States.[17] Importantly, though, it points to gaps in European asylum and refugee policy. In particular, it is forcing the EU to see these issues in the context of forced migration and to look at the global picture. For example, the European Commission's Communication

[16] UNHCR is attempting to direct the agenda by focusing upon safe interdiction policies: see UNHCR, *Refugee Protection and Mixed Migration: A 10-Point Plan of Action* (Revision 1, January 2007).

[17] M Garlick, 'The EU Discussions on Extra-Territorial Processing: Solution or Conundrum?' (2006) 18 *International Journal of Refugee Law* 601 at 614.

on migration and development recognises the positive side of migration in the global context by acknowledging the role of remittances in the 'North–South' diaspora. UNHCR has urged the European Commission to recognise the relationship between development and refugees:

> Refugees in regions of origin are often the beneficiaries of humanitarian aid, but they are frequently excluded from development programmes. Yet ignoring the potential of refugees and returnees to participate in the development of regions in which they are living—or to which they are returning—may hamper efforts to attain the Millennium Development Goals.[18]

Both UNHCR (under the Agenda for Protection) and the EU are focusing upon comprehensive approaches and solutions to this problem of forced migration. In the case of the EU, this arises from the external dimension of its policy which was launched under the Hague Programme in late 2004.[19] This aspect of the programme has been very much led by the Mediterranean situation and developments on its eastern borders described above. There are two main elements of this external policy: measures to enhance the protection capacity of areas close to refugees' regions of origin, and a joint EU resettlement programme.

A 2005 Communication from the European Commission to the Council and the European Parliament proposed the establishment of Regional Protection Programmes ('RPPs') to 'enhance the capacity of areas close to regions of origin to protect refugees'.[20] RPPs are intended to comprise

[18] UNHCR, 'UNHCR Observations on the European Commission's Communication on "Migration and Development: Some Concrete Orientations" [COM (2005) 390 final, 1 September 2005]' (10 October 2005). The Communication from the Commission to the Council and the European Parliament, 'Implementing the Hague Programme: The Way Forward', COM (2006) 331 final (28 June 2006) s 2.3 further recognises the link between migration and development. (Although this is not expressly linked to asylum issues, it follows discussion of that issue.)

[19] The Hague Programme, also known as Tampere II, is the second phase in the creation of a Common European Asylum System. The first phase was the product of the European Council's meeting in Tampere in 1999, when Member States committed to creating a common asylum system based on the full and inclusive application of the Refugee Convention and respect for the principle of *non-refoulement*, according to the timetable set by the Treaty of Amsterdam. The first stage led to the adoption of the following instruments: Council Directive 2003/9/EC of 27 January 2003 laying down Minimum Standards for the Reception of Asylum Seekers [2003] OJ L31/18; Council Regulation (EC) No 343/2003 of 18 February 2003 establishing the Criteria and Mechanisms for Determining the Member State Responsible for Examining an Asylum Application Lodged in One of the Member States by a Third-Country National [2003] OJ L50/1; Council Directive 2004/83/EC of 29 April 2004 on Minimum Standards for the Qualification and Status of Third Country Nationals or Stateless Persons as Refugees or as Persons Who Otherwise Need International Protection and the Content of the Protection Granted [2004] OJ L304/12; and Council Directive 2005/85/EC of 1 December 2005 on Minimum Standards on Procedures in Member States for Granting and Withdrawing Refugee Status [2005] OJ L326/13.

[20] Communication from the Commission to the Council and the European Parliament, 'Regional Protection Programmes', COM (2005) 388 final (1 September 2005).

the two elements of protection close to refugees' regions of origin and resettlement. The States that have been identified as possible participants are Ukraine, Moldova and Belarus (as regions of transit) and Tanzania (as a region of origin). The Commission has been working on a separate proposal to enhance Libya's protection capacity, which includes the funding of camps.

In contrast to Australia, European countries on the whole have traditionally not been involved in resettling refugees. The EU has been better known for its 'reticence' to engage with asylum-related activities abroad. Thus, the idea of RPPs represents a change of focus which is significant, despite the modesty of the proposals.[21] In its response, UNHCR has given cautious support for the idea of RPPs. The High Commissioner, António Guterres, remarked that it will be important to ensure full co-ordination of these programmes with other initiatives and, in particular, to ensure consultation with the countries concerned. He warned that 'building protection capacity in third countries cannot replace asylum in Europe'.[22]

Thus, although there are no concrete proposals for joint processing of asylum seekers, extraterritorial processing is very much on the EU agenda. In this context, the EU and Member States have looked to the Australian model. Under Australia's Pacific Strategy,[23] extraterritorial processing is aimed at preventing and punishing secondary movements from countries of first asylum and preventing access to Australia's legal system. It also involves the use of mandatory detention, as well as processes which arguably provide less protection against *refoulement* than those provided under Australian law. If an asylum seeker is granted protection in Australia, the status conferred is temporary and the rights attached to it are arguably less than those contemplated by the 1951 Refugee Convention. The deterrent rationale under this model is clear.

With this context in mind, I turn now to a re-examination of the bases of the STC notion.

III. A RE-EXAMINATION OF STC—LEGAL BASES

The use of the STC notion has its origins in collective European practices dating from the 1990s, aimed at restricting access to national asylum

[21] See Garlick (n 17 above).

[22] Guterres (UNHCR) (n 8 above).

[23] See further S Kneebone, 'The Pacific Plan: The Provision of Effective Protection?' (2006) 18 *International Journal of Refugee Law* 696. The Pacific Strategy arose as a response to the arrival of the *MV Tampa* in Australian waters in late August 2001, with a cargo of 433 asylum seekers from the Middle East who had passed through Indonesia. The strategy was put in place by legislation that enabled the interdiction of asylum seekers intending to land on Australian shores and their subsequent transfer to offshore places, such as Nauru, for processing.

procedures. This was historically the period when 'asylum fatigue' began to set in as the number of asylum seekers in Europe escalated. In this period a number of other restrictions were introduced, such as sanctions on carriers, detention and abbreviated asylum procedures. In 1993, the influential German scholar, Kay Hailbronner, published an article supporting the use of the STC notion to prevent the European asylum system from collapsing.[24]

Official recognition of the STC notion dates from the 1990 Dublin Convention[25] and the 1992 EU Ministers' resolution.[26] Under the terms of the resolution, EU Member States agreed to incorporate the 'safe third country' principle into their national legislation. The effect of this was to impose an obligation on Member States to identify whether such a country existed before undertaking a substantive examination of the application for asylum. Thus, the premise of the STC notion is that the obligation or responsibility to process the asylum seeker rests with another country.[27]

The use of the STC notion is now institutionalised in European law and practice to such an extent that one commentator has suggested that it has the status of a 'customary international law' principle.[28] The notion is recognised in the EU Reception Directive and the Qualification Directive, which refer to persons applying for protection as 'third country nationals'.[29] It is directly referred to in the 2005 Asylum Procedures Directive.[30]

The use and practice of the STC notion under the Dublin Convention has been subject to criticism.[31] With time, the application and practice of the STC notion appears to have fewer safeguards and to be open to greater misuse.[32] For example, whilst the Preamble to the Dublin

[24] K Hailbronner, 'The Concept of "Safe Country" and Expeditious Asylum Procedures: A Western European Perspective' (1993) 5 *International Journal of Refugee Law* 31.

[25] Convention Determining the State Responsible for Examining Applications for Asylum Lodged in One of the Member States of the European Communities (adopted 15 June 1990, entered into force 1 September 1997) [1997] OJ C254/1.

[26] Resolution on a Harmonized Approach to Questions Concerning Host Third Countries (1 December 1992).

[27] S Legomsky, 'Secondary Refugee Movements and the Return of Asylum Seekers to Third Countries: The Meaning of Effective Protection' (2003) 15 *International Journal of Refugee Law* 567 at 570.

[28] S Taylor, 'Australia's "Safe Third Country" Provisions: Their Impact on Australia's Fulfillment of its Non-Refoulement Obligations' (1996) 15 *University of Tasmania Law Review* 196.

[29] See n 19 above.

[30] See n 19 above, preambular paras 17, 18, 21, Arts 29, 30, 31 (on safe countries of origin); and preambular paras 23, 24, Arts 27, 36 (on safe third countries).

[31] R Byrne and A Shacknove, 'The Safe Third Country Notion in European Asylum Law' (1996) 9 *Harvard Human Rights Journal* 185; A Hurwitz, 'The 1990 Dublin Convention: A Comprehensive Assessment' (1999) 11 *International Journal of Refugee Law* 646.

[32] Executive Committee, 'Note on International Protection', UN Doc A/AC.96/914 (7 July 1999) para 19.

Convention provided that applicants were *guaranteed* an examination of their claim for asylum by a Member State, under the Dublin Regulation[33] and Procedures Directive,[34] such a provision is missing.[35]

There is no provision in the 1951 Refugee Convention which directly supports the STC notion. However, it is said that in the absence of an enforceable duty to process asylum seekers in either the 1951 Refugee Convention or Article 14 of the Universal Declaration of Human Rights ('UDHR'),[36] States are free to return asylum seekers to a STC provided the *non-refoulement* obligation is respected. By extension, they are also able to intercept and to move asylum seekers to STCs, provided the *non-refoulement* obligation is not breached. The critics of Australia's actions arising out of the *Tampa* episode[37] assume the correctness of this proposition and accept the supposed corollary, namely, that asylum seekers have no right to choose their destination. The fact that interdiction results in asylum seekers being detained and transported against their will appears to be of little note.[38]

Apart from Article 33 of the 1951 Refugee Convention and Article 14 of the UDHR, there are other relevant legal sources to consider in assessing the STC notion. In addition to Article 31 of the 1951 Refugee Convention, there is considerable guidance to be gained from various UNHCR Executive Committee Conclusions and statements over a 30-year period which reinforce the basic duty of States parties to the 1951 Refugee Convention to respect the right to seek asylum. This argument is also supported by the duty of States parties to implement their Convention obligations in good faith.[39] Additionally, there is guidance from general human rights principles to be considered. In the next three sub-sections I examine the limits of the legal bases of the STC notion with the aid of these extra perspectives.

[33] See n 19 above.

[34] *Ibid*.

[35] Garlick (n 17 above) also lists delays and disagreements among States with respect to the interpretation of the provisions. Greece, for example, applies a national law under which persons returned are assumed to have withdrawn claims and thus do not receive substantive examination of their claims.

[36] Universal Declaration of Human Rights (adopted 10 December 1948) UNGA Res 217A (III).

[37] See n 23 above; T Magner, 'A Less Than "Pacific" Solution for Asylum Seekers in Australia' (2004) 16 *International Journal of Refugee Law* 53.

[38] CM Bostock, 'The International Legal Obligations Owed to the Asylum Seekers on the MV Tampa' (2002) 14 *International Journal of Refugee Law* 279 at 286 refers to the fact that the asylum seekers were under the 'effective control' of the Australian government, but concludes that the interdiction was not strictly a breach of international law, even if contrary to the 'humanitarian' objects and purposes of the 1951 Refugee Convention.

[39] Vienna Convention on the Law of Treaties (adopted 23 May 1969, entered into force 27 January 1980) 1155 UNTS 331, Art 31.

A. The Right to Seek Asylum and the Country of First Asylum Principle

There are three suggested limits or qualifications to the 'right' to seek asylum in Article 14 of the UDHR which are used to justify the STC notion. First, Article 14 is said to contain an empty right without a corresponding duty.[40] Secondly, the right is said to be qualified by a duty to apply for asylum in the country of first refuge or asylum ('CFA'). The third qualification, which derives from the CFA 'principle', is the duty to come 'directly' to the country of asylum. The overall justification for these qualifications is the problem of 'secondary' or irregular movements. I deal first with the nature of the 'right', before turning to the second and third qualifications.

Whilst some scholars assume that the right to seek asylum in Article 14 of the UDHR is simply the corollary of the State's duty of *non-refoulement*,[41] and is therefore very limited, many are today prepared to argue that the right to seek asylum has a substantive basis. For example, Bostock argues that it is a principle of customary international law, on the basis of the responsibility of States to those within their territory or under their de facto control.[42] This is an extension of the 'territorial–sovereignty nexus' argument, which is discussed more fully below. Blake, by contrast, refers to the history of State practice in relation to the recognition of the right to seek asylum, and argues that it was 'generous enough to assume that there was a right'.[43] Edwards, on the other hand, argues for the existence of the right on the basis of a human rights analysis.[44] As she cogently argues, refugee law and human rights 'form part of the same legal schema and tradition'.[45] Referring to the drafting history of the 1951 Refugee Convention, she says that it is 'arguable' that the right to seek and enjoy asylum is 'implicit in the very existence of the 1951 Convention'.[46] Interestingly, Edwards argues that the right to seek asylum is 'reinforced' by the inclusion of the *non-refoulement* provision in the 1951 Refugee Convention, and 'assisted' by the express right to leave

[40] G Noll, 'Seeking Asylum at Embassies: A Right of Entry under International Law?' (2005) 17 *International Journal of Refugee Law* 542 at 548.

[41] Magner (n 37 above). It is sometimes also pointed out that the UDHR is 'merely' declaratory.

[42] Bostock (n 38 above) 283–6.

[43] N Blake, 'The Dublin Convention and the Rights of Asylum Seekers in the EU' in E Guild and C Harlow (eds), *Implementing Amsterdam: Immigration and Asylum Rights in EC Law* (Oxford, Hart Publishing, 2001) 99.

[44] A Edwards, 'Human Rights, Refugees, and the Right to "Enjoy" Asylum' (2005) 17 *International Journal of Refugee Law* 293.

[45] *Ibid*, 299.

[46] *Ibid*, 298.

a country, contained in Article 13(2) of the UDHR and Article 12(2) of the International Covenant on Civil and Political Rights.[47] These views are a powerful counterweight to the argument that the right in Article 14 of the UDHR rests on a dubious legal basis.

In contrast to the 1951 Refugee Convention, the right of asylum is specifically mentioned in the 1969 Organization of African Unity Convention Governing the Specific Aspects of Refugee Problems in Africa.[48] To take the political 'sting' out of asylum, Article 2(2) states that the grant of asylum is 'a peaceful and humanitarian act'. In 2004, UNHCR reiterated this view in the Executive Committee's General Conclusion on International Protection.[49] With the waning of the tradition of granting asylum over the last couple of decades, UNHCR since at least 2000 has strongly emphasised the importance of asylum in the international refugee protection regime.

UNHCR's Executive Committee Conclusions are a valuable source of refugee law. They reflect contemporary refugee issues and are very instructive in recording the development of approaches to asylum. From the 1970s onwards, refugee crises in parts of the world other than Europe—largely in developing countries affected by decolonisation and independence movements—provided substantial challenges to the international refugee protection regime.[50] In 1974, UNHCR estimated that there were 2.4 million refugees, but by 1984 the figure was 10.5 million.[51] Up to 3 million people fled from Indo-China in the two decades after 1975.[52]

The central importance of asylum was reinforced during the Indo-Chinese refugee crisis in the 1970s and 1980s. The Comprehensive Plan of Action for Indo-Chinese refugees ('CPA'), which was agreed upon in Geneva in June 1989 by UNHCR, countries of first asylum and 50 resettlement countries in the west, followed a renewed surge in Vietnamese departures between 1987 and 1988. An important factor in the success of the CPA was the granting of asylum by countries in the region.[53] Executive

[47] *Ibid*, 301, citing International Covenant on Civil and Political Rights (adopted 16 Dec 1966, entered into force 23 March 1976) 999 UNTS 171.

[48] Organization of African Unity Convention Governing the Specific Aspects of Refugee Problems in Africa (adopted 10 September 1969, entered into force 20 June 1974) 1001 UNTS 45, Art 2(2).

[49] Executive Committee Conclusion No 99 (LV), 'General Conclusion on International Protection' (2004) para (n), recalling Executive Committee Conclusion No 94 (LIII), 'Civilian and Humanitarian Character of Asylum' (2002).

[50] L Barnett, 'Global Governance and the Evolution of the International Refugee Regime' (2002) 14 *International Journal of Refugee Law* 249.

[51] *Ibid*.

[52] UNHCR, *The State of the World's Refugees 2000: Fifty Years of Humanitarian Action* (Oxford, Oxford University Press, 2000) 79.

[53] *Ibid*, ch 4.

Committee Conclusion No 15 of 1979[54] was contemporaneous with this crisis. Paragraph (a) stated that 'States should use their best endeavours to grant asylum to bona fide asylum seekers'. However, another factor in the success of the CPA was that the countries of first asylum were assured that their obligations were temporary, as resettlement would follow.

The 'principle' that an asylum seeker should apply for asylum in the first safe country that he or she reaches is also to be found in Conclusion No 15. It suggests that if an asylum seeker

> already has close links with another State, he may if it appears fair and reasonable be called upon first to request asylum from that State.[55]

Historically, it seems this CFA principle was the basis of the Dublin Convention and was derived from a reading of Article 14 of the UDHR.[56] The 'right to seek asylum' was construed as conferring an obligation to do so in the first 'safe' place of asylum.

To this so-called principle of CFA was added the obligation to go 'directly' to a country of asylum. For example, Executive Committee Conclusion No 5 of 1977,[57] reflecting the Indo-Chinese crisis, applauded States for 'generally' following 'liberal asylum practices', and appealed to them to continue such practices in granting permanent 'or at least temporary asylum to refugees who have come *directly* to their territory'(emphasis added).[58] Shortly after this, Conclusion No 15 (1979) touched on the issue of 'secondary' or irregular movements. Paragraph (k) stated:

> Where a refugee who has already been granted asylum in one country requests asylum in another country on the ground that he has compelling reasons for leaving his present asylum country due to the fear of persecution or because his physical safety or freedom are endangered, the authorities of the second country should give favourable consideration to his asylum request.

The gentle tone of this direction contrasts with later statements on the issue of secondary movements.

In the 1980s, as refugee crises escalated, the emphasis of refugee protection changed from an 'exilic' basis to a 'source control bias'.[59] Executive Committee Conclusion No 22 of 1981, dealing with situations of mass influx,[60] emphasises the need to protect asylum seekers according to

[54] Executive Committee Conclusion No 15 (XXX), 'Refugees without an Asylum Country' (1979).

[55] *Ibid*, para (h)(iv).

[56] Blake (n 43 above) 98–9.

[57] Executive Committee Conclusion No 5 (XXVIII), 'Asylum' (1977).

[58] *Ibid*, para (d) .

[59] TA Aleinikoff, 'State Centred Refugee Law: From Resettlement to Containment' (1992) 14 *Michigan Journal of International Law* 120 at 125.

[60] Executive Committee Conclusion No 22 (XXXII), 'Protection of Asylum-Seekers in Situations of Large-Scale Influx' (1981).

'basic human standards' and 'fundamental civil rights', even during the provision of temporary protection. However, the tone of Executive Committee Conclusion No 58 of 1989[61] is quite different. Whilst it refers to the need to respect 'basic human standards'[62] in relation to irregular 'movers', its focus is upon the 'destabilizing effect' that such movements have 'on structured international efforts to provide appropriate solutions for refugees'.[63] Conclusion No 58 reflects the escalating crisis in Indo-China. Around this period, the emphasis of refugee protection changed to 'containment' in countries of origin or CFA.

Conclusion No 22 (1981) cross-references Article 31 of the Refugee Convention. Article 31 is relied upon as a legal basis for the STC concept[64] and the related CFA concept.[65] Article 31 applies to refugees 'unlawfully' in the country of refuge,[66] and contains a prohibition on the conferment of 'penalties' on refugees 'coming directly from a territory where their life or freedom was threatened', provided 'they present themselves without delay to the authorities and show good cause for their illegal entry or presence'. The provision has been relied upon as a justification for detaining persons before transferring them to a STC, and for interdicting and transferring asylum seekers. This interpretation arises from stressing the words 'coming directly'.

However, this interpretation of Article 31 is strongly contested. Goodwin-Gill and others conclude that the words 'coming directly from a territory where their life or freedom was threatened' were not intended to be construed literally.[67] The provision does not link the threat to the asylum seeker's country of origin, but—significantly—to a 'territory'. That Article 31 contemplates both direct and indirect flight can be gleaned from the context of the article and the reference to 'good cause' for the flight, which refers to the reasons for leaving. This is consistent with Conclusion No 15

[61] Executive Committee Conclusion No 58 (XL), 'The Problem of Refugees and Asylum Seekers Who Move in an Irregular Manner from a Country in Which They Had Already Found Protection' (1989).

[62] *Ibid*, para (f).

[63] Executive Committee Conclusion No 58 (XL) (n 61 above) para (a).

[64] C Costello, 'The Asylum Procedures Directive and the Proliferation of Safe Country Practices: Deterrence, Deflection and the Dismantling of International Protection?' (2005) 7 *European Journal of Migration and Law* 35 at 39.

[65] Hailbronner (n 24 above); Byrne and Shacknove (n 31 above).

[66] GS Goodwin-Gill, 'Article 31 of the 1951 Convention Relating to the Status of Refugees: Non-Penalization, Detention, and Protection' in E Feller, V Türk and F Nicholson (eds), *Refugee Protection in International Law: UNHCR's Global Consultations on International Protection* (Cambridge, Cambridge University Press, 2003) 216 explains that the prohibition on imposing penalties in Art 31 extends to States which exercise de facto control or jurisdiction over a person and thus may cover persons attempting to enter a territory if such control or jurisdiction is exercised.

[67] *Ibid*; Blake (n 43 above) 99; JC Hathaway, *The Rights of Refugees under International Law* (Cambridge, Cambridge University Press, 2005) 399.

(1979) on the issue of 'secondary' or irregular movements, which refers to 'compelling reasons for leaving' a country of asylum.[68] Similarly, even the severe Conclusion No 58 (1989) says that there may be 'exceptional cases' in which a person may 'justifiably' claim that he or she fears persecution or that his or her 'physical safety or freedom are endangered in a country where he or she has previously found protection'.[69]

As Goodwin-Gill has emphasised, a State must first examine a claim for asylum to ensure that its international obligations are being met.[70] Otherwise, its actions in detaining or interdicting a person as a preliminary step to invoking the STC notion may amount to a 'penalty' (quite apart from the risk of *refoulement*). Extraterritorial processing may involve other penalties or discrimination. For example, under the Pacific Strategy, the Australian government denies asylum seekers access to its domestic jurisdiction and its refugee status determination procedures (including independent merits review and access to judicial review). Additionally, the regime of Temporary Protection Visas ('TPVs') introduced by the Australian government penalises and discriminates against this group of asylum seekers. This regime denies access to some basic services and to family reunion.[71] TPV-holders are vulnerable to re-processing of their visas and to the Australian government's convenient use of Article 1C(5) of the Refugee Convention.[72] Further, the detention of asylum seekers under the Pacific Strategy breaches Article 31(2) of the Refugee Convention by imposing unnecessary restrictions on their freedom of movement.[73] As Conclusion No 22 (1981) recognises, such restrictions are only justified in the interests of 'public health and public order'.[74]

In conclusion, it appears that the suggested limits or qualifications to the 'right' to seek asylum in Article 14 of the UDHR which are used to justify the STC notion can all be challenged. It is not my argument that Article 14 imposes a positive duty on States to process asylum seekers. However, the negative proposition, that Article 14 imposes no obligations on States, can be questioned. Further, UNHCR has made it clear that the practice of STC must be balanced by respect for the rights of asylum seekers, and the need to avoid the imposition of penalties. In particular, the

[68] Executive Committee Conclusion No 15 (XXX) (n 54 above) para (k).

[69] Executive Committee Conclusion No 58 (XL) (n 61 above) para (g).

[70] Goodwin-Gill (n 66 above) 187.

[71] Kneebone (n 23 above).

[72] See *Minister for Immigration and Multicultural and Indigenous Affairs v QAAH of 2004* [2006] HCA 53.

[73] As holders of Special Purpose Visas, it could be argued that the asylum seekers on Nauru were 'lawful' refugees who were denied the right to freedom of movement on Nauru in addition to being 'unlawfully' detained. See also *Ruhani v Director of Police (No 2)* [2005] HCA 42; and Refugee Convention, Art 26.

[74] Executive Committee Conclusion No 22 (XXXII) (n 60 above) s II2(a).

right to seek asylum must be respected.[75] As Crisp has observed, as the underpinnings of asylum that existed in the past two decades have been progressively dismantled

> [o]ne of the most striking features of the asylum issue in the industrialised states is the extent to which it is impervious to the usual instruments of public policy.[76]

Governments are all too ready to characterise refugee situations as mass influxes and to read the Refugee Convention in such as way as to support their practices. Article 31 of the Refugee Convention is the strongest source to rely upon to reject the CFA and 'direct flight' principles.

B. The Right to 'Enjoy' Asylum

Article 14 of the UDHR refers not only to the right to 'seek' asylum, but also to 'enjoy' asylum. The question that is considered in this section is whether the right to enjoy asylum requires the personal preferences and needs of the asylum seeker to be considered.[77] As stated above, it is often suggested that the exercise of choice by an asylum seeker is 'forum shopping' and an indication of 'abuse' of the asylum system. However, there are studies which suggest that some asylum seekers will make choices of destination on the basis of family, language and cultural connections, as will migrants whose flight is not forced. There are some indications that the legitimate preferences of the asylum seeker are a relevant issue in determining 'durable solutions'.[78] If that is a valid proposition, it weakens the legal argument for the STC notion which is based on the CFA idea and an obligation to proceed 'directly' to the place of asylum.

The drafting history of the UDHR shows that the word 'granted' was replaced by 'to enjoy'. As Edwards explains, this changed 'the tone and ramifications of the provision'. She says that the right to enjoy asylum 'suggests at a minimum a right "to benefit from" asylum'.[79] Conclusion

[75] The Australian government interprets its obligation under the Refugee Convention to apply only when it is the 'last resort': Department of Immigration, Multicultural and Indigenous Affairs, 'The Principle of Effective Protection in the Australian Domestic Legal and Policy Context' in UNHCR, 'Discussion Paper: The Principle of Effective Protection Elsewhere' (No 1, 2004) 4–5 <http://www.unhcr.org.au/pdfs/dpaper012004.pdf> (accessed 20 June 2007).

[76] J Crisp, 'A New Asylum Paradigm? Globalization, Migration and the Uncertain Future of the International Refugee Regime', UNHCR, *New Issues in Refugee Research*, Working Paper No 100 (2003) 9.

[77] The issue of what amounts to 'effective protection' against *non-refoulement*, which includes guarantees, is discussed by Legomsky (n 27 above).

[78] One such indication would be a right to family unity, which is generally assumed to be one of the standards for 'effective protection'.

[79] Edwards (n 44 above) 302.

No 15 (1979) lends support to this as it states that identifying the country 'responsible for determining the asylum request' should 'as far as possible' take into account the intentions of the asylum seeker, and also consider whether it is 'fair and reasonable' for the asylum seeker to request asylum from a third State where he or she already has 'close links with another State'.[80]

There are indications from the Refugee Convention which support Conclusion No 15. If, as argued above, it is correct that Article 31 of the Convention refers to both direct and indirect flight, it provides additional support for the relevance of choice. Hathaway accepts the argument that the absence of a CFA or direct flight requirement in the Refugee Convention means that refugee law 'effectively allows most refugees to choose for themselves the country in which they will claim refugee status'.[81] The exclusion clause in Article 1E of the Refugee Convention, which provides that the Convention does not apply to a person who has 'taken residence' in another country where he or she has 'the rights and obligations which are attached to the possession of the nationality of that country', is also relevant. In Australia, Article 1E has been interpreted as incorporating the STC concept into Australian law.[82] Article 1E supports the proposition that an asylum seeker's choice is indeed relevant.[83] Implications about choice can be drawn also from Article 1C of the Refugee Convention, which recognises that a refugee may 'voluntarily' change his or her status by actions amounting to choice of nationality or residence. Article 1C, together with the refugee definition in Article 1A(2) and Article 34, strongly suggests that refugees granted protection should be 'assimilated' into their new State. Assimilation implies integration and choice by the asylum seeker, as well as acceptance into a community.[84]

Blake has pointed out that the question whether a person has a 'substantial connection' with a third country was considered to be a very relevant consideration in the United Kingdom prior to 1990. At that time, the policy was based on whether an 'alternative *appropriate* country with appropriate links existed'.[85] Further, the Dublin Convention prescribed family connections as a criterion for selecting the Member State responsible for examining the asylum claim. Although this was not

[80] Executive Committee Conclusion No 15 (XXX) (n 54 above) para (h).

[81] JC Hathaway, *The Law of Refugee Status* (Toronto, Butterworths, 1991) 46.

[82] *Minister for Immigration v Thiyagarajah* (2000) 169 ALR 515 (HCA).

[83] See J Vedsted-Hansen, 'Non-Admission Policies and the Right to Protection: Refugees' Choice versus States' Exclusion?' in F Nicholson and P Twomey (eds), *Refugee Rights and Realities: Evolving International Concepts and Regimes* (Cambridge, Cambridge University Press, 1999).

[84] S Kneebone, 'The Rights of Strangers: Refugees, Citizenship and Nationality' (2004) 10 *Australian Journal of Human Rights* 33.

[85] Blake (n 43 above) 100–01.

implemented in practice, it is further evidence that personal connections are relevant to a decision about asylum. It is a short step from acknowledging the relevance of personal connections to acknowledging the legitimate role of the individual's preference or choice. Indeed, the practice under the Dublin Convention *in fact* was to allow asylum seekers the choice of destination country.

The consistent position taken by UNHCR is that asylum seekers should not be returned to countries with which they lack sufficient connection.[86] UNHCR has, for example, stressed the importance of 'family connections, cultural ties, knowledge of the language, the possession of a residence permit and the applicant's previous periods of residence'.[87] It rejects the proposition that mere transit through a territory is sufficient for this purpose. Legomsky's view is that whilst these criteria rest on 'sensible and humane policy considerations',[88] they do not 'express binding principles of international law'.[89] Legomsky appears to be persuaded by the arguments based on Article 14 of the UDHR and Article 31 of the Refugee Convention which have been analysed and critiqued above. However, it can be argued that the underlying principles on which Legomsky relies are themselves contestable. He deals with the negative proposition for Article 31 by asking whether it is a penalty to return people to countries with which they have insufficient links.[90] As explained below, the relevant issue is whether the person will be discriminated against.

In Australia, the government (and the courts) have taken the view that even a transitory stay in a CFA may be sufficient to deprive a person of the right to seek asylum in Australia.[91] Many people have been returned to countries with which they have no real links and only a fragile status, effectively leaving them stateless.[92] As UNHCR has stressed, it cannot be assumed that a person has effective protection in a CFA: it is necessary to

[86] UNHCR, 'UNHCR Observations on the European Commission's Proposal for a Directive on Common Standards and Procedures in Member States for Returning Illegally Staying Third-Country Nationals (COM (2005) 291 final)' (December 2005).

[87] UNHCR, 'UNHCR's Observations on the European Commission's Proposal for a Council Regulation establishing the Criteria and Mechanisms for Determining the Member State Responsible for Examining an Asylum Application Lodged in One of the Member States by a Third Country National (COM (2001) 447 final)' (February 2002) para 7.

[88] Legomsky (n 27 above) 664.

[89] *Ibid*, 665.

[90] *Ibid*, 666.

[91] Migration Act 1958 (Cth), s 36(3) provides that even a temporary 'right to enter and reside' in another country may deprive the person of the right to seek asylum in Australia. This is inconsistent with Australia's position about transitory stops during the Comprehensive Plan of Action period: GS Goodwin-Gill and J McAdam, *The Refugee in International Law*, 3rd edn (Oxford, Oxford University Press, 2007) 150 fn 80.

[92] See, eg *Minister for Immigration v Al-Sallal* (1999) 94 FCR 549 (FCA), and the discussion of that case and others in Kneebone (n 84 above).

examine the individual circumstances to ensure that he or she will not be penalised or discriminated against in any way in that country.[93]

Mathew concludes that an accurate reading of the law requires a view somewhere between the extremes of choice–no choice.[94] For that purpose, Conclusion No 15 supplies guidance. But to formulate policy on the basis that individual asylum seekers never have a choice, thus enabling States to avoid their responsibilities under the Refugee Convention, is not sound. The proposition that the STC notion rests on the lack of choice of asylum destination cannot be sustained.

C. The Limits of the *Non-Refoulement* Principle

Although there is no provision in the Refugee Convention which directly supports the STC concept, it is thought to arise from implications about the limits of the *non-refoulement* obligation in Article 33, and the non-enforceable nature of the right to seek asylum in Article 14 of the UDHR. It is frequently acknowledged that the right to seek asylum amounts to a right to have access to refugee status determination.[95] If that access is denied, then constructive *refoulement* may occur.[96]

States tend to read the extent of their *non-refoulement* obligations narrowly by reference to a territorial–sovereignty nexus. Therefore, States feel free to move their borders, and to define the extent of their international obligations, according to their own domestic or national standards. This appears to be justified on a reading of thc 1967 Declaration on Territorial Asylum, which clearly makes the link between asylum and territory. Article 3(1) reads:

> No person [entitled to invoke Article 14 of the UDHR] shall be subjected to such measures as rejection at the frontier or, if he [or she] has entered the territory … expulsion or compulsory return to any State where he [or she] may be subjected to persecution.

However, there is general consensus that the Article 33 *non-refoulement* obligation extends beyond the actual territory and territorial waters of a State.

[93] See UNHCR Regional Office (Canberra), 'Australia's Protection Obligations: Only a Last Resort?' in UNHCR (n 75 above) 3. UNHCR detailed other instances in this paper of Australia assuming that 'effective protection' existed 'elsewhere'. *The Michigan Guidelines on Protection Elsewhere* (n 12 above) state that policies must ensure that refugees enjoy the rights set out in Arts 2–34 of the Refugee Convention.

[94] P Mathew, 'Australian Refugee Protection in the Wake of Tampa' (2002) 96 *American Journal of International Law* 661 at 668.

[95] In *Victorian Council for Civil Liberties Inc v Minister for Immigration and Multicultural Affairs* [2001] FCA 1297, (2001) 110 FCR 452, discussed in the text below, the government's purpose in refusing the asylum seekers access to Australian territory was to deny them access to the procedures provided for under Australian law.

[96] *Amuur v France* (1996) 22 EHRR 533 (ECtHR).

Article 33 applies to any situation where the State has 'effective control'[97] of the asylum seekers—as Australia clearly did in the *Tampa* case and other situations where it has interdicted asylum seekers. Furthermore, the excision of territory in domestic law does not affect the obligations owed by a State under international law. This is, of course, separate from the question of whether removal to a STC amounts to *refoulement*. The *non-refoulement* obligation is explained by reference to the territorial–sovereignty nexus and the extension of that idea, namely the de facto exercise of jurisdiction.[98]

The use of the territorial–sovereignty nexus is clear from the decision in *Ruddock v Vardalis*,[99] which arose out of the *Tampa* incident. In that case, the asylum seekers (who were labelled 'rescuees') clearly made a claim for asylum, but the Australian government refused to process them. In the subsequent action for habeas corpus, on the basis that the asylum seekers were illegally detained against their will, the Australian government argued that they had the right to expel them from the Australian border, using the analogy of the sovereign right to expel 'enemy aliens'. It also argued that their plight was 'self-inflicted'.[100]

The action on behalf of the asylum seekers succeeded before North J at first instance.[101] However, on appeal to the Full Federal Court, the decision was reversed by 2:1.[102] In the appeal proceedings, the argument turned largely upon the question of sovereignty and the authority to expel the asylum seekers. The majority accepted the authority to expel argument,[103] and rejected the habeas corpus–detention argument. In a passage which overlooked the significance of Article 14 of the UDHR, French J said that the asylum seekers' argument begged the question of release 'from what?'. In his opinion, the asylum seekers had neither the right nor the freedom to travel to Australia. The second judge in the majority, Beaumont J, thought that Article 33 of the Refugee Convention was the only relevant provision, but he considered that there was no risk of *refoulement*. In an interesting postscript, he said:

> Finally, it should be added that this is a municipal, and not an international, court. Even if it were, whilst customary international law imposes an obligation upon a coastal State to provide humanitarian assistance to vessels in distress, international law imposes no obligation upon the coastal State to resettle those

[97] Bostock (n 38 above) 287.

[98] Hathaway (n 67 above) 336.

[99] *Ruddock v Vardalis* [2001] FCA 1329, (2001) 110 FCR 491 (FCA).

[100] *Victorian Council for Civil Liberties* (n 95 above) para 64.

[101] *Victorian Council for Civil Liberties* (n 95 above).

[102] *Ruddock v Vadarlis* (n 99 above) (Black CJ, Beaumont and French JJ).

[103] This was based upon a reading of the executive power under the Australian Constitution. See P Billings, 'Refugees, Rule of Law and Executive Power: A(nother) Case of the Conjuror's Rabbit?' (2001) 54 *Northern Ireland Legal Quarterly* 412.

rescued in the coastal State's territory. This accords with the principles of the Refugee Convention. By Art 33, a person who has established refugee status may not be expelled to a territory where his life and freedom would be threatened for a Convention reason. Again, there is no obligation on the coastal State to resettle in its own territory. Any extra-judicial assessment of Executive policy in the present circumstances should be seen in this context.[104]

With respect, this statement understates the obligations and responsibilities owed by States under the Refugee Convention. Because States interpret the limits of the *non-refoulement* obligation so narrowly, they only recognise a de facto duty to admit, or to grant asylum to, persons who turn up at the border or in a territory. This accounts for a narrow reading of the right to seek asylum under Article 14 of the UDHR. In that context we can see that the territorial–sovereignty nexus tends to lead to circular arguments about rights and duties. We therefore leave the legal scene and turn to consider political theory and the ethical implications of extraterritorial processing.

IV. THE ETHICAL IMPLICATIONS

It has been suggested above that the perspective of global justice is at the fore of determining what is 'ethical' in the treatment of asylum seekers, and for evaluating proposals for extraterritorial processing. The discussion has shown that it is difficult to construct an argument around the choice of the individual. This is because there is a conflict between liberal principles and the individual's autonomy or liberty. One such 'liberty' is the right to freedom of movement.[105] This has given rise to a theoretical debate between supporters for and against the notion of 'open' versus 'closed' borders.[106] For example, the argument presented above for acknowledging the legitimate choice of an asylum seeker in some circumstances might be seen as advocating open borders. Similarly, support is also seen to arise for open borders from 'utilitarian' arguments and 'cosmopolitans', who stress issues of global justice and universal human rights in determining the rights of refugees.[107]

The argument for closed borders is one that resonates with State interests. It has two relevant aspects: it assumes both the existence of a

[104] *Ruddock v Vadarlis* (n 99 above) para 126.

[105] F Whelan, 'Citizenship and Freedom of Movement: An Open Admission Policy?' in M Gibney (ed), *Open Borders? Closed Societies?: The Ethical and Political Issues* (Westport, CT, Greenwood Press, 1998).

[106] M Walzer, *Spheres of Justice: A Defence of Pluralism and Equality* (Oxford, Martin Robertson, 1983) ch 2, and J Carens, 'The Case for Open Borders' (1987) 49 *The Review of Politics* 251 represent the arguments for closed and open borders respectively.

[107] P Singer and R Singer, 'The Ethics of Refugee Policy' in Gibney (n 105 above).

'bounded' territory, and the right of the 'community' to exclude those who are not its members. The latter involves the right to confer membership on newcomers. The first feature is familiar to legal language—it is explicitly represented by the territorial–sovereignty nexus idea, which was discussed above. The second feature, the idea of 'community' and conferment of 'membership', is implicit in refugee law. Refugees are consistently defined in policy by exclusion, that is, as persons outside the legal system. They are defined by way of 'inclusive exclusion',[108] as non-citizens. However, as the discussion of *Ruddock v Vardalis* illustrates, the two ideas of the territorial–sovereignty nexus and community are linked. There the asylum seekers were excluded on the analogy of 'enemy aliens'.

There are many aspects to the 'open' versus 'closed' borders debate which cannot be explored here, involving theories of justice and the 'State'. The main purpose of this discussion is to draw attention to the views of a political scientist, Matthew Gibney,[109] which provide useful tools for critiquing the legal implications of the issue.

As Gibney explains, the argument for 'closed' borders needs to be more nuanced. Gibney's aim is to determine the limits of the right of States to control entry to their territory. He argues that to allow asylum seekers untrammelled access to refugee status determination procedures by granting a 'right of asylum' would lead to inequality on a global scale by creating inequalities between States, because the 'burden' of asylum would fall inequitably on them (as, for example, it did in the case of Germany in the early 1990s). He also argues that, from a moral perspective, privileging those who turn up at the border over those who do not is arbitrary. Moreover, he argues that the moral issues raised by refugeehood do not require more than that the people concerned are provided with a secure new State, not necessarily one of their own choosing. Thus, he opposes the idea that refugees can have a moral right to choose their destination.

Gibney's definition of 'ethical' in this context is 'a moral standard or value' which also takes into account the political reality of asylum policies. He attempts to define normative prescriptions for action that take into account what States could actually do. He expresses concerns about what is 'politically possible',[110] in terms of how States might be persuaded to respond more ethically (and consequently more generously) to the refugee problem. Gibney develops a 'humanitarian principle' to modify the

[108] Kneebone (n 84 above) 40.
[109] MJ Gibney, *The Ethics and Politics of Asylum: Liberal Democracy and the Response to Refugees* (Cambridge, Cambridge University Press, 2004).
[110] *Ibid*, 17.

traditional sovereign State exclusionist argument, by pointing to the responsibility of States to respect the *non-refoulement* principle and to resettle refugees. He argues that States have an obligation to assist refugees when the costs of doing so are low.[111] He says: 'Humanitarianism has no respect for distance; it is owed to all refugees on the basis of need alone'.[112]

Gibney's argument is thus clearly addressed to industrialised States in particular. Their responsibility to asylum seekers is explained through the 'harm' principle, which stresses the importance of such States as agents in the creation of the refugee problem.[113] States have a responsibility for asylum seekers when there is a risk of *refoulement*, or where there is a causal link between their actions and the reasons for people seeking refuge. As Gibney explains, States are more than a culture or a territory. They are actors and agents in an interconnected global environment. Gibney advocates that States should respond by more generous resettlement of refugees, as a means of sharing the burden in a global crisis.

Gibney develops two powerful critiques which are useful for assessing the legal implications discussed above. First, he offers insights into the territorial–sovereignty argument. He is concerned that arguments which are used to exclude people on the basis of control of territory should not be overstated. This is partly because the moral claim to such territory is often contested.[114] However, he recognises that a territorial nexus may be relevant to create a proximate relationship or causal link, so as to engage the *non-refoulement* obligation and the harm principle. Under his 'harm principle', physical proximity is but one way in which a causal relationship can arise. There is room in Gibney's analysis for freedom of choice for those asylum seekers who have no alternative but to flee and who *need* protection. But unless extraterritorial processing is fair and effective, those needs will not be identified.

The ideas of community and membership are more important reasons, in Gibney's view, for including or excluding people from a territory. He develops a model of community membership which is based upon the idea of a 'political culture', rather than one based on culture as such. He is concerned that exclusion–inclusion on the basis of culture and ethnicity should not be overstated as a reason for membership.[115] Rather,

[111] *Ibid*, 231.

[112] *Ibid*, 240.

[113] *Ibid*, 50–56. For example, Gibney refers to the role of industrialised States in the creation of the circumstances leading to the mass outflow of refugees in Indo-China in the 1960s and 1970s.

[114] *Ibid*, 39–40. JA Scanlan and OT Kent, 'The Force of Moral Arguments for a Just Immigration Policy in a Hobbesian Universe: The Contemporary American Example' in Gibney (n 105 above) argue that a defensive concept of the State is embedded in nations which have acquired territory through force.

[115] Gibney (n 109 above) 43.

he emphasises the political nature of the State's institutions, through the bonds of membership. He recognises that these institutions or bonds, in turn, may not be completely independent of cultural and ethnic ties. Thus, his concern is with protecting the interests of voting citizens *because* this is a means of preserving the important political institutions of a State. He considers that States are only justified in restricting entry of non-citizens in order to protect the institutions and values of the liberal democratic welfare State.[116] Importantly, he analyses this concept of political community as a collective extension of the individual's right to self-determination.[117]

In the field of international refugee law, it is often stressed that protection under the Refugee Convention is a surrogate for the bond of 'trust, loyalty and protection' which has broken down between the citizen and her or his State.[118] Shacknove argues that the basic needs of refugees include 'liberty of political participation', in addition to physical security.[119] Gibney's argument develops this idea of political participation. It is an inclusive view which contrasts with that of scholars such as Scanlan and Kent, who privilege citizens per se against outsiders because of their status: 'universal moral principles must be reducible to the interests of citizens'.[120] For them, the 'ethical' equals the 'interests of citizens'.

At the end of his book, Gibney deals with a potential objection to his views, namely that they could be seen as encouraging temporary protection and detention of refugees by 'trading' their rights to asylum in the interests of global justice.[121] However, he concludes that

> [a]s long as *refoulement* is guarded against, the desire of asylum seekers to go to the country of their choice ... should not scupper all proposals for international burden sharing on grounds such as the 'commodification' of refugees.[122]

In a subsequent paper, Gibney deals further with the 'commodification' objection.[123] Whilst he dismisses objections which rely upon the freedom and dignity of the individual and free choice for the reasons stated above (namely their potential to encourage the application of unethical standards leading to global inequality), he accepts a proviso to his views.

[116] *Ibid*, 195.

[117] *Ibid*, 26.

[118] A Shacknove, 'Who is a Refugee?' (1985) 95 *Ethics* 274.

[119] *Ibid*, 280.

[120] Scanlan and Kent (n 114 above) 77.

[121] Gibney (n 109 above) 249. Note that this follows a passage in which he describes the Australian government's response to the *Tampa* incident in strongly critical terms.

[122] *Ibid*, 253.

[123] MJ Gibney, 'Forced Migration, Engineered Regionalism and Justice between States' in S Kneebone and F Rawlings-Sanaei (eds), *New Regionalism and Asylum Seekers: Challenges Ahead* (Oxford/New York, Berghahn Books, 2007).

This is that, provided asylum seekers are not treated as a negative value which affects how they are treated if they are admitted to a country,[124] the 'commodification' objection should be rejected.

Gibney also recognises that there is a potential danger in burden sharing arrangements when richer States pay poorer ones to take their refugees, effectively enabling richer States to opt out of their international obligations. That is the challenge for plans for extraterritorial processing. They must be developed in the interests of global justice, but with respect for the right to seek asylum and the basic needs of asylum seekers.

V. CONCLUSION

The STC notion has developed as a practice whereby States deny asylum seekers access to their national processes and instead seek to pass their responsibility on to other States. It is an attack on the fundamental principle of asylum, a principle which is vital to international refugee protection. Although the STC practice is widespread, it does not have any firm legal basis except by implication from the limits of the negative *non-refoulement* obligation in Article 33 of the Refugee Convention. The STC notion is thought to be supported by two 'principles'—the 'country of first asylum' and the obligation to proceed 'directly' to the place of asylum. However, there is no direct support for such principles in the Refugee Convention, including Article 31 of the Convention (the 'no penalty' provision), which is typically relied upon for this purpose. A reading of Article 31 in the light of guidance from UNHCR's Executive Committee supports the view that refugees may proceed directly or indirectly to a country of asylum, subject to 'good reasons' for doing so. The Executive Committee's Conclusions indicate that State practice should always take into account the rights of individuals, rather than approach refugee protection from a deterrent perspective, even in situations of mass influx.

Another limb of the argument for a STC notion relies upon the absence of a clear right to seek asylum in Article 14 of the UDHR, and its corollary—the right to choose the place of asylum. However, the view that there is no substantive right to seek asylum can be questioned. Further, there are indications that the personal preferences of an asylum seeker are relevant in determining 'durable solutions'. Without going so far as to argue that there is a substantive right to seek asylum, it is clear that the proposition that the STC notion rests on the lack of choice of asylum cannot be sustained.

The legal justifications for the STC notion and for interdiction and removal to an STC stress the 'territorial–sovereignty nexus', or the right

[124] Gibney uses the analogy of 'toxic waste': *ibid*, 73.

of the State to exclude. A consideration of the ethical implications of extraterritorial processing of asylum seekers questions the limits of this notion. The concept of a 'political community' is a sounder basis for exclusive–inclusive policies towards refugees, rather than those based upon territory or status alone. Without advocating open borders, a position which respects the rights and genuine needs of asylum seekers must be reached in order to accommodate the interests of the individual and global justice. This can be achieved by stressing the responsibility of States to assist refugees. Extraterritorial processing as practised under the Australian Pacific Strategy extends the STC notion to countries which are not truly 'third countries', but rather offshore sites under Australia's control. These serve the purpose of denying asylum seekers access to domestic refugee status determination procedures. The Pacific Strategy does not arise from a sense of responsibility, but rather *denies* responsibility. As such, it is unlikely to lead to international burden sharing.

It is to be hoped that the EU will take a comprehensive and multi-pronged approach to refugee flows, viewing them as part of forced migration generally. If extraterritorial processing ultimately forms part of the EU's response, then it must heed the ethical implications and respect the rights of individuals in conformity with the Refugee Convention.

6

Re-thinking the Paradigms of Protection: Children as Convention Refugees in Australia

MARY CROCK*

I. INTRODUCTION

THE INCREASING NUMBER and mobility of refugees around the world has created new challenges for countries of asylum in the form of children who are travelling without parents or any other legal or customary guardian/carer. These children—persons under the age of 18 years—present either embedded in groups of obvious asylum seekers or (more problematically) as the victims of people trafficking. The United Nations High Commissioner for Refugees ('UNHCR') estimates that approximately half of the world's refugees are children.[1] While most refugee children flee their homes with their families, between two and five per cent are 'unaccompanied' or 'separated' children,[2] and in some countries

* This chapter borrows extensively from ch 12 of M Crock, *Seeking Asylum Alone: Australia: A Study of Australian Law, Policy and Practice regarding Unaccompanied and Separated Children* (Sydney, Themis Press, 2006); and from ch 7 of J Bhabha and M Crock, *Seeking Asylum Alone: A Comparative Study: Unaccompanied and Separated Children and Refugee Protection in Australia, the UK and the US* (Sydney, Themis Press, 2006). As in the *Australian Report*, I acknowledge here the particular contribution made by Professor Jacqueline Bhabha, my partner in the *Seeking Asylum Alone* project. It is Professor Bhabha who has done the pioneering theoretical work in this area. See, eg J Bhabha, 'Demography and Rights: Women, Children and Access to Asylum' (2004) 16 *International Journal of Refugee Law* 1; and J Bhabha, 'Boundaries in the Field of Human Rights: International Gatekeepers?: The Tension Between Asylum Advocacy and Human Rights' (2002) 15 *Harvard Human Rights Journal* 155.

1 UNHCR Refugee Children Co-ordination Unit, 'Summary Note on UNHCR's Strategy and Activities concerning Refugee Children' (Geneva, May 2002).

2 The term 'separated children' is used in addition to the term 'unaccompanied children', as experience has shown that refugee children may be accompanied by an extended family member or other adult, but still face risks similar to unaccompanied refugee children: UNHCR's Global Consultations on International Protection, 'Refugee Children' UN Doc EC/GC/02/9 (25 April 2002); UNHCR Refugee Children Co-ordination Unit (n 1 above) 3.

in recent years the figures have been as high as 15 per cent.[3] Although Australia's experience of asylum seekers has always been modest in world terms,[4] it has not been immune to these trends. Between 1 July 1999 and 28 February 2003, 4089 children arrived in Australia and sought protection as refugees. Of these, 290 were classified as 'unaccompanied minors' (a category which generally corresponds to that of 'separated children' as defined by UNHCR). The vast majority were males aged between 15 and 17 years of age.[5] This chapter explores the deficits in the protection afforded to children who seek asylum alone. In so doing, attention is drawn to a more general failure to think about children as refugees in their own right—most particularly within the construct of the Convention relating to the Status of Refugees ('Refugee Convention') and its attendant Protocol ('Protocol').[6]

The particular vulnerability of unaccompanied and separated child asylum seekers has encouraged research in many countries around the world—most recently in the United States, the United Kingdom and Australia.[7] The studies demonstrate that no country can yet lay claim to laws and policies that are truly sensitive to the experiences and needs of these young people. Children travelling alone are seen first through the lens of immigration control, in many instances with damaging consequences for children in need of protection.[8]

[3] UNHCR, 'Trends in Unaccompanied and Separated Children Seeking Asylum in Europe, 2000' (November 2001) <http://www.unhcr.org/statistics/STATISTICS/3c060c804.pdf> (accessed 10 June 2007).

[4] See M Crock, B Saul and A Dastyari, *Future Seekers II: Refugees and Irregular Migration in Australia* (Sydney, Federation Press, 2006) ch 3, esp 34.

[5] Department of Immigration and Multicultural Affairs' response to questions on notice from Senator Harradine, Additional Senate Estimates Hearing (Cth of Australia, 11 February 2003) (copy on file with author). See the discussion in M Crock, *Seeking Asylum Alone: Australia: A Study of Australian Law, Policy and Practice regarding Unaccompanied and Separated Children* (Sydney, Themis Press, 2006) ('*Australian Report*') 39–42. Over a similar period (2000–04), 38,700 asylum claims were lodged in Australia, with 14,926 coming from individuals who arrived in Australia without authorisation: Crock, Saul and Dastyari (n 4 above) 31, 34.

[6] Convention relating to the Status of Refugees (adopted 28 July 1951, entered into force 22 April 1954) 189 UNTS 137; Protocol relating to the Status of Refugees (adopted 31 January 1967, entered into force 4 October 1967) 606 UNTS 267.

[7] See J Bhabha and S Schmidt, *Seeking Asylum Alone: United States: Unaccompanied and Separated Children and Refugee Protection in the US* (Cambridge, MA, Harvard Centre for Human Rights, 2006); J Bhabha and N Finch, *Seeking Asylum Alone: United Kingdom: Unaccompanied and Separated Children and Refugee Protection in the UK* (Sydney, Themis Press, 2006) ('*UK Report*'); *Australian Report* (n 5 above); and J Bhabha and M Crock, *Seeking Asylum Alone: A Comparative Study: Unaccompanied and Separated Children and Refugee Protection in Australia, the UK and the US* (Sydney, Themis Press, 2006) ('*Comparative Report*'). The reports are all available online at <http://www.humanrights.harvard.edu/index> and <http://www.law.usyd.edu.au/scigl.index/>.

[8] Of the three countries studied in the Seeking Asylum Alone project, the United Kingdom stood out as the nation most willing to see the phenomenon of child migrants first and foremost as a child protection issue. Unaccompanied children in that country are placed immediately into foster care and appointed a guardian and legal advisor.

There can be little dispute that unaccompanied and separated children are often exquisitely vulnerable. In many countries, such children face an increased risk of military recruitment, sexual violence, exploitation and abuse, becoming forced labour, denial of access to education and basic assistance and detention.[9] The focus of this chapter, however, is the problems that such children face in their quest for protection outside of their country of origin. In many countries, few or no concessions are made for children who seek asylum alone. Without adequate assistance, it is hardly surprising that many children find the cultural and linguistic challenges of the foreign administrative process insurmountable. Of equal concern is the failure of decision-makers to look at the Refugee Convention from the perspective of the child. Refugee jurisprudence, like asylum processes around the world, has developed with the adult asylum seeker as the norm. While recent years have seen decision-makers becoming more sensitive to interpreting the Convention so as to acknowledge the experiences of women,[10] the specific claims and experiences of persecuted children have been largely unseen and unheard.[11] For a child travelling without a responsible adult guardian, this oversight can mean a failure to gain protection.[12]

For the Refugee Convention to be recognised as relevant to the claims of children, care must be taken to consider the specific nature of the harms

In most cases they are not interviewed unless this is to elicit very basic information about their identity and immediate needs. Even then, however, a reluctance to recognise these children as asylum seekers was identified as a pervasive problem. A mere two per cent of unaccompanied and separated children in that country gain recognition as refugees, with access to all the entitlements that flow from that status under the Refugee Convention. The balance gain a temporary status based on minority, leaving those who pass their 18th birthday in a peculiar limbo. See *Comparative Report* (n 7 above) ch 5.2; and *UK Report* (n 7 above) chs 18 and 19.

[9] See W Ayotte, *Separated Children Coming to Western Europe: Why They Travel and How They Arrive* (London, Save the Children, 2000); *Australian Report* (n 5 above) ch 2; *Comparative Report* (n 7 above) ch 2.

[10] See, eg H Crawley, *Refugees and Gender: Law and Process* (Bristol, Jordans, 2001); T Spijkerboer, *Gender and Refugee Status* (Aldershot, Burlington, 2000); and C Dauvergne, 'The Dilemma of Rights Discourses for Refugees' (2000) 23 *University of New South Wales Law Journal* 56.

[11] On the dangers inherent in interpreting the term 'refugee' from an adult-centred perspective, marginalising the specific claims and experiences of persecuted children, see J Bhabha, 'Demography and Rights: Women, Children and Access to Asylum' (2004) 16 *International Journal of Refugee Law* 1; J Bhabha, 'Boundaries in the Field of Human Rights: International Gatekeepers?: The Tension Between Asylum Advocacy and Human Rights' (2002) 15 *Harvard Human Rights Journal* 155; and S Ruxton, *Separated Children Seeking Asylum in Europe: A Programme for Action* (Stockholm, Save the Children, 2000) 79–80.

[12] In this context, see, eg the statistics provided in relation to the unaccompanied children sent to Nauru for the processing of their refugee claims. Unlike similar children processed on the Australian mainland, these children were given no access to legal advice or assistance. The result was that 32 of the 55 recorded as unaccompanied children at point of entry were returned to Afghanistan in 2001–03: *Australian Report* (n 5 above) 43–4.

that can and do befall them. A child-centred approach to the definition of 'refugee' requires two modifications to most of the asylum processes around the world. Decision-makers need to consider the *procedural* concessions that are necessary if children are to be able to tell their stories and to articulate the dangers that they do (or should) fear.[13] Just as importantly, decision-makers need to read the Refugee Convention with the image of the child front and centre.

The chapter begins by examining the factors that have created an institutional blindness to the experiences of refugee children in many asylum States, using Australia as a case study. The body of the chapter (part 3) is devoted to a reading of the Convention definition of 'refugee' from the perspective of the dispossessed and endangered child. Again, Australia is used as the case study. The chapter concludes in part 4 by outlining the benefits that should flow from adopting the approach advocated.

II. LOST CHILDREN

Although orphaned and abandoned children have always been a distressing by-product of war and natural disasters,[14] the number of children and young people today travelling alone in search of protection is without precedent. How is it that countries of asylum everywhere have been blind to the phenomenon, or at least slow to respond?

In Australia, perhaps the most immediate problem for young asylum seekers has been their novelty. As a country used to receiving *adult* asylum seekers—or, at best, children embedded in family groups seeking refuge—it has been physically and conceptually ill-prepared to deal with children travelling alone.[15] Children have been brought to Australia over many years as part of organised programmes.[16] However, such children have not been agents of their own movement. Indeed, in the days of large-scale child migration, the children were in many respects commodified both in the process of selection abroad and in their resettlement, training

[13] It is beyond the scope of this chapter to explore the procedural aspects of refugee claims for children. These matters are dealt with in the *Australian Report* (n 5 above) pt 3; *Comparative Report* (n 7 above) ch 5. See also M Crock, 'Lonely Refuge: Judicial Responses to Children Seeking Refugee Protection in Australia' (2004) 22 *Law in Context* 120.

[14] See EM Ressler, N Boothby and DJ Steinbock, *Unaccompanied Children: Care and Protection in Wars, Natural Disasters, and Refugee Movements* (New York, Oxford University Press, 1988); *Comparative Report* (n 7 above) ch 2.1; and *Australian Report* (n 5 above) ch 2.

[15] Note that children have arrived as unaccompanied minors over many years, and have generally arrived singly or in pairs. The cases of Simon Odhiambo, Peter Martizi and 'X and Y' in the 1990s are examples in point: see discussion in Crock (n 13 above) 129–32.

[16] See *Australian Report* (n 5 above) ch 2.2.1.

and engagement in Australia.[17] Children presenting as asylum seekers are the antithesis of such child migrants insofar as they come uninvited, and without the guiding and controlling hand of a responsible adult.

Australia's prior experience of asylum seekers was (and to some extent still is) manifest in laws, policies and physical structures framed with adults as the norm. For example, until July 2005, the Migration Act 1958 made no mention of and no concessions for children seeking asylum. The national obsession with the incarceration of non-citizens present in the country without a visa applied equally to adults and children.[18]

The country's resistance to changing its harsh laws and policies in the face of the obvious need and vulnerability of child asylum seekers seems to have its roots in a series of factors that have coloured both the perception of these children and the responses they have engendered.

The first, and perhaps most important, issue has been the general concern about the emergence of the Refugee Convention as a vehicle for subverting the sovereign right of a nation to control its borders. Australia's identity as an island continent, and its geographical isolation from many of the world's trouble-spots, means that its experience of asylum seekers (or mobile refugees in search of refuge) has been very limited. For many Australians, 'refugees' have been a category of migrant, brought into the country through organised humanitarian programmes.[19] Persons entering the country without visas and invoking the Refugee Convention so as to avoid removal have engendered both alarm and deep distrust. While a small number have come directly from countries of alleged persecution,[20] the majority of recent asylum seekers in Australia have passed through various 'safe' countries before arrival. This has led to a discourse on asylum seekers as (abusive) persons who use the Refugee Convention to achieve 'immigration outcomes' rather than to seek protection from immediate danger.[21]

[17] For an account of the grief caused by these programs in the UK, see M Humphreys, *Empty Cradles* (London, Corgi Books, 1983), re-published as *Empty Cradles: One Woman's Fight to Uncover Britain's Most Shameful Secret* (London, Doubleday, 1994). The children transhipped under these programs suffered just as badly: see Senate Community Affairs References Committee, *Lost Innocents: Righting the Record: Report on Child Migration* (Canberra, Cth of Australia, 2001).

[18] The facilities established for the detention of 'unauthorised arrivals' have been the subject of endless debate and controversy because of the generic failure to accommodate the needs of children and vulnerable adults. See Crock, Saul and Dastyari (n 4 above) ch 10.

[19] For an account of Australia's offshore refugee resettlement program, see *ibid*, ch 2, esp 15–17.

[20] A particularly contentious group of such arrivals in recent years has been fugitives from West Papua. In early 2006, the grant of asylum to 42 West Papuans invoked a furious response from Indonesia, leading to a flurry of diplomatic and legislative responses from Australia, which, in turn, engendered passionate disagreement from government back-benchers.

[21] For a sophisticated exposition of this attitude of distrust towards asylum seekers, see Department of Immigration and Multicultural and Indigenous Affairs, *Interpreting the Refugees Convention: An Australian Contribution* (Canberra, Cth of Australia, 2002).

Against this background of general distrust, the second problem is that child asylum seekers have been characterised specifically as vehicles of manipulation and abuse. A most egregious example is the so-called 'children overboard' affair that occurred shortly before the federal election in Australia in October 2001. The 'interdiction' programme instituted in August 2001 to repel unauthorised boat arrivals from Australia gave rise to (unfounded) allegations that asylum seekers had thrown their children into the sea in an attempt to force the Australian navy to rescue them and to bring them to Australia.[22] The children were presented not as objects of pity, but as a means by which the adults in the group might take advantage of the country's 'good nature'. The 'natural' urge to respond with compassion was presented as something to be resisted: any form of compassionate response might be regarded as weakness or foolishness on the country's behalf. For unaccompanied children within Australia, such attitudes have been apparent in a tendency to view the children as 'anchors' for their parents, sent ahead to secure the eventual passage to Australia of the whole family. Again, this is seen as abusive in the sense that an 'immigration outcome' is sought by individuals who would not otherwise meet the criteria for entry to Australia.[23] In the United States, such thinking is apparent in a visa created especially for unaccompanied children, which permanently bars them from sponsoring their foreign parent(s) as a migrant.[24]

A third, related challenge for children seeking asylum alone is the notion that assisting a smuggled or trafficked child will only encourage the parents of other children to consign their offspring to people smugglers or traffickers in the hope of finding a haven abroad. In a variation of a 'you have to be cruel to be kind' argument, a hard line against unaccompanied children is justified as a necessary deterrent to practices that in many instances are abusive of the children involved.

Fourthly, children travelling without a responsible adult can be characterised as threats to civil society—as 'little devils' who lack any form of moral compass or sense of restraint. A restrictive response in this context is seen as elementary self-interest on the part of a receiving State. In many countries, children travelling alone come from backgrounds that are threatening as well as abusive. Children who have been conscripted

[22] The best account of this period in Australia's recent history is D Marr and M Wilkinson, *Dark Victory* (Sydney, Allen & Unwin, 2003). See also P Weller, *Don't Tell the Prime Minister* (Melbourne, Scribe Short Books, 2002).

[23] See the comments of David Manne (solicitor) and Michael Walker (migration agent) interviewed by researchers for the *Australian Report* (n 5 above) ch 3.3.

[24] See the Special Immigrant Juvenile Status Visas, discussed in *Comparative Report* (n 7 above) ch 8.2.

to fight in wars or who have lived in street gangs are a challenge to any host society.[25]

If these preconceptions and challenges have worked against child asylum seekers in Australia, they do not represent the biggest obstacles to ensuring protection outcomes. The research in that country suggests that the negative experiences of children owe more to benign neglect than to hostile ideation. Until recently, there has been a general cultural failure to think about children as agents and as refugees in their own right. Within family groups the tendency was (and still is) to tie the fate of children to that of their responsible adult relatives. Unaccompanied and separated children have forced decision-makers to face the issues of children's entitlements to protection. Even so, the jurisprudence on children as refugees is recent and poorly developed. As the following section demonstrates, many issues have yet to be considered at an appellate level in Australia. In this context, there is much that Australian decision-makers can take from the emerging jurisprudence in comparative jurisdictions.[26]

III. READING CHILDREN INTO THE REFUGEE CONVENTION

The idea that the Refugee Convention can be read so as to accommodate children is neither new nor radical as an idea. UNHCR has issued policies and guidelines on asylum seeker and refugee children in order to ensure that they receive appropriate and effective treatment and assistance.[27] Its 'Guidelines on Policies and Procedures in Dealing with Unaccompanied Children Seeking Asylum' were first published in February 1997. In assessing a child's refugee claims, the Guidelines recommend that

> particular regard ... be given to circumstances such as the child's stage of development, his/her possibly limited knowledge of conditions in the country of origin, and their significance to the legal concept of refugee status, as well as his/her vulnerability.[28]

In Australia, these Guidelines have been adopted to some extent in policies promulgated at both the level of first instance decision-making

[25] See I Cohn and GS Goodwin-Gill, *Child Soldiers: The Role of Children in Armed Conflicts* (Oxford, Oxford University Press, 1994); MS Gallagher, 'Soldier Boy Bad: Child Soldiers, Culture and Bars to Asylum' (2001) 13 *International Journal of Refugee Law* 310; and Bhabha 'Demography' (n 11 above).

[26] See *Comparative Report* (n 7 above) ch 7.

[27] UNHCR Executive Committee, 'UNHCR Policy on Refugee Children' UN Doc E/SCP/82 (6 August 1993); UNHCR, *Refugee Children: Guidelines on Protection and Care* (Geneva, UNHCR, 1994); see also *Australian Report* (n 5 above) ch 4.3.

[28] UNHCR, 'Guidelines on Policies and Procedures in Dealing with Unaccompanied Children Seeking Asylum' (February 1997) para 8.6.

and appellate review.[29] The extent and practical impact of those policies, however, is an open question.

In this section, particular attention is paid to three broad aspects of the Convention definition of 'refugee': (i) the requirement that an individual demonstrate a 'well-founded fear'; (ii) what will be recognised as 'persecution'; and (iii) the grounds on which persecution must be feared. The section will conclude with some brief comments on issues relating to the identity of the persecutor.

A. 'Well-Founded Fear'

The Convention requirement that a refugee exhibit a fear that is 'well-founded' creates problems for children in two respects. Depending on the age of a child, the expectation that a child exhibit fear as an emotion can be misplaced. Fear requires an understanding of a situation and the cognitive ability to apprehend future harm. For very young children this may not be possible. The phenomenon of child soldiers reflects a different facet of cognitive development in this regard: children are often chosen to fight for rebel armies precisely because some do not experience fear in the same way as adults do.[30]

This primary aspect of the refugee definition is relatively easy to adapt to the situation of children: many policies in Australia and in comparative countries of asylum note that the subjective fears expressed by a child (or not expressed, as the case may be) should be given less weight than the objective evidence available about the likely personal safety of a child. The Australian Refugee Review Tribunal's 'Guidelines on Children Giving Evidence' acknowledge that 'child applicants in a refugee matter may not be able to express a subjective fear of persecution in the same manner as an adult applicant'.[31]

They also recognise that children may be unable to present evidence in support of their claims because of their age, gender, cultural background or other circumstances. The Guidelines state that greater allowances should be made for inconsistencies in the evidence of children.

These Guidelines should provide a useful reference point for Australian courts and tribunals. The problem is that decision-makers

[29] For a discussion, see *Australian Report* (n 5 above) ch 6.3, esp 88–90.

[30] Nor do they have the moral compass of the adult to apprehend that what they are doing is both dangerous and 'wrong': see generally Cohn and Goodwin-Gill (n 25 above).

[31] Refugee Review Tribunal, 'Guidelines on Children Giving Evidence' para 5.2 <http://www.rrt.gov.au/publications/RRT%20Guidelines%20on%20Children%20Giving%20Evidence.pdf> (accessed 5 June 2007).

retain substantial discretion in determining what latitude to allow for this purpose, and without greater recognition of the particular needs of unaccompanied and separated child applicants, policies set by domestic or international bodies are unlikely to be applied with any regularity in these cases.[32] The Australian research uncovered at least one case where a young female asylum seeker from Afghanistan was initially 'screened out' of the refugee status process in 2001 because of a failure to express a credible claim. With the conditions in Afghanistan prevailing at the time in question, it should have been obvious that the child had the potential to invoke Australia's protection obligations.[33]

In addition to the requirement that a refugee possess a subjective fear, the test posed by Article 1A(2) of the Refugee Convention implies that 'fear' must also have an objective element, in that the fear of persecution must be 'well-founded'. In Australia, the test has consequently been paraphrased as the question whether there is a 'real chance' of persecution.[34] This second aspect can also pose problems for children because of the general tendency across many societies not to 'hear' children—most particularly when there are adult voices of authority in conflict with the child's view.

For children, the challenge is that their testimony will often be disregarded in favour of objective evidence. For example, the assertion that conditions have changed in a country of origin can be virtually impossible for a child to contest. The Afghan children whose cases were examined for the Australian study are examples in point: regime change in Afghanistan presented substantial obstacles to proving the existence of a well-founded fear of persecution.[35] Even where there have not been changes in the country of origin, the existence of objective evidence that contradicts the lived experience of the child can be an insuperable obstacle. In some respects this situation—and the frustrations it entails—is not peculiar to children.

[32] For example, in one case the Federal Magistrates Court found that aspects of the UNHCR, *Handbook on Procedures and Criteria for Determining Refugee Status under the 1951 Convention and the 1967 Protocol relating to the Status of Refugees* UN Doc HCR/IP/4/Eng/Rev.1, 2nd edn (Geneva 1992) that might have assisted the applicant would have no force in Australian law. Accordingly, no error of law could be identified in the Tribunal's failure to refer to those model procedures when dealing with separated children: see *VFAA v Minister for Immigration and Multicultural and Indigenous Affairs ('MIMIA')* [2003] FMCA 389; and *WAEF v MIMIA* [2002] FCA 1121. Note that s 91X of the Migration Act 1958 (Cth) prohibits the publication of the names of refugee claimants. The letters are the case descriptors used by the Federal and High Courts.

[33] When the child was eventually discovered by a refugee advocate and given assistance, she was promptly recognised as a refugee. See discussion of 'Halimi's' experience in the *Australian Report* (n 5 above) ch 8.2.

[34] *Chan Yee Kin v Minister for Immigration and Ethnic Affairs* (1989) 169 CLR 379 (HCA).

[35] *Australian Report* (n 5 above) chs 11.2 and 11.3 (examining how the children were tested in the refugee status determination process).

However, the obstacle for children will be even more pronounced than for adults, for the simple reason that adult testimony will almost always be preferred over a child's.

Another problem associated with the objective element of the definition and the way 'country information' is used at an appellate level in Australia is the legislation governing both merits review and legal challenges (in the form of judicial review). The country information relied upon by the Refugee Review Tribunal ('Tribunal') is generally a matter for that tribunal. The federal courts, on the other hand, are confined in their power to rule Tribunal decisions unlawful. The insertion into the Migration Act 1958 of a privative clause[36] in 2001 means that the courts will only intervene if it is possible to show that a decision is affected by 'jurisdictional error'—a fundamental legal error. If there is any legal basis at all for the Tribunal's decision, obtaining the intervention of the courts will be impossible.

The difficulties in demonstrating a legal error serious enough to meet the definition of 'jurisdictional error' is illustrated in cases such as *WAEF v Minister for Immigration and Multicultural and Indigenous Affairs* ('*MIMIA*').[37] In that matter, French J held that irregularities in the linguistic analysis relied upon by the decision-maker in the case of an unaccompanied minor were not sufficient to constitute jurisdictional error. His Honour ruled further that the decision-maker did not commit a jurisdictional error in failing to follow guidelines created by UNHCR in assessing the credibility of the young asylum seeker.

In each of the Federal Court decisions studied in the Australian research, the court declined to intervene in the Tribunal's application of particular country information. The case of *SCAW v MIMIA*[38] is an example in point. There, the Tribunal referred to BBC Monitoring Reports when considering the contemporary situation of Hazaras in Afghanistan. These reports quoted a Hazara leader, who expressed happiness at the Taliban's downfall and the newfound freedom of Hazaras to participate in political processes. Citing these reports, the Tribunal found that there was no longer an objective basis for the fears expressed by the applicant. On appeal to the Federal Court, these sources were taken to support the Tribunal's finding against the applicant. It was not necessary for

[36] This is a legislative provision which states on its face that decisions are final and cannot be called into question on any basis in a court of law: Migration Act 1958 (Cth) pt 8. See also C Beaton-Wells, 'Judicial Review of Migration Decisions: Life after s 157' (2005) 33 *Federal Law Review* 141; and M Crock and E Santow, 'Privative Clauses and the Limits of the Law', in M Groves and HP Lee (eds), *Australian Administrative Law: Fundamentals, Principles and Doctrines* (Melbourne, Cambridge University Press, 2007) ch 19.

[37] *WAEF v MIMIA* (n 32 above).

[38] *SCAW v MIMIA* [2002] FCA 810.

the Tribunal to locate reports favouring the applicant's position. It had reached a legitimate finding of fact on the material before it.

Just how durable the change in country circumstances must be before the applicant's fear of persecution loses its objective basis is a contentious matter in many cases. The case of *SFTB v MIMIA* is representative of the jurisprudence examined in the Australian study. In that case, the Tribunal declined to consider the 'durability', significance or effectiveness of the changed circumstances in the applicant's home province of Ghazni in Afghanistan.[39] On appeal to the Full Federal Court, this finding was upheld: the Tribunal was not obligated to consider the durability of peace in the region. It had reached a legitimate finding of fact on the material before it.[40]

The challenge for decision-makers and for those acting for children seeking asylum alone is to reflect carefully on both the selection and interpretation of available objective evidence. For example, there can be a tendency in some cases to focus on changes in a country of origin while failing to acknowledge changes in the asylum-seeking child's situation, which might be equally apposite to the child's protection needs. The child might have become acculturated to the asylum country, placing him or her at risk if he or she were returned to the country of origin.[41] A child-centred approach in these cases would place weight both on what is known of the persecutory experiences of a child in the past, and on how the child is likely to be received as he or she now presents, taking into account both changes in the country of origin and changes in the child himself or herself.[42]

There can also be a tendency to accept evidence presented by apparent experts as probative. Although this response may not disadvantage children more than adults on the face of things, the problem is that the opinion of experts seems to be sought out more often in cases involving children than adults. In Australia, this has been demonstrated by the tendency to subject recordings of interviews with children to language analysis by a private Swedish laboratory as a means of determining the child's country of origin. The same children might also be subjected to intrusive x-rays and bone scans with the objective of determining age.

[39] *SFTB v MIMIA* [2003] FCAFC 108, (2003) 129 FCR 222.

[40] On the issue of changed circumstances, see further *Australian Report* (n 5 above) ch 14.2.1.

[41] The transformation apparent in the young Afghan boys studied for the *Australian Report* (n 5 above) was used as a ground for claiming asylum in some cases, generally without success. See, eg *MIMIA v VFAY* [2003] FCAFC 191; and *STQB v MIMIA* [2004] FCA 882.

[42] For an example of good practice of such an approach in the United States, see *Matter of Chen* Int Dec 3102 (BIA 1989), where a Chinese citizen was granted asylum on the basis of his past experiences of persecution which the Board found to be exacerbated by his youth or identity as a child.

Although both types of scientific inquiry can be very unreliable, there are few cases in Australia where reliance on such tests has been challenged successfully by a child applicant.[43]

B. 'Persecution'

The next requirement is that the child show that what he or she fears amounts to 'persecution'. The recognition of the requisite fear—real or imputed—of a refugee child requires a modification of the decision-maker's behaviour and expectations when assessing children, and a reconsideration of the meaning of 'persecution' from the perspective of a child. The term is not defined in international law, although it has been 'interpreted' under Australian domestic law through a non-exhaustive definition. As Bhabha has argued, the indeterminacy of this central term seems to be deliberate:[44] a recognition of the almost infinite variety in the way human beings mistreat each other.

In Australia, both the legislation and the jurisprudence from the courts have favoured a broad interpretation. In section 91R of the Migration Act 1958, for example, persecution is said to constitute 'serious harm', defined in turn to include (the definition is not exhaustive):

(a) a threat to the person's life or liberty;
(b) significant physical harassment of the person;
(c) significant physical ill-treatment of the person;
(d) significant economic hardship that threatens the person's capacity to subsist;
(e) denial of access to basic services, where the denial threatens the person's capacity to subsist;
(f) denial of capacity to earn a livelihood of any kind, where the denial threatens the person's capacity to subsist.[45]

[43] See, eg *SBBR v MIMIA* [2002] FCA 842; *SBBS v MIMIA* [2002] FCA 842; *WAEF v MIMIA* (n 32 above) (language testing); and *Applicant VFAY v Minister for Immigration* [2003] FMCA 289 (on the use of x-rays).

[44] See Bhabha 'Demography' (n 11 above); Bhabha 'Boundaries' (n 11 above); and *Comparative Report* (n 7 above) ch 7.2.

[45] In the case of *Minister for Immigration and Multicultural Affairs v Ibrahim* [2000] HCA 55, (2000) 204 CLR 1, McHugh J stated (at para 65) that, ordinarily, persecution is:

'— unjustifiable and discriminatory conduct directed at an individual or group for a Convention reason
— which constitutes an interference with the basic human rights or dignity of that person or the persons in the group
— which the country of nationality authorises or does not stop, and
— which is so oppressive or likely to be repeated or maintained that the person threatened cannot be expected to tolerate it, so that flight from, or refusal to return to, that country is the understandable choice of the individual concerned.'

In *Applicant S*, the High Court of Australia confirmed that the characterisation of persecutory behaviour is to be determined by the standards of human rights law and the extent to which an individual is subjected to discriminatory treatment. This, in turn, has given rise to questions about when (if ever) validly enacted laws will (or could) amount to persecution. In the same case, Gleeson CJ, Gummow and Kirby JJ noted that the more 'ad hoc and random' the infliction of harm, the more likely it is that an individual is being subjected to persecution rather than a 'law of general application'.[46] The test is whether a general law has a legitimate objective and uses means proportionate to the objects desired. In *Chen Shi Hai*, the court stated:

> Whether the different treatment of different individuals or groups is appropriate and adapted to achieving some legitimate government objective *depends* on the different treatment involved and, *ultimately, whether it offends the standards of civil societies which seek to meet the calls of common humanity* (emphasis added).[47]

For unaccompanied and separated children seeking asylum alone, this approach has the benefit of expanding the categories of persecutory behaviour to include actions that might be taken in line with either broadscale policies or with the tolerance of the authorities. The relevant standard to be applied is that of the 'civilised and organised society'.

The expansive and inclusive conception implicit in this approach is important, since human rights violations that affect asylum seekers may well fall outside the range of experience and be unfamiliar to domestic fact-finders and decision-makers. It is not just spectacular individual acts that constitute persecution. Lesser measures that do not individually amount to persecution can nevertheless cumulatively constitute persecution where they operate incrementally and in aggregate. This principle is well established in both international and domestic law.

Australia's legislative scheme contains elements that work both for and against children seeking asylum alone. Section 91R of the Migration Act 1958 defines the term 'persecution' in a way that focuses attention on personal violence and traditional types of harm, but also includes other deprivations affecting the ability of a claimant to subsist. This is a non-exclusive definition that could work well for children seeking asylum alone. The problem seems to be that not enough attention has been paid to considering the issue of persecution from the perspective of a child, in a way that acknowledges and prioritises the special vulnerability of children. On the other hand, section 91S of the Migration Act 1958

[46] *Applicant S v MIMIA* [2004] HCA 25, (2004) 217 CLR 387, paras 39–49, discussing the High Court ruling in *Minister for Immigration and Multicultural Affairs v Israelian* (2001) 206 CLR 323 (HCA).

[47] *Chen Shi Hai v Minister for Immigration and Multicultural Affairs* [2000] HCA 19, (2000) 201 CLR 293, 317.

operates to restrict the ability to rely on the persecutory experiences of family members (alive or dead) where these cannot be tied directly to the Refugee Convention definition of 'refugee'.

In the case of unaccompanied and separated children, the denial of family protection, education and other citizenship rights clearly constitutes an interference with basic human rights and dignity within the meaning of section 91R. As noted earlier, unaccompanied and separated children face an increased risk of a variety of harms, including detention and denial of access to education and basic assistance.[48] These are matters which have the potential to affect the right of such children to subsist.

There are at least three ways in which 'persecution' can manifest itself for children.[49] Children can face persecution that is similar or identical to the types of persecution faced by adults. However, they can also be at risk because of persecution that only applies to children. For example, only children can be victims of the various iterations of child abuse, and only children can be forced into under-age marriage or be conscripted as child soldiers or as members of child street gangs. Finally, there are threatened or actual harms that might not constitute persecution for adults, but that become persecutory in the case of children because of their special vulnerability.

It is a striking feature of the cases studied for the Australian study that the persecution feared tended to be similar or identical to the types of persecution feared by adults. For the 85 children whose cases were examined, persecutory conduct included the abduction, conscription and murder of male relatives by the Taliban, and direct physical threats to the children themselves. For male applicants, fear of being conscripted or killed overwhelmingly provided the impetus for fleeing.

In such instances, even when children are unaccompanied or separated from their families, the persecution alleged may not need to include reference to any child-specific features. Though the separated status of children may give rise to special procedural problems, it does not necessarily constitute an issue for the substantive adjudication of the asylum claim. No special account of child persecution is therefore required. However, even in these 'mainstream' cases, child-specific issues may arise and be neglected. For example, a child may be persecuted as part of an oppressed minority group in order to increase pressure on politically prominent or targeted parents. Officials and judges who ignore child-specific factors may miss such a dynamic and overlook the particular risks facing such a child.

International instruments that are protective of children—most particularly the United Nations Convention on the Rights of the

[48] Cohn and Goodwin-Gill (n 25 above); Gallagher (n 25 above); Bhabha 'Demography' (n 11 above).

[49] See further *Comparative Report* (n 7 above) chs 7.2 and 7.3.

Child[50]—have been invoked in many cases involving unaccompanied children seeking asylum. In the most contentious cases, the focus of argument appears to have been on using these instruments to invoke rights on behalf of the child: for example, to assert a child's right to be released from detention or to have appointed an effective legal guardian. However, there have also been cases in which the denial of rights enshrined in this treaty has been invoked as evidence of persecution.[51]

i. Persecution That Only Applies to Children

Situations of persecution that are specific to children arise when the fact that the applicant is a child is central to the harm inflicted or feared. The most obvious examples involve persecution that can only be inflicted on a child. Only children can be conscripted as child soldiers, subjected to child abuse, recruited into gangs of street children, threatened with infanticide or pre-puberty female circumcision, subjected to child sale or marriage, or made to suffer persistent discrimination as 'second children' or as street children.

In these cases, an understanding of child-specific persecution is critical to the success of an asylum claim. Until recently, many of the categories of child-specific persecution listed above were not considered to fall within the asylum rubric at all. This is not because the behaviour concerned did not have the hallmarks of serious harm or a threat to life and freedom, but because a traditional conception of the limits of persecution hampered both advocates and decision-makers in pursuing and advancing such claims. Given the rapidly expanding scope of human rights norms, and of global knowledge of rights violations inflicted on children, it is critical that the concept of persecution central to the adjudication of asylum claims keeps in step.

In Australia, the High Court has recognised that children born in contravention of China's 'one child policy' can be refugees in their own right. However, it did not do so until adverse findings had been made in a string of 'one child policy' cases, in which it would appear that no-one thought to lodge *separate* refugee claims for such children. In the late 1990s, considerable controversy arose in Australia over whether key aspects of the Chinese policy—including practices of forced abortion and sterilisation—could amount to persecution, given that the policy was one of general application. The High Court overruled lower courts on this point in 1997, stating that the test should be the nature of the harms inflicted, and not the question whether the harms were caused by government officials following

[50] Convention on the Rights of the Child (adopted 20 November 1989, entered into force 2 September 1990) 1577 UNTS 3.

[51] See, eg RRT Reference: V96/04554 (12 July 1996) and V96/04555 (12 July 1996). Compare RRT Reference: V04/17382 [2005] RRTA 51 (28 April 2005).

orders.[52] It was not until three years later that the same court accepted that children excluded from key aspects of participation in Chinese society (because they were born in contravention of the 'one child policy') could be refugees.[53] The change came only after a major scandal in which a Chinese woman, denied asylum in Australia and returned to China, was forced to have her unborn child aborted at 38 weeks' gestation.[54] Ironically, the child recognised in *Chen Shi Hai* as a refugee in 2000 was born to a refugee family who arrived in Australia on the same boat as the ill-fated Chinese woman. They managed to avoid removal.

ii. Behaviour Which Constitutes Persecution for a Child but Not an Adult

The third, and perhaps most contentious, category of child persecution involves situations where the behaviour complained of should be considered persecution when inflicted on or threatened against a child, even though the same behaviour may not rise to the level of persecution in the case of an adult. Although courts in the United States have begun to explore this concept,[55] the jurisprudence in Australia has yet to venture into this territory.

What is advocated here is the recognition that persecution should be regarded as a relative term, with an appropriate inquiry directed at consideration of the personal impact of the harm inflicted. In tort law, an equivalent rule might be the 'eggshell skull' rule, which recognises that the perpetrator of harm must face the consequences even if a victim is unusually vulnerable because of a physical attribute of some kind.[56] In the same way, consideration needs to be given to the particular

[52] *Applicants A and B v Minister for Immigration and Multicultural Affairs* (1997) 190 CLR 225 (HCA). Note, however, that the High Court ruled in that case that parents fleeing China to escape the persecutory practices associated with the policy were not refugees. This was because the parents could not demonstrate that they were being persecuted for one of the five Convention reasons. The court ruled that the parents could not be said to belong to a 'particular social group' because such groups must be seen to exist independently of a shared experience of persecution. See M Crock, 'Apart from Us or a Part of Us: Immigrants' Rights, Public Opinion and the Rule of Law' (1998) 10 *International Journal of Refugee Law* 49; and C Dauvergne, 'Chinese Fleeing Sterilisation: Australia's Response against a Canadian Backdrop' (1998) 10 *International Journal of Refugee Law* 77.

[53] *Chen Shi Hai* (n 47 above).

[54] The scandal spawned a major Senate inquiry into Australia's refugee program: Senate Legal and Constitutional References Committee, *A Sanctuary under Review: An Examination of Australia's Refugee and Humanitarian Processes* (Canberra, Cth of Australia, 2000).

[55] See, eg *Mei Dan Liu v Ashcroft* 380 F 3d 307 (7th Cir 2004). Note that while the court agreed that age can be a significant factor in determining whether an incident amounts to persecution, it rejected the contention that what the applicant had experienced amounted to persecution. The court held: 'There may be situations where children should be considered victims of persecution though they have suffered less harm than would be required for an adult. But this is not such a case. Though a minor, Mei Dan was near the age of majority—she was sixteen—at the time the events took place. Whatever slight calibration this may warrant in our analysis is insufficient to transform her experiences with the Chinese authorities from harassment to persecution'.

[56] See *Smith v Leech Brain & Co Ltd* [1962] 2 QB 405 (CA).

sensitivities of children, taking into account their youth, life experiences and developmental stage. For children seeking asylum alone, regard must be had to the extra vulnerability of children who are without the usual protection of a responsible adult.

While a threat that involves relatively minor beatings, incarceration or aggressive questioning might not constitute persecution for an adult, it could do for a child. What is required is a consideration of how a vulnerable child might respond to the treatment complained of. What is likely to be the emotional response evoked and how is a child likely to be affected in the longer term? A child-centred perspective would identify behaviour that is likely to affect a child in the longer term as persecution. A contrasting approach might miss the significance of the experience to the child and/or trivialise its impact on the applicant. It is not only conduct directed at a child that can elicit this heightened response. Actions that target close relatives, such as parents or siblings, may also terrorise and traumatise a child so as to constitute persecution, in circumstances where an adult would not be so affected.

Children's vulnerability in the face of separation or loss of family is widely acknowledged. Forced separation from parents, such as where the latter are detained or where children are abandoned or neglected, may in some circumstances constitute persecution for a child where similar separation for an adult could not be so considered. The same argument applies to children who become homeless as a result of domestic abuse or family destitution and who are, as a result, deprived of basic social and economic rights, such as access to schooling, housing and health care. They are not merely clear candidates for welfare protection or foster care, as a matter of immediate social provision. Where such domestic protection is unavailable, these children may meet the 'persecutory' requirements of the Convention definition of 'refugee'. Again, international benchmarks such as the Convention on the Rights of the Child should be used as guidance in determining what might constitute persecutory experiences, in the event that these rights are not available in the receiving or home State.

As far as the statutory definition of 'persecution' is concerned in the Australian context, the issue here is the interpretation of what constitutes 'serious harm' for a child for the purposes of section 91R of the Migration Act 1958. Put simply, there is nothing in Australian domestic law that prevents decision-makers from adopting different standards according to whether a claimant is an adult or a child. The issue, rather, seems to be that decision-makers and advocates have not been thinking seriously enough about children.

C. The Convention 'Grounds'

The next step for children seeking asylum is to tie the persecution feared to one of the five Refugee Convention grounds—race, religion, nationality, membership of a particular social group or political opinion. Each raises issues for children, and for children seeking asylum alone in particular.

i. Race, Religion and Nationality

The grounds invoked most frequently in children's refugee claims are those involving unchanging characteristics on the part of the claimant, which can accommodate either adults or children. In a country torn apart by racial, ethnic or religious divisions, it is often relatively easy to demonstrate the requisite nexus between the persecution feared and the race, religion or nationality grounds. Successful claims in these cases do not always require applicants to do anything: it is enough that a person is *perceived* to belong to a particular sect or religion and is liable to be persecuted for this reason.[57]

Cases involving claims based on nationality can raise issues of persecution that are specific to children. For example, a child might be denied all forms of schooling because of his or her nationality (or lack of nationality), or a child might face deportation to a dangerous location from the only country he or she has known as home due to immigration rules excluding the child and/or the family. Children of mixed marriages in segregated societies can be at risk from both sides of a racial divide. These examples demonstrate either harms specific to childhood, or actions that have the potential to cause harm to a child that is disproportionate to the impact that the same event might have on an adult.

Children from minority nationalities can also face discrimination that is particularly harsh in its impact on their cultural or linguistic identity: forcing children to speak or learn in the language of a dominant group is a potent weapon in the destruction of the social fabric of a minority group. Such children can also be denied access to work and involvement in the broader community. Again, a child-centred approach to the definition of 'refugee' might recognise these experiences as persecution on the basis of nationality. In Australia, much will depend on what a decision-maker is prepared to recognise as seriously harmful to a child.[58]

ii. Political Opinion

The political opinion ground in the Convention definition of 'refugee' represents problems for children where decision-makers approach a case with their own cultural bias or assumptions about the roles that children play in society. Whereas children in affluent western societies

[57] See *Kuldip Ram v Minister for Immigration and Ethnic Affairs* (1995) 130 ALR 314 (FCAFC).

[58] See *Chen Shi Hai* (n 47 above).

often exist in a sphere that is ignorant of and totally removed from the world of politics, this is simply not true of children in many developing societies and, more significantly, in societies that are rent by conflict. In such cases, it can be erroneous to assume that a child is too young or immature to hold a political opinion, or indeed to be of interest to an opposition party.

The challenge here is for decision-makers to be sensitive not just to the conditions prevailing in a particular country, but also to the cultural mores, expectations and realities as they affect children. Researchers for the Australian study collected evidence from one practitioner whose young client's case was dismissed by a decision-maker who had openly compared her own child's behaviour and abilities to those asserted by the young asylum seeker.[59]

A child's capacity to hold a political opinion is a question of fact that needs to be determined in a way that takes into account cultural understandings and practices, as well as the child's maturity, intelligence and ability to articulate thoughts. In some very conflicted societies, such an analysis could almost start from the presumption that children are politically engaged. By the same token, much will also depend on the experiences of the children involved. The children considered for the Australian study did not fall neatly into categories for this purpose. Some were acutely aware of the politics of their situation, both in Afghanistan and in Australia. However, a significant number suffered in their asylum claims because their parents had been overprotective of them, forcing them to live cosseted lives in both physical and political terms.[60]

A second issue for children in these matters is the assumption that persecutors do not target children for political reasons because of their inferior place in society. Such attitudes miss the obvious point that children can be targeted because they are good 'soft' targets. Easy to harm, the targeting of children is also an effective mechanism for inducing stress in a targeted community—both at the intimate level of family and in the broader community. Many refugees attest that harms perpetrated on children have a greater impact on them than direct physical harm to their own person. In many countries, children have no option but to immerse themselves in the political battles of their kin. Children may have political opinions attributed or imputed to them, and this may also lead to persecution. Decision-makers need to be alert to these realities.

59 Author interview with Mary Anne Kenny (Southern Communities Advocacy Legal and Education Service, Perth, Western Australia) (24 November 2004).

60 See, eg young people like 'GS', whose story is described in the *Australian Report* (n 5 above) ch 3.3, esp 57.

iii. Particular Social Group

One of the most interesting and potentially fruitful grounds for refugee children is the catch-all 'membership of a particular social group' category. The starting point in interpreting the phrase 'particular social group' has been traditionally to seek out groups with some 'immutable' or unchanging characteristics on the one hand or, on the other, association between members of a group. The Canadian Supreme Court in *Canada v Ward*[61] provided three examples of such groupings: (a) groups identified by an innate or unchangeable characteristic; (b) groups whose members associate voluntarily for reasons fundamental to their human dignity; and (c) groups associated by a former voluntary status, unalterable due to its historical permanence. The Australian courts have expanded these categories by confirming that association between members is not a prerequisite for a 'social group'. Because the Convention requirement is that persecution be *by reason of* membership of a social group, it is accepted that the existence or otherwise of a group is less important than the *perception* that such a group exists.[62]

In some cases, group membership for the child asylum applicant will be defined by a child's minority and a form of child-specific persecution. As noted earlier, there are many ways in which children in unsettled societies can be targeted for harmful practices. The street children in many South American countries are periodically persecuted by governments, and across the world, children are conscripted as soldiers, with devastating impacts on them. On the other hand, a government's indifference to or acquiescence in harmful practices can be equally damaging to children. One example is the governmental failure in many developing countries to proscribe female circumcision, child marriage or other abusive treatment of children. Malignant intent on behalf of a government in such cases is not a requirement for an individual to be entitled to protection as a refugee.[63]

While the Taliban were in control in Afghanistan, the vast majority of the young Afghan asylum seekers in Australia had little difficulty in gaining recognition as refugees on the same bases as their adult counterparts. Many were Shiite Hazara—members of a group widely accepted as being at risk of persecution from the predominantly Pashtun Taliban on grounds of both ethnicity and religion. After the fall of the Taliban-controlled government, however, the children lost the comfort of the broad

[61] *Canada v Ward* [1993] 2 SCR 689 (SCC).

[62] See *Kuldip Ram* (n 57 above) 317; *Chen Shi Hai* (n 47 above) and *Minister for Immigration and Multicultural Affairs v Zamora* (1998) 85 FCR 458 (FCA).

[63] In the US context, see, eg *Matter of Kasinga* 21 I & N Dec 357 (BIA 1996); *Pitcherskaia v INS* 118 F 3d 641 (9th Cir 1997).

and accepting approach that had until then been taken towards Afghan asylum seekers.

The predominant view in the lower federal courts has been that unaccompanied and separated children cannot be identified as belonging to a 'particular social group' in their own right for the purposes of the refugee definition. In 2003, the Full Federal Court heard two cases that raised precisely these issues. *Applicants SHBB v MIMIA*[64] and *MIMIA v VFAY*[65] concerned unaccompanied children who claimed to have fled forcible conscription by the Taliban. Different arguments were raised about the social groups to which young people in the applicants' situation might belong. However, in both instances the court upheld the rejection of the boys' claims on the basis that the undisputed vulnerability of unaccompanied and separated children did not mean that they faced persecution *by reason of* their membership of a cognisable social group. In *SHBB*,[66] the court held that the Tribunal had made a defensible finding of fact that Afghan society does not recognise 'young males without a protector' as a social group. In *VFAY*, the court ruled that it was not enough to show that the general conditions in Afghanistan might have a differential impact on some groups. A well-founded fear in itself does not create refugee status. The fear of persecution must be *by reason of* the individual's membership of a particular social group.

A subsequent ruling from the High Court of Australia suggests that these Federal Court rulings may no longer represent good law in Australia.[67] The case of *Applicant S* concerned a young Afghan male of Pashtun ethnicity who fled Afghanistan after twice narrowly avoiding recruitment by the Taliban.[68] The Tribunal rejected the man's refugee claim on the basis that he was not 'targeted to the extent that he was listed or registered for recruitment' by the Taliban. He was merely seen as a young, able-bodied man who was available in a particular area at a particular time. The High Court upheld the first instance ruling by Carr J to the effect that this characterisation of the applicant's case revealed a failure to consider at all whether the applicant belonged to a 'particular social group' for the purposes of the Refugee Convention.[69]

64 *Applicants SHBB v MIMIA* [2003] FMCA 82, (2003) 175 FLR 304.

65 *MIMIA v VFAY* (n 41 above).

66 *Applicants SHBB v MIMIA* (n 64 above) para 57.

67 In fact, both *Applicants SHBB v MIMIA* (n 64 above) and *VFAY* (n 41 above) appealed to the High Court of Australia. After the ruling in *Applicant S* (n 46 above) their cases were settled by consent before going to hearing.

68 *Applicant S* (n 46 above).

69 *Ibid*. See also *Applicant S v Minister for Immigration and Multicultural Affairs* [2001] FCA 1411.

The High Court concluded that both the Full Federal Court and the Tribunal fell into legal error in their characterisation of the claimant's status. The Full Court had erroneously advocated a subjective test (perceptions of individuals *by the Afghan community*), while the Tribunal had asked itself the wrong questions by failing to consider whether young, able-bodied men in Afghanistan emerge as a distinct group when seen in the light of 'legal, social, cultural and religious norms prevalent in Afghan society'.[70]

For the unaccompanied children at the heart of the applications in *SHBB* and *VFAY*, the ruling in *Applicant S* provides cause for hope. In a society where family ties and clan allegiances determine virtually all aspects of a person's daily existence, such children take on dramatically different characteristics depending on whether a subjective (inter-societal) perspective or an objective (third party) perspective is used. Stripped of clan relationships and protection, unaccompanied children are at once manifestly at risk and invisible within Afghan society. The adoption of the subjective test approach explains why the Tribunal in both *SHBB* and *VFAY* found that the young people did not constitute a particular social group. If an *objective* test is used, however, the results are starkly different. The children stand out as a 'particular social group' not because their youth makes them vulnerable, but because social, cultural and legal factors within Afghan society mark the children as different or distinct within the community. The dislocation of the children distinguishes them from the wider body of children in Afghanistan with whom they share the heightened vulnerability to harm common to all children in situations of war and deprivation.

There is another aspect of the High Court's ruling in *Applicant S* that is likely to benefit children who seek asylum alone in Australia. The court also considered the question whether laws or policies of general application, or behaviours that are not predicated on 'enmity or malignity', can ever constitute persecution for the purposes of the Refugee Convention. In *Applicant S*, the Minister argued that young, able-bodied men could not be refugees because the Taliban 'merely sought to harness the valued resource of those capable of fighting'.[71] The fact that young conscripts might die or suffer harm in the fighting did not mean that the regime was trying to rid itself of the young men. The court rejected this submission in a ruling that provides a welcome indication that legal formalism should not be allowed to override basic notions of human rights in the interpretation of the Refugee Convention.

If children can constitute a particular social group for the purposes of the Refugee Convention, there is one respect in which they stand in

[70] See *Applicant S* (n 46 above) para 50.
[71] *Ibid*, para 37.

a somewhat unique position. If the phrase has been interpreted so as to favour individuals with immutable characteristics of some kind, children stand apart in that childhood is a transient state. Children can therefore 'age out' of a particular social group as they reach their majority.

D. State Involvement in Persecution Feared

There is one other aspect of the Convention definition of 'refugee' that can operate as a barrier to children seeking asylum. In Australia, as in many countries of asylum, issues have arisen about the status of people who fear harm at the hands of individuals who may not be acting immediately as agents of a State's government. Although opinions have varied among the judiciary, the dominant view in Australia is that random violence at the hands of non-State actors will not entitle a person to recognition as a refugee. This is because the view has been taken that the Refugee Convention operates to secure the protection of persons who are in some way denied the natural protection of the State. Absent some link back to the State, 'simple' victims of human rights abuse are not regarded as refugees.

This approach represents a problem for children because children are more likely to suffer harm at the hands of private actors. Examples include children sold by their parents to traffickers, and children at risk of being forced into prostitution, slave labour or other abusive conditions if returned to their countries of origin. In many instances the harms feared occur largely in the 'private' domain, rather than at the hands of government operatives.

Recent decisions in cases involving women victims of domestic violence demonstrate that it is not impossible to find scope for the Refugee Convention to apply in situations where harms occur, or are likely to occur, at the hands of non-State actors.[72] In these cases, attention was drawn to the role played by the State in supporting perpetrators of the harms feared and, conversely, the tendency for harms inflicted on women to be trivialised or ignored altogether. For children in many countries, it would not be difficult to identify similar patterns of malign neglect or abuse being actively ignored by State authorities.[73] The trouble for children, as for women in years past, is that decision-makers in countries of asylum have failed to look for or to see these realities.

[72] *Minister for Immigration and Multicultural Affairs v Khawar* [2002] HCA 14, (2002) 187 ALR 574.

[73] For example, see the critiques made about the gendered nature of the definition, summarised most recently and comprehensively in Crawley (n 10 above). See also Spijkerboer (n 10 above); K Walker, 'New Uses of the Refugees Convention: Sexuality and Refugee Status' in S Kneebone (ed), *The Refugees Convention 50 Years On: Globalisation and International Law* (Aldershot, Ashgate Publishing, 2003).

In 2004, arguments were made in one case that went some way to characterising child-specific persecution.[74] The child in question was born after the (negative) assessment of her parents' claim, which is how she came to seek asylum in her own right. Even though the child's parents were found not to be refugees, it was argued that the disadvantages that would be visited on the child if removed from Australia should be regarded as persecution. Interestingly, the Tribunal accepted the child's refugee claim in spite of the parents having received an adverse assessment. However, it did so after carefully dismissing the submissions made about child-specific persecution involving generic assertions of harms done to 'children born into a family in difficult circumstances' or to the 'children of dissident families'. The Tribunal rejected arguments that the child was at increased risk of being abused, physically and sexually, either through being kidnapped and sold into trafficking, or forced ultimately into prostitution. It held that:

> Both perspectives rely on state complicity or indifference to bring the applicant's anticipated exploitation within the scope of the Convention. However, the Tribunal is not satisfied by the evidence from external sources … that either the government of XXX or its agents are commonly involved in the exploitation of children or indifferent to children at risk of exploitation.[75]

In essence, the Tribunal relied on new information advanced about the persecution that the parents would face if forced to return to the country from which they had fled, using this as the basis for accepting that the child would face serious discrimination in matters such as housing, access to education and the ability to earn a livelihood. The child was therefore recognised as a refugee on the basis of her parents' (implied) refugee status and her membership of the particular social group constituted by her family.[76] The child's parents were subsequently granted Protection Visas on the basis of the new information.

It is important to note that the norm among both legal advisers and government decision-makers has not been to insist on the articulation of separate refugee claims by children embedded in a family group. Until this occurs, it is difficult to see how the refugee claims of children will be given the attention they deserve. The case discussed above suggests that decision-makers remain wary about expanding the categories of cases in which refugee status will be recognised. In a political environment where asylum seekers and irregular migrants remain deeply unpopular, such attitudes are not surprising, although they are disappointing.

[74] See *Case N04/49908* (13 January 2005) (copy on file with author).
[75] *Ibid*, 40.
[76] See *Case N04/49908* (n 74 above).

IV. CONCLUSION

The refugee definition of the Refugee Convention must be interpreted in an age- and gender-sensitive manner, taking into account the particular motives for, and forms and manifestations of, persecution experienced by children. Persecution of the kin; under-age recruitment; trafficking of children for prostitution; and sexual exploitation or subjection to female genital mutilation are some of the child-specific forms and manifestations of persecution which may justify the granting of refugee status if such acts are related to one of the Refugee Convention grounds. States should, therefore, give utmost attention to such child-specific forms and manifestations of persecution, as well as gender-based violence, in national refugee status determination procedures.[77]

Although the phenomenon of children seeking asylum alone is beginning to force consideration of children as Convention refugees in their own right, it is fair to say that for a long time children have been unseen and unheard in refugee status determination processes around the world. Recent research suggests that Australia does not present an exception to the rule, even though some interesting case law has begun to emerge. The fundamental problem is that insufficient attention has been paid to the plight of displaced children. Just as importantly, insufficient use has been made of the flexibility within the international definition of 'refugee'.

In Australia, no effective concessions were made for children at all until the middle of 2005, when the policy of the indiscriminate detention of all unauthorised arrivals (regardless of age, health or level of risk) was modified so as to allow for the presumptive release of children. Policies have now been drafted which acknowledge the special challenges that inhere in any process requiring children to be interviewed. What is needed now is a more comprehensive overhaul of immigration and refugee status determination processes, to place children front and centre in the minds of politicians and policy-makers.

Perhaps most importantly, efforts need to be made to increase the general knowledge about conditions affecting children in countries of origin. Attention needs to be drawn to the plight of children in countries affected by war, internal unrest and other disruptions to civil society. A new discourse needs to develop on 'child persecution' within the jurisprudence on refugee protection. Within the administrative process, arrangements need to be put in place to ensure that children are afforded the support and advice they need in order to give an appropriate account of their

[77] Committee on the Rights of the Child, 'General Comment No 6: Treatment of Unaccompanied and Separated Children outside Their Country of Origin' UN Doc CRC/GC/2005/6 (1 September 2005).

situation. In addition to the appointment of guardians and legal advisers, more attention needs to be given across the board to the training of all officials involved in the reception and evaluation of children seeking protection. The deficiencies identified in the course of the Australian research into unaccompanied and separated children occurred at every level in the asylum process. By and large, advocates assigned to assist children have been as ill-equipped to handle children's cases and as ignorant of the child protection potential of the Refugee Convention as officials and bureaucrats. What is needed is a reorientation in approach to the situation of children within the asylum regime, acknowledging harms when they threaten children, and hearing the voices of children when they speak. This needs to occur both at the level of decision-making and advocating the claims of children seeking asylum—most particularly children seeking asylum alone.

7

Wearing Thin: Restrictions on Islamic Headscarves and Other Religious Symbols

BEN SAUL

ORDINARILY, WHAT ONE chooses to wear is a personal matter, influenced by cultural questions of taste, fashion, the household budget, climate and workplace conformism, but not normally circumscribed by law or State intervention. There have always been some regulatory limits on clothing, such as garments required, or prohibited, for occupational health and safety reasons. Normally, such rules are easily comprehended and well understood; few doubt the wisdom of banning neckties when operating high-speed machinery, or requiring white gowns in industries where hygiene is paramount. Restrictions of this kind usually generate little protest, though they may sometimes be inconvenient, or offend one's personal sense of style.

In recent years, it is ironic that something as innocuous as a simple headscarf has been elevated to an iconic symbol of civilisational struggle, a site of political, cultural, religious, social and legal controversy not only in Western Europe, but across Asia, the Middle East, the Americas and borderlands such as Turkey. Particularly as Muslims have migrated as refugees or as other migrants to new societies, or come to live alongside other religious groups in pluralistic societies (including outside the west), the headscarf has come to function as a metonym for an acutely perceived collision of different cultural and religious forms. It has played a part in triggering extensive debates about the future of multiculturalism, integration, assimilation, the scope and limits of religious freedom, the risks of fundamentalism, and the values of secular, liberal democratic orders and their commitment to human rights.

In some ways, the wearing of the Islamic headscarf has attracted public prominence out of all proportion to its objective significance, as it has become an emotive question of values, sentiment and prejudice, as much as it may be a legitimate question of human rights, religious freedom or public order in some circumstances. Particularly after the terrorist attacks of 11 September 2001, the popular association of radical Islam with terrorism has invested the headscarf with potent new meanings and anxieties, 'securitising' it and demarcating it as a highly visible sign of a seemingly existential threat to western civilisation. One Italian politician seamlessly suggested that anti-terrorism laws forbidding the wearing of masks should apply to the wearing of the Islamic veil,[1] as if the two were an equivalent and indistinguishable threat.

Of course, wearing (or not wearing) the headscarf, or other forms of Islamic dress, carries very different consequences and connotations in different parts of the world. Being veiled or unveiled in the Taliban's Kabul, Mecca or Tehran is very different from being veiled or unveiled in London, Paris or Berlin. Certainly in some contexts, there is an undercurrent of extremism swirling around headscarves, which occasionally erupts in ugliness. In Pakistan, the Punjab's Minister for Social Welfare, Zilla Huma Usman, was shot dead in early 2007 for not wearing a veil at a public meeting.[2] Before shooting her, the gunman asked: 'Why aren't you in Islamic dress?'.

While the meaning of wearing a headscarf (and there are many different types) is inevitably context-specific, in western popular and political discourse it is often too easily portrayed as uni-dimensional: the wearer being a fanatic and proselytiser, burdened by it at the insistence of men, and threatened with stoning or acid should she take it off. The paradox in such stereotyping is manifest: the Muslim woman is at once a victim (of men) and an aggressor (forcing the veil on to others).[3] Yet, for some women, invisibility is a blessing not a curse; choosing to wear the veil can be an act of empowerment and a realisation of gender equality, rather than its antithesis, and certainly not some kind of false consciousness in which women fail to understand that they are acting as passive instruments of male desire.

What is extraordinary in the global public discourse about Islamic headscarves is the degree to which those not wearing headscarves have felt it their place to criticise those who wear them, regardless of the specific circumstances of different wearers. The former British Foreign Minister, Jack Straw, famously called for Islamic women in his constituency

[1] C Fraser, 'Protection for Italy Veil Row MP' BBC News (23 October 2006) <http://news.bbc.co.uk/2/hi/europe/6078392.stm> (accessed 25 June 2007).

[2] B Loudon, 'Preacher Kills MP over Veil' *The Australian* (22 February 2007) <http://www.theaustralian.news.com.au/story/0,20867,21266579-2703,00.html> (accessed 25 June 2007). Ms Usman was in fact wearing a traditional shalwar kameez (a tunic and baggy pants), which is acceptable to most religious scholars, but the gunman believed she should have been wearing a dupatta (a traditional veil covering the head).

[3] C Evans, 'The "Islamic Scarf" in the European Court of Human Rights' (2006) 7 *Melbourne Journal of International Law* 52 at 72.

to stop wearing the full veil (niqab) over their faces, since it was a 'a visible statement of separation and of difference' which made 'better, positive relations between the two communities difficult'.[4] Former British Prime Minister, Tony Blair, agreed that it is 'a mark of separation',[5] while the former, Australian Prime Minister, John Howard, described the full burqa as 'confronting' (without giving reasons).[6] When another Australian politician called for headscarves to be banned in schools, the Prime Minister did not disagree on principle, but merely said that it would be 'impractical' since it might also affect Jews and Sikhs.

If the wearing of religious clothing has become a cultural and political flashpoint, it has also generated considerable efforts at regulation in many societies. In Egypt, where Islam is the State religion and Sharia law is the main source of legislation, women who wear the headscarf are nonetheless banned from presenting programmes on State-owned television,[7] in an effort to contain the growth of radical Islam. In Tunisia, the government has begun to enforce a 1981 decree that bans women from wearing Islamic headscarves in schools and government offices, again in order to constrain extremism.[8] Singapore recently banned headscarves in schools to prevent tensions between the ethnic Chinese majority and the Malay Muslim minority; while the Malaysian Federal Court in the *Serban case* in 2006 confirmed the expulsion of three students who disobeyed school regulations which prohibited wearing Islamic turbans (serban).[9]

In Europe, there has been a long and well-known debate in France about restricting the headscarf in schools, and since 2006 France has banned 'signs and dress that conspicuously show the religious affiliation

[4] M Taylor and V Dodd, '"Take off the Veil", Says Straw—to Immediate Anger from Muslims' *The Guardian* (6 October 2006) 1.

[5] J Shaulis, 'UK Teaching Aide to Appeal Tribunal Ruling on Muslim Veil Suspension' *Jurist* (20 October 2006) <http://jurist.law.pitt.edu/paperchase/2006/10/uk-teaching-aide-to-appeal-tribunal.php> (accessed 25 June 2007).

[6] F Farouque, 'Howard Wants to See the Back of Burqa' *The Age* (28 February 2006) <http://www.theage.com.au/news/national/pm-wants-to-see-the-back-of-burqa/2006/02/27/1141020024463.html> (accessed 25 June 2007).

[7] M Abdelhadi, 'Egypt TV "Bans Veiled Presenters"' BBC News (6 September 2003) <http://news.bbc.co.uk/1/hi/world/middle_east/3087220.stm> (accessed 25 June 2007); H Saleh, 'Egypt Minister in Headscarf Row' BBC News (21 November 2006) <http://news.bbc.co.uk/2/hi/africa/6169170.stm> (accessed 25 June 2007). The Egyptian Culture Minister was, however, pressured to resign by his own ruling party after stating that wearing the headscarf was 'regressive' and not required by Islam.

[8] H Saleh, 'Tunisia Moves against Headscarves' BBC News (15 October 2006) <http://news.bbc.co.uk/2/hi/africa/6053380.stm> (accessed 25 June 2007); M Abdelhadi, 'Tunisia Attacked over Headscarves' BBC News (26 September 2006) <http://news.bbc.co.uk/2/hi/africa/5382946.stm> (accessed 25 June 2007).

[9] J Pantesco, 'Malaysia High Court Rules Turban Ban in Schools Constitutional' *Jurist* (12 July 2006) <http://jurist.law.pitt.edu/paperchase/2006/07/malaysia-high-court-rules-turban-ban.php> (accessed 25 June 2007). See also n 61 below.

of students'.[10] Also in 2006, the German Constitutional Court ruled that existing laws did not permit schools to exclude Muslim teachers for wearing headscarves, but found that it was open to the German states to pass such legislation. Subsequently, an administrative tribunal found that Baden-Württemberg's ban on female teachers wearing the Islamic headscarf (ostensibly to protect children against fundamentalist influences) was discriminatory, since Catholic nuns were not similarly affected.[11]

In late 2006, the Netherlands proposed a complete ban on burqas and other Islamic veils in public, on the grounds that

> [t]he cabinet finds it undesirable that garments covering the face—including the burqa—should be worn in public in view of public order [and] the security and protection of fellow citizens.[12]

Whereas the law may seem like an overreaction given that only an estimated 30 Dutch Muslim women wear full burqas,[13] that effort must be understood in the context of the murder of Dutch film director Theo van Gogh, a strident critic of Islam, in 2004 by an extremist. The purported public order rationale may have some weight, if one thinks, for example, of CCTV footage of one of the unsuccessful 21 July bombers in London, Yassin Omar, leaving London a day after the failed attacks dressed in a full burqa.[14] Whether a total public ban is necessary and proportionate, however, is another question, and begs the question whether long trench-coats and woollen winter scarves also should be banned. Equally, it is difficult to understand the objective rationale for the sacking of a supermarket check-out operator in Denmark for wearing a headscarf at work, notwithstanding its strict legal basis in a contractual dress code.

In other situations, more concrete and plausible justifications for restricting headscarves have been accepted. For instance, a Florida court found constitutional the revocation of a Muslim woman's driver's licence

[10] 'French Cabinet Backs Scarf Ban' BBC News (28 January 2004) <http://news.bbc.co.uk/2/hi/europe/3437133.stm> (accessed 25 June 2007).

[11] 'German State Overturns Ban on Headscarves' DPA (7 July 2006) <http://www.expatica.com/actual/article.asp?subchannel_id=26&story_id=31414> (accessed 25 June 2007). The law prohibited 'outward expressions that undermine the neutrality of the government or peace between political and religious creeds in school'. The teacher wore a scarf tied loosely around her head like a hat, rather than in an overtly religious way, and there had been no complaints in her 10 years at the school.

[12] A Hudson, 'Dutch Plan to Impose Burqa Ban Unveiled' *The Sun-Herald* (19 November 2006) <http://www.smh.com.au/news/world/dutch-plan-to-impose-burqa-ban-unveiled/2006/11/18/1163266833749.html> (accessed 25 June 2007). Dutch law previously restricted the wearing of burqas and other complete coverings in schools and on public transport.

[13] B Hibbitts, 'Dutch Government Promises Burqa Ban after Election' *Jurist* (18 November 2006) <http://jurist.law.pitt.edu/paperchase/2006/11/dutch-government-promises-burqa-ban.php> (accessed 25 June 2007).

[14] 'Bomb Accused Dressed in Burka', *The Australian* (22 February 2007) <http://www.theaustralian.news.com.au/story/0,20867,21266555-2703,00.html> (accessed 25 June 2007).

after she refused to remove her full-face veil (niqab) for the identity photograph.[15] As Judge Thorpe stated, 'the momentary raising of her veil for the purpose of the ID photo does not constitute a substantial burden on her right to exercise her religion', and was necessary to prevent criminal activities and security threats.[16] While a Russian court overturned a ban on women wearing the headscarf in identification photos in 2005,[17] that decision related to scarves which did not cover the face and therefore render identification impossible.

Other situations may be less clear-cut: for example, a US appeal court overturned a district court judge's dismissal of a civil action brought by a Muslim woman who refused to take off her niqab while testifying, where the judge believed he needed to see her face to determine the truth of her testimony.[18] Likewise, the Chief Justice of the Peshawar High Court in Pakistan banned female lawyers from wearing the hijab in court, stating that

> [y]ou are professionals and should be dressed as required of lawyers … . We cannot identify veiled woman lawyers and suspect that veiled lawyers appear to seek adjournment of proceedings in other lawyers' cases.[19]

The judge also noted that it was difficult to hear lawyers from behind the veil. In contrast, some female judges in the North West Frontier Province of Pakistan wear the hijab, while many female legislators in the area also wear it. Such cases must involve careful appreciation of specific factual circumstances, and general rules are rarely adequate; the availability of less invasive means will also require close scrutiny.

In the face of controversy, less inflammatory examples of quiet accommodation may attract less attention: the introduction of burqa-style clinical gowns in some British hospitals, to make some Muslim women more at ease; the establishment of Muslim hospitals in the Netherlands; or the cordoning-off of women-only beaches in Italy. In Australia, members of the New South Wales state police force may apply for permission to wear

[15] The judge stated further that '[t]he state's need to be able to immediately identify subjects of investigative traffic stops and criminal and intelligence investigations outweighs anyone's need to pose for a driver's licence photo wearing any garb that cloaks all facial features except the eyes'.

[16] For another case where such a restriction for photo identification purposes on a licence was found to be lawful (to avert fraud and falsification), see *Association United Sikhs et M Shingara Mann Singh*, No 289947, Ordonnance du juge des référés du 6 mars 2006 (French Conseil d'Etat).

[17] 'Headscarves in the Headlines' BBC News (10 February 2004) <http://news.bbc.co.uk/1/hi/world/europe/3476163.stm> (accessed 25 June 2007).

[18] 'Woman Given Veil Choice Gets New Hearing' Associated Press (24 January 2007) <http://www.civilrights.org/press_room/buzz_clips/page.jsp?itemID=29332876> (accessed 25 June 2007).

[19] Quoted in R Olden, 'Pakistan Judge Forbids Muslim Veils in Courtroom' *Jurist* (4 November 2006) <http://jurist.law.pitt.edu/paperchase/2006_11_04_indexarch.php#116267514020519128> (accessed 25 June 2007).

religious attire such as crucifixes, the hijab or a turban. The policy has caused little difficulty, with only one application having been made—to wear a turban—and which was granted without incident.[20]

Some efforts to restrict religious clothing have been of general application, and have not specifically targeted Muslims. There was a furore when it was reported that British Airways had banned Christian crosses worn on chains by airline staff, unless they could be concealed underneath the BA uniform.[21] In fact, the uniform policy provided that personal items of jewellery could only be worn underneath the uniform, whereas hijabs and turbans were not affected because they were not jewellery. After much public controversy, the airline allowed staff to wear discreet religious symbols such as lapel pins and symbols on chains.

The headscarf issue has attracted increasing scholarly attention.[22] It plainly raises a host of complex and inter-related legal issues, as well as empirical, theoretical and ethical problems concerning the boundaries of secularism and religion, and of cultural pluralism and multicultural difference; ideas about integration and assimilation; the threat posed by Islamic fundamentalism and the means through which it works; the connection (if any) to contemporary terrorism; and the proper scope of government regulation. Within a human rights framework, the key recurrent issues in the case law on headscarves and other religious symbols have centred on freedom to manifest one's religion, the right to education, and gender equality, with a broader underlying tension between 'equal rights and the right to difference based on a claim of authenticity'.[23]

This chapter critically examines three key recent cases of superior courts concerning restrictions on religious symbols: a prohibition on wearing headscarves in Turkish universities, upheld by the Grand Chamber of the European Court of Human Rights (*Şahin v Turkey*);[24] a restriction on a

[20] H Alexander, 'It's a Sign of the Times: What We Wear Can Trigger an Unholy Row' *Sydney Morning Herald* (17 October 2006) <http://www.smh.com.au/news/national/its-a-sign-of-the-times-what-we-wear-can-trigger-an-unholy-row/2006/10/16/1160850872598.html> (accessed 25 June 2007).

[21] 'BA Drops Ban on Wearing Crosses' BBC News (19 January 2007) <http://news.bbc.co.uk/2/hi/uk_news/6280311.stm> (accessed 25 June 2007); see also D Smith, 'BA Faces Legal Action over Worker's Crucifix Ban' *The Guardian* (15 October 2006) <http://www.guardian.co.uk/religion/Story/0,,1922925,00.html> (accessed 25 June 2007).

[22] D McGoldrick, *Human Rights and Religion: The Islamic Headscarf Debate in Europe* (Oxford, Hart Publishing, 2006); I Ward, 'Headscarf Stories' (2006) 29 *Hastings International and Comparative Law Review* 315; Evans (n 3 above); L-A Thio and J Ling-chien Neo, 'Religious Dress in Schools: The Serban Controversy in Malaysia' (2006) 55 *International and Comparative Law Quarterly* 671; T Poole, 'Of Headscarves and Heresies: The Denbigh High School Case and Public Authority Decision-Making under the Human Rights Act' [2005] *Public Law* 685; M Sunder, 'Piercing the Veil' (2003) 112 *Yale Law Journal* 1399.

[23] M Loughlin, 'Constitutional Theory: A 25th Anniversary Essay' (2005) 25 *Oxford Journal of Legal Studies* 183 at 199.

[24] *Şahin v Turkey* App No 44774/98 (ECtHR: Grand Chamber, 10 November 2005).

particular kind of Islamic dress in an English school, upheld by the British House of Lords (*R (on the Application of Begum) v Headteacher and Governors of Denbigh High School*);[25] and an absolute ban on wearing a Sikh kirpan (a symbolic dagger) in a Québecois school, struck down by the Canadian Supreme Court (*Multani v Commission Scolaire Marguerite-Bourgeoys*).[26]

Each case focused on similar arguments about freedom to manifest one's religion, and dealt with subsidiary arguments about the impact of the respective restrictions on the right to education. While each case proceeded from different factual circumstances, there were considerable differences in the courts' approaches to what were essentially the same human rights law questions. The decision of the European Court of Human Rights is the least satisfactory in both its reasoning and its result; the House of Lords arguably reached the correct result but its reasoning was abbreviated; and the Canadian Supreme Court properly reasoned its way to a correct result. Each case is analysed in turn, drawing contrasts and comparisons where relevant.

I. EUROPEAN COURT OF HUMAN RIGHTS: *ŞAHIN v TURKEY* (2005)

Leyla Şahin was a young Turkish, Muslim woman who believed it was her religious duty to wear a headscarf. In her fifth year of medicine at Istanbul University, the Vice-Chancellor issued a circular in February 1998 which provided that

> students whose heads are covered (who wear the Islamic headscarf) and students ... with beards ... must not be admitted to lectures, courses or tutorials.[27]

She continued to wear her headscarf and was consequently denied access to lectures and exams at the university. The university also took disciplinary action against her for her involvement in protests against the dress code, resulting in her suspension, although she subsequently benefited from an amnesty in 2000. Her application to set aside the circular was dismissed by the Istanbul Administrative Court in March 1999, which held that under Turkish legislation the Vice-Chancellor had power to

[25] *R (on the Application of Begum) v Headteacher and Governors of Denbigh High School* [2006] UKHL 15.

[26] *Multani v Commission Scolaire Marguerite-Bourgeoys* [2006] 1 SCR 256, 2006 SCC 6.

[27] Quoted in *Şahin* (n 24 above) para 16. 1994 Rules of the University also stated: 'The rules governing dress in universities are set out in the laws and regulations. The Constitutional Court has delivered a judgment which prevents religious attire being worn in universities'. In addition, a university resolution of July 1998 reaffirmed this legal basis (para 1) and stated (in para 2) that '[s]tudents shall not wear clothes that symbolise or manifest any religion, faith, race, or political or ideological persuasion in any institution or department of the university, or on any of its premises'.

regulate students' dress to maintain order at the university, and that the circular did not conflict with the Turkish Constitution. By September 1999, Şahin had enrolled at the University of Vienna to continue her higher education.

By way of background, religious dress had been regulated by Turkish law as early as 1925 and again in 1934,[28] as part of the drive to establish a modern, secular Turkish Republic from 1923. Wearing Islamic headscarves in schools and universities only became increasingly common in the 1980s, and soon generated public controversy in a climate of increasingly organised Islamic political movements. A 1981 Turkish law required employees of public organisations, and staff and female students of State institutions, to wear ordinary, sober and modern dress, and excluded veils in educational institutions. A 1982 circular by the Higher Education Authority banned Islamic headscarves during lectures, and the circular was found to be lawful by the Supreme Administrative Court in 1984, which stated that:

> Beyond being a mere innocent practice, wearing the headscarf is in the process of becoming the symbol of a vision that is contrary to the freedoms of women and the fundamental principles of the Republic.[29]

A further higher education law of 1988 provided that:

> Modern dress or appearance shall be compulsory in the rooms and corridors of institutions of higher education, preparatory schools, laboratories, clinics and multidisciplinary clinics. A veil or headscarf covering the neck and hair may be worn out of religious conviction.[30]

The latter part of that provision was found to be unconstitutional by the Turkish Constitutional Court in March 1989, being contrary to constitutional guarantees of secularism, equality before the law and freedom of religion, as well as the principle of sexual equality implicit in the values of a republican and revolutionary Constitution. Significantly, the court held that secularism was essential to Turkish democracy and ensured freedom of religion and equality before the law. A person's freedom to manifest his or her religion (including by wearing religious dress) could be restricted on public order grounds in order to defend secularism, at least outside the private sphere of individual conscience.[31] A provision which legally recognised a religious symbol (the Islamic headscarf) in universities was incompatible with the requirement of neutrality in State education, since it would generate conflict between students of different religious beliefs. Subsequently, a 1990 law provided that:

[28] See *Şahin* (n 24 above) paras 30–35.
[29] Quoted in *ibid*, para 37.
[30] Quoted in *ibid*, para 38.
[31] *Ibid*, para 39.

> Choice of dress shall be free in institutions of higher education, provided that it does not contravene the laws in force.

A later Constitutional Court judgment in 1991 interpreted that provision as taking into account its own prior decision of 1989 (as a law in force), to the effect that:

> In institutions of higher education, it is contrary to the principles of secularism and equality for the neck and hair to be covered with a veil or headscarf on grounds of religious conviction.[32]

In challenging the ban on the headscarf before the European Court of Human Rights, Şahin alleged that it amounted to an unjustified interference with her right to manifest her religion or beliefs under Article 9(2) of the European Convention on Human Rights ('ECHR'),[33] which provides that:

> Freedom to manifest one's religion or beliefs shall be subject only to such limitations as are prescribed by law and are necessary in a democratic society in the interests of public safety, for the protection of public order, health or morals, or for the protection of the rights and freedoms of others.

In addition, Şahin alleged that the ban constituted a violation of her right to education under Article 2 of Protocol No 1 to the ECHR: 'No person shall be denied the right to education'. On both grounds, in June 2004 a judgment of the Chamber of the European Court of Human Rights found against Şahin. While the ban amounted to an interference with Şahin's right to manifest her religion, it was found to be duly prescribed by law, pursuing a legitimate aim under Article 9(2), and necessary and proportionate. The Chamber further found that no separate question arose under Protocol No 1, since 'the relevant circumstances were the same as those it had examined in relation to Article 9, in respect of which it had found no violation'.[34]

For the same reason, Şahin's allegations of violations of Articles 8, 10 and 14 of the ECHR (concerning respect for private life, freedom of expression and non-discrimination) were summarily rejected.[35]

On appeal to the Grand Chamber of the European Court of Human Rights, the judgment focused on the alleged violation of Article 9(2) of the ECHR, but it also separately considered the alleged violation of Article 2 of Protocol No 1 (unlike in the Chamber). The allegations of violations of Articles 8 and 10 were, however, still treated as a 'mere reformulation' of

32 Quoted in *ibid*, para 41.

33 Convention for the Protection of Human Rights and Fundamental Freedoms (European Convention on Human Rights, as amended) (4 November 1950) ETS No 5.

34 *Şahin* (n 24 above) para 127.

35 *Ibid*.

the complaints under Article 9 of the ECHR and Article 2 of Protocol No 1, in relation to which, as explained below, the Grand Chamber found there to be no violations. The Grand Chamber noted that no detailed pleadings were made on the Article 14 allegation, and in any event, the reasoning relevant to Article 9 and Protocol No 1 would apply to Article 14. In an arguably more sound analytical approach, in their concurring opinion, two judges of the Grand Chamber preferred to regard freedom to manifest religion as 'the obvious *lex specialis* covering the facts of the case', such that the corollary allegation of a Protocol No 1 violation could not be considered to raise a separate issue.[36]

A. Freedom to Manifest Religion

The Grand Chamber first accepted the Chamber's view that regulations restricting Şahin's right to wear the Islamic headscarf in universities amounted to an interference in her right to manifest her religion, on the basis that her decision to wear it 'may be regarded as motivated or inspired by a religion or belief', since she believed that she was obeying a religious precept and was attempting to comply strictly with the duties of her Islamic faith.[37] The Chamber noted, however, that it was not deciding whether 'in every case' the decision to wear a headscarf was in order to fulfil a religious duty. Secondly, the Grand Chamber found that the interference was 'prescribed by law' since the circular found its legal basis in the 1990 Turkish law (mentioned above), in conjunction with the relevant Turkish case law (above).[38] Such laws were accessible and sufficiently precise so as to make the restriction and its consequences foreseeable. Thirdly, the parties agreed that the interference pursued the legitimate aim of protecting the rights and freedoms of others and protecting public order.[39]

The central controversy concerned whether the restriction was 'necessary in a democratic society', including whether the infringement was proportionate to the legitimate objectives pursued. The Grand Chamber observed that freedom of religion is a foundation of 'democratic society' under the ECHR and is 'one of the most vital elements that go to make up the identity of believers and their conception of life', as well as being a 'precious asset for atheists, agnostics, sceptics and the unconcerned', since it entails a freedom whether to believe and practise

[36] See the Concurring Opinion of Judges Rozakis and Vajić in *Şahin* (n 24 above).
[37] *Şahin* (n 24 above) para 78.
[38] *Ibid*, paras 84–98.
[39] *Ibid*, para 99.

or not.[40] Freedom to manifest one's religion under the ECHR expressly includes freedom of worship, teaching, practice and observance, although it does not protect every act motivated or inspired by religion.[41]

Further, the Grand Chamber reiterated that restrictions on manifesting one's religion may be necessary in a democratic society of multiple religions 'to reconcile the interests of the various groups and ensure that everyone's beliefs are respected'.[42] In this regard, the State acts as a 'neutral and impartial organiser of the exercise of various religions', in the interests of public order, religious harmony and tolerance, without assessing the legitimacy of any particular beliefs.[43] In addition, the court noted that '[p]luralism and democracy must also be based on dialogue and a spirit of compromise necessarily entailing various concessions' between different actors.[44]

At this point, the Grand Chamber emphasised the importance of deference to national authorities on religious questions:

> Where questions concerning the relationship between State and religions are at stake, on which opinion in a democratic society may reasonably differ widely, the role of the national decision-making body must be given special importance.[45]

The margin of appreciation accorded to national decision-makers was considered particularly important in 'the choice of the extent and form' of regulations on the wearing of religious symbols in educational institutions, in light of the diversity of national approaches to the issue in Europe (which precluded any 'uniform conception of the significance of religion in society').[46] Such conclusion was reached after the Grand Chamber had briefly reviewed State practice in various European countries.[47]

Oddly, the review of practice objectively indicated that there was a general lack of restriction on the wearing of headscarves by students in universities in most European countries, including in Austria, Germany, the Netherlands, Spain, Sweden, Switzerland and the United Kingdom. In some other countries, the issue had not arisen, as in the Czech Republic, Greece, Hungary, Poland and Slovakia. Where restrictions did exist, they related to the different context of schools rather than universities, as in France and Belgium, or to teachers rather than to students. Restrictions in universities were only identified in Turkey, Azerbaijan and Albania,[48]

[40] *Ibid*, para 104.
[41] *Ibid*, para 105.
[42] *Ibid*, para 106.
[43] *Ibid*, para 107.
[44] *Ibid*, para 108.
[45] *Ibid*, para 109.
[46] *Ibid*.
[47] *Ibid*, paras 55–65.
[48] In addition, note that the UN Human Rights Committee has previously criticised Uzbekistan for restrictions on headscarves in universities: see Communication No 931/2000, UN Doc CCPR/C/82/D/931/2000 (18 January 2005).

which were exceptions to the norm. If anything, there was a fair European consensus in favour of *not* preventing students from wearing headscarves in universities, and the lack of a 'uniform conception of the significance of religion in society' is a rather more general, different (and arguably irrelevant) question from the narrower issue of (adult) student clothing in universities. The distinction is important because, as Judge Tulkens noted in dissent, young adults in universities are 'less amenable to pressure' than young children in schools.[49]

Given the margin of appreciation, the Grand Chamber saw its role as determining whether national measures 'were justified in principle and proportionate', in light of the need to ensure the survival of democracy by protecting the rights and freedoms of others, preserving public order and securing civil peace and religious pluralism.[50] The Grand Chamber also invoked earlier case law in the European human rights system in support of permissible restrictions on freedom to manifest religion.[51] The relevance of those cases is questionable given the different circumstances. For instance, *Karaduman* concerned a need to remove headscarves for the purpose of photographic identification on graduation certificates, in order to avoid fraud.

Further, the second case cited, *Dahlab*, involved a suggestion that a headscarf worn by a teacher in a class of young children might constitute a (detrimental) 'powerful external symbol' with a proselytising effect and an impact on gender equality and non-discrimination, since it appeared to be a religious imposition on women. Such a situation self-evidently raises rather different issues from the context of an adult student at university, where there is no question of influencing vulnerable or impressionable young children, where the student is not a role model in a position of authority over others,[52] and where the woman wearing the headscarf is well-educated and consciously chooses to wear it.

In addition, any purported proselytising effect is questionable in the absence of any attempt by the headscarf wearer to convert others or spread her religion, since there is nothing innate or inherent in wearing it that has such an effect. So far as young children are concerned, exposing them to a diversity of religious clothing and beliefs—rather than shielding them from it—is arguably an essential part of building a culture of citizens who respect and appreciate diversity and plurality, and who are not fearful or suspicious of it. So far as Şahin herself was concerned, there was no suggestion, on the evidence, that she ever engaged in proselytising activities or pressured other women to wear the headscarf.

[49] *Şahin* (n 24 above) para 3 (Dissenting Opinion of Judge Tulkens).

[50] *Şahin* (n 24 above) para 110.

[51] *Karaduman v Turkey* (1993) 74 DR 93 (ECtHR); *Dahlab v Switzerland* App No 42393/98 (15 February 2001) (ECtHR).

[52] In dissent in *Şahin* (n 24 above) para 7 (Dissenting Opinion of Judge Tulkens), Judge Tulkens alluded to this issue.

Having set out its approach to the legal issues, the Grand Chamber then cited with approval the March 1989 decision of the Turkish Constitutional Court, which had emphasised the importance of secularism in guaranteeing democratic values, including liberty and equality.[53] That decision had viewed the State as an impartial arbiter which was prohibited from preferring one religion over another, and which protected individuals from pressure by extremist movements, including by restricting the freedom to manifest religion where necessary.[54] The Grand Chamber approved of the Chamber's invocation of the principle of secularism, deriving from the Constitutional Court's decision, as 'consistent with the values underpinning' the ECHR and necessary to protect democracy in Turkey.[55]

Indeed, the Grand Chamber restated and affirmed the approach of the Chamber[56] without adding much further reasoning. The Chamber had suggested that the protection of women and gender equality under the Turkish Constitution and the ECHR were threatened by the wearing of the headscarf, given the 'impact which wearing such a symbol, which is presented or perceived as a compulsory religious duty, may have on those who choose not to wear it'.[57]

Here the Chamber identified the rights and freedoms of others and the maintenance of public order as the interests at stake, in a country where a majority of the population, 'while professing a strong attachment to the rights of women and a secular way of life, adhere to the Islamic faith'.[58]

Restrictions on the wearing of the headscarf were thus seen as 'meeting a pressing social need by seeking to achieve those two legitimate aims', particularly in light of extremist political Islamic movements in Turkey 'which seek to impose on society as a whole their religious symbols and conception of a society founded on religious precepts'.[59]

After quoting at length from the Chamber's decision, the Grand Chamber glossed those extracts by concluding for itself that:

> It is the principle of secularism ... which is the paramount consideration underlying the ban on the wearing of religious symbols in universities. In such a context, where the values of pluralism, respect for the rights of others and, in particular, equality before the law of men and women are being taught and applied in practice, it is understandable that the relevant authorities should

[53] *Şahin* (n 24 above) para 113.
[54] *Ibid.*
[55] *Ibid*, para 114.
[56] *Ibid*, para 115.
[57] Quoted in *ibid.*
[58] *Ibid.*
[59] *Ibid.*

> wish to preserve the secular nature of the institution concerned and so consider it contrary to such values to allow religious attire, including … the Islamic headscarf, to be worn.[60]

The Grand Chamber next proceeded to find that the ban was proportionate to the legitimate aim pursued. The first factor in its analysis was its finding that Muslim students remained

> free, within the limits imposed by educational organisational constraints, to manifest their religion in accordance with habitual forms of Muslim observance.[61]

Secondly, other forms of religious attire (such as beards) were also forbidden, implying that the restriction was not discriminatory on gender grounds (although begging the question whether the ban was necessary for gender equality).

Thirdly, it was suggested that special public order constraints applied to medical courses.[62] This appears to be a reference to the origins of the ban at Istanbul University, in which students in a midwifery course in 1994 were instructed that the Ministry of Health required uniforms for midwives and nurses.[63] In the words of the Vice-Chancellor at the time:

> Imagine a student of midwifery trying to put a baby in or remove it from an incubator, or assisting a doctor in an operating theatre or maternity unit while wearing a long-sleeved coat.[64]

These practical concerns were coupled with fears of disorder and unrest arising from a campaign on campus to wear headscarves.

Fourthly, the Grand Chamber found that the restrictions were the result of a lengthy process of debate in Turkey and in the teaching profession, and in its decision-making process the university

> sought to adapt to the evolving situation in a way that would not bar access to the university to students wearing the veil, through continued dialogue with those concerned, while at the same time ensuring that order was maintained.[65]

The essential flaws in the majority judgment were accurately dissected by Judge Tulkens in dissent. Foremost was the Grand Chamber's excessive deference to the views of Turkey, as the better-placed national authority. While Judge Tulkens did not contest the doctrine of the margin of appreciation itself, she argued that 'European supervision seems quite simply to be absent

[60] *Ibid*, para 116.

[61] *Ibid*, para 118. A similar factor was considered relevant by the Malaysian Federal Court in the *Serban case* (2006) <http://www.malaysianbar.org.my/content/view/3526/27/> (accessed 25 June 2007), which noted that students could wear turbans in the school prayer room and after school.

[62] *Şahin* (n 24 above) para 119.

[63] *Ibid*, para 43.

[64] Quoted in *ibid*.

[65] *Ibid*, para 120.

from the judgment', notwithstanding that the issue was not merely local but of significance for all European States.[66] It is true that much of the majority judgment rests on untested assertions about the potency of the headscarf as a symbol of both extremism and gender inequality, which somehow threatens to destabilise secular democracy. Yet, the majority judgment never comes close to showing how. In large part, it is content to defer to the national authorities on this point, without interrogating those assumptions for itself to see whether indeed those views are reasonably supported by evidence.

Consequently, Judge Tulkens argued that the headscarf ban was not 'necessary in a democratic society',[67] given the exceedingly thin ground on which the justification for the ban was constructed. In particular, she argued that the ban was not necessary to meet a pressing social need, since it was premised on 'worries or fears' about its impact on secularism rather than concrete examples or 'indisputable facts and reasons whose legitimacy is beyond doubt'.[68] Şahin herself neither disputed nor (by her actions) contravened the principle of secularism, and certainly did not infringe the rights of others by wearing the headscarf ostentatiously, aggressively, provocatively or to proselytise, propagandise or undermine others' religious convictions.[69] Nor was there any evidence that her wearing it disrupted public order on campus.

While acknowledging the real threat of extremist Islam, Judge Tulkens cautioned the majority against automatically associating the headscarf with fundamentalism, particularly on the facts of this case where Şahin herself was not a radical, did not pressure others into wearing the headscarf, and was an educated adult who 'might reasonably be expected to have a heightened capacity to resist pressure'.[70] The majority's concern about the impact of wearing the headscarf manifested itself as a rather abstract or generalised fear, allowing freedom of religion to become 'absorbed by the public interest in fighting extremism'.[71]

Here, Judge Tulkens highlighted two possible problems in the jurisprudence of the court: first, it tends to be more protective of religious *beliefs* than *practices*, the latter receiving only 'subsidiary' protection,[72] even though the symbolic significance of clothing may differ greatly in different religions. Secondly, freedom of religion is seen as somehow less important than the freedom of expression, as the following analogy suggests:

> [T]he Court has never accepted that interference with the exercise of the right to freedom of expression can be justified by the fact that the ideas or views concerned are not shared by everyone and may even offend some people.[73]

66 *Şahin* (n 24 above), para 3 (Dissenting Opinion of Judge Tulkens).
67 *Ibid*, para 13.
68 *Ibid*, para 5.
69 *Ibid*, paras 7–8.
70 *Ibid*, para 10.
71 *Ibid*.
72 *Ibid*, para 6.
73 *Ibid*, para 9.

There is nothing rational about according greater protection to political speech than religious practice in a democracy; political views can often be as unfathomable as religion, and both are deserving of at least equal protection in a democratic order premised on respect for the moral autonomy and life choices of all of its members, without descending into paternalistic interference.

As for the purported detrimental impact of wearing the headscarf on gender equality, Judge Tulkens was similarly sceptical of the majority's assertions. Invoking the decision of the German Constitutional Court in September 2003,[74] she noted that 'wearing the headscarf has no single meaning; it is a practise that is engaged in for a variety of reasons', and may represent the emancipation of women as much as their alienation or submission to men.[75] The majority seems to homogenise the experience of all Muslim women, possibly based on the judges' own stereotypes or perceptions about the nature of Islam and the position of women within it. The majority's assertion, derived from *Dahlab*, that the headscarf is hard to reconcile with equality, tolerance, respect and non-discrimination, is abstract, generalised and paternalistic, rather than particular to the facts at hand.[76] Şahin freely chose to wear it, and as a puzzled Judge Tulkens stated:

> I fail to see how the principle of sexual equality can justify prohibiting a woman from following a practice which, in the absence of proof to the contrary, she must be taken to have freely adopted. Equality and non-discrimination are subjective rights which must remain under the control of those who are entitled to benefit from them.[77]

Logically, in her view, the State would be required to prohibit the headscarf in all places if really violated the principle of gender equality.[78]

B. Right to Education

In analysing the right to education, the Grand Chamber noted its fundamental importance and its applicability to higher education.[79] While accepting

[74] *Teacher Headscarf case* BVerfG, 2 BvR 1436/02 (German Constitutional Court, 24 September 2003); see also case note by C Skach in (2006) 100 *American Journal of International Law* 186.

[75] *Şahin* (n 24 above) para 11 (Dissenting Opinion of Judge Tulkens).

[76] *Ibid*, para 12. See *Dahlab v Switzerland* (n 51 above).

[77] *Şahin* (n 24) para 12.

[78] *Ibid*.

[79] *Şahin* (n 24 above) paras 129, 134, 136–7, 141.

that the State has a positive obligation to ensure respect for the right, and to render the right 'practical and effective', it acknowledged that

> the development of the right ... whose content varies from one time or place to another, according to economic and social circumstances, mainly depends on the needs and resources of the community.[80]

Further, the court accepted that the right is not absolute but may be subject to limitations, and that States enjoy a margin of appreciation in this respect.[81] In particular, the right

> does not in principle exclude recourse to disciplinary measures, including suspension or expulsion from an educational institution in order to ensure compliance with its internal rules.[82]

In this context, the Grand Chamber transplanted much of its reasoning on the justifiability of the infringement of Şahin's freedom to manifest her religion to its analysis of the right to education.[83] In doing so, it appeared to accept that her right to education had indeed been infringed. It accordingly found that the restriction was foreseeable and in pursuit of a legitimate aim (protecting the rights and freedoms of others and maintaining public order)—that is, to preserve secularism in universities. The restriction was also proportionate since it did not prevent students from 'performing the duties imposed by the habitual forms of religious observance'; the university's decision-making process appropriately weighed up the competing interests; there were safeguards of conformity with statute law and judicial review; and the restriction and its consequences were reasonably foreseeable to Şahin.[84]

In contrast, in dissent Judge Tulkens found that Şahin had been deprived de facto of her 'indispensable' right to access to education, on grounds which were neither 'relevant nor sufficient'.[85] Şahin had not sought exemption from, or modifications to, any aspects of her university course, but merely sought to continue her studies under the conditions in force at the time she enrolled (that is, prior to the ban on headscarves). Further, it was problematic for the majority to simply analyse the right to education as though it raised identical considerations to freedom of religion. While both may be subject to limitations, in dissent, Judge Tulkens argued that additional elements affect the proportionality of restrictions on the right to education.[86] Specifically, it was suggested that the university should have attempted to secure Şahin's compliance with the

[80] *Ibid*, para 136.
[81] *Ibid*, para 154.
[82] *Ibid*, para 156.
[83] *Ibid*, paras 157–9.
[84] *Ibid*, paras 159–60.
[85] *Şahin* (n 24 above) para 15 (Dissenting Opinion of Judge Tulkens).
[86] *Ibid*, para 17.

ban through alternative, less invasive means (such as mediation) before effectively excluding her from her education.

Secondly, Şahin was left with no alternative solutions, since the consequence of the ban was her complete exclusion from university education in Turkey, and she was forced to study abroad. Unlike in the *Begum case*, discussed below, there was no possibility of moving to another Turkish university, since the ban now applied to all public and private universities. Thirdly, the majority did not sufficiently weigh up the competing interests, namely the damage suffered by Şahin and the benefit to Turkey of the ban on headscarves. Judge Tulkens also suggested that the infringement of Şahin's right to education might constitute religious discrimination,[87] although little reasoning was provided for this assertion and there was no consideration of whether secularism or public order might provide legitimate grounds for differentiation between religions.

The broader policy concerns raised by Judge Tulkens are important. There is an irony in banning headscarves 'in the name of secularism and equality' with the result that a student is excluded 'from precisely the type of liberated environment in which the true meaning of these values can take shape and develop'.[88]

Further, depriving students of their autonomy 'echo[es] that very fundamentalism these measures are intended to combat', with the risks of radicalising beliefs and a return to fundamentalism: 'intolerance breeds intolerance', whereas the 'the best means of preventing and combating fanaticism and extremism is to uphold human rights'.[89] The ban arguably also contributes to 'the climate of hostility' against Muslims.[90]

The Grand Chamber's decision was of considerable practical significance, given that up to 65 per cent of Turkish women wear a headscarf, and more than 1000 Turkish women had already made similar applications to the courts to challenge the ban on headscarves.[91] More than 10,000 women in Istanbul alone are estimated to have been denied access to university.[92] Others have resorted to removing their headscarf before entering university and replacing it with a wig.[93]

In light of the level of controversy surrounding the issue in Turkey, it may seem unremarkable that the majority of the Grand Chamber elected to defer to the position of the Turkish authorities, perhaps

[87] *Ibid*, para 18.
[88] *Ibid*, para 19.
[89] *Ibid*, paras 19–20.
[90] *Ibid*, para 20.
[91] 'Court Backs Turkish Headscarf Ban' BBC News (10 November 2005) <http://news.bbc.co.uk/2/hi/europe/4424776.stm> (accessed 25 June 2007).
[92] T Morgan, 'Scarf Conundrum Grips Turkey' BBC News (25 February 2004) <http://news.bbc.co.uk/1/hi/world/europe/3513259.stm> (accessed 25 June 2007).
[93] *Ibid*.

conscious of its own legitimacy in the eyes of the Turkish State. However, in providing such thin reasoning for its position, which seems contradicted by the empirical evidence, the Grand Chamber may paradoxically succeed in damaging its credibility in the eyes of its real constituents—European human beings.

II. HOUSE OF LORDS: *R (ON THE APPLICATION OF BEGUM) v HEADTEACHER AND GOVERNORS OF DENBIGH HIGH SCHOOL* (2006)

Moving away from universities and into schools, Shebina Begum was a student at Denbigh High School in England, who claimed that she was excluded from her school as a result of a school uniform policy which did not allow her to wear the Islamic clothing of her choice. The school was non-denominational and its students were diverse, comprising 21 ethnic groups and 10 religions, with about 79 per cent of students being Muslim.[94] The school uniform was thought to help in

> securing high and improving standards, serving the needs of a diverse community, promoting a positive sense of communal identity and avoiding manifest disparities of wealth and style.[95]

It was adopted in 1993 after consultation with the school community and local imams, and one of the three options approved, the shalwar kameeze (a sleeveless dress and loose trousers), was considered to constitute modest dress for Muslim girls.[96] In addition, certain headscarves were also permitted. The policy was repeatedly notified to parents and students.

For two years, Begum wore the shalwar kameeze to school without protest, but in late 2002 her brother and another man accompanied her to school and insisted that she be allowed to wear the jilbab (a longer garment not approved under the uniform policy). The school refused and legal proceedings ensued after other efforts to resolve the dispute were unsuccessful. Begum alleged that the decision of the head teacher and school governors not to admit her to the school while wearing the jilbab constituted a violation of her freedom to manifest her religion or beliefs (under Article 9 of the ECHR) and her right not to be denied an education (under Article 2 of Protocol No 1), as in the *Şahin case*.

A. Freedom to Manifest Religion

In the House of Lords, Lord Bingham, in his leading opinion, reiterated the fundamental importance of freedom of religion in a pluralistic,

[94] *Begum* (n 25 above) para 3.
[95] *Ibid*, para 6.
[96] *Ibid*, para 7.

multicultural society and noted that whereas the right to hold a belief is absolute, the right to manifest a belief is qualified by the various grounds of legitimate restriction under Article 9(2).[97] It was accepted by the parties that Begum's religious belief was sincerely held, and the key issues in dispute were whether her freedom to manifest her belief had been limited or interfered with and, if so, whether such interference was justified.

On the question of interference, Lord Bingham noted that not every act motivated or inspired by religion or belief is protected, and that the specific situation of an individual is relevant to his or her exercising the freedom to manifest religion.[98] Lord Bingham then cited 'a coherent and remarkably consistent body of authorities' which indicated that the existence of interference with freedom to manifest religion is difficult to establish.[99] In part, this led to his conclusion that there had been no interference with Begum's right to manifest her belief in practice or observance, since she had voluntarily attended the school with knowledge of the uniform policy, and had indeed followed that policy for two years. Further, it was open to her to attend another of the various schools in the area at which the jilbab was permitted.[100] Lord Hoffmann agreed that Begum could have chosen to attend a school where she could wear a jilbab, or where Islam did not require her to wear a jilbab (for instance, an all-girls school).[101] Freedom to manifest one's religion was not considered to entail the freedom to do so at any time and any place, and only if it was impossible to manifest religion was there an interference.[102]

Here, Lord Hoffmann revealed frustration towards Begum's insistence on enforcing her rights,[103] asserting that '[c]ommon civility also has a place in the religious life' and that 'people sometimes have to suffer some inconvenience for their beliefs'. Further, he argued for an 'expectation of accommodation, compromise, and, if necessary, sacrifice in the manifestation of religious beliefs', rather than pursuing confrontation.[104] Unlike in the *Şahin case*, where the ban on headscarves applied in all Turkish universities, in this case it was at least possible (and not difficult, according to Lord Hoffmann) for Begum to move to another school where her choice of Islamic clothing would be permitted.

In contrast to the majority, Lord Nicholls and Baroness Hale both found that the uniform policy amounted to an interference with Begum's right.

[97] *Ibid*, para 20.
[98] *Ibid*, para 22, citing *Kalac v Turkey* (1997) 27 EHRR 552 (ECtHR) para 27.
[99] *Begum* (n 25 above) paras 23–4.
[100] *Ibid*, para 25.
[101] *Ibid*, para 50 (Lord Hoffmann).
[102] *Jewish Liturgical Association Cha'are Shalom Ve Tsedek v France* (2000) 9 BHRC 27 (ECtHR) para 80.
[103] *Begum* (n 25 above) para 52 (Lord Hoffmann). A similar factor was considered relevant by the Malaysian Federal Court in the *Serban case* (n 61 above), which noted that students could choose to attend a different school, such as a *pondok* school where turbans were allowed.
[104] *Begum* (n 25 above) para 54 (Lord Hoffmann).

Lord Nicholls cautioned against over-estimating how easy it would be for Begum to move to another school, and against under-estimating how much it would disrupt her education.[105] Baroness Hale was uneasy about the majority view that Begum had voluntarily chosen her school with knowledge of its uniform policy given 'the reality … that the choice of secondary school is usually made by parents', while the child's views may not be decisive nor fully developed in the sense of 'capacity to make autonomous moral judgements'.[106]

The majority judges arguably exhibited a lack of sensitivity and empathy towards the position of Begum herself as a young teenage child, both in terms of her capacity and the upheaval involved in moving schools—no doubt as a result of the court's impatience with the confrontational behaviour of Begum's adult relatives. Despite finding that there was no interference, Lord Bingham proceeded to consider whether interference would have been justified. After dealing with an initial procedural controversy over the proper approach to proportionality,[107] Lord Bingham found that the school's actions were 'fully justified', since it took 'immense pains to devise a uniform policy which respected Muslim beliefs but did so in an inclusive, unthreatening and uncompetitive way'.[108] The policy had been subject to little complaint and appeared acceptable to 'mainstream' Muslim opinion.[109]

Lord Hoffmann agreed that the uniform policy was necessary to protect the rights and freedoms of others, in light of evidence suggesting that some Muslim girls at the school did or would feel pressure to wear a jilbab, either within or outside the school.[110] That evidence had included a protest outside the school by an extreme Muslim group, leading to complaints of interference and harassment by students; and concerns that allowing different Islamic clothing would differentiate students according to the strictness of their beliefs and could result in the formation of cliques.[111]

In arriving at his conclusion, Lord Bingham substantially deferred to the school authorities, who were 'best placed' to make decisions of this nature, stating that it would be

> irresponsible of any court, lacking the experience, background and detailed knowledge [of the school authorities] … to overrule their judgment on a matter as sensitive as this.[112]

105 *Ibid*, para 41 (Lord Nicholls).
106 *Ibid*, paras 92–3 (Baroness Hale).
107 *Ibid*, paras 26–31.
108 *Ibid*, para 34; see also para 44 (Lord Hoffmann).
109 *Ibid*, para 34.
110 *Ibid*, para 58 (Lord Hoffmann).
111 *Ibid*, para 18.
112 *Ibid*, para 34.

Lord Hoffmann explained this deferential approach not as a formal application of the margin of appreciation, developed in the context of European human rights supervision of national authorities, but as 'comparable' to it in a domestic context.[113] In Britain, where there is no national law on Islamic clothing, individual schools are empowered to make decisions about uniforms. In this context, it is for the British courts 'to decide how the area of judgment allowed by that margin should be distributed between the legislative, executive and judicial branches', and for reasons of democracy the judiciary may defer to the expert decision-making body.[114]

Curiously, Lord Bingham's judgment pays little attention to the legal grounds of limitation under Article 9(2) of the ECHR, failing to explore specifically whether the policy was 'prescribed by law', 'necessary in a democratic society', and to protect public order or the rights and freedoms of others. The Court of Appeal had been criticised by Lord Hoffmann in particular for improperly focusing on the process of legal reasoning on human rights questions that the school ought to have followed. In his view, freedom of religion concerned substance not procedure, and the result was what mattered, not the way in which the decision was made (as is usual in administrative law matters).[115] As he pithily stated:

> Head teachers and governors cannot be expected to make such decisions with textbooks on human rights law at their elbows.[116]

That may well be right, but it does not absolve judges of their duty to follow the required steps of legal reasoning which are inherent in the text of the ECHR itself, and instead, as Lord Bingham did, to make impressionistic judgements simply about whether the school did the right thing, in some kind of opaque, common-sense fashion.

Moreover, the lead judgments make much of the fact that the uniform policy was adopted as a result of a process of community consultation and dialogue. Yet, if human rights review is concerned with substance and not procedure, it is difficult to discern the relevance of the way in which the policy decision was made—either it is a proportionate infringement, or it is not—and the process by which that substantive result was reached has little bearing on whether a right is justifiably infringed. This problem highlights the defect in approaching the case without following closely the legal steps required in evaluating the justifiability of a limitation on a right, and instead somehow divining its lawfulness by agreeing with the policy's good sense.

[113] *Ibid*, paras 62–4 (Lord Hoffmann).
[114] *Ibid*.
[115] *Ibid*, para 68.
[116] *Ibid*.

Baroness Hale agreed with the rest of the House of Lords that the interference she had identified was justified, since it pursued the legitimate aim of protecting the rights of others,[117] although her reasons were rather more nuanced. She found the dissenting judgment of Judge Tulkens in the *Şahin case* 'very persuasive'[118] in its acknowledgment that many Muslim women voluntarily choose to wear the headscarf and do not have it imposed upon them by religious patriarchs, and notwithstanding the objections of some western feminists that Islamic clothing is oppressive. Conversely, she noted that strict dress codes are sometimes imposed on women for ostensibly religious reasons, but in ways which deny equal treatment and free choice, and conceal political and social power relations.[119]

Baroness Hale did, however, regard the issue of Islamic dress in schools as different from debates about the wearing of Islamic clothing by adults and in other contexts. Schools were seen as having a role in educating the young to achieve their full potential, promoting harmony amidst diversity, and fostering community and cohesion: 'A uniform dress code can play its role in smoothing over ethnic, religious and social divisions', and a good school should enable and support young girls from different backgrounds to make their own choices.[120] In this context, Denbigh High School's uniform policy was viewed as a fair compromise which balanced such values as freedom, equality, cultural diversity, and child and parent rights; it promoted social cohesion while respecting cultural and religious diversity, and was 'a thoughtful and proportionate response to reconciling the complexities of the situation'.[121]

The search for social cohesion and community is clearly a question of emphasis and degree. An alternative view might be that, over the long term, cohesion and harmony are not possible if policies are accepted which eradicate difference, or render it invisible. Ultimately, harmony in a diverse society can only be built upon respect for difference, rather than its suppression in the name of public order or the pursuit of a vision of social cohesion that reflects a majoritarian view. By way of stark analogy, some people find homosexuals confrontational or a threat to the community and social cohesion, but that is no reason to require them to conceal defining characteristics of their identity and autonomy.[122]

That children are impressionable and vulnerable is not so much a reason to shield them from difference, but to inculcate in them a deep respect

[117] *Ibid*, para 94 (Baroness Hale).
[118] *Ibid*.
[119] *Ibid*, para 95–6.
[120] *Ibid*, para 97.
[121] *Ibid*, para 98.
[122] For an analysis of persecution on the grounds of sexual orientation, see the judgment of the High Court of Australia in *S395/2002 v Minister for Immigration and Multicultural Affairs* [2003] HCA 71, (2003) 216 CLR 473.

for it. Radical Islam poses a much greater threat in Turkey than in Britain and, in the absence of a comparable level of threat, British decision-makers should arguably be even more cautious than their Turkish counterparts in resorting to restrictions on religious expression. On one view, it is rather difficult to see how a young girl in a long robe genuinely threatens public order or social cohesion in a country such as England. On the other hand, despite their numerical minority in the British population, some polls suggest that 40 per cent of British Muslims want to be governed by Sharia law; but it is a considerable leap to equate Sharia law with extreme, radical fundamentalism.

B. Right to Education

The House of Lords gave relatively little attention to separately analysing the right to education. Lord Bingham held that the school's actions had not denied Begum access to the general level of education available in Britain,[123] since on existing authority, the right to education is not a right to attend a particular school.[124] The two-year interruption in her schooling resulted from her unwillingness to comply with the school's permissible uniform policy and her failure to enrol elsewhere; there was no statutory (disciplinary) exclusion from the school as such, which remained willing to allow her attendance if she complied with the uniform policy.[125]

Most of the judges tended to blur the analysis, exploring in a general way the policy justifications for the uniform policy without specifically examining whether those justifications separately authorised the limitation of both freedom to manifest religion and the right to education. Where analysis was specific, it tended to relate primarily to freedom of religion rather than the right to education, which was dismissed rather too easily as unfounded, on account of there being other schools in England which permitted the jilbab.

In other English cases dealing with the headscarf, the bases for its restriction have been rather more concrete than the generalised need for social cohesion at the root of the uniform policy in the *Begum case.* In 2006, an employment tribunal of a Yorkshire local council upheld a school's decision to suspend a Muslim teaching assistant for refusing to remove a full veil (hijab) during class, on the ground that it made her speech difficult for students to understand in her position as a bilingual

[123] *Begum* (n 25 above) para 36; see also para 69 (Lord Hoffmann).

[124] *Ibid*, para 69 (Lord Hoffmann), citing *Adbul Hakim Ali v Head Teacher and Governors of Lord Grey School* [2006] UKHL 14.

[125] *Begum* (n 25 above) para 38.

support worker.[126] The school had only required her to remove the veil while in direct contact with children, and there had been complaints from children, many of whom came from non-English speaking backgrounds and for whom learning English was vital. Here, there appears to be a more easily identifiable, legitimate occupational reason for restricting the wearing of the veil, assuming that the evidence does actually support the contention that the veil impedes communication.

Similarly, in another case, a 12-year-old school girl did not succeed in challenging a Buckinghamshire school's ban on the full-face veil.[127] The ban was considered to be a proportionate restriction of her rights because it prevented teachers from seeing the facial expressions of students (which was a necessary part of classroom interaction); it provided a sense of equality and identity for girls of different faiths; it ensured security by preventing strangers from moving incognito around the school; and it helped to avoid peer pressure on girls to wear the veil. In yet another case, school uniform policies cut the other way—a new Islamic school in Leicester will require non-Muslim students to wear the hijab,[128] and following the *Begum* decision, the starting point must be that students consent to such restriction by choosing to attend that school.

III. CANADIAN SUPREME COURT: *MULTANI v COMMISSION SCOLAIRE MARGUERITE-BOURGEOYS* (2006)

While in the *Begum case* Lord Bingham distinguished, without explanation, the 'different facts' of the *Multani* decision in the Canadian Supreme Court,[129] that decision is in many ways a model of good decision-making on freedom to manifest religion, and offers considerable lessons for both the European Court of Human Rights in *Şahin* and the House of Lords in *Begum*. *Multani* involved an orthodox Sikh child in Québec, Gurbaj Singh, who believed that his religion required him always to wear a kirpan, which is a religious object similar to a metal dagger. After Singh dropped his kirpan (which he wore underneath his clothes) at his school, Ecole Sainte-Catherine-Labouré, in 2001, the school board wrote to his parents authorising him, as a 'reasonable accommodation', to wear the

[126] Shaulis (n 5 above); see also 'Veil Teacher "Should Be Sacked"' BBC News (15 October 2006) <http://news.bbc.co.uk/1/hi/england/bradford/6050392.stm> (accessed 25 June 2007); R Mutton, 'Schools Veil Row Deepens Cultural Rift' *Sydney Morning Herald* (16 October 2006) <http://www.smh.com.au/news/world/schools-veil-row-deepens-cultural-rift/2006/10/15/1160850814579.html> (accessed 25 June 2007); 'School Suspends Woman over Veil', BBC News (13 October 2006) <http://news.bbc.co.uk/1/hi/england/bradford/6046992.stm> (accessed 25 June 2007).

[127] 'Schoolgirl Loses Veil Legal Case' BBC News (21 February 2007) <http://news.bbc.co.uk/1/hi/education/6382247.stm> (accessed 25 June 2007).

[128] See Mutton (n 126 above).

[129] *Begum* (n 25 above) para 34.

kirpan to school according to certain conditions. In particular, the kirpan was required to be sealed or sewn inside his clothing, and the boy and his parents agreed.

In early 2002, however, the school's governing board rejected the agreement for breaching the prohibition on the carrying of weapons in the school's code of conduct (*Code de vie*), and that decision was confirmed by the school board's council of commissioners. The council allowed Singh only to wear a symbolic kirpan-shaped pendant or a kirpan made of a harmless material, such as plastic or wood (but not metal). On application by his father, in 2002 the Superior Court overturned the council's decision and allowed Singh to wear his kirpan on the following conditions:

— that the kirpan be worn under his clothes;
— that the kirpan be carried in a sheath made of wood, not metal, to prevent it from causing injury;
— that the kirpan be placed in its sheath and wrapped and sewn securely in a sturdy cloth envelope, and that this envelope be sewn to the guthra (shoulder strap);
— that school personnel be authorised to verify, in a reasonable fashion, that these conditions were being complied with;
— that he keep the kirpan in his possession at all times, and that its disappearance be reported to school authorities immediately; and
— that in the event of a failure to comply with the terms of the judgment, he would definitively lose the right to wear his kirpan at school.

In 2004, a unanimous Québec Court of Appeal set aside that judgment and restored the council's decision, finding that its decision was a justifiable infringement of Singh's freedom of religion under section 2 of the Canadian Charter of Rights and Freedoms[130] and section 3 of Québec's Charter of Human Rights and Freedoms.[131] Justice Lemelin found that the decision was motivated by a pressing and substantive objective (the safety of students and staff), and that the prohibition on wearing the kirpan was directly and rationally connected to that objective. The danger posed by the kirpan could only be delayed, but not eliminated, by the proposed conditions on its wearing, thus reducing safety standards at the school and increasing exposure to risks. She believed that safety concerns in schools were no less serious than those in courts or on aircraft, and the council's position was not unreasonable. Further, the Court of Appeal did not separately consider the right to equality because the same justifications as those for restricting freedom of religion were considered to apply.

[130] Canadian Charter of Rights and Freedoms, Pt I of the Constitution Act 1982, being Schedule B to the Canada Act 1982 (UK) .

[131] Québec Charter of Human Rights and Freedoms, RSQ c C-12.

On further appeal, in March 2006, the Canadian Supreme Court set aside the Court of Appeal's decision and declared the decision of the council of commissioners null.

A. Infringement of the Freedom to Manifest Religion

In approaching freedom of religion, a majority of five (of eight sitting) judges on the Supreme Court first emphasised its importance, including the freedom to manifest religious belief by worship and practice or by teaching and dissemination, subject only to those limitations necessary to protect public safety, order, health, morals or the rights and freedoms of others.[132] Individuals must determine for themselves the nature of their religious obligations, and enjoy the freedom to undertake practices which they sincerely believe are connected with their religious beliefs, regardless of whether they are officially or formally required by the religion.[133] In this respect, the Canadian court applied a less intensive or invasive approach than that of the Malaysian Federal Court in the *Serban case* of 2006, where the asserted religious duty to wear the turban was closely scrutinised.[134] The Malaysian court observed that wearing a turban was only a commendable (sunat) Islamic practice not a mandatory (wajib) one, and that it was more a symbol of nationality than of religion.[135]

For the Canadian Supreme Court, however, freedom of religion is infringed if a person sincerely believes that a practice is connected with religion (and even if others in the religion practise differently), and the conduct of another interferes 'in a manner that is non-trivial or not insubstantial' with that practice.[136] The belief must be asserted in good faith and must not be fictitious, capricious or an artifice.[137] On the facts, it was not contested that Singh sincerely believed that his religion required him to wear a metal kirpan at all times, and it was accepted that the orthodox Sikh religion, indeed, requires it.[138] While the court acknowledged that

[132] *Multani* (n 26 above) para 32, citing *R v Big M Drug Mart Ltd* [1985] 1 SCR 295, 336–7

[133] *Multani* (n 26 above) para 33, citing *Syndicat Northcrest v Amselem* [2004] 2 SCR 551, 2004 SCC 47, para 46.

[134] See Pantesco (n 9 above).

[135] Judge Abdul Hamid held that the Koran (*Al Quran*) does not require it and that 'Islam is not about turban and beard'. The President noted that turbans 'are not only worn by Arabs' but were historically worn by peoples in desert areas such as the Afghans and Persians, often to cover the head and face from the heat, dryness and dust. The President further argued that today 'the turbans, distinguished by their designs and the way they are tied or worn, symbolise the nationality of the persons wearing them, for example whether they are Saudis, Sudanese, Afghans, Omanis etc'. In Malaysia, it was observed that few muftis or Sharia court judges wear the turban; see the *Serban case* (n 61 above).

[136] *Multani* (n 26 above) paras 34–5.

[137] *Ibid*, para 35, citing *Syndicat Northcrest v Amselem* (n 133 above) para 52.

[138] *Multani* (n 26 above) para 36.

the kirpan is a bladed weapon capable of causing injury, it accepted that it is primarily a religious symbol.[139] It was not considered capricious for Singh to refuse to wear a non-metal kirpan where he believed it would not comply with his religion, regardless of whether other Sikhs would have accepted it.[140] Furthermore, the interference with Singh's freedom to manifest his religion was regarded as neither trivial nor insignificant, since it deprived him of his right to attend a public school.[141]

It is readily apparent that the Canadian Supreme Court analysed the issue of infringement at a level of detail and sophistication which eluded the House of Lords in the *Begum case*. The fact that Singh could have attended another school was not considered a relevant factor in whether his freedom to manifest his religion had been infringed, unlike in *Begum* where it was given considerable emphasis by those judges who found that there had been no infringement. The House of Lords appeared to require a higher threshold test for establishing the existence of an infringement, whereas the Canadian court weighted the protection of constitutional rights more highly. At the same time, the question of voluntarily choosing the school did not arise in *Multani*, since the ban on the kirpan only arose after Singh had dropped the kirpan at school and not, as in Begum, after the student had already enrolled in the school with knowledge of its uniform policy. As such, the Canadian school's policy was not prospectively foreseeable to him in the way that the uniform policy was in the case of Denbigh High School, and where it played an important role in the Lords' rights analysis.

B. Infringement Not Justified

Having identified an infringement, the court considered whether it amounted to a reasonable limit prescribed law and demonstrably justified in a free and democratic society, as required under section 1 of the Canadian Charter of Rights and Freedoms. That provision imports two requirements: first, the legislative objective must be sufficiently important to justify limiting the right, and secondly, the means chosen must be proportional to that objective (meaning that the means must be rationally connected to the objective and must only minimally impair the right or freedom affected).[142]

Applying this test, the court found that the infringement was not justifiable. First, it accepted that the infringement pursued a pressing and

[139] *Ibid*, para 37.
[140] *Ibid*, para 39.
[141] *Ibid*, para 40.
[142] *Ibid*, para 43, citing *R v Oakes* [1986] 1 SCR 103 and *R v Edwards Books and Art Ltd* [1986] 2 SCR 713.

substantial objective, that is, ensuring a reasonable degree of safety in schools.[143] The court did not accept that a higher standard of safety in schools applied, such as absolute safety, which might have required metal detectors and banning all potentially dangerous items (including scissors, compasses, baseball bats and knives in the cafeteria), and, more importantly, which could jeopardise universal access to public education.[144]

Secondly, in applying its proportionality analysis, the court accepted that the measure was rationally connected with the objective of reasonable safety in schools, in light of the character of the kirpan as a bladed weapon which could cause injury.[145] However, the infringement did not minimally impair freedom of religion, since it did not fall within the range of reasonable alternatives.[146] The council of commissioners had imposed an absolute ban on wearing the kirpan to school, which was not a reasonable alternative, given the very low risk of violence if the kirpan was worn under the conditions earlier proposed, and which had been accepted by the student who had no evident behavioural problems.[147]

The risk of other students taking and using his kirpan was also very low, since a student would

> first have to physically restrain him, then search through his clothes, remove the sheath from his guthra, and try to unstitch or tear open the cloth enclosing the sheath in order to get to the kirpan.[148]

In addition, the court observed that there are many other more readily available objects in schools which could be used to commit violence, including scissors, pencils and baseball bats.[149]

Objectively, the court observed that there was no evidence of any violence in schools involving a kirpan in the 100 years since Sikhs had attended Canadian schools. While it was accepted that preventive measures are sometimes necessary before harm occurs, any threat must be 'unequivocally established' to justify infringing a constitutional right.[150] Kirpans worn under conditions were not inherently dangerous, and, in addition, the relationships between staff and students in school environments allowed staff to exercise greater control over potential threats than, for instance, was possible among strangers on board an aircraft or in a courtroom.[151]

143 *Multani* (n 26 above) para 48.
144 *Ibid*, para 46.
145 *Ibid*, para 49.
146 *Ibid*, paras 50–51, citing *RJR-MacDonald Inc v Canada (Attorney General)* [1995] 3 SCR 199, para 160. The infringement need not, however, be the least intrusive means.
147 *Multani* (n 26 above) paras 54, 57.
148 *Ibid*, para 58.
149 *Ibid*.
150 *Ibid*, para 67.
151 *Ibid*, para 65.

A further argument that allowing the kirpan to be worn might have a 'ripple effect'—encouraging other students to bring defensive weapons to school—was dismissed, on the basis that it was speculative and unsupported by evidence.[152] Neither was it accepted that the kirpan should be prohibited as a symbol of violence, given its 'purely symbolic nature' and the importance of respect for multiculturalism and tolerance of religious pluralism in Canada.[153] Far from banning symbols of difference, the court stated that it is the role of schools to ensure respect for them:

> Religious tolerance is a very important value of Canadian society. If some students consider it unfair that Gurbaj Singh may wear his kirpan to school while they are not allowed to have knives in their possession, it is incumbent on the schools to discharge their obligation to instil in their students this value that is … at the very foundation of our democracy.[154]

In the final analysis, the court found that the school had applied its code of conduct 'literally' and without considering alternative means of rendering the kirpan safe, thus making an unreasonable decision.[155]

Because the court found that the infringement was not justified, it was not necessary to proceed to balance positive and negative effects of the measure.[156] Nonetheless, the court went on to remark that '[t]he deleterious effects of a total prohibition thus outweigh its salutary effects'.[157] This was because an absolute prohibition on the kirpan would impair values such as multiculturalism, diversity, tolerance, impartiality and the development of an educational culture respectful of the rights of others.[158] In this regard, the court quoted from *R v M (MR)*:

> These values are best taught by example and may be undermined if the students' rights are ignored by those in authority.[159]

Likewise, it invoked the earlier decision of *Trinity Western University*, which held that:

> teachers are a medium for the transmission of values. … Schools are meant to develop civic virtue and responsible citizenship, to educate in an environment free of bias, prejudice and intolerance.[160]

In this light, the court stated:

> A total prohibition against wearing a kirpan to school undermines the value of this religious symbol and sends students the message that some religious

152 *Ibid*, paras 68–9.
153 *Ibid*, paras 70–77.
154 *Ibid*, para 76.
155 *Ibid*, para 99.
156 *Ibid*, para 78.
157 *Ibid*, para 79.
158 *Ibid*, para 78.
159 *R v M (MR)* [1998] 3 SCR 393, para 3 quoted in *ibid*.
160 *Trinity Western University v British Columbia College of Teachers* [2001] 1 SCR 772, 2001 SCC 31, para 13.

> practices do not merit the same protection as others. On the other hand, accommodating Gurbaj Singh and allowing him to wear his kirpan under certain conditions demonstrates the importance that our society attaches to protecting freedom of religion and to showing respect for its minorities.[161]

Also at issue in *Multani* was the threshold question whether a constitutional or administrative law standard of review was applicable to the matter at hand. The majority found that because the complaint was founded on freedom of religion under the Canadian Charter (a constitutional question), the Court of Appeal erred in applying an (irrelevant) administrative law standard of reasonableness to the matter.[162] By contrast, two judges in the Supreme Court, Deschamps and Abella JJ, found that a constitutional law justification is not appropriate in assessing an administrative body's decision (that of the council of commissioners) relating to human rights. In their view, despite the overlap identified by the majority between the concepts of 'reasonable accommodation' (an administrative law standard) and 'minimal impairment' (a constitutional standard), the two concepts should be seen as 'different analytical categories' involving different values.[163] The former considers the specific circumstances and interests of individual parties and allows for dialogue between them, whereas the latter considers broader societal interests.[164] To put it another way, '[a]n administrative law analysis is microcosmic [or individual], whereas a constitutional law analysis is generally macrocosmic [or public]'.[165]

IV. CONCLUSION

Recent cases about headscarves and other religious symbols continue to highlight the tension in pluralistic democratic societies between communal solidarity and diversity,[166] equality and culture,[167] gender and religion, and general and specific laws.[168] Some judicial decisions involving religious practices have struggled to reconcile these competing interests within a human rights framework, while others, such as the *Multani* decision in the Canadian Supreme Court, have done better than most in rationalising and balancing the rights and interests at stake.

[161] *Multani* (n 26 above) para 79.
[162] *Ibid*, paras 15–23; see also the concurring view of Lebel J at paras 141–4 and 153–5.
[163] *Ibid*, paras 129, 132.
[164] *Ibid*, paras 130–34.
[165] *Ibid*, para 132.
[166] D Goodhart, 'Discomfort of Strangers' *The Guardian* (24 February 2004) <http://www.guardian.co.uk/comment/story/0,,1154650,00.html> (accessed 25 June 2007).
[167] D McGoldrick, 'Multiculturalism and its Discontents' (2005) 5 *Human Rights Law Review* 27 at 38, citing B Barry, *Culture and Equality: An Egalitarian Critique of Multiculturalism* (Cambridge, MA, Harvard University Press, 2002).
[168] McGoldrick (n 167 above) 37.

While a fundamental challenge to the theory of multiculturalism may well be 'the issue of supporting illiberal cultures, particularly those that do not have at least a formal premise of gender equality',[169] it is equally a challenge for liberal courts to respect relatively harmless minority religious practices without stamping them out, whether in the name of some vaguely articulated interest in public order or social cohesion. Courts should not abandon their supervision of human rights too easily, lest the untested assertions of governments and decision-makers are allowed to pass as empirical truths about the existence of threats to legitimate public interests.

Where there is no evidence that banning Islamic dress would appreciably reduce the risk of extremism, the law should not step in. Indeed, in such circumstances restrictions may well provoke a backlash which genuinely encourages extremism. Merely finding someone's clothing 'confronting' or a 'mark of separation' is the flimsiest reason for banning it. Such statements reflect a crude aversion to visible signs of difference, which is the slightest step away from the more sinister impulse to eradicate that difference. It sends a message to Muslim citizens and migrants that they are only welcome in society as long as they set their differences, including their clothing—and thus, in part, their identity and beliefs—aside.

Such incivility and intolerance may play well to parts of the electorate, particularly those obsessed with policing the boundaries of a 'mainstream' community identity. But no respectable national identity can be built upon the exclusion and marginalisation of cultures that are different from 'ours'. An identity of that kind fails to value individual autonomy and inevitably compromises liberal democracy itself. People are entitled to freely express their personal and religious identity through their clothing, and to have their choices respected. Courts in liberal democratic societies should proceed very carefully before telling people what not to wear; if not, then justifications for restricting clothing will begin to wear dangerously thin.

[169] *Ibid*, 36.

8

Subjectivity and Refugee Fact-Finding

ARTHUR GLASS*

DECIDING REFUGEE CLAIMS involves the bringing together of the law—basically the Refugee Convention definition[1]—with the facts of the case.[2] At times, the meaning of the law may be unclear. More often the difficulties lie with the other moment of this process—the finding of facts. This is the subject of this chapter, and in it I ask: How do fact-finders come to have some confidence in their decisions? And how can others share or dispute this confidence?[3]

Decision-making is based on factual findings. But of course facts are not just found as one locates stones on the ground, and they cannot be found through the application of impersonal procedures. For, despite the name—fact-finding—this is an evaluative task. Finding the facts means selecting the relevant facts from the irrelevant, and the more plausible facts from the less plausible. As these judgements are made by a particular person—the decision-maker—there is an immediate and inevitable subjective component to this activity. Different people may well disagree as to which facts are salient, or which parts of the testimony are more likely to be true. But how can we have confidence in a practice of fact-finding explained in subjective terms? The inconstancy and variability of personal opinion has somehow to be turned into persuasive fact-finding.[4]

* I thank Giles Short, a Senior Member of the Australian Refugee Review Tribunal, for discussing these matters with me. Any errors are, of course, mine.

[1] Convention relating to the Status of Refugees (adopted 28 July 1951, entered into force 22 April 1954) 189 UNTS 137, in conjunction with the Protocol relating to the Status of Refugees (adopted 31 January 1967, entered into force 4 October 1967) 606 UNTS 267 (together 'Refugee Convention').

[2] See UNHCR, *Handbook on Procedures and Criteria for Determining Refugee Status under the 1951 Convention and the 1967 Protocol relating to the Status of Refugees* UN Doc HCR/IP/4/Eng/Rev.1, 2nd edn (Geneva 1992) para 29.

[3] As the paper is about fact-finding in general, I ignore the ways in which law-finding and fact-finding are connected. For example, the categories generated by the law via its interpretation will become important categories for fact-finding (see, eg, the role that 'discreet behaviour' has played in claims based on religion or homosexuality). And, going in the other direction, the law obtains its meaning through its application in particular cases.

[4] GS Goodwin-Gill and J McAdam, *The Refugee in International Law*, 3rd edn (Oxford, Oxford University Press, 2007) 551.

This problem, familiar to all legal fact-finding, is compounded in refugee decision-making. For a number of reasons, fact-finding here is more difficult. First, a fact-finder will be interested in the personal history of the applicant and the circumstances in his or her country of origin. With both of these matters there will be 'evidentiary voids'.[5] Applicants will give an account of what happened to them, but there is likely to be little corroborating evidence, such as documents or eye-witness testimony. And the general information—'country information'—is usually just that, general. Inferences must be drawn to link this material to the applicant's personal account.

Secondly, the inquiry will be concerned not just with what happened to the applicant, but ultimately with what might happen. What are the potential risks of persecution? This makes the process more speculative. It is not only focused backwards with a view to determining which facts probably or possibly occurred; the ultimate question is orientated towards the future. What are the risks to the applicant if he or she returns to his or her country of origin?

Thirdly, where there is so little to go on, the evidence provided by the applicant is central. Issues of credibility are thus crucial to the inquiry. Decision-makers will ask: Are the applicant's claims about X credible? Or, possibly, is the applicant credible?

Fourthly, the applicant and the decision-maker will more than likely have quite different cultural backgrounds. This compounds the chance of misunderstanding. If the decision-maker and applicant are to communicate with each other, interpreters usually will be needed. Moreover, as we will see, notions such as 'plausibility' play a key role in fact-finding. And what is plausible from one perspective may be implausible from another.

Fifthly, obtaining evidence from the applicant may prove difficult because of the applicant's experiences and present health, or possibly because of the unfamiliar or intimidating nature of the fact-finding proceedings.

Fact-finding is always *subjective*, in the sense that someone, a particular person, is doing it. However, if we read a statement of reasons for a refugee status decision and we have a different view of the facts of the case from the decision-maker, we do not see this simply as a difference of taste for which there can be no accounting.[6] The claim that the fact-finding is defective carries the implication that it is defective for specific reasons.

[5] JC Hathaway, *Rebuilding Trust: Report of the Review of Fundamental Justice in Information Gathering and Dissemination at the Immigration and Refugee Board of Canada* (Ottowa, Immigration and Refugee Board of Canada, 1993) 6.

[6] About matters of taste there is no disputing (*de gustibus non disputandum est*): Seneca.

'Wrong', here, is not just an expression of the critic's personal dislike. To make this point from the side of the decision-maker, the finding of facts in this context is not just a claim that the decision-maker sincerely believes these to be the facts. It is a claim that the findings are reasonable and that others would decide the facts in the same way, faced with the same material. In other words, fact-finding is an appeal to *inter-subjective* criteria. The variability of personal opinion is turned into *reasonable* fact-finding through the application of inter-personal standards. My aim is to give an account of some of these.[7]

However, to make these kinds of points I need a specific example of refugee decision-making, for with regard to these matters not all refugee decision-making is the same. That is the point: this regulatory framework is made up of understandings and expectations that arise out of the particular legal and bureaucratic setting. True, refugee fact-finding has certain characteristics; I have just noted five of these. But these commonalities are not in themselves sufficient to determine how fact-finding should be carried out.

For reasons of convenience I turn to the Australian Refugee Review Tribunal ('Tribunal'), although much of the following discussion will equally apply to refugee decision-making elsewhere. This body provides merits review for onshore Protection Visa refusals.[8] Its decision-making procedures usually involve a hearing with the applicant,[9] as well as a consideration of the documentary material from the applicant and 'country information' from various sources.[10] As the Tribunal is not bound by the rules of evidence, it is open to individual Members[11] to take account of whatever material they consider relevant. The process is non-adversarial and this places even more responsibility upon the decision-maker. In addition, Members sit alone. Hearings often involve only the Member, the applicant and an interpreter.

[7] What follows is a description of these standards. For a recent account that argues for the ideological way in which these standards can be used to conceal the constructive nature of refugee fact-finding, see JA Sweeney, 'The Lure of "Facts" in Asylum Appeals' in SR Smith (ed), *Applying Theory to Policy and Practice: Issues for Critical Reflection* (Aldershot, Ashgate Publishing, 2007).

[8] And in some circumstances, Protection Visa cancellations.

[9] The right to a hearing can be lost if the applicant fails to respond to Tribunal requests for information or comment.

[10] The Tribunal itself has a Country Information Unit that provides material and answers specific questions. I am told that a Member has access to the Department of Immigration's Country Information Service that draws on reports of human rights organisations, journals, newspapers, the Australian Department of Foreign Affairs and Trade, and UNHCR. Available also electronically are most of the reports from national and international bodies, such as the US State Department, UK Home Office, Danish Immigration Service, International Helsinki Federation for Human Rights, Amnesty International, Human Rights Watch, and so on.

[11] This is the name given to the Tribunal's decision-makers.

More people fail before the Tribunal than succeed. The Tribunal affirmed only 63 per cent of the Department of Immigration's decisions in the years 2004–05 and 2005–06.[12] There are many reasons why a review may fail—the applicant is believed but his or her fears are not Convention-related, the applicant fails to attend a hearing, and so on—but with every claim there is the possibility that it is supported by material that is not true. Awareness of this possibility is a starting assumption.[13]

The principles that set the framework for fact-finding are those dealing with the onus of proof and standard of proof. Material before decision-makers is often equivocal. Yet, in this state of uncertainty, cases can be decided with some degree of confidence only because the party with the burden of proof either has (or has not) established the facts in issue to the requisite degree. Without these default rules there often could be no decision one way or the other.[14]

We are familiar in other contexts with the onus of proof being on the plaintiff or the Crown, and the standard of proof being expressed as 'on the balance of probabilities' or 'beyond reasonable doubt'. But there is nothing inevitable about those rules. They reflect the particular values and interests considered to be at stake in, for example, negligence cases or criminal cases. Refugee law generates different values and interests. In refugee determinations the costs of error are high (possibly death) and the applicant labours under evidentiary disadvantages. Demanding too much evidence would undermine the point of the Refugee Convention—that States should protect persons in specified dire circumstances.

In this context, any reference to onus of proof in refugee determinations is said to be misplaced. For it would be wrong to treat refugees as we treat other legal applicants and place on them the burden of making out a case.[15] We will see below that this difficulty is acknowledged in the rules concerning the standard of proof and in the limited duty of inquiry imposed upon the Tribunal. However, an onus of some sort remains with the applicant: the Member must be satisfied that the facts as established bring the applicant within the legal definition of 'refugee'. If the Member is not satisfied, the applicant loses; that is the default rule.

However, the standard of proof is lower than 'on the balance of probabilities'. To establish a 'well-founded' fear of persecution, applicants have only to show that they face a 'real chance' of persecution, where a

[12] *Migration Review Tribunal and Refugee Review Tribunal: Annual Report 2005–06* (Canberra, Cth of Australia, 2006) 29, 30 <http:www.rrt.gov.au/publications/annrpts/0506/MRTRRTAR0506.pdf> (accessed 9 June 2007).

[13] The Tribunal's review follows on from a negative decision from the Department of Immigration, and the Department's decision may have turned on this very point.

[14] For an account of these procedures as a response to the 'burden of ignorance', see R Gaskins, *Burdens of Proof in Modern Discourses* (New Haven, Yale University Press, 1992).

[15] UNCHR Handbook (n 2 above) para 196.

'real chance' is understood as a degree of likelihood somewhere between 'not far-fetched' and a 'reasonable possibility'.[16] But how is this relaxed standard of proof passed down to the activity of finding the facts upon which this test operates? Do these facts have to be established on the balance of possibilities, or the balance of probabilities? The High Court of Australia in *Minister for Immigration and Ethnic Affairs v Guo Wei Rong*[17] accepted that the Tribunal must often come to a view about whether past events occurred and the likelihood of future events occurring. In doing this, it must weigh the evidence and on balance choose one set of events over another. Possibly this can be explained as doing something different from balancing the probabilities—perhaps as balancing the possibilities. But however it is described, it is still an evaluative process through which the 'more likely' is chosen over the 'less likely'.

Guo connects the 'real chance' test and the weighing of the factual evidence as follows. The degree of confidence the decision-maker has in these findings will be a factor when considering whether there is a 'real chance' of persecution. For example, the more confident the finding that persecution has not occurred to date, the less there is a 'real chance' of persecution in the future.[18]

This degree of confidence (or lack thereof) in the findings is expressed in another established approach that proceeds as follows. If the decision-maker cannot be satisfied that the applicant's claims did not occur, then the application should be assessed on the basis that it is *possible* that the events occurred as claimed.[19] In other words, a proper application of the 'real chance' test calls upon the decision-maker to take account of possibilities, even if these are considered unlikely.[20]

At times it has been suggested that the assessment of the facts should better reflect the difficult position of refugees. The applicant's account should be accepted—presumed to be true—it is said, unless there is good reason not to do so.[21] The risks of uncertainty would then fall on the State rather the applicant. The UNHCR Handbook suggests that

> [i]f the applicant's account appears credible, he should, unless there are good reasons to the contrary, be given the benefit of the doubt.[22]

[16] In other words, below 50 per cent: see *Chan v Minister for Immigration and Ethnic Affairs* (1989) 169 CLR 379 (HCA).

[17] *Minister for Immigration and Ethnic Affairs v Guo Wei Rong* (1997) 191 CLR 559 (HCA).

[18] But of course a claim of possible future persecution can be made out without the claim of past persecution. This is obviously the case with many *sur place* claims.

[19] *Rajasundaram v Minister for Immigration and Multicultural Affairs* [1998] FCA 565, (1999) 51 ALD 682; *Minister for Immigration and Multicultural Affairs v Rajalingam* [1999] FCA 719, (1999) 93 FCR 220.

[20] This still leaves the question (assuming these facts): Is the Convention definition satisfied?

[21] I Durst, 'Lost in Translation: Why Due Process Demands Deference to the Refugee's Narrative' (2000) 53 *Rutgers Law Review* 127.

[22] UNHCR Handbook (n 2 above) para 196.

It is quite appropriate to begin with the assumption that the applicant is telling the truth. But this cannot be conclusive of the issue. For the mere fact that the applicant claims a fear of persecution does not establish that the fear is well-founded, or, for that matter, that the fear is genuinely held.[23] Some of what is claimed may be false. Even a presumption of truth approach concedes this, since it only applies 'if the applicant's account appears credible' and 'unless there are good reasons to the contrary'. In other words, the Tribunal cannot avoid testing the evidence placed before it, including the applicant's account.[24]

The above discussion establishes that the Tribunal finds facts through such notions as 'is the Member satisfied?', 'real chance', 'weighing material on balance', and 'not satisfied that the claims did not occur'. While different decision-makers may have different views as to how these ideas apply to particular facts, this is the vocabulary that orientates all of their thinking. Without these basic concepts, reasonable fact-finding would have no stable meaning.

As information relevant to the review is scarce, much turns upon the applicant's evidence. This makes assessments of credibility crucial in refugee determinations. Is the applicant credible?[25] Or, more likely, is a *part* of the applicant's evidence credible?

One way of assessing an applicant's credibility is through a consideration of his or her demeanour when giving evidence. Demeanour provides a context in everyday life for determining a speaker's meaning. But this is more likely to be a way of determining the speaker's attitude to what is said: 'Is the speaker joking?', 'Is he or she being ironic?', rather than: 'Is the speaker telling the truth?'. In any event, testing the applicant's evidence in this way is dangerous, particularly in a jurisdiction where the decision-maker and the applicant have different cultural backgrounds and where the evidence is received via an interpreter.[26] There could be many reasons for an applicant's confidence or hesitancy, clarity of thought or confusion, calmness or nervousness. Clearly no findings should be based on these points alone.[27] Furthermore, decision-makers should be discouraged from believing that experience on the job can give them a 'sixth sense'

[23] *Minister for Immigration and Ethnic Affairs v Guo Wei Rong* (n 17 above) 596 (Kirby J).

[24] D Martin, 'Reforming Asylum Adjudication: On Navigating the Coast of Bohemia' (1990) 138 *University of Pennsylvania Law Review* 1247 at 1287.

[25] As Michael Kagan points out, it is more objective to put the question as 'Is the material credible?', rather than 'Do I believe this material?': M Kagan, 'Is Truth in the Eye of the Beholder? Objective Credibility Assessment in Refugee Status Determination' (2003) 17 *Georgetown Immigration Law Journal* 367 at 381.

[26] For a nice statement of this point, see Gray J in *Kathiresan v Minister for Immigration and Multicultural Affairs* [1998] FCA 159.

[27] G Coffey, 'The Credibility of Credibility Evidence at the RRT' (2003) 15 *International Journal of Refugee Law* 377 at 386ff, 414–15.

about these things.[28] I cannot say that these sorts of considerations play no role in the Tribunal's decision-making, but they *should* play no role in it or in the statement of reasons for the decision.[29]

More familiar ideas that figure in assessments of credibility are assessments of the *plausibility* of the applicant's account and the *consistency* of the applicant's evidence. The basis for these regulatory ideas is straightforward. Conventional wisdom has it that the reasonable is more likely to be true than the unreasonable, and a detailed account is more likely to be true than one less detailed. Consistency is also important, for truth is consistent and coherent with itself, while falsity is not. But while these ideas are commonplace, the risks of applying them in this setting are also obvious: sometimes the unreasonable or the general is true, sometimes inconsistencies are irrelevant.[30] And what is considered unreasonable, or not sufficiently specific, or inconsistent, may be a reflection not of the evidence itself, but of the inadequacies of the decision-maker.[31]

By the plausibility of the evidence, I have in mind two things. Is the evidence sufficiently specific? And does the evidence make sense? As a regulatory assumption, specificity strengthens the account and a lack of detail can weaken it. There may be good reasons for the lack of detail, and the lack of sense may be due to the decision-maker's failure of imagination, rather than any failings of the applicant. At the least, these matters must be put to the applicant to learn what these reasons might be. The response will at times explain away the misunderstanding; at other times, puzzles will remain. The issue then becomes: What weight should be given to these puzzles?

Inconsistencies are generated when the applicant has provided information at a number of points in time and this information cannot all stand together. Perhaps there are direct inconsistencies between these accounts. Possibly the problem is a lack of coherence, in that it does not all hang together. A typical example of a potential lack of coherence is where the claims raised at the hearing are late claims; they were not made, say, in the initial interview with the Department of Immigration. Again, there may be good reasons for this and due process demands that these matters be

28 Kagan (n 25 above) 378ff.

29 Section 91V of the Migration Act 1958 (Cth) is presumably a response to this kind of criticism. In my view, it is an ill-conceived response, and as far as I can gather, is little used.

30 This is because they do not relate to the central issues of the review, or, possibly, because they can be attributed to the applicant's ill-health or the stress of the proceedings.

31 J Cohen, 'Questions of Credibility: Omissions, Discrepencies and Errors of Recall in the Testimony of Asylum Seekers' (2002) 13 *International Journal of Refugee Law* 293; C Rousseau, F Crepeau, P Foxen and F Houle, 'The Complexity of Determining Refugeehood' (2002) 15 *Journal of Refugee Studies* 43; and Amnesty International (UK), *Get It Right: How Home Office Decision Making Fails Refugees* (February 2004) <http://www.amnesty.org.uk/uploads/documents/doc_15239.pdf> (accessed 9 June 2007).

explored with the applicant. But if inconsistencies or incoherence remain, this will weaken the applicant's account.

A common form of potential inconsistency is where the applicant's claims conflict with country information. There may be occasions when the inconsistency is false, as the Tribunal has relied on inadequate information.[32] No doubt some material is better than other material (more reliable, more detailed, more up-to-date, and so on). One would expect the Tribunal's Country Information Unit to assist the Member to find the better materials—material that accurately reflects the conditions in the country of origin. But the approach of the Country Information Unit is to *provide* information, not to *evaluate* information.[33] Investigations of country information will often disclose conflicting accounts. Here the Member has to reconcile these differences by ranking the material—on the basis of age or source—or possibly finding the mean between rival accounts. If accepted country information produces facts inconsistent with the applicant's account, and these remain after obtaining the applicant's response, then there is a problem. A choice has to be made as to which to accept. Members of the Tribunal will often choose the country information over the applicant's account. But the issue still remains as to what weight to give to these findings.

As noted above, proper fact-finding will provide an opportunity for the applicant to respond to potentially adverse information. Hearing the other side assists in the disclosure of the relevant facts and it helps avoid misunderstandings.[34] Examples of adverse material include information from 'concerned members of the community' (such as 'dob-in' letters), apparent inconsistencies between statements given by the applicant at different points in time, and inconsistencies between the country information and the applicant's account. Judicial review has established that adverse material does not encompass the reasoning process of the decision-maker. The reasons why the account is found implausible or inconsistent do not have to be disclosed for comment prior to the decision.[35]

The Tribunal has a double obligation to disclose adverse material, and this can lead to confusion on the part of the applicant and the Member. Section 424A of the Migration Act 1958 imposes a specific obligation to provide to the applicant

[32] Examples of this can be found in J Millbank, 'Imagining Otherness: Refugee Claims on the Basis of Sexuality in Canada and Australia' (2002) 26 *Melbourne University Law Review* 144; and C Dauvergne and J Millbank, 'Burdened by Proof' (2003) 31 *Federal Law Review* 299.

[33] I am told, however, that the Country Information Unit will provide advice as to possible bias in particular sources, and this will assist the Member when attributing weight to the material.

[34] It is also the appropriate way for decision-makers to treat the people before them.

[35] *Re Minister for Immigration and Multicultural Affairs; ex parte Applicant S154/2002* [2003] HCA 60, (2003) 201 ALR 437.

particulars of information that the Tribunal considers would be the reason, or part of the reason, for affirming the decision under review.

This provision is testament to the accidentality of law reform. It was proposed in 1997 in a Bill that took away the right of the review applicant to a hearing.[36] Section 424A protected an aspect of due process in the anticipated circumstances of a paper review. As it turned out, the Senate blocked the changes to the right to a hearing but section 424A was implemented nonetheless.

Section 424A has exceptions. There is no need to provide adverse information which is in the form of general information, or information that was given by the applicant for the purpose of the review. In other words, inconsistencies between the applicant's account and country information, or between different accounts given by the applicant to the Tribunal, do not have to be disclosed under section 424A. But these matters must be disclosed as part of the due process associated with a fair hearing. When matters fall within section 424A, its obligations operate independently from the requirements for holding a fair hearing. Due process with regard to these matters must be given twice.[37] While this is a little odd, section 424A has proved to be a simple way in which courts can supervise aspects of due process. Failure to comply with section 424A is a common source of jurisdictional error, even if due process was given at the hearing.[38]

As refugee applicants face difficulties in providing evidence for their claims, the decision-maker has some responsibilities. The UNHCR Handbook states that 'the duty to ascertain and evaluate all the relevant facts is shared between the applicant and the examiner'.[39] Judicial review has clarified the extent of this obligation in the Australian context. The Tribunal has a limited duty to inquire (where the Tribunal is in a better position to obtain information and it can do so without much difficulty).[40] Material considerations are also relevant. The Tribunal will have a view as to when investigations become too costly.[41]

[36] Whether a hearing was held or not was left to the discretion of the Presiding Member: see Migration Legislation Amendment Bill (No 4) 1997 (Cth).

[37] This does not mean that the applicant always has notice of potential problems *before* the hearing, since both s 424A and the common law obligations of due process can be satisfied via correspondence after the hearing. There is also, of course, a difference between receiving notice of difficulties and being in the position to respond to them.

[38] See *SAAP v Minister for Immigration and Multicultural and Indigenous Affairs* [2005] HCA 24, (2005) 215 ALR 162; *SZEEU v Minister for Immigration and Multicultural and Indigenous Affairs* [2006] FCAFC 2, (2006) 150 FCR 214.

[39] UNHCR Handbook (n 2 above) para 196.

[40] *Sun Zhan Qui v Minister for Immigration and Ethnic Affairs* (1997) 81 FCR 71 (FCFCA); *Minister for Immigration and Ethnic Affairs v Singh* (1997) 74 FCR 553 (FCFCA).

[41] S Taylor, 'Informational Deficiencies Affecting Refugee Status Determinations' (1994) 3 *University of Tasmania Law Review* 43 at 79, says that provisions like s 424A only require the provision of *adverse* information. There is no obligation to provide material that might

I have described, if only briefly, a number of basic assumptions and regulatory principles that guide Tribunal fact-finding: the expectation that the evidence will be tested, the onus and standard of proof rules, standards of plausibility and consistency for assessing credibility, the obligation to allow for a response to adverse material and the obligation for the Tribunal to itself inquire into the facts.

These guiding norms are more than personal criteria, for they exist independently from and stand over individual Members. Members are not free to disregard these ideas. Additionally, what is a reasoned finding of facts will take its meaning from these regulatory principles. A reasoned finding of facts will *appropriately* test the evidence, *sensibly* weigh the evidence against the *relevant* standard of proof, *reasonably* assess credibility through the ideas of plausibility and consistency, give the *appropriate* due process and fulfil the *obligation* to independently inquire into the facts.

A descriptive account of these regulatory norms can answer the question posed at the beginning of the chapter, namely, how fact-finders can come to have some confidence in their decisions. And it discloses criteria through which others can share or dispute this confidence.

Nevertheless, a *descriptive* account of fact-finding practices immediately gives rise to the following questions. Are the fact-finding practices in place good enough? How successfully do the Members apply these standards? How can Members be encouraged to apply these standards appropriately?

There is an available body of material, often critical, responding to the first and second questions.[42] Here I can only comment on the third

strengthen the applicant's case. Further, the Tribunal's responsibility to share relevant information does not extend in Australia, as it does in Canada, to making the country information held by the Tribunal available to he public: Dauvergne and Millbank (n 32 above) 339.

[42] Taylor (n 41 above), referring to over-reliance on Department of Foreign Affairs and Trade material, and failure to understand legitimate reasons for inconsistent testimony; S Kneebone, 'The Refugee Review Tribunal and the Assessment of Credibility' (1998) 5 *Australian Journal of Administrative Law* 78, referring to over-emphasis on country information; C Colborne, 'The RRT: A Personal View' (1999) 75 *Reform* 27, referring to lack of disclosure of relevant material; Millbank (n 32 above) referring to lack of understanding of claims based on sexuality, the use of 'discreet', improperly policing sexual mores, and the unfavourable comparison with Canada; Dauvergne and Millbank (n 32 above), referring to inconsistent approaches to evaluating evidence, improper use of biased or inadequate country information, the unfavourable comparison with Canada, and specific changes proposed; and Coffey (n 27 above), referring to examples of poor decision-making, wrong use of demeanor, and guidelines for evaluating credibility. Less critical is the report of the Senate Legal and Constitutional References Committee, *A Sanctuary under Review: An Examination of Australia's Refugee and Humanitarian Determination Processes* (Canberra, Cth of Australia, 2000) ch 5. Partly as a response to these criticisms, the Tribunal recently formulated and publicised its own 'Guidelines on the Assessment of Credibility' (October 2006) <http://www.rrt.gov.au/publications/CredibilityGuidanceOct06.pdf> (accessed 9 June 2007).

question: How can Members be encouraged to apply these standards appropriately? Appoint suitable people in the first place. Adequately train new Members. Re-train old Members—for experience can bring certain pathologies.[43] Have some cases decided by more than one person—for personal idiosyncrasies have less influence on a two- or three-Member panel, and seeing how others do their work should encourage self-reflection. These are all obvious suggestions, but no less worthy for that reason.

I conclude with the following observation. Ultimately, what guides the application of the fact-finding principles I have discussed is the Member's understanding of the purpose of the review. It makes a large difference to how the fact-finding is approached depending on whether the point of the review is seen as correctly identifying *valid* claims, or whether it is seen as correctly identifying *invalid* claims.[44] Both tasks are involved, of course, but the point is which has priority. The briefest familiarity with the Tribunal's work will disclose that some Members are more worried than others that they may be fooled by an applicant. Some Members are more confident than others that they can uncover the truth. While these are matters of personal temper, much turns on this basic attitude. Every effort should be made to promote the idea that the point of refugee fact-finding is to identify valid claims. The greater worry is that genuine refugees are found to be otherwise.

[43] Such as 'compassion fatigue', over-confidence, and a mechanical processing of claims.
[44] A point made by Taylor (n 41 above) 63.

9

Towards Convergence in the Interpretation of the Refugee Convention: A Proposal for the Establishment of an International Judicial Commission for Refugees

ANTHONY M NORTH AND JOYCE CHIA*

I. INTRODUCTION

THERE ARE, AS most of us know, many problems with the Refugee Convention.[1] This chapter will not discuss all of them. Nor, indeed, will it solve any of them. Rather, its purpose is to suggest one way of addressing a critical problem. The problem is that while the Convention is a universal humanitarian treaty, designed to offer universal protection, the *interpretation* of the treaty differs from country to country, and even within countries. The result is that a refugee in Canada may not be a refugee in the United States, and vice versa. Seeking asylum, in the words of the European Council on Refugees and Exiles, becomes a 'dangerous lottery'.[2]

* We gratefully acknowledge in particular the invaluable assistance of Elizabeth Lacey, a previous Associate at the Federal Court of Australia; Bianca Hill, a former Research Associate at the Federal Court of Australia; and Jessica Howard, Lecturer, University of Melbourne. We extend our appreciation for the helpful comments of Professor James Hathaway, Professor Philip Alston, Professor Hilary Charlesworth and the referees. All errors and omissions remain our own.

[1] Convention relating to the Status of Refugees (adopted 28 July 1951, entered into force 22 April 1954) 189 UNTS 137; in conjunction with the Protocol relating to the Status of Refugees (adopted 31 January 1967, entered into force 4 October 1967) 606 UNTS 267 (together 'Convention or Refugee Convention').

[2] European Council on Refugees and Exiles, 'Europe Must End Asylum Lottery: Refugee NGOs' PR6/11/2004/EXT/RW (Press Release, 4 November 2004) <http://www.ecre.org/press/asylumlot.pdf> (accessed 10 June 2007).

In this chapter, we propose a practical way of addressing this issue. We acknowledge that our proposal will not solve the problem of conflicting interpretations. In the present climate, the obvious solution—an international court with the power to bind States parties—is not a practical one. Rather, we hope to create an international forum in which different interpretations can be discussed, and from which may be built an international consensus on the interpretation of the Convention.

The proposal is simple. We suggest that the United Nations High Commissioner for Refugees ('UNHCR') establish an independent international judicial commission, comprised of a small number of eminent jurists and experts in refugee law. The function of the commission would be to provide carefully reasoned opinions on major questions relating to construction of the Convention. These opinions would be neither binding nor enforceable. Rather, their authority would be derived from their institutional mandate and their intellectual and practical quality.

In essence, this proposal continues and expands the second track of the Global Consultations process convened by UNHCR in 2001–02,[3] in which experts discussed difficult issues regarding the interpretation of the Convention and from which, subsequently, UNHCR produced legal guidance in the form of Guidelines on International Protection.[4]

Such a commission would provide useful international 'soft law', alongside the UNHCR Handbook, UNHCR Executive Committee Conclusions and the Guidelines on International Protection. It would, however, have significant advantages over these other sources of soft law. As a

[3] The Global Consultations on International Protection were an initiative of UNHCR which aimed to 'rise to modern challenges confronting refugee protection, to shore up support for the international framework of protection principles, and to explore the scope for enhancing protection through new approaches': E Feller, 'Preface' in E Feller, V Türk and F Nicholson (eds), *Refugee Protection in International Law: UNHCR's Global Consultations on International Protection* (Cambridge, Cambridge University Press, 2003) xvii. They consisted of three 'tracks', the second of which consisted of expert roundtables held during 2001.

[4] For a summary, see V Türk, 'Introductory Note to UNHCR Guidelines on International Protection' (2003) 15 *International Journal of Refugee Law* 303. UNHCR has issued the following Guidelines, available at <http://www.unhcr.org>: 'Gender-Related Persecution within the Context of Article 1A(2) of the 1951 Convention/or Its 1967 Protocol relating to the Status of Refugees' UN Doc HCR/GIP/02/01 (7 May 2002); '"Membership of a Particular Social Group" within the Context of Article 1A(2) of the 1951 Convention/or Its 1967 Protocol relating to the Status of Refugees' UN Doc HCR/GIP/02/02 (7 May 2002); '"Internal Flight or Relocation Alternative" within the Context of Article 1A(2) of the 1951 Convention and/or 1967 Protocol relating to the Status of Refugees' UN Doc HCR/GIP/03/04 (23 July 2003); 'Cessation of Refugee Status under Article 1C(5) and (6) of the 1951 Convention relating to the Status of Refugees (the "Ceased Circumstances" Clauses)' UN Doc HCR/GIP/03/03 (10 February 2003); 'Application of the Exclusion Clauses: Article 1F of the 1951 Convention relating to the Status of Refugees' UN Doc HCR/GIP/03/05 (4 September 2003); and 'Religion-Based Refugee Claims under Article 1A(2) of the 1951 Convention and/or the 1967 Protocol relating to the Status of Refugees' UN Doc HCR/GIP/04/06 (28 April 2004).

permanent body, it would be able to address on-going issues of interpretation in a detailed way, based on an extensive knowledge of the principles and practice of refugee law. Our hope is that these opinions will begin to shape the direction of domestic interpretations, and thus move us towards the convergence of interpretations of the Convention.

The aims of this chapter are to make a case for further convergence in interpretation of the Convention and to attempt to formulate a method to promote such convergence. We hope to provoke and stimulate both debate and action. As such, the chapter focuses on the practical aspects of the proposal, instead of attempting a scholarly disquisition on the niceties of treaty interpretation or international judiciaries. It is also, we emphasise, a *proposal*; namely, it is open to improvements, criticisms and changes.

The chapter begins with an exploration of why, in our view, further convergence in the interpretation of the Convention is desirable, although it is not the purpose of this chapter to discuss this at length. We then examine the prospects for further convergence through existing efforts and mechanisms, concluding that the prospects are inherently limited. In the third section, we explain the principles underlying our proposal, with reference to the experience of existing international judicial bodies. Finally, we set out the details of the proposal.

II. THE NEED FOR CONVERGENCE IN INTERPRETATION

In this section of the chapter, we establish why, in our view, there is an unacceptable degree of diversity in the interpretation of the Convention.

A. Like Cases Treated Alike

It is an elementary principle of fairness that like cases ought to be treated alike in the application of laws. It is elementary common sense that a refugee, recognised as such pursuant to the definition in Article 1A of the Convention, should also be recognised as a refugee in another country using the same definition. As will be discussed later, this is far from the position today. As a consequence, the application of the Convention is unfair. It is unfair to refugees, who may be treated differently depending on which country they happen to end up in. It is also unfair to States that adopt more generous interpretations. This unfairness is most obvious in the case of refugee recognition, but it also extends to interpretation of other aspects of the Convention. For example, the loss of refugee status or the exclusion of refugees under the Convention should not depend upon quirks of national interpretation. It goes without saying that unfairness in these matters has very real ramifications for refugees and for States.

Of course, the principle that like cases be treated alike does not compel uniformity of interpretation. Interpretation, we recognise, is a dynamic process, in which diversity of opinion is a necessary and healthy element. It is important, however, that in interpreting an international treaty designed to offer universal protection we do not lose sight of this fundamental, and easily overlooked, principle of justice.

In the case of international refugee law, the present degree of diversity undermines this principle of justice. While diversity exists in domestic legal systems, the balance is held in check by forces such as the notion of precedent in common law systems. The pressures in favour of convergence are much looser in international law, where treaty interpretation is left up to States parties and any adjudicatory mechanism they decide to adopt, subject to the accepted principles of treaty interpretation. As the UN Human Rights Committee has noted in relation to reservations, these principles do not operate adequately in relation to human rights treaties, because in those treaties State interests are rarely at stake.[5] Indeed, the Human Rights Committee has felt it necessary to perform the role of treaty interpretation in relation to reservations itself, vividly illustrating the need for greater consistency in treaty interpretation.

The purpose of the proposed commission is to correct the balance between uniformity and diversity in interpretation in respect of the Convention. It would encourage convergence of interpretation by exposing differences in interpretation of the Convention, and expounding and explaining the preferable construction.

We recognise that convergence of interpretation in itself will not remedy other aspects of unfairness, such as different procedures for refugee determination, which also have important effects on the fairness of the regime. However, while the convergence of interpretation will not solve all the world's ills, it will be a concrete and achievable step towards improving the fairness of the current refugee regime.

B. The Special Position of Refugee Law

It may be argued that the rules of treaty interpretation, which confer the right of interpretation upon States parties, do not place much emphasis on the principle that like cases be treated alike. However, there are at least four good reasons why international refugee law requires a different approach.

[5] Human Rights Committee, 'General Comment No 24: Issues relating to Reservations Made upon Ratification or Accession to the Covenant or the Optional Protocols thereto, or in relation to Declarations under Article 41 of the Covenant' UN Doc CCPR/C/21/Rev.1/Add.6 (4 November 1994).

First, while the obligations under the Convention are owed by States to each other, they are owed *in relation to* refugees, who are the substantive beneficiaries of the Convention.[6] While there may be some position of equality in the case of States parties, which all have the right to interpret the treaty, clearly this is not true in the case of refugees themselves.

Secondly, the Convention is designed to be a universal humanitarian instrument, offering a regime of international protection to the most vulnerable. In this respect, the aims and context of the treaty are fundamentally undermined if there are substantial differences between the views taken by States parties of their obligations. Obviously, the rights of the refugee are impaired. Further, other States parties may be forced to shoulder a heavier burden. A stark illustration of this may be seen in the case of *R v Secretary of State for the Home Department, ex parte Adan*,[7] in which three asylum seekers who claimed persecution by non-State actors transited through Germany and France before arriving in the United Kingdom. At that time, unlike the United Kingdom, Germany and France did not recognise persecution by non-State actors as a Convention basis for refugee status. It was held that the UK Secretary of State was unable to authorise the asylum seekers' return to either Germany or France because they were not 'safe third countries', resulting in the United Kingdom having greater obligations than other States parties.

The same case also illustrates the third point, namely that international refugee law includes a framework in which refugees are 'shared around' through the mechanisms of settlement and regional agreements. This international framework of refugee burden-sharing is impeded by the fact that a refugee in one country may not be considered a refugee in another country. Divergences in interpretation do not always favour the interests of States. The recent European Union Directive on the qualification for refugee status[8] indicates that States may, in the context of regional burden-sharing and forum-shopping agreements, have a greater interest in harmonisation than in divergence.

Finally, while in some cases diversity in interpretation has roots in the recognition of legitimate differences, this is not true of interpretation of the Convention. Federalism and the doctrine of the 'margin of

[6] But see the views of the majority of the High Court of Australia in *NAGV and NAGW of 2002 v Minister for Immigration and Multicultural and Indigenous Affairs* [2005] HCA 6, (2005) 213 ALR 668, para 27, and contrast the position of Kirby J at para 68.

[7] *R v Secretary of State for the Home Department, ex parte Adan* [1999] EWCA Civ 1948, [1999] 4 All ER 774; affirmed [2001] 2 AC 477 (HL).

[8] Council Directive 2004/83/EC of 29 April 2004 on Minimum Standards for the Qualification and Status of Third Country Nationals or Stateless Persons as Refugees or as Persons Who Otherwise Need International Protection and the Content of the Protection Granted [2004] OJ L304/12.

appreciation' in the European Union, for example, permit variations between States and on the basis of different values and systems that ought to be given due recognition. Such values may well justify differences in the procedures for refugee determination, but they do not sustain the more general differences in interpretation of the Convention, which rarely, if ever, arise out of such due deference.

C. The Present State of Divergence in the Interpretation of the Convention

The next logical step is to demonstrate that the present balance between consistency and diversity in interpretation is inappropriate. To many, this may be self-evident. As has been said, 'the interpretation of the criteria for granting refugee status and asylum displays almost as many variations as there are countries'.[9]

This section of the chapter sketches some of the areas of debate to demonstrate that the difficulties—and their impact—are substantial.

One indication of the extent of the difficulties is the existence of debate about the broad interpretative approach taken to the Convention. Judges of the High Court of Australia, for example, have disagreed whether the interpretation of the Convention should be confined by its original historical meaning, or whether an evolutionary approach should be taken.[10]

The most notable controversies, however, concern the definition of 'refugee', enshrined in Article 1A(2) of the Convention, which states that a 'refugee' is a person who,

> owing to well-founded fear of being persecuted for reasons of race, religion, nationality, membership of a particular social group or political opinion, is outside the country of his nationality and is unable or, owing to such fear, is unwilling to avail himself of the protection of that country; or who, not having a nationality and being outside the country of his former habitual residence as a result of such events, is unable or, owing to such fear, is unwilling to return to it.

Perhaps the most controversial element of this definition is the category of 'membership of a particular social group', which is the subject of one

[9] E Arboleda and I Hoy, 'The Convention Refugee Definition in the West: Disharmony of Interpretation and Application' (1993) 5 *International Journal of Refugee Law* 66 at 76, quoting Report of the Lawyers Committee for Human Rights, *The UNHCR at 40: Refugee Protection at the Crossroads* (February 1991).

[10] *Minister for Immigration and Multicultural Affairs v Ibrahim* (2000) 204 CLR 1 (HCA) 46–57 (Gummow J) and 70–71 (Kirby J). See generally E Lauterpacht and D Bethlehem, 'The Scope and Content of the Principle of *Non-Refoulement*: Opinion', in Feller, Türk and Nicholson (n 3 above) 104–06.

set of UNHCR Guidelines.[11] Does the particular group have to exist outside of a social perception of a group?[12] Most common law jurisdictions require it to, except Australia,[13] and the United States has applied two different tests in different circuits.[14] In contrast, European civil law jurisdictions such as France, Germany and the Netherlands have avoided analysis of this ground.[15] The difference between approaches may result in differential recognition among, for example, women opposed to a prevalent practice of genital mutilation.[16]

Even where the case law is consistent, it is 'lost in a mosaic when these definitions are applied to certain categories of persons',[17] perhaps best illustrated by the controversy over China's 'one child policy'.[18] In Australia, these asylum seekers are not 'members of a particular social group',[19] although children born in contravention of that policy are members.[20] In the United States, the courts have rejected such claims made either on

[11] See, eg *Applicant A v Minister for Immigration and Ethnic Affairs* (1997) 190 CLR 225 (HCA) 259. This area is usefully summarised in UNHCR's Guidelines on Membership of a Particular Social Group (n 4 above). See also P Dimopoulos, 'Membership of a Particular Social Group: An Appropriate Basis for Eligibility for Refugee Status' (2002) 7 *Deakin Law Review* 367.

[12] TA Aleinikoff, 'Protected Characteristics and Social Perceptions: An Analysis of the Meaning of "Membership of a Particular Social Group"' in Feller, Türk and Nicholson (n 3 above) 263.

[13] *Applicant A* (n 11 above).

[14] The line of authority in the Ninth Circuit differed from that adopted by the Board of Immigration Appeals ('BIA') and other circuits. The Ninth Circuit required a 'cohesive, homogeneous group': *Sanchez-Trujillo v INS* 801 F 2d 1571 (9th Cir 1986), while the BIA and other circuits required 'a group of persons all of whom share a common, immutable characteristic': *Matter of Acosta* 19 I & N Dec 211 (1 March 1985). In *Hernandez-Montiel v INS* 225 F 3d 1984 (9th Cir 2000) 1093 the Ninth Circuit seemed to combine the two standards, holding that a particular social group was 'one united by a voluntary association, including the former association, or by an innate characteristic that is so fundamental to the identities and consciences of its members that members either cannot or should not be required to change it'. See generally Aleinikoff (n 12 above) 275–80.

[15] See Aleinikoff (n 12 above) 280–85. This also appears true of Austria and Spain, while Belgium prefers the 'protected characteristics' approach and Denmark interprets the term very strictly: J-Y Carlier, D Vanheule, K Hullman and C Peña Galiano (eds), *Who is a Refugee?: A Comparative Case Law Study* (The Hague, Kluwer Law International, 1997) 49 (Austria), 100–01 (Belgium), 330 (Denmark), 368 (Spain). In H Crawley and T Lester, 'Comparative Analysis of Gender-Related Persecution in National Asylum Legislation and Practice in Europe' (UNHCR Evaluation Report, EPAU/2004/5, May 2004) para 379, it is said that only four of the surveyed countries had case law guidance on this definition (namely, France, Lithuania, the Netherlands and the United Kingdom).

[16] See Aleinikoff (n 12 above) 298.

[17] See Carlier and others (n 15 above) 713.

[18] *Applicant A* (n 11 above) 261–3.

[19] *Ibid*. Whether they could rely on the ground of political opinion has not been definitively settled: see *Minister for Immigration and Ethnic Affairs v Guo Wei Rong* (1997) 191 CLR 559 (HCA).

[20] *Chen Shi Hai v Minister for Immigration and Multicultural Affairs* (2000) 201 CLR 293 (HCA).

the ground of 'political opinion' or on the ground of 'membership of a particular social group', but Congress has overturned that interpretation.[21] In Canada, the courts are divided on the issue.[22] Such claims have been accepted in the Netherlands,[23] but not in France.[24]

Changes in methods of persecution have resulted in divergent views on the Convention's application to cases of civil war[25] and to non-State agents of persecution,[26] while changes in perception, such as the more recent concern with gender-sensitive interpretations of the Convention, have also resulted in differences among countries,[27] even where gender guidelines have been issued.[28]

Recently, attention has shifted to the exclusion[29] and cessation[30] clauses (Articles 1F and 1C) of the Convention. Article 1F excludes the application

[21] P Mathew, 'Conformity or Persecution: China's One Child Policy and Refugee Status' (2000) 23 *University of New South Wales Law Journal* 103 at 114. The US definition was amended by the Illegal Immigration Reform and Immigrant Responsibility Act 1996, 8 USC § 1101(a)(42).

[22] Compare *Cheung v Canada* [1993] 2 FC 314, (1993) 102 DLR (4th) 214 with *Chan v Canada* [1993] 3 FC 675, 692–3.

[23] Aleinikoff (n 12 above) 284, citing Afdeling Bestuursrechtspraak van de Raad van State (Administrative Law Division of the Council of State) RV 1996, 6 GV 18d-21 (7 November 1996).

[24] Aleinikoff (n 12 above) 281, citing *Zhang*, CRR, SR, Dec No 2228044 (8 June 1993); *Wu*, CRR, SR, Dec No 218361 (19 April 1994).

[25] See, eg *Ibrahim* (n 10 above) (a 4:3 decision) esp 63–6 (Kirby J, dissenting); cf *R v Secretary of State for the Home Department, ex parte Adan* [1998] UKHL 15, [1999] AC 293; cf *Salibian v Canada (Minister of Employment and Immigration)* [1990] 3 FC 250.

[26] See, eg Arboleda and Hoy (n 9 above) 86–7; *R v Secretary of State for the Home Department, ex parte Adan* [2001] 2 AC 477 (HL) esp 490–93 (on the position of the UK in contrast to other European countries); European Council on Refugees and Exiles, 'Non-State Agents and the Inability of the State to Protect: The German Interpretation' (London, September 2000) <http://www.ecre.org/research/nsagentsde.pdf> (accessed 10 May 2007).

[27] See, eg K Luopajärvi, 'Gender-Related Persecution as Basis for Refugee Status: Comparative Perspectives', Åbo Akademi University, Finland, Institute of Human Rights Research Report No 19 (2003); Crawley and Lester (n 15 above); A Macklin, 'Cross-Border Shopping for Ideas: A Critical Review of United States, Canadian, and Australian Approaches to Gender-Related Asylum Claims' (1998) 13 *Georgetown Immigration Law Journal* 25; R Haines, 'Gender-Related Persecution' in Feller, Türk and Nicholson (n 3 above).

[28] Macklin (n 27 above).

[29] See generally Lawyers Committee for Human Rights, 'Safeguarding the Rights of Refugees under the Exclusion Clauses: Summary Findings of the Project and a Lawyers Committee for Human Rights Perspective' (2000) 12 *International Journal of Refugee Law* 317 at 324–5; PJ van Krieken (ed), *Refugee Law in Context: The Exclusion Clause* (The Hague, TMC Asser Press, 1999); G Gilbert, 'Current Issues in the Application of the Exclusion Clauses' in Feller, Türk and Nicholson (n 3 above); J Handmaker, 'Seeking Justice, Guaranteeing Protection and Ensuring Due Process: Addressing the Tensions between Exclusion from Refugee Protection and the Principle of Universal Jurisdiction' (2003) 21 *Netherlands Quarterly of Human Rights* 677.

[30] See generally J Fitzpatrick and R Bonoan, 'Cessation of Refugee Protection' in Feller, Türk and Nicholson (n 3 above); D Milner, 'Exemption from Cessation of Refugee Status in the Second Sentence of Article 1C(5)/(6) of the 1951 Refugee Convention' (2004) 16 *International Journal of Refugee Law* 91.

of the Convention in respect of those who have committed prohibited acts in certain categories, all three of those categories having no accepted definition.[31] All three are also subject to different procedures in terms of determining refugee status prior to applying the clause,[32] balancing the seriousness of the alleged crime against that of the feared persecution,[33] the level of evidence that constitutes 'serious reasons for considering',[34] and whether decision-makers can infer 'serious reasons' merely from the asylum seeker's membership of a particular organisation.[35]

Attention has also moved outside the text of the Convention to the practices of the 'safe third country',[36] the doctrine of 'effective protection',[37] and the 'internal flight' or 'internal protection' alternative.[38] As already noted, the 'safe third country' approach depends on a similarity

[31] See Gilbert (n 29 above) 434–57; W Kälin and J Künzli, 'Article 1F(b): Freedom Fighters, Terrorists, and the Notion of Serious Non-Political Crimes' (2000) 12 (Spec Issue) *International Journal of Refugee Law* 46.

[32] The UK says that the exclusion clauses should be applied after considering whether a person is a refugee; France increasingly agrees; Belgium's practice is inconsistent; while in the US and Canada there is normally no obligation to consider refugee status prior to applying the exclusion clauses: M Bliss, '"Serious Reasons for Considering": Minimum Standards of Procedural Fairness in the Application of the Article 1F Exclusion Clauses' (2000) 12 *International Journal of Refugee Law* 92 at 106–8. The Netherlands has put in place a special procedure for exclusion that precludes an inquiry into whether a person is a refugee: Handmaker (n 29 above) 685–6.

[33] Generally European countries engage in a balancing exercise, but this is not the case in common law countries: see *T v Secretary of State for Home Department* [1996] AC 742 (UK); *INS v Aguirre-Aguirre* 526 US 415 (1999) (US); *Applicant NADB of 2001 v Minister for Immigration and Multicultural Affairs* (2002) 126 FCR 453 (Australia); *Malouf v Canada (Minister of Citizenship and Immigration)* [1995] 1 FC 537 (Canada).

[34] There is a conflict in Canada between 'lower ... than the balance of probabilities': *Ramirez v Canada* [1992] 2 FC 306 at 311–13, and 'clear and convincing evidence': *Cardenas v Canada* (1994) 23 Imm LR (2d) 244; in the UK the evidence must 'point ... strongly to his guilt': *T's case* (n 33 above); and in the US 'probable cause' is enough: *Ofosu v McElroy* 933 F Supp 237 (SDNY 1995). UNHCR itself has proposed a 'more likely than not' test in its own practice: Lawyers Committee for Human Rights (n 29 above) 329.

[35] Contrast, eg the US Immigration and Naturalization Act § 219(a), 8 USC § 1189(a)(l) with *T's case* (n 33 above). In the Netherlands, in practice the determination body predetermines whether the organisation, and by association, the applicant, has a 'cruel purpose': Handmaker (n 29 above) 687.

[36] See, eg G Bordelt, 'The Safe Third Country Practice in the European Union: A Misguided Approach to Asylum Law and Violation of International Human Rights Standards' (2002) 33 *Columbia Human Rights Law Review* 473.

[37] The doctrine was first developed in *Minister for Immigration and Multicultural Affairs v Thiyagarajah* (1997) 80 FCR 543. This was strongly questioned, although followed, in *NAGV v Minister for Immigration and Multicultural and Indigenous Affairs* [2003] FCAFC 144, and the appeal was allowed by the High Court in *NAGV and NAGW* (n 6 above). The legislature has also intervened, amending the Migration Act 1958 (Cth) to include its own 'safe third country' exception: see s 36. See generally R Germov and F Motta, *Refugee Law in Australia* (Melbourne, Oxford University Press, 2003) 463–75.

[38] JC Hathaway and M Foster, 'Internal Protection/Relocation/Flight Alternative' in Feller, Türk and Nicholson (n 3 above).

of interpretation between countries. Under the recent 'safe third country' agreement between the United States and Canada,[39] for example, different treatment of gender-related claims could result in Canada breaching its obligations under the Convention, as defined by Canadian law.

While diversity in interpretation is mainly a result of legitimate differences in judicial interpretation, there is a trend for governments to provide legislative definitions of key terms of the Convention. Foreign policy and domestic xenophobia often inform these definitions. Such legislative definitions obviously limit the extent to which convergence is possible, although a commission could examine whether such definitions are in breach of international law. Nevertheless, the majority of these conflicting interpretations are within the province of refugee decision-makers and judges, and it is this interpretative community that the international judicial commission would address.

It is, of course, impossible to gauge the numbers likely to be affected by these divergences, although it is fair to infer from the divergences' range and depth that the numbers are not insignificant. Wide variations in acceptance rates by different countries seem to support this inference,[40] although of course—as with all statistics—the numbers can be deceptive.[41] In 2004, for example, Jordan recognised 90 per cent of Iraqis as refugees, Belgium recognised 66.3 per cent as refugees, and the United Kingdom recognised 0.1 per cent as refugees.[42] Indeed, the European Council on Refugees and Exiles declares that, even after five years of harmonisation, 'a person can have a 90% chance of being accepted as a refugee in one EU country, while her chances are virtually nil next door'.[43]

D. Redressing the Balance

The preceding review suggests that there are significant differences in the interpretation of the Convention. These differences are, in the main,

[39] Agreement between the Government of Canada and the Government of the United States of America for Co-operation in the Examination of Refugee Status Claims from Nationals of Third Countries (signed 5 December 2002, entered into force 29 December 2004).

[40] Arboleda and Hoy (n 9 above) 80–81.

[41] See, eg P Mares, 'The Generous Country? Asylum Seeking in Australia: Myths, Facts and Statistics', Lecture, Storey Hall RMIT, Melbourne (13 September 2001) <http://www.carad-wa.org/library/mares131101.htm> (accessed 20 April 2007).

[42] UNHCR, *2004 Global Refugee Trends: Overview of Refugee Populations, New Arrivals, Durable Solutions, Asylum-Seekers, Stateless and Other Persons of Concern to UNHCR* (Geneva, UNHCR, 17 June 2005) Table 8, available from UNHCR's website: <http://www.unhcr.org>.

[43] European Council on Refugees and Exiles (n 2 above).

unjustified, particularly as the Convention is designed as a universal instrument of humanitarian protection. That the degree of divergence appears to lead to dramatically different results of acceptance in neighbouring countries offends the normative goals of equality before the law, certainty and stability. It does so with, one can only imagine, tragic consequences. In the arena of refugee law, we need to tilt the balance between consistency and divergence in favour of greater consistency.

III. PROSPECTS FOR FURTHER CONVERGENCE

If further convergence is desirable, the next question is whether we can achieve such convergence through existing initiatives and mechanisms. In this section, we review these and conclude that, while they are of some significance, their potential is limited.

A. UNHCR

UNHCR has, of course, already made significant efforts in the area of interpretation. It publishes the leading soft law instrument, commonly known as the Handbook.[44] It has issued the previously-mentioned Guidelines on International Protection, as well as a variety of position papers.[45] Occasionally, UNHCR intervenes in and presents amicus curiæ briefs in significant cases.[46] Lastly, the Executive Committee sometimes gives interpretative guidance in its Conclusions.[47]

This work demonstrates the value of international soft law. These sources of guidance have substantially impacted upon the interpretation of the Convention, due to their institutional authority, their global nature and their wide dissemination. The Handbook is routinely referred to by decision-makers. It is considered by the Council of the European

44 UNHCR, *Handbook on Procedures and Criteria for Determining Refugee Status under the 1951 Convention and the 1967 Protocol relating to the Status of Refugees* UN Doc HCR/IP/4/Eng/Rev.1, 2nd edn (Geneva 1992).

45 These can be accessed from the UNHCR website: <http://www.unhcr.org>.

46 UNHCR has been involved in eg *R v Immigration Officer at Prague Airport, ex parte European Roma Rights Centre* [2004] UKHL 55, [2005] 2 AC 1; *Sepet v Secretary of State for the Home Department* [2003] UKHL 15, [2003] 3 All ER 304; *El-Ali v Secretary of State for the Home Department* [2002] EWCA Civ 1103, [2003] 1 WLR 95; *Suresh v Canada (Minister of Citizenship and Immigration)* [2002] 1 SCR 3, 2002 SCC 1; *Islam v Secretary of State for the Home Department* [1999] 2 AC 629 (HL); and *Haitian Centers Council v McNary* 969 F 2d 1326 (2nd Cir 1992) vacated as moot, 113 S Ct 3028 (1993). UNHCR's documents for these can be found on its website: <http://www.unhcr.org>.

47 See generally J Sztucki, 'The Conclusions on the International Protection of Refugees adopted by the Executive Committee of the UNHCR Programme' (1989) 3 *International Journal of Refugee Law* 285.

Union as 'a valuable aid'.[48] The House of Lords views it as having 'high persuasive authority',[49] while the Canadian Supreme Court views it as 'highly relevant authority',[50] and it provides 'significant guidance' to the US Supreme Court.[51]

Such enthusiasm has not always been universal, as comments by Lord Bridge of Harwich[52] and a former Australian Chief Justice evidence.[53] Indeed, one Australian judge recently suggested that 'a certain conservatism should attend' usage of the Handbook, because of a 'general lack of enthusiasm for using the Handbook' among judges (a comment that was, however, disapproved of on appeal).[54] It remains true, at least in Australian courts, that where there is a conflict of opinion, greater weight is generally accorded to decisions of other common law courts and learned commentators.[55]

It is perhaps too early to say whether the recent Guidelines on International Protection carry more authority,[56] although in a recent Australian case they were considered to be 'statements that should

[48] 'Joint Position of 4 March 1996 defined by the Council on the Basis of Article K.3 of the Treaty on European Union on the Harmonized Application of the Definition of the Term "Refugee" in Article 1 of the Geneva Convention of 28 July 1951 relating to the Status of Refugees' [1996] OJ L63/2.

[49] *Adan* (n 26 above) 520.

[50] *Chan v Canada (Minister of Employment and Immigration)* [1995] 3 SCR 593, 620, 628. See also *Canada (Attorney-General) v Ward* [1993] 2 SCR 689, 713–14.

[51] *INS v Cardoza-Fonseca* 480 US 421 (1987) 439 fn 22.

[52] See, eg *Bugdaycay v Secretary of State for the Home Department* [1987] AC 514 (HL) 524.

[53] *Chan v Minister for Immigration and Ethnic Affairs* (1989) 169 CLR 379 (HCA) 392.

[54] *Savvin v Minister for Immigration and Multicultural Affairs* (1999) 166 ALR 348 (FCA) 358 (Dowsett J); on appeal, *Minister for Immigration v Savvin* (2000) 98 FCR 168 (FCAFC) 192–3.

[55] See, eg *Applicant NADB* (n 33 above); *Minister for Immigration and Multicultural Affairs v WABQ* (2002) 121 FCR 251 (FCAFC) 275–8. In particular, the texts by JC Hathaway, *The Law of Refugee Status* (Toronto, Butterworths, 1991) and GS Goodwin-Gill and J McAdam, *The Refugee in International Law*, 3rd edn (Oxford, Oxford University Press, 2007) are often cited.

[56] As at July 2007, the Global Consultations and the resulting Guidelines on International Protection have had some impact on jurisprudence in common law jurisdictions. In Australia, the Global Consultations were cautiously cited in support in *QAAH v Minister for Immigration and Multicultural and Indigenous Affairs* [2005] FCAFC 136, (2005) 145 FCR 363, 373–7 (Wilcox J), an approach adopted also in the Federal Magistrates Court in *VXAJ v Minister for Immigration and Multicultural and Indigenous Affairs* [2006] FMCA 234, para 15, and *MZWLH v Minister for Immigration* [2005] FMCA 1200, paras 16–18. They were also cited in support in dissenting judgments in *Minister for Immigration and Multicultural and Indigenous Affairs v QAAH of 2004* [2006] HCA 53, (2006) 231 ALR 340, paras 73–81 (Kirby J); *STCB v Minister for Immigration and Multicultural and Indigenous Affairs* [2006] HCA 61, (2006) 231 ALR 556, para 79 (Kirby J); *NBGM v Minister for Immigration and Multicultural and Indigenous Affairs* [2006] FCAFC 60, (2006) 150 FCR 522, 563–4 (Allsop J); and *Minister for Immigration and Multicultural Affairs v Applicant S* (2002) 124 FCR 256, 269 (North J). In the US, the Guidelines have been cited four times as at July 2007. They were cited in support by the Court of Appeals in *Castillo-Arias v United States AG* 446 F 3d 1190 (11th Cir 2006); *Mohammed v Gonzales* 400 F 3d 785 (9th Cir 2005); *Zhang v Ashcroft* 388 F 3d 713 (9th Cir 2004); and *Castellano-Chacon v INS* 341 F 3d 533 (6th Cir 2003) 548–9, where the court noted that the

be taken into account' by decision-makers, as they were 'documents prepared by experts published to assist States ... to carry out their obligations under the Convention'.[57] The Conclusions of the Executive Committee are in a slightly different position. In the United Kingdom they are regularly invoked,[58] but in Australia they are rarely used.[59]

Although there is potential to improve the acceptance of UNHCR instruments by decision-makers, there remain inherent limitations. These instruments are published as and when time and resources permit. The Handbook has not been updated for more than 10 years. This limits its usefulness as circumstances throw up new challenges for interpretation and as jurisprudence evolves.[60] Even if it were updated more regularly, the Handbook can never be comprehensive and, to retain its utility, it must remain concise and therefore, to some degree, abstract. The Conclusions of the Executive Committee are only adopted at yearly

definition of 'membership of a particular social group' might evolve along the path indicated by the Guidelines. In Canada, the Guidelines were cited in support in *Ventocilla v Canada (Minister of Citizenship and Immigration)* [2007] FC 575, para 14; *Avila v Canada (Minister of Citizenship and Immigration)* [2006] FC 359, para 24; *Joseph v Canada (Solicitor General)* [2006] FC 165, paras 17–18; *Nagamany v Canada (Minister of Citizenship and Immigration)* [2005] FC 1554, para 53; and *Rahaman v Canada (Minister of Citizenship and Immigration)* [2002] 3 FC 537, 561–3. The UK has been most receptive, with endorsements of the Guidelines by the House of Lords in *K v Secretary of State for the Home Department* [2006] UKHL 46, [2007] 1 AC 412, paras 15, 52, 85, 98–103, 118–20; *Januzi v Secretary of State for the Home Department* [2006] UKHL 5, [2006] 2 AC 426, paras 20–21 (with some caution) and 67; and *R (on the Application of Hoxha) v Secretary of State for the Home Department* [2005] UKHL 19, [2005] 4 All ER 580, paras 31–5. They were also cited in support in *HH (Iraq) v Secretary of State for the Home Department* [2006] EWCA Civ 1374, para 42. They were discussed but not found to have a significant impact in *Hamid v Secretary of State for the Home Department* [2005] EWCA Civ 1219, paras 19–27. A Guideline was dismissed in *L v Secretary of State for the Home Department* [2004] EWCA Civ 1441, [2004] All ER (D) 43 (Nov).

57 *QAAH* (n 56 above) para 46 (Wilcox J).

58 See, eg *European Roma Rights Centre* (n 46 above); *A v Secretary of State for Home Department* [2004] UKHL 56, [2005] 2 AC 68; *R v Special Adjudicator, ex parte Hoxha* [2005] UKHL 19, [2005] 4 All ER 580. They were also cited in *Rahaman v Canada* (n 56 above) para 45.

59 In the Federal Court of Australia, since 1995 (as at July 2007) they have only been cited in *Rezaei v Minister for Immigration and Multicultural Affairs* [2001] FCA 1294, para 52, and *Patto v Minister for Immigration and Multicultural Affairs* (2000) 106 FCR 119, 128, and noted in *Thiyagarajah* (n 37 above) 561, *Guo Wei Rong v Minister for Immigration and Ethnic Affairs* (unreported, Sackville J, 4 May 1995), and *Wu v Minister for Immigration and Ethnic Affairs* (1996) 64 FCR 245, 295. They were referred to in passing in *Applicants M160/2003 v Minister for Immigration and Multicultural and Indigenous Affairs* [2005] FCA 195, (2005) 219 ALR 140 paras 17–18. They were also cited in *QAAH* (n 56 above) para 118, *Re Woolley; ex parte Applicants M276/2003 by Their Next Friend GS* [2004] HCA 49, (2004) 210 ALR 369, para 107 fn 127, and *Minister for Immigration and Multicultural Affairs v Khawar* [2002] HCA 14, (2002) 210 CLR 1, para 127 fn 114.

60 See, eg in Australia *Minister for Immigration and Multicultural Affairs v Mohammed* (2000) 98 FCR 405, 413; in Canada *Xie v Canada* (*Minister of Citizenship and Immigration*) [2004] 2 FCR 372, para 25; and *Pushpanathan v Canada* (*Minister of Employment and Immigration*) [1996] 2 FC 49, para 22; reversed on appeal [1998] 1 SCR 982.

intervals, and although the Executive Committee's inter-governmental character may lend it greater legitimacy, it also inhibits a consensus on politically controversial questions.[61] These instruments, therefore, cannot provide the kind of on-going, context-specific jurisprudential reasoning that would be of particular use to the interpreters of the Convention.

B. European Union Common Asylum Policy

In the European Union, the much wider project of converging asylum and immigration policies[62] has included a Directive on minimum standards for the qualification of refugee status and other forms of international protection ('Qualification Directive'),[63] which deals with some significant areas of divergence in interpretation. As this will have a direct effect on the domestic law of the Member States,[64] it is a much more effective method of harmonisation. Given the size of the European Union, the Directive is bound to have a significant impact on the deliberations of the proposed commission.

Nevertheless, although the Qualification Directive will reduce divergence in interpretation, it suffers from the same inherent limitations as the UNHCR publications: it cannot hope to anticipate all future scenarios to provide future guidance, it is not comprehensive, and it speaks in general terms only.

Three other significant limitations arise. First, such a method cannot be exported outside of the European Union. Secondly, there is the potential for regional interpretations to undermine a universal regime. Thirdly, and perhaps most importantly, the method of achieving such convergence is by political negotiation and compromise, rather than by the proper construction of the Convention, using the accepted tools of legal reasoning. Unfortunately, this can lead to a lowering of protection, a charge made by

[61] 'The 44th Session of the UNHCR Executive Committee: A View from the Side' (1994) 6 *International Journal of Refugee Law* 63.

[62] The Tampere programme, which began in 1999, concluded in 2004: see 'Area of Freedom, Security and Justice: Assessment of the Tampere Programme and Future Orientations' COM(2004) 0401 final (2 June 2004) and its Annex I, 'List of the Most Important Instruments Adopted' SEC(2004) 680 (2 June 2004). The next phase, the Hague Programme, aims for a common European asylum system: see the Presidency Conclusions (4–5 November 2004). For a recent overview, see P Shah (ed), *The Challenge of Asylum to Legal Systems* (London, Cavendish, 2005); E Guild, 'Seeking Asylum: Storm Clouds between International Commitments and EU Legislative Measures' (2004) 29 *European Law Review* 198.

[63] See n 8 above.

[64] See generally S Douglas-Scott, *Constitutional Law of the European Union* (Harlow, Pearson Education, 2002) 288–91.

many observers. For example, a leading commentator ended a review of the harmonisation process on this bitter note:

> [W]hen one comes to examine the developing EU acquis in the field one has the impression that the Member States are seeking to draw up a whole new acquis unencumbered by their international commitments. Indeed, the Member States have insisted on the inclusion in EU measures of provisions which either have already been criticised by the supra-national courts … or by national courts … . They thereby give the impression that they wish to re-write the rules to get rid of inconvenient human rights issues. Some Member States appear to be seeking the right to crush protection seekers like soft drink cans which are no longer wanted.[65]

C. Other Efforts

Two further types of initiatives are worth mentioning. The first is other regional approaches, such as the work of the Council of Europe's Ad Hoc Committee of Experts on the Legal Aspects of Territorial Asylum, Refugees and Stateless Persons ('CAHAR').[66] CAHAR has issued several recommendations and resolutions directly relevant to the interpretation of the Convention.[67] Much less intensive (and not particularly useful) regional approaches exist in Africa, Latin America[68] and South Asia.[69] These suffer from the same limitations already mentioned, and also suffer from a lesser institutional authority.

The other category consists of efforts made by non-governmental organisations, academic experts and legal associations. These include

[65] Guild (n 62 above) 218; see also Shah (n 62 above).

[66] For a recent summary of the activities of the Council of Europe generally, see M Ochoa-Llidó, 'Recent and Future Activities of the Council of Europe in the Fields of Migration, Asylum and Refugees' (2004) 5 *European Journal of Migration and Law* 497.

[67] See, eg Committee of Ministers, Recommendation No R (2004) 9 on the Concept of 'Membership of a Particular Social Group' (MPSG) in the context of the 1951 Convention relating to the Status of Refugees (30 June 2004); Recommendation No 4 (97) 22 to Member States containing Guidelines on the Application of the Safe Third Country Concept; Recommendation No (98) 13 on the Right to an Effective Remedy by Rejected Asylum-Seekers against Decisions on Expulsion in the Context of Article 3 of the European Convention on Human Rights; Recommendation No R (99) 23 to Member States on Family Reunion for Refugees and Other Persons in Need of International Protection. For a full list, see <http://www.coe.int/T/E/Legal%5FAffairs/Legal%5Fco%2Doperation/Foreigners%5Fand%5Fcitizens/Asylum%2C%5Frefugees%5Fand%5Fstateless%5Fpersons/Texts%5Fand%5Fdocuments/> (accessed 10 June 2007).

[68] See generally JH Fischel de Andrade, 'Regional Policy Approaches and Harmonization: A Latin American Perspective' (1998) 10 *International Journal of Refugee Law* 391; and the San José Declaration on Refugees and Displaced Persons, adopted by the International Colloquium in Commemoration of the 'Tenth Anniversary of the Cartagena Declaration on Refugees' (San José, 5–7 December 1994).

[69] See generally P Oberoi, 'Regional Initiatives on Refugee Protection in South Asia' (1999) 11 *International Journal of Refugee Law* 193.

position papers by the European Council on Refugees and Exiles,[70] guidelines published by the University of Michigan,[71] a project on the exclusion clauses funded by 'Human Rights First',[72] and workshops conducted by the International Association of Refugee Law Judges.[73] While these efforts are all valuable, and altruistically motivated, they lack institutional authority, are not always widely disseminated and, once again, are limited by their generality and abstraction from facts.

D. Existing Institutions with Competence

The interpretation of the Convention is already within the institutional competence of a number of bodies. The International Court of Justice ('ICJ') has direct institutional competence,[74] as does the Inter-American Court of Human Rights.[75] Refugee-related issues may be raised indirectly before the UN Human Rights Committee, the European Court of Human Rights, the European Court of Justice ('ECJ') (through the Qualification Directive) and the UN Committee against Torture.

Of these, the ICJ would be the preferred forum for resolving disputes about the interpretation of the Convention because of its truly international character, its institutional competence as the court of the United Nations and its judicial expertise. However, this jurisdiction of the ICJ has never been invoked, and the prospects of it being used are remote. States or even UNHCR[76] are unlikely to go to the trouble and expense of beginning long and complex proceedings over these issues of interpretation, particularly as it is of no tangible benefit to States. The adversarial procedure would be an extremely inefficient process of harmonisation, even if the docket of the court were not already 'full'.[77]

[70] European Council on Refugees and Exiles, 'Position on the Interpretation of Article 1 of the Refugee Convention' (September 2000) <http://www.ecre.org/policy/position_papers.shtml> (accessed 10 June 2007).

[71] JC Hathaway, 'The Michigan Guidelines on the Internal Protection Alternative' (1999) 21 *Michigan Journal of International Law* 131. There are also Guidelines on 'well-founded fear', and on 'nexus': <http://www.refugeecaselaw.org/fear.asp> (accessed 12 June 2007).

[72] Previously 'Lawyers Committee for Human Rights' (see n 29 above).

[73] See JC Hathaway, 'A Forum for the Transnational Development of Refugee Law: The IARLJ's Advanced Refugee Law Workshop' (2003) 15 *International Journal of Refugee Law* 418.

[74] Under Arts 36(2) and 65 of its Statute; see also Art 38 of the Refugee Convention.

[75] American Convention on Human Rights (adopted 22 November 1969, entered into force 18 July 1978) 1144 UNTS 123, Art 64(1), which allows for interpretation of 'other treaties concerning the protection of human rights in the American states'.

[76] At present, UNHCR is not authorised to request an advisory opinion, but this could be permitted by a resolution of the UN General Assembly. Further, it could ask a State party to raise the matter, as suggested by W Kälin, 'Supervising the 1951 Convention relating to the Status of Refugees: Article 35 and Beyond' in Feller, Türk and Nicholson (n 3 above) 653.

[77] At the time of writing, there were 12 cases pending: see <http://www.icj-cij.org/docket/index.php?p1=3&p2=1>.

For this reason, it seems unprofitable to pursue convergence by adjudication. These comments apply a fortiori to the other courts, which suffer the additional problem of providing only regional solutions and, with respect to the European courts, would involve interpreting the Convention indirectly through the lens of the Qualification Directive (in the case of the ECJ) or the European Convention on Human Rights (in the case of the European Court of Human Rights).[78] The European courts also suffer from large backlogs. Although these latter defects do not affect the Inter-American Court of Human Rights, disharmonies in interpretation are less pronounced in its Member States since UNHCR assesses most of the claims for asylum, and because of the broader regional refugee definition.[79]

The problems of indirect interpretation and large backlogs also attend the use of the Human Rights Committee and the Committee against Torture, which are increasingly being used for refugee issues in the absence of a specific supervisory mechanism for the Convention.[80] (Indeed, most cases before the Committee against Torture now involve asylum seekers.[81]) Additionally, the committees only meet part-time and their opinions have less normative force than the judgments of courts.

E. Conclusion

Current prospects for minimising divergent interpretations of the Convention using existing mechanisms are not, in our view, promising. There are significant limitations in using general guides, which are not timely or context-specific; political methods of harmonisation appear

[78] Convention for the Protection of Human Rights and Fundamental Freedoms (European Convention on Human Rights, as amended) (4 November 1950) ETS No 5.

[79] See Cartagena Declaration on Refugees (22 November 1984) in Annual Report of the Inter-American Commission on Human Rights OAS Doc OEA/Ser.L/V/II.66/doc.10, rev.1, 190–93 (1984–85).

[80] See, eg J Fitzpatrick (ed), *Human Rights Protection for Refugees, Asylum-Seekers, and Internally Displaced Persons: A Guide to International Mechanisms and Procedures* (Ardsley, Transnational Publishers, 2002); O Andrysek, 'Gaps in International Protection and the Potential for Redress through Individual Complaints Procedures' (1997) 9 *International Journal of Refugee Law* 392; S Takahasi II, 'Recourse to Human Rights Treaty Bodies for Monitoring of the Refugee Convention' (2002) 20 *Netherlands Quarterly of Human Rights* 53; and Amnesty International and the International Service for Human Rights, *The UN and Refugees' Human Rights: A Manual on How UN Human Rights Mechanisms Can Protect the Rights of Refugees* AI Index 30/02/97 (August 1997) <http://web.amnesty.org/library/pdf/IOR300021997ENGLISH/$File/IOR3000297.pdf> (accessed 15 June 2007).

[81] Of the 18 decisions made on the merits reported in the 2004 report of the Committee against Torture to the UN General Assembly, 15 concerned asylum seekers. The other three were cases brought by Tunisian nationals granted refugee status in Switzerland: *Report of the Committee against Torture*, UN General Assembly Official Records ('GAOR'), 59th session, Annex VII, UN Doc A/59/44 (2004).

undesirable in the present climate; and convergence by adjudication is not an efficient method of harmonisation.

However, this review does indicate that there is value in international soft law as a method of guidance. It also points to the following conclusions:

— The interpretation of the Convention should be global, not regional, in character.
— In order for such interpretation to be accepted by national decision-makers, it should be arrived at by accepted judicial techniques and have an authority derived from the expertise and integrity of the institution.
— Such interpretations should address practical factual circumstances rather than general and abstract questions.
— There should be an on-going interpretative body, to ensure continuity over time and relevance to the current needs of decision-makers.
— Such interpretations must be widely promoted and publicised to ensure that they come to the attention of decision-makers.

These conclusions have informed the design of the proposal, which is developed below.

IV. THE PRINCIPLES OF THE PROPOSAL

A. The Purpose of the Commission

The ultimate aim of this proposal is to promote greater consistency in the interpretation of the Convention, for the reasons outlined. This aim has shaped our proposal in distinctive ways.

The first distinctive feature is the judicial character of the commission. While the commission would not be a court, we aim to emphasise features that draw from the tradition of the judiciary, and in that broad sense the commission could be called 'judicial'. This is partly for the practical reason that, in many countries, interpretation of the Convention is the province of the judiciary, and if we are to promote convergence of interpretations, the people who are best equipped to persuade judges are fellow jurists and experts. More importantly, however, the judicial character of the commission would endow it with particular values such as independence, impartiality, intellectual integrity and legal expertise. These are qualities that are essential to the enterprise of interpreting the Convention.

This feature draws upon the demonstrated value of present international judicial institutions. These perform useful functions in international law: they adjudicate disputes, interpret the law, supervise the development of the law and legitimate the system by ensuring independent and (at least in theory) apolitical oversight. International judicial institutions have been responsible for greatly elaborating the content and extending the reach of international law, as well as providing an alternative discourse for international politics and the legitimacy of State actions. These would all be valuable additions to the present refugee regime.

The second distinctive feature is that, unlike most international judicial bodies, this body would not be an adjudicatory forum. The aim of promoting consistency can be more effectively achieved by addressing divergences directly, rather than waiting for applications to raise issues relevant to the development of the jurisprudence of refugee law.

Such a view is supported by the experience of the UN treaty committees. Among the many useful functions of these supervisory committees has been their elaboration of the various treaties that they monitor, primarily through the issuing of General Comments and consideration of individual complaints. However, the effectiveness of the committees has been undermined by large backlogs of complaints.[82] Further, such elaboration is an incidental function of the committees, and as a result the guidance given by these bodies in this respect, although useful, tends to be ad hoc and reactive.

In addition, the scale of resources required for adequate adjudication is immense, as the increasing workload of the European Court of Human Rights evidences.[83] Prior to its reform in 1998, the court and its partner, the European Commission of Human Rights, had delivered a total of 38,389 decisions and judgments in 44 years; within the first five years of its operation since then, the court had delivered 61,633 judgments.[84]

Although there is, of course, a practical value in allowing individual adjudication, the present proposal takes as its basis the primary purpose of convergence in interpretation. Adjudication is, as experience shows, a costly and time-consuming route to such interpretation, and for those reasons the proposed body would not have an adjudicatory function.

A third distinctive feature of the proposal is that the mission of the commission would be to promote reasoned discussion on the major interpretative controversies. The use of expository reasoned opinions should promote debate, and use a method of intellectual persuasion rather than the power of compulsion. By explaining different interpretations within these opinions, the commission's opinions would allow room for the expression and testing of a diversity of opinions.

[82] See, eg P Alston and J Crawford (eds), *The Future of UN Human Rights Treaty Monitoring* (Cambridge, Cambridge University Press, 2000); and AF Bayefsky, *The UN Human Rights System: Universality at the Crossroads* (The Hague, Kluwer Law International, 2001).

[83] See, eg P Mahoney, 'New Challenges for the European Court of Human Rights resulting from the Expanding Case Load and Membership' (2002) *Penn State International Law Review* 101.

[84] *Ibid.*

B. Legitimacy

Two of the key measures of the success of an international (and indeed a domestic) court or tribunal are its legitimacy and its effectiveness. The two dimensions are, of course, related: illegitimacy undermines effectiveness, and ineffectiveness undermines legitimacy. However, the distinction is useful for analytical purposes.

Legitimacy involves the acceptance of the authority of the international judicial institution. The importance of legitimacy to the effectiveness of an institution is vividly illustrated by the routine protestations of illegitimacy against international criminal tribunals by defendants such as Milosevic.[85] Legitimacy may be assessed in relation to the different actors involved: the parties; those directly affected by the outcome of the proceedings; the international political elite; States; the broader international legal community; and the population in general. From the perspective of the Rwandan government, for example, there have been serious doubts about the legitimacy of the ad hoc tribunal for Rwanda: the government voted against the establishment of the International Criminal Tribunal for Rwanda,[86] and recently denounced a controversial acquittal.[87] Nor have the ad hoc tribunals necessarily gained legitimacy in the eyes of the communities they are meant to serve, with one opinion poll finding that 32 per cent of Serbs think that the International Criminal Tribunal for the former Yugoslavia's major goal is 'to place all the blame for war suffering on Serbs'.[88] By contrast, the extremely heavy workload of the European Court of Human Rights indicates a perception of success among litigants.

Legitimacy may have different sources. An important, although not sole, source is institutional authority. For example, the ICJ enjoys great institutional authority as the principal judicial organ of the UN. The Statute of the International Criminal Court ('ICC') is a source of great legitimacy, evincing as it does the consent of a large number of States to a pioneering court, a consent strengthened by its speedy ratification.

[85] For an excellent account see P Hazan, *Justice in a Time of War: The True Story behind the International Criminal Tribunal for the Former Yugoslavia* (College Station, Texas A & M University Press, 2004) 159–70.

[86] SW Tiefenbrun, 'The Paradox of International Adjudication: Developments in the International Criminal Tribunals for the Former Yugoslavia and Rwanda, the World Court, and the International Criminal Court' (1999–2000) 25 *NCJ International Law and Commercial Regulation* 551.

[87] 'Thousands Demonstrate against UN Tribunal' (29 February 2004) <http://www.globalpolicy.org/intljustice/tribunals/rwanda/2004/0229against.htm> (accessed 15 June 2007).

[88] A Uzelac, 'Hague Prosecutors Rest Their Case' (27 December 2004) <http://www.globalpolicy.org/intljustice/tribunals/yugo/2004/1227rest.htm> (accessed 15 June 2007).

The global character of the human rights treaties and their widespread ratification[89] confers legitimacy on the UN treaty committees.

In contrast, the institutional legitimacy of the ad hoc criminal tribunals has been questioned, based as they are on resolutions of the UN Security Council passed in a frenzied political climate.[90] This has hampered their functioning, with some nations refusing to assist the tribunals in their work.[91]

However, the experience of the ad hoc tribunals also demonstrates that legitimacy need not merely be conferred: it can be self-generated. The persistence of dedicated personnel has generated more confidence about the usefulness of ad hoc tribunals among the human rights community and among States, a confidence that eventually enabled the fulfilment of the dream of the ICC.[92]

Another key source of legitimacy is the relationship between States and the institution. The textbook criticism of the ICJ, for example, is that too few States submit to its jurisdiction,[93] and too many States attack or ignore its decisions.[94] The institutional legitimacy conferred by treaties may be undercut by the political negotiations and compromises inherent in them, as was demonstrated by the lengthy negotiating process involved in the creation of the ICC, the flaws of which have been described at length elsewhere.[95] The UN treaty committees have complained of the delayed compliance or non-compliance of States with their obligations to report and their implementation of decisions on communications.[96]

[89] Bayefsky (n 82 above) 7. The statistics for non-participation of UN Member States by treaty given in that text are: one per cent for the Convention on the Rights of the Child, 13 per cent for the Convention on the Elimination of All Forms of Discrimination against Women, 19 per cent for the Convention on the Elimination of All Forms of Racial Discrimination, 23 per cent for the International Covenant on Civil and Political Rights, 25 per cent for the International Covenant on Economic, Social and Cultural Rights, and 35 per cent for the Convention against Torture and Other Cruel, Inhuman or Degrading Treatment or Punishment.

[90] The International Criminal Tribunal for the Former Yugoslavia was established by United Nations Security Council ('UNSC') res 827 (25 May 1993). The International Criminal Tribunal for Rwanda was established by its Statute annexed to and adopted by UNSC res 955 (8 November 1994).

[91] For a vivid account, see Hazan (n 85 above).

[92] L Arbour and A Neier, 'History and Future of the International Criminal Tribunals for the Former Yugoslavia and Rwanda' (1997–98) 15 *American University International Law Review* 1495 at 1496–7.

[93] As at 31 July 2006, only 67 of the 192 UN members had adhered to the ICJ's compulsory jurisdiction, and the UK is the only permanent member of the Security Council that maintains a declaration under Art 36(2) of the ICJ's statute: *Report of the International Court of Justice, 1 August 2005–31 July 2006*, UN GAOR, 61st sess, UN Doc A/61/4 (2006) para 45.

[94] The Israeli reaction to the recent judgment on the Israeli security barrier is an example: see C McGreal, 'Israel Lashes out at EU for Backing UN Vote on Wall' *The Guardian* (22 July 2004).

[95] See M Cherif Bassiouni, 'Negotiating the Treaty of Rome on the Establishment of an International Criminal Court' (1999) 32 *Cornell International Law Journal* 443.

[96] See, eg the statement of 'deep concern' at the situation in the *Report of the Human Rights Committee*, UN GAOR, 59th sess, UN Doc A/59/40 (2004) para 256.

State co-operation is vital to the success of the institution. Governments have obstructed the ad hoc tribunals from investigating, arresting[97] and extraditing suspects,[98] and the tribunals continue to rely on political and financial pressure from the United States and European countries to procure reluctant co-operation.[99] Although it is too early to judge the success of the ICC, its legitimacy has been undermined by the United States' wide-ranging attack on it,[100] and the failure by certain States to ratify it. The Inter-American Court of Human Rights was undermined when its rulings led to Peru seeking to withdraw from its jurisdiction[101] and Trinidad and Tobago denouncing it.[102]

In contrast, one of the reasons for the success of the European Court of Human Rights and the ECJ is the general support and compliance of their Member States. A recent review of the European Court of Human Rights, for example, found that only a few decisions were not complied with for political reasons.[103]

[97] Arbour and Neier (n 92 above) 1501–2.

[98] Tiefenbrun (n 86 above) 582; C Jeu, 'A Successful Permanent International Criminal Court ... "Isn't it Pretty to Think So?"' (2004) 26 *Houston Journal of International Law* 411 at 426.

[99] See, eg 'EU Keeps Pressure on Croatia before Entry Talks' (Reuters, 21 February 2005) <http://www.alertnet.org/thenews/newsdesk/L21710159.htm> (accessed 15 June 2007); 'Serbia and Montenegro Assistance' (23 January 2005) <http://www.voanews.com/uspolicy/archive/2005-01/a-2005-01-24-8-1.cfm> (accessed 15 June 2007).

[100] This includes a UN Security Council resolution that for one year from its establishment, the ICC will not begin or proceed with investigations or prosecutions against current or former officials and personnel from a State contributing to a UN peacekeeping mission but not a party to the Rome Statute: UNSC Res 1422 (12 July 2002); bilateral 'impunity' agreements purporting to invoke Art 98(2) of the Rome Statute: see C Eubany, 'Justice for Some? US Efforts under Article 98 to Escape the Jurisdiction of the International Criminal Court' (2003) 27 *Hastings International and Comparative Law Review* 103; the American Servicemembers' Protection Act of 2002, which essentially proscribes American co-operation with the ICC: 22 USC §7421–32; and attempts to revise the status of forces agreements. See generally RT Alter, 'International Criminal Law: A Bittersweet Year for Supporters and Critics of the International Criminal Court' (2003) 37 *International Law* 541 at 547–50; Jeu (n 98 above); and DF Orentlicher, 'Judging Global Justice: Assessing the International Criminal Court' (2003) 21 *Wisconsin International Law Journal* 495 at 495–6.

[101] On 9 July 1999, President Fujimori presented Peru's declaration of withdrawal to the Secretary-General of the Organization of American States, in response to its judgment in *Castillo Petruzzi*. However, on 9 February 2001, the new Peruvian government presented the court with a note reaffirming its acceptance of the contentious jurisdiction, without interruption, since its original declaration was deposited. See CM Cerna, 'The Inter-American System for the Protection of Human Rights' (2003) 16 *Florida Journal of International Law* 195 at 204, 206–8.

[102] See G McGrory, 'Reservations of Virtue? Lessons from Trinidad and Tobago's Reservation to the First Optional Protocol' (2001) 23 *Human Rights Quarterly* 769.

[103] Committee on Legal Affairs and Human Rights, Parliamentary Assembly of the Council of Europe, 'Report on the Execution of Judgments of the European Court of Human Rights', Doc 8808 (28 September 2000), reprinted in (2000) 21 *Human Rights Law Journal* 275; European Commission for Democracy through Law (Venice Commission), 'Opinion 209: Implementation of the Judgments of the European Court of Human Rights', reprinted in (2003) 24 *Human Rights Law Journal* 249.

The independence of members of the institution is also an important component of legitimacy. Allegations of horse-trading at the UN treaty committees and of close links between States and their representatives affect the perception of the committees, and therefore their legitimacy. External pressure has also been cited for the high rate of resignations of officials at the ad hoc tribunal for Rwanda.[104]

Legitimacy also depends upon the extent to which international judicial institutions are supported, not only by States but also by an international legal community and broader activist and popular communities. Although governments of States are frequently embarrassed by, or constrained by, international judicial institutions, support outside of the government encourages recognition of the normative force of the decisions, and in turn compliance with them. This is evidenced by recent studies that have concluded that the decisions of the ICJ are generally effective.[105]

Perhaps the importance of broader political support is most vividly illustrated in the differences between the European Court of Human Rights and the Inter-American equivalent. The European Court of Human Rights is supported by, and promotes, a well-versed human rights culture that accepts the authority of its decisions and the importance of human rights. Its high-profile cases receive significant media attention and have worked dramatic changes on domestic laws, as the recent ruling on the requirement for legal aid in the long-running British 'McLibel' case demonstrates.[106]

The Inter-American Court of Human Rights has been notably less successful, having made decisions in only 86 cases,[107] although a large number of cases are dealt with by the Inter-American Commission on Human Rights. This is largely because States are reluctant to submit to the court's contentious jurisdiction,[108] and its work was thus confined mostly to an advisory jurisdiction during many of the worst abuses in the 1980s.[109] The obvious

[104] 'Rwanda Alarmed by Resignation of Top Tribunal Officials' Hirondelle News Agency (18 May 2004) <http://www.globalpolicy.org/intljustice/tribunals/rwanda/2004/0518external.htm> (accessed 15 June 2007).

[105] C Paulson, 'Compliance with Final Judgments of the International Court of Justice since 1987' (2004) 98 *American Journal of International Law* 434; C Schulte, *Compliance with Decisions of the International Court of Justice* (Oxford, Oxford University Press, 2004).

[106] *Steel and Morris v United Kingdom*, App No 68416/01 (15 February 2005); M Oliver and agencies, 'McLibel Two Win Legal Case' *The Guardian* (15 February 2005).

[107] See the list of judgments at <http://corteidh.or.cr/casos.cfm>, as at 10 July 2007. 17 of those judgments were in 2006 alone. This calculation includes only judgments on the merits.

[108] See generally AS Dwyer, 'The Inter-American Court of Human Rights: Towards Establishing an Effective Regional Contentious Jurisdiction' (1990) 13 *Boston College of International and Comparative Law Review* 127.

[109] See generally *ibid*; and D Shelton, 'Improving Human Rights Protections: Recommendations for Enhancing the Effectiveness of the Inter-American Commission and Inter-American Court of Human Rights' (1988) 3 *American University of International Law and Policy* 323.

reason for this comparative lack of success is the lack of support of relevant institutions and a hostile political climate. People involved in cases in the 1980s, for example, were sometimes threatened or even murdered.[110] As the region has become more democratic, the court's effectiveness has revived, although States are still rarely prepared to investigate, try and punish the perpetrators.[111]

The difficulty for our proposal is that the traditional international law source of legitimacy for such an international judicial body, namely the consent of States in the form of a treaty, is likely to affect negatively its legitimacy in terms of its acceptance by the broader refugee advocacy community. The increasingly restrictive temper of many governments makes it more than likely that they would wish to control the composition of any commission and seek to influence its opinions in their perceived national interest. The form of the proposal therefore places emphasis on other sources of legitimacy.

(i) Creation under the Supervisory Mandate of UNHCR

First, and foremost, it is proposed that the body be created under the supervisory mandate of UNHCR. Paragraph 8 of the UNHCR Statute provides that the High Commissioner

> shall provide for the protection of refugees falling under the competence of his Office by … promoting the conclusion and ratification of international conventions for the protection of refugees, *supervising their application* and proposing amendments thereto (emphasis added).[112]

Articles 35 and 36 of the Convention provide for the corresponding obligations of States to co-operate with UNHCR in this respect.[113] The creation of the limited body we have described falls within that supervisory mandate, as described more fully by Kälin.[114] In essence, the proposal involves little more than giving the Global Consultations process a permanent form.

This method of creation has a number of advantages. First, the commission is designed to *supplement*, rather than usurp, the function of UNHCR. As mentioned earlier, it is in essence a continuation and expansion of UNHCR's own supervisory efforts. Such a supplementary role would

110 Dwyer (n 108 above) 148.

111 Cerna (n 101 above) 203–4.

112 Statute of the Office of the United Nations High Commissioner for Refugees, UNGA Res 428 (V) of 14 December 1950.

113 See V Türk, 'UNHCR's Supervisory Responsibility', UNHCR, *New Issues in Refugee Research*, Research Paper No 67 (October 2002) 19.

114 Kälin (n 76 above).

also preserve the coherence of the international refugee regime, and ensure that the commission would be international in character.

Secondly, the mandate of UNHCR is created by treaty. The creation of a commission within that mandate would not, therefore, trespass on sovereign rights. Rather, it would serve to fulfil the expectations of the treaty.

Thirdly, courts and decision-makers already refer to the 'soft law' created by UNHCR in fulfilment of its mandate. As has been discussed, the weight placed upon UNHCR's interpretations varies. Nevertheless, UNHCR has an unrivalled *institutional* legitimacy in the minds of courts and decision-makers.

Fourthly, there are some very considerable practical advantages in utilising UNHCR's extensive experience in refugee law. UNHCR is in touch with changing refugee realities and would inform the priorities of the commission.

Fifthly, this more flexible method of creation would allow the commission to evolve with changing circumstances and needs. Experience often demonstrates flaws in the best-laid plans. Experience may also breed trust. As States and decision-makers become more comfortable with the new commission, changes in the commission's function might become desirable. The evolution of the European Court of Human Rights, for example, suggests that we also take an evolutionary perspective in designing the commission.

(ii) Judicial Character

A second source of legitimacy is the judicial character of the commission, which was briefly mentioned earlier. Two aspects of this warrant further discussion: (a) the separation of powers; and (b) the discipline of the law.

The principle of separation of powers has, to some extent, been translated at the international level[115] through the recent proliferation of international judicial and quasi-judicial bodies.[116] Independent experts have increasingly been entrusted with the job of monitoring

[115] See, eg P Mahoney, 'Separation of Powers in the Council of Europe: The Status of the European Court of Human Rights vis-à-vis the Authorities of the Council of Europe' (2003) 24 *Human Rights Law Journal* 152.

[116] See generally CP Romano, 'The Proliferation of International Judicial Bodies: The Pieces of the Puzzle' (1999) 31 *New York University Journal of International Law and Politics* 709; T Buergenthal, 'Proliferation of International Courts and Tribunals: Is It Good or Bad?' (2001) 14 *Leiden Journal of International Law* 267; P-M Dupuy, 'The Danger of Fragmentation of Unification of the International Legal System and the International Court of Justice' (1998–99) 31 *New York University Journal of International Law and Politics* 791; and JI Charney, 'The Impact on the International Legal System of the Growth of International Courts and Tribunals' (1998–99) 31 *New York University Journal of International Law* 697.

the implementation of treaties, and independent dispute settlement mechanisms have either been introduced or strengthened in respect of a large number of important treaties. While the significance and practical effect of these institutions are often exaggerated, the trend expresses the value of an independent dispute settler in a way analogous to that of the domestic dispute settler.

The doctrine of separation of powers expresses the value of fragmenting the functions of governance. Adjudication of disputes is accepted as fair if, among other things, the adjudicator is impartial and independent. The independence of the judiciary, although not necessarily in the short-term interests of a government, legitimates executive power in the long run.

But the separation of the judiciary does more than simply legitimate the system of governance. It allows disputes to be resolved that cannot be resolved politically, not only in cases of high political importance such as the election of a President, but also in the detail of interpreting nuances of legislation and regulating the private disputes of citizens.

Unlike other major human rights treaties, the Refugee Convention presently does not have a separation of executive and interpretative power. Yet such a separation suits the hybrid nature of UNHCR. Presently, UNHCR is open to the charge that its operational needs undermine its authority as an interpreter of the Convention. A natural pressure exists upon UNHCR not to condemn a country that allows it to operate within its territory, nor to condemn the handful of donor countries.[117] UNHCR could more effectively achieve both its supervisory and operational objectives by devolving some of its supervisory responsibility to an independent judicial body.[118]

Another factor underpinning the legitimacy of an independent judicial body is the special authority of law.[119] There is no hard and fast line between law and politics, and the notion of law as a morally or politically neutral sphere has long ago been exploded. Yet the law is a discipline and the rules of law are different from the rules of politics. The law is concerned with reasoning from principles and rules using accepted legal techniques, and the loyalty of lawyers and judges is to the law itself. Judges are servants of the law and owe their allegiance to it, not to the political masters of the day. In particular, they have

[117] According to UNHCR, 10 donors provide 80 per cent of its funding, with three donors covering 53 per cent of its funding: UNHCR, *Global Appeal 2007: Strategies and Programmes* (Geneva, UNHCR, 2007) 57–8 <http://www.unhcr.org/publ/PUBL/4565a6872.pdf> (accessed 10 July 2007).

[118] See generally Takahasi (n 80 above) 61–3.

[119] See MN Shaw, 'The International Court of Justice: A Practical Perspective' (1997) 46 *International and Comparative Law Quarterly* 831 at 853.

a function in ensuring the legality of government and in restraining arbitrary exercises of power, a function and value that has special importance in the current age.[120]

(iii) International Composition and Representation

Of course, to some extent the value of the judiciary is already present in the international refugee regime, as in many countries the judiciary plays a leading role in the interpretation of the Refugee Convention. However, an international judicial body would have other benefits. An international judicial body dedicated to refugee law would benefit from the special expertise of its members in international law and by its sole focus on refugee law.

An international judicial body would also be particularly appropriate given the international nature of the Convention, and in light of the present state of disharmony that has resulted from divergent national interpretations. By looking at the Convention directly, rather than through the distorting lens of national legislation, an international body could see the Convention for what it is, namely, an international humanitarian instrument. It is likely that an international judicial body would have greater capacity to resist the politicisation of refugee law by national governments and would be able to expose breaches of international law with greater authority than national courts. The normative influence of a persuasive international judicial body is a resource for national courts, as recent judgments of the House of Lords demonstrate.[121] The principled development of international refugee law would promote a certainty and predictability that could only enhance the legitimacy of national judicial decisions.

(iv) The Legitimacy of Expertise

The contemporary world is the age of the expert. There are good reasons for this, but expertise is not a prerequisite for those currently involved in the interpretation of the Refugee Convention. While superior appellate courts often engage in sophisticated analyses of the Convention, this is not an option for most primary decision-makers. Refugee law also poses particular problems that even senior appellate judges may struggle to overcome. It lies at the intersection of humanitarian law and international law, two areas that have developed significantly since most judges were

[120] See, eg J Steyn, 'Guantanamo Bay: The Legal Black Hole' (2004) 53 *International and Comparative Law Quarterly* 1. For case law examples, see *A v Secretary of State for Home Department* (n 58 above); *Zaoui v Attorney-General (No 2)* [2006] 1 NZLR 289 (NZSC); *Rasul v Bush* 542 US 466 (2004); and *Rumsfeld v Padilla* 542 US 426 (2004).

[121] See, eg *A v Secretary of State for Home Department* (n 58 above).

educated. Moreover, a sophisticated analysis requires access to, and understanding of, material across a variety of jurisdictions and a range of international instruments. There are some landmark refugee cases that may have been decided differently had an expert in refugee law been sitting.

(v) The Thorny Issue of State Involvement

Despite the foregoing, it may be desirable to have some form of State involvement to assist in developing the legitimacy of the commission. States supporting the creation of such a body might, for example, have privileges in relation to the appointment of members, or standing to make submissions to the commission. It might be desirable to bring together interested States parties for consultation prior to the creation of the commission, and it would be advisable to liaise with them through the process. However, a balance must be struck between co-operation and dialogue with States, and impermissible interference by States. Furthermore, while engagement with States might be useful, the primary target audience of the commission would be decision-makers and the judiciary. It would also be necessary to develop good working relationships with these people.

(vi) Absence of Enforceability

It might be objected that the legitimacy of the commission would be greatly undermined by its lack of powers to enforce its views. To lawyers familiar with domestic courts, the enforcement powers of courts appear to be fundamental to their authority, and international bodies are often criticised for being no more than talking shops.

There are, however, insuperable difficulties in the way of establishing a body capable of delivering binding judgments. Specific consent by States parties would be required in order to make the opinions binding. Such consent is not likely to be forthcoming, and in some cases may be constitutionally impossible. The experience of the ICJ, and the small number of States parties that have agreed to accept its compulsory jurisdiction,[122] indicates the magnitude of the task.

Nevertheless, the experiences of the ICJ and other international bodies illustrate the normative value and political influence of judicial opinions,[123] even when their judgments are defied. What is more important, in our view, would be political and cultural acceptance of the legitimacy of the commission's decisions.

[122] See n 93 above.
[123] See n 105 above.

Although enforcement is not a practical possibility, some powers could be assigned to the body by UNHCR. UNHCR could make the interpretations determinative for the purposes of the refugee status determination which it conducts in many countries.[124] By making the opinions of the commission enforceable in this area, there would exist the potential to stimulate a pattern of State acquiescence.

The lack of power to enforce its opinions would have two positive aspects for the commission. It would make the creation of the body simpler. The consent of States, which is essential for the creation of a court that renders binding judgments, would not be necessary. And non-binding opinions attract less controversy, and hence less resistance, from States jealous of their sovereign powers.

C. Effectiveness

Three aspects of effectiveness are addressed here. First, in order to be effective at all, the proposal has to be politically feasible. Secondly, effectiveness measures the gap between the objectives of the body and its performance. Thirdly, effectiveness depends partly upon the efficiency of the body.

The first aspect explains why the proposal is modestly framed, with the commission's function being limited to a traditionally judicial task, and with the commission being designed to supplement the existing refugee regime. It also explains why we do not favour the method of treaty creation. As the experience of the ICC has shown, such a method has as many risks as it has rewards. It also explains why we have opted for an advisory model.

The second aspect supports the narrow focus on the objective of promoting convergence in interpretation. Such narrow objectives are much more easily fulfilled than wide-ranging and broad ones. This is supported by the experience of the UN treaty committees, in which grand objectives and multiple functions are placed upon part-time committees, with the inevitable result that few of the objectives can realistically be achieved. This tends to undermine the legitimacy of the bodies.

The third, related, aspect is the question of efficiency. Narrower objectives permit more carefully targeted use of resources. As already explained, the absence of an adjudicatory function promotes efficiency. In the case of an adjudication, applications have to be received and processed, parties given due time to prepare and argue cases, and, if necessary, appeal. Where such applications are made in relation to human

[124] See generally M Alexander, 'Refugee Status Determination Conducted by UNHCR' (1999) 11 *International Journal of Refugee Law* 251.

rights treaties with broad jurisdiction, there is almost invariably a mismatch between the number of applications and resources. Another mismatch also often occurs, in which petitioners from particular countries are over-represented, because they are aware of, and have greater access to, such courts and bodies. An obvious example is the difference in workload between the Inter-American Court of Human Rights and the European Court of Human Rights, which clearly does not reflect a difference in the extent of human rights abuses in the various regions.

The proposal takes into account the critical importance of resources. A persistent criticism of the UN treaty committees[125] and the ad hoc criminal tribunals[126] has been that resources are inadequate to meet the demands of wide-ranging briefs. The need for resources often also diminishes legitimacy, as the States that hold the purse strings can attach conditions to their financial support. In the case of the ad hoc criminal tribunals, overdue payments by States have resulted in large funding gaps,[127] and escalating costs have partly motivated the decision to close the tribunals by 2010.[128]

We recognise that UNHCR's budget is stretched. For that reason, we have felt it important to develop a funding model that seeks support from committed private sources such as universities, law firms, and professional organisations and foundations. Further, the commission would seek to establish its secretariat within one or two academic centres devoted to refugee studies. It would be possible for appointees to serve part-time and to minimise the costs of meeting by utilising electronic communications. A further advantage of such a model is that an independently *funded* commission would emphasise the independence of the body, thereby assisting the body to gain further legitimacy.

[125] See generally E Evatt, 'Ensuring Effective Supervisory Procedures: The Need for Resources', and M Schmidt, 'Servicing and Financing Human Rights Supervisory Bodies' in Alston and Crawford (n 82 above).

[126] See the (first) *Annual Report of the International Tribunal for the Prosecution of Persons Responsible for Serious Violations of International Humanitarian Law Committed in the Territory of the Former Yugoslavia since 1991*, UN GAOR, 49th sess, UN Doc A/49/342–S/1994/1007 (1994) 28–51.

[127] See *Ninth Annual Report of the International Criminal Tribunal for the Prosecution of Persons Responsible for Genocide and Other Serious Violations of International Humanitarian Law Committed in the Territory of Rwanda and Rwandan Citizens Responsible for Genocide and Other Such Violations Committed in the Territory of Neighbouring States between 1 January and 31 December 1994*, UN GAOR, 59th sess, UN Doc A/59/183–S/2004/601 (2004); *Eleventh Annual Report of the International Tribunal for the Prosecution of Persons Responsible for Serious Violations of International Humanitarian Law Committed in the Territory of the Former Yugoslavia since 1991*, UN GAOR, 59th sess, UN Doc A/59/215–S/2004/627 (2004).

[128] UNSC Res 1534 (26 March 2004).

V. THE PROPOSAL

A. Foundational Principles

The essence of the proposal is that an international judicial commission be created under the supervisory mandate of UNHCR, for the primary purpose of promoting convergence in the interpretation of the Refugee Convention by the method of producing authoritative opinions. A secondary purpose of such a commission would be to promote discussion about the interpretation of the Convention. It would not be involved in determining applications made by individual asylum seekers.

In order to achieve the primary objective, the commission would produce compelling opinions analysing, and providing practical legal guidance in relation to, current divergences in interpretation. Such opinions, directed towards interpretation rather than adjudication, would consolidate and draw upon all sources of international and domestic law, and provide guidance both at the level of general principle and in relation to particular factual situations.

While presently the primary difficulties with divergence in interpretation focus upon the definition of refugees, the commission would also be well placed to consider the question of refugee rights, an issue that will probably become more prominent in the future. Indeed, the commission could fill a critical void on this subject.

As discussed above, the authority of the commission would depend upon a mixture of its institutional mandate, its judicial character, its international composition, and—to a lesser extent—involvement by States parties to the Refugee Convention. It would also depend on the quality of its appointees and its overall conduct. It is imperative, therefore, that the commission be independent and composed of judges (including former and serving judges, as well as experts with academic or practical expertise) of the highest skill, reputation and integrity.

B. The Role of UNHCR

As already explained, it is proposed that the commission be created pursuant to the existing supervisory mandate of UNHCR. In this way, the commission would supplement the authority of the UNHCR, and recognise its fundamental role in the international refugee regime. At the same time, the funding arrangements for the commission are designed to avoid adding to the financial burden on UNHCR.

The commission could be created informally by UNHCR or perhaps by way of a formal resolution. The commission's proposed function is clearly within the supervisory mandate of UNHCR. Creation by treaty would, even if all States could be persuaded to participate, significantly delay the creation of the commission. Not all States would be persuaded to ratify, thereby fragmenting a universal regime. More importantly, there would probably be compromises caused by bargaining between States, and the present trends in the refugee policies of many States—as well as the experience of the process of developing a common asylum policy in the European Union—suggest that the negotiation of any treaty may undermine, rather than strengthen, the protections of the Refugee Convention.

It is expected that UNHCR would play a significant role in the operation of the commission. We would suggest that UNHCR have a role in making appointments to the commission; have the right to apply for an opinion of the commission; and have the right to make submissions on any question before the commission. Former UNHCR officials would also be considered for appointment to the commission. The opinions of the commission could be used by UNHCR where it undertakes refugee status determination.

However, the commission would have to be, and be seen to be, independent of UNHCR in the formulation of its opinions. Indeed, by separating the function of providing interpretations of the Refugee Convention from the other work of UNHCR, the commission would benefit UNHCR by allowing it to concentrate on its protection mandate.

C. Engagement with Interested Parties

The special relationship between the commission and UNHCR would give the commission a certain immediate recognition. This would be a starting point for dialogue and liaison between the commission and the participants in the world of refugee status determination and protection. As the commission would be a new and unique body, it would need to advocate its reason for existence widely in order to gain the necessary acceptance. While the most persuasive form of advocacy would come from the quality of its opinions, certain arrangements might be necessary to advance the cause of the commission.

It is proposed that a UN rapporteur be appointed to disseminate information about the work of the commission. A retired Chief Justice or like person would be ideal. The rapporteur would visit judges and decision-makers the world over to explain the work of the commission and encourage understanding of its opinions and their use in domestic decision-making. In the early stages there would be a place for a liaison officer to assist the rapporteur, while the reputation of the commission is being built.

D. Methods of Operation

This section of the paper makes some concrete proposals as to the operation of the commission. However, as we have noted, this remains a framework only, and one that is open to change. In particular, this proposal is directed towards the initial stage of setting up the commission. We envisage that, as with all institutions, the commission would evolve over time. The proposal therefore addresses the operation of the commission at the stage of inception.

(i) Composition of the Commission

For the reasons already canvassed, the members of the commission should be eminent experts in international refugee law, whether that expertise be derived from academic, judicial or practical experience (such as former high-level UNHCR officials). Minimum legal qualifications would be required. However, a mixture of academic, judicial and practical experience is desirable.

The commission should initially comprise nine judges, in view of the heavy workload likely to be involved in establishing the institution and determining priorities in the early stages. A small number of judges is more practical, as they require fewer resources, are likely to produce opinions more quickly and more likely to achieve agreement. A larger number is not necessary as the task of the commission is quite confined, and because we propose that it have broad powers to set its priorities and organise its workload.

For similar reasons, part-time appointments are preferable. First, higher calibre personnel would more likely be available, as many academics and sitting judges would be capable of engaging in the task part-time but be unwilling or unable to give up their full-time positions. Secondly, such judges might well be able to rely on the institutional support of their staff in their full-time positions, thereby minimising the resources required by the body. Thirdly, such appointments would not require full-time judicial salaries.

Part-time appointments have caused difficulty in other international bodies, most notably with the UN treaty committees. This is largely because of the increase in workload, although it has also been said that committee members are unable to devote the requisite time because of the demands of their primary employment. However, this may be suitably addressed at the appointment stage. Candidates unable to dedicate a certain amount of time to the task, or who have a potential conflict of interest, could be eliminated during the appointment process, and the terms of office might require that candidates who find themselves unable to fulfil their duties for whatever reason must resign.

As discussed earlier, part of the legitimacy of the commission would derive from its representation of different regions, cultures, legal systems and genders. This is particularly important given that much of refugee law is context-dependent and involves dealing with a wide range of cultures.

(ii) Appointment and Conditions of Office

The appointment process, and the terms and conditions of office, should conform to the recently published International Law Association's 'Burgh House Principles on the Independence of the International Judiciary'.[129] In particular, in contrast to other international judicial bodies, States should not have control over the appointments process, although some form of State involvement might be desirable.

The experience of other institutions has been that selection by States has resulted in politicking. The political influence is said to be 'omnipresent', for example, in elections to the ICJ,[130] although judges are usually well qualified.[131] The European Court of Human Rights recently found it necessary to make reforms to counter criticisms of the independence of its judges.[132] Procedures such as standard curricula vitæ and informal examination of the candidates[133] might be usefully adopted.

Appointments should be made by an appointments commission. The composition of this commission would be critical. It should include representatives of relevant organisations, such as the International Association of Refugee Law Judges, and involve sitting members of the commission. It may also be desirable to involve government representatives to some degree.

In order to engage the wider refugee advocacy community, the first stage of the process might involve open nominations, in which individuals, non-governmental organisations, judges, legal practitioners and academics could formally propose names to the appointments commission. Vacancies, and the criteria for appointment, would be widely published.

[129] 25 November 2004 <http://www.pict-pcti.org/FINAL%2025%20November%202004%20ILA%20Study%20Group%20Principles.doc> (accessed 10 June 2007).

[130] N Blokker and S Muller, 'The 1996 Elections to the International Court of Justice: New Tendencies in the Post-Cold War Era?' (1998) 47 *International and Comparative Law Quarterly* 211 at 213.

[131] See generally CF Amerasinghe, 'Judges of the International Court of Justice: Elections and Qualifications' (2001) 14 *Leiden Journal of International Law* 335. Contrast the earlier comments by GM Wilner and TJ Schoenbaum, however, which questioned the quality and independence of the judges: 'Forum: American Acceptance of the Jurisdiction of the International Court of Justice: Experiences and Prospects' (1989) 19 *Georgia Journal of International and Comparative Law* 489 at 497–500.

[132] Interights, 'Judicial Independence: Law and Practice of Appointments to the European Court of Human Rights' (2003) 24 *Human Rights Law Journal* 262.

[133] See A Drzemczewski, 'The European Human Rights Convention: A New Court of Human Rights in Strasbourg as of November 1, 1998' (1998) 55 *Washington and Lee Law Review* 697 at 723–4.

The appointments commission would adopt a transparent procedure for selection that would include consultation with relevant organisations and individuals.

Appointments would be for a term of five years, although this could be left up to the discretion of the appointments commission since it would depend on the preferences of candidates. As the appointment process would not be politically determined, some flexibility in the length of terms and re-appointment could be permitted without undue interference. The appointments commission would have the power to require a resignation in the event of incapacity, misconduct, conflict of interest and similar specified circumstances.

In order to attract the highest calibre candidates, it would be necessary to remunerate them appropriately for their time. The conditions of office should be similar to those available to other international judges, albeit with appropriate recognition of the part-time nature of the duties.

(iii) Selection of Cases

Given that the primary purpose of the commission would be to promote convergence, it would isolate the major areas of debate over the construction of the Refugee Convention and prioritise the delivery of its opinions accordingly. The commission would invite suggestions from UNHCR, leading academic commentators, governments, the legal profession and NGOs concerning appropriate issues for consideration.

Additionally, the commission might find it useful to allow certain parties, such as UNHCR, to ask the commission for an opinion. The commission would have the discretion to accept or refuse such an application, so as to avoid becoming a tool for political causes and to manage its resources wisely.

The commission should also be able to review or re-open opinions if it appeared necessary to do so.

(iv) The Deliberation Process

The rules of the commission would be flexible, allowing it to choose the best procedure for determining each case. In some instances it might be appropriate to conduct oral hearings, but many issues could be determined from written submissions from invited parties and research papers prepared for the commission.

The commission would have power to invite submissions from any source it considered could usefully contribute, and would usually invite submissions from UNHCR, NGOs, concerned governments, leading academic commentators and refugee law practitioners. As judges are likely to be spread across the world, there might be a place for hearings by telephone or video-conferencing. However, there would also be value in providing for the members of the commission to meet and discuss the issues for opinion.

(v) Single or Multiple Opinions?

The civil law method that generally envisages the production of a single opinion by a judicial body has the value of certainty and of providing clear guidance for future cases. This system avoids the morass of separate opinions, which often arrive at the same conclusion with barely distinguishable paths of reasoning. Such decisions generate confusion in the administration of the law.

The virtue, however, of the common law tradition that allows for dissenting opinions is that it exposes contrary standpoints, and thereby stimulates the development of the jurisprudence.

Given that the purpose of the commission would be to promote convergence of interpretations, it is envisaged that initially, at least, it would produce joint opinions. However, such a rule need not be inflexible, particularly as the commission would not finally determine individual applications.

(vi) Funding and Support of the Commission

In order to hasten the creation of the commission, it is envisaged that public financial support would be minimal. Private foundations, leading law firms and commercial organisations with an interest in the project would be invited to fund the salaries and travelling expenses of judges, a limited number of registry and support staff, as well as a space for its headquarters. Such a space could be usefully located in an academic centre for refugee studies, allowing access to expertise and relevant resources.

A novel approach to the funding of research support would be taken. Thus, the commission would offer to a recognised faculty or faculties a memorandum of understanding whereby academic staff would be made available to support the work of the commission. The support might also extend to the provision of information technology and translation facilities.

VI. CONCLUSION

As was noted in the Global Consultations process, 'the viability of a universal commitment to protection [in refugee law] is challenged by divergence in State practice'.[134] This chapter has set out a modest, and practical, proposal to address one aspect of divergence: the interpretation of the Refugee Convention.

[134] Hathaway and Foster (n 38 above) 358.

The present inconsistency in the Convention's interpretation is both undesirable and unjustifiable. The universal regime of international law envisaged by the Convention is, in practice, fragmented by diverging national interpretations. As has become evident in relation to many other international instruments, an international judicial authority is an essential element of a regime based on international law. This is not a problem that, as the present proposal indicates, demands significant resources or political will. It is a problem that is eminently capable of resolution by the international legal community. Indeed, it is a problem that can be addressed at minimal cost, and not at the expense of the pressing material needs of refugees.

For many commentators, the prospect of an international refugee court has been a pipe dream. Looked at closely, however, what is needed is not yet another *court* to determine refugee status, but an authoritative interpreter of the Refugee Convention. That fundamental insight informs the proposal. A small number of internationally-renowned experts in refugee law, endowed with the authority of UNHCR and with their own formidable intellectual, analytical and rhetorical gifts, would be an invaluable asset in the task of promoting convergence in the interpretation of the Convention. Funded by civil society and the legal community in particular, untainted by the political control of States, and untroubled by the procedural and administrative difficulties of deciding real cases, such a body would avoid many of the difficulties experienced by other international courts and tribunals. Instead, it could focus clearly on the task at hand: interpreting the Refugee Convention by the fearless and authoritative application of legal knowledge and rules.

10

The Refugee Convention as a Rights Blueprint for Persons in Need of International Protection

JANE McADAM

SINCE ITS ENTRY into force in 1954, the Refugee Convention ('Convention')[1] has been the central international instrument on refugee status, supplemented by the 1967 Protocol[2], which extended its temporal and (with respect to some States) its geographical application. In the half-century since the Convention's inception, international human rights law has evolved as a sophisticated system of rights and duties between the individual and the State, affecting traditional notions of State sovereignty and behaviour in an unprecedented manner.[3] Despite the influence of international human rights law on the regulation of States' conduct, however, there has been a general reluctance by States, academics and institutions to view human rights law, refugee law and humanitarian law as branches of an interconnected, holistic regime,[4] particularly when it comes to triggering eligibility for protection beyond the scope of Article 1A(2) of the Convention.

Complementary protection is largely about this intersection. A feature of most western protection regimes,[5] it describes protection granted by

[1] Convention relating to the Status of Refugees (adopted 28 July 1951, entered into force 22 April 1954) 189 UNTS 137.

[2] Protocol relating to the Status of Refugees (adopted 31 January 1967, entered into force 4 October 1967) 606 UNTS 267.

[3] Eg the Human Rights Act 1998 (UK).

[4] It is refreshing to note, however, that the 2006 International Law Association (British Branch) conference considered these issues under the general conference theme: 'Tower of Babel: International Law in the 21st Century—Coherent or Compartmentalised?'. See also the work of the International Law Commission on fragmentation in international law: <http://untreaty.un.org/ilc/guide/1_9.htm> (accessed 20 June 2007).

[5] Australia is exceptional in having no formal system of complementary protection, despite a recognised need for it: see, eg Senate Legal and Constitutional Affairs Committee, *Administration and Operation of the Migration Act 1958* (Canberra, Cth of Australia, 2006)

States to individuals with international protection needs falling outside the 1951 Convention framework. It may be based on human rights treaties, such as the express prohibition on *refoulement* in Article 3 of the Convention against Torture ('CAT')[6] and its implied prohibition in Article 7 of the International Covenant on Civil and Political Rights ('ICCPR'),[7] or on more general humanitarian principles, such as providing assistance to persons fleeing generalised violence.[8] (It is on this latter basis that temporary protection in mass influx situations is premised.) Importantly, complementary protection derives from legal obligations preventing return, rather than from compassionate reasons or practical obstacles to removal. Even though these latter instances of 'protection' may be humanitarian in nature, they are not based on international protection obligations per se and therefore do not fall within the legal domain of 'complementary protection'.

At first glance, it appears that international law has little to say about the relatively amorphous concept of complementary protection. Although there is long-standing State practice of protecting extra-Convention refugees, encompassed by such terms as 'de facto refugees', 'B status

Recommendation 33, para 4.50ff; Senate Select Committee on Ministerial Discretion in Migration Matters, *Report* (Canberra, Cth of Australia, 2004) esp ch 8. See further J McAdam, *Complementary Protection in International Refugee Law* (Oxford, Oxford University Press, 2007) 3, 131–4; UNHCR Regional Office (Australia, New Zealand, Papua New Guinea and the South Pacific), 'Discussion Paper: Complementary Protection' (No 2, 2005) <http://www.unhcr.org.au/pdfs/Discussion22005.pdf> (accessed 20 June 2007); Refugee Council of Australia and others, 'Complementary Protection: The Way Ahead' (April 2004) <http://www.refugeecouncil.org.au/docs/current/comp-protection-model.pdf > (accessed 21 June 2007); and National Council of Churches in Australia, 'Fact Sheet: Introducing the Complementary Protection Model' (2007) <http://www.ncca.org.au/__data/page/993/Complementary_Protection_Fact_Sheet_2007.pdf> (accessed 20 June 2007). Senator Andrew Bartlett of the Australian Democrats (a minor party) introduced a Bill on complementary protection into the Australian Parliament on 13 September 2006: Migration Legislation Amendment (Complementary Protection Visas) Bill 2006. It is unlikely to receive sufficient support to become law. New Zealand is in the process of introducing a legislative system of complementary protection regime: Department of Labour, 'Immigration Act Review: Discussion Paper' (April 2006) s 14; 'Immigration Change Programme: Immigration Act Review' (Cabinet Recommendations) (November 2006) 4, 27–8 <http://www.dol.govt.nz/PDFs/immigration-act-review-cabinet-paper.pdf> (accessed 20 June 2007). A Bill was intended to be introduced into Parliament in April 2007, but as at June 2007, had not been: Hon David Cunliffe, 'Comprehensive Immigration Law Closer' (Press Release, 5 December 2006) <http://www.beehive.govt.nz/ViewDocument.aspx?DocumentID=27894> (accessed 20 June 2007).

[6] Convention against Torture and Other Cruel, Inhuman or Degrading Treatment or Punishment (adopted 10 December 1984, entered into force 26 June 1987) 1465 UNTS 85.

[7] International Covenant on Civil and Political Rights (adopted 16 Dec 1966, entered into force 23 March 1976) 999 UNTS 171.

[8] See D Perluss and JF Hartman, 'Temporary Refuge: Emergence of a Customary Norm' (1986) 26 *Virginia Journal of International Law* 551; and GS Goodwin-Gill, '*Non-Refoulement* and the New Asylum Seekers' (1986) 26 *Virginia Journal of International Law* 897; cf K Hailbronner, '*Non-Refoulement* and "Humanitarian" Refugees: Customary International Law or Wishful Legal Thinking?' (1986) 26 *Virginia Journal of International Law* 857.

refugees', 'OAU and Cartagena-type refugees' and 'humanitarian refugees', the term 'complementary protection' appears in no international treaty and has no singular connotation in State practice.[9] An Executive Committee Conclusion adopted in October 2005 specifically refers to 'complementary protection', but does not define it.[10]

The first binding, supranational instrument on complementary protection, the 'Qualification Directive', was concluded in April 2004 by the European Union, but it adopts the term 'subsidiary protection' instead.[11] Beneficiaries of subsidiary protection are defined as those facing a real risk of the 'death penalty or execution', 'torture or inhuman or degrading treatment or punishment' in the country of origin, or a 'serious and individual threat to [their] life or person by reason of indiscriminate violence in situations of international or internal armed conflict',[12] and who do not meet the Convention definition of 'refugee'. Significantly, the Qualification Directive also sets out the rights to which beneficiaries are entitled. This is a considerable step forward for some EU Member States, which had previously simply 'tolerated' the presence of non-removable persons but had not granted them a formal legal status. There are well-documented cases of the financial, social and psychological hardships suffered by persons left in legal limbo.[13] However, rather than recognising the *need* for protection as triggering protection entitlements equivalent to

[9] See the survey of State practice in R Mandal, 'Protection Mechanisms outside of the 1951 Convention ("Complementary Protection")', UNHCR Legal and Protection Policy Research Series, PPLA/2005/02 (June 2005). Refugees under the Cartagena Declaration include 'persons who have fled their country because their lives, safety or freedom have been threatened by generalized violence, foreign aggression, internal conflicts, massive violation of human rights or other circumstances which have seriously disturbed public order': Cartagena Declaration on Refugees (22 November 1984) in *Annual Report of the Inter-American Commission on Human Rights* OAS Doc OEA/Ser.L/V/II.66/doc.10, rev.1, 190–93 (1984–85) Conclusion 3. On OAU Convention refugees, see the text to n 74 below.

[10] Executive Committee Conclusion No 103 (LVI), 'The Provision of International Protection including through Complementary Forms of Protection' (2005). For background discussion paper, see Mandal (n 9 above); and Executive Committee Standing Committee, 'Providing International Protection including through Complementary Forms of Protection', UN Doc EC/55/SC/CRP.16 (2 June 2005); on the original recommendation for an Executive Committee Conclusion, see UNHCR, *Agenda for Protection*, 2nd edn (March 2000) 34; for the text of the preliminary draft, see Global Consultations on International Protection, 'Complementary Forms of Protection', UN Doc EC/GC/01/18 (4 September 2001) para 11.

[11] Council Directive 2004/83/EC of 29 April 2004 on Minimum Standards for the Qualification and Status of Third Country Nationals or Stateless Persons as Refugees or as Persons Who Otherwise Need International Protection and the Content of the Protection Granted [2004] OJ L304/12.

[12] *Ibid*, Art 15.

[13] See, eg *Ahmed v Austria* (1997) 24 EHRR 278 (ECtHR), and discussion in O Andrysek, 'Gaps in International Protection and the Potential for Redress through Individual Complaints Procedures' (1997) 9 *International Journal of Refugee Law* 392.

those of Convention refugees, part of the political compromise reached in drafting the Qualification Directive was the dilution of standards for beneficiaries of *subsidiary* protection. While certain delegations sought to justify a secondary status on the ground that subsidiary protection needs are of a more temporary nature—an assertion not supported by empirical evidence—ultimately no legal justification was offered to support the establishment of a protection hierarchy.[14] In addition to the unjustified dilution of subsidiary protection beneficiaries' rights, differentiation in treatment may lead to States favouring subsidiary protection by 'defining out' categories of persons who legitimately fall within Article 1A(2), so as to avoid the more stringent obligations required for Convention refugees. Procedurally, it may also create an incentive for appeal by beneficiaries of subsidiary protection, attempting to 'upgrade' their status.[15]

This chapter establishes the fundamental conceptual connections between international refugee law and human rights law in order to argue that under *international* law, beneficiaries of protection—whether as Convention refugees or otherwise—are entitled to an identical status.[16] While there are clear policy reasons why this should be the case, there are also cogent legal arguments that support the extension of Convention status to extra-Convention refugees. These are based on a conceptualisation of international law as a body of interrelated norms that must be interpreted in relation to, and be informed by, each other.

The discussion begins with a reflection on the inadequacy of human rights law in providing a legal *status* for beneficiaries of complementary protection. It is argued that while human rights attach to all persons in principle—irrespective of their nationality or formal legal status[17]—in practice such characteristics can significantly affect the extent of rights

[14] GS Goodwin-Gill and A Hurwitz, 'Memorandum' in Minutes of Evidence Taken before the EU Committee (Sub-Committee E) (10 April 2002) para 19, in the House of Lords Select Committee on the EU, *Defining Refugee Status and Those in Need of International Protection* (London, The Stationery Office, 2002) Oral Evidence 2–3. This is contrasted with Canadian practice relating to 'protected persons': Immigration and Nationality Act 2001, ss 95–97.

[15] House of Lords Select Committee (n 14 above) paras 102, 111. The Minister (Angela Eagle MP, Parliamentary Under Secretary of State at the Home Office) acknowledged that this already happens. For a discussion of appeal processes, see J McAdam, 'Complementary Protection and Beyond: How States Deal with Human Rights Protection', UNHCR, *New Issues in Refugee Research*, Working Paper No 118 (2005).

[16] This chapter does not address the more complicated situation of persons who, though protected by human rights-based *non-refoulement*, would be excluded under Art 1F of the Refugee Convention on the basis of their conduct. It is not legally defensible to suggest that they are entitled to Convention status, since they are expressly excluded from it. For an analysis of the status to which they might be entitled under international law, see McAdam (n 5 above) ch 6.

[17] Certain exceptions exist with respect to political rights reserved for citizens: see ICCPR, Arts 12(3), 13, 25. See also Human Rights Committee, 'General Comment 15: The Position of Aliens under the Covenant' (11 April 1986), reinforced by Human Rights Committee,

an individual is actually accorded. In reality, States *do* differentiate between the rights of citizens and the rights of aliens (and even between different categories of aliens), premising this on their sovereign right to determine who remains in their territories and under what conditions. While the rights set out in the Refugee Convention are not inherently superior to those in the universal human rights treaties, being largely based on the latter,[18] they are applied in a different way. Whereas a grant of Convention status entitles the recipient to the full gamut of Convention rights, no comparable status arises from recognition of an individual's protection need under a human rights instrument. Human rights law lacks a fundamental feature of the Refugee Convention: a status required by international law.[19]

Thus, though it might initially seem appropriate to point to human rights law as offering a complementary and, in part, more generous set of rights than the Refugee Convention, the generality and vagueness of those rights, combined with a lack of implementing mechanisms at the domestic level, make them in practice comparatively weak. Although the universal human rights instruments grant a comprehensive set of rights to all persons within a State's jurisdiction,[20] international human rights law is strong on principle but weak on delivery.[21]

'General Comment 31 on Article 2 of the Covenant: The Nature of the General Legal Obligation Imposed on States Parties to the Covenant' (29 March 2004) UN Doc CCPR/C/21/Rev.1/Add.13 (26 May 2004) para 10; Committee on the Elimination of Racial Discrimination, 'General Recommendation XI on Non-Citizens (Art 1)' (19 March 1993) in UN Doc A/46/18.

[18] Many of the provisions of the Convention were based on the UDHR (n 46 below) and the draft ICCPR (n 7 above) and ICESCR (n 36 below): see nn 49 and 50 below.

[19] H Lambert, 'Protection against *Refoulement* from Europe: Human Rights Law Comes to the Rescue' (1999) 48 *International and Comparative Law Quarterly* 515 at 519; *Ahmed v Austria* (n 13 above); *BB v France* App No 30930/96 (9 March 1998). It is not surprising that treaties such as the CAT do not articulate a resultant status for those who benefit from human rights-based *non-refoulement*. For example, the purpose of the CAT was not to enumerate the rights of persons protected from *refoulement*, but rather to strengthen the existing prohibition of torture and other cruel, inhuman or degrading treatment or punishment under international law through a number of supportive measures. See JH Burgers and H Danelius, *The United Nations Convention against Torture: A Handbook on the Convention against Torture and Other Cruel, Inhuman or Degrading Treatment or Punishment* (Dordrecht, Martinus Nijhoff Publishers, 1988). Hathaway argues that refugee rights consist of 'an amalgam of principles drawn from both refugee law and the [human rights] Covenants', and that refugee 'status' should now be understood as comprising a combination of these: JC Hathaway, *The Rights of Refugees under International Law* (Cambridge, Cambridge University Press, 2005) 9. Certainly, where this is the case, that more comprehensive status should also be accorded to beneficiaries of complementary protection for the same reasons as advanced above.

[20] With the exception of certain rights granted to citizens only: see n 17 above.

[21] Thanks to Professor Christopher McCrudden (Lincoln College, University of Oxford) for this description.

It is for this reason that the chapter then demonstrates, through historical analysis, why the status set out in the Refugee Convention should attach to all those whom the principle of *non-refoulement* protects. This should not be viewed as an attempt to broaden the scope of Article 1A(2), but rather as recognition that the widening of *non-refoulement* under treaties and customary international law[22] requires a concomitant consideration of the status which beneficiaries acquire. Though a specialist treaty, the Refugee Convention nevertheless forms part of the corpus of human rights law, both informing and being informed by it. Accordingly, with respect to the status it confers on protected persons, the Convention acts as a type of *lex specialis*. It does not seek to displace the *lex generalis* of international human rights law, but rather complements and strengthens its application.

I. THE INADEQUACY OF '*NON-REFOULEMENT* PLUS HUMAN RIGHTS LAW' ALONE

Beyond providing a widened threshold for claiming protection, international human rights law alone is an inadequate alternative source of substantive protection. Many States undertake human rights obligations at the formal level, but do not ensure that the rights subscribed to can actually be claimed.[23] Unless special measures are taken to ensure that such provisions are translated into national law, then certain benefits may be inaccessible.[24] Even where individuals may not be barred from enjoyment of a right,

> they are in practice often deprived of it inasmuch as it is dependent on the fulfillment of certain formalities, such as production of documents, intervention of consular or other authorities, with which … they are not in a position to comply.[25]

While human rights law requires States to respect the rights it sets out in relation to *all* persons within its jurisdiction or territory, the quality of each right may vary depending on the individual's legal position vis-à-vis the State. Thus, while the *standard* of compliance with human

[22] On which, see GS Goodwin-Gill and J McAdam, *The Refugee in International Law*, 3rd edn (Oxford, Oxford University Press, 2007) 345–54; and E Lauterpacht and D Bethlehem, 'The Scope and Content of the Principle of *Non-Refoulement*: Opinion' in E Feller, V Türk and F Nicholson (eds), *Refugee Protection in International Law: UNHCR's Global Consultations on International Protection* (Cambridge, Cambridge University Press, 2003) paras 217–53.

[23] GS Goodwin-Gill and J Kumin, 'Refugees in Limbo and Canada's International Obligations' (Caledon Institute of Social Policy, September 2000) 4.

[24] *Ibid*, 5.

[25] Ad Hoc Committee on Statelessness and Related Problems, 'A Study of Statelessness' UN Doc E/1112, E/1112.Add.1 (New York, August 1949); Andrysek (n 13 above) 411.

rights law is international, the State retains discretion in its choice of *implementation*[26]—namely, whether and how to incorporate treaty provisions into domestic law.

There is therefore a gap between the theory of human rights and the ability to enjoy those rights.[27] As Hathaway notes, '[t]he divergence between the theory and the reality of international human rights law is strikingly apparent'.[28] At the international level, the content of rights is very broad and ill-defined, and it may be possible for States to 'guarantee' such rights without doing much towards their positive implementation. A common problem is that State constitutions often guarantee rights only to 'citizens',[29] making the enforcement of non-citizens' rights difficult. In 1967, Weis described international measures for safeguarding human rights as 'modest',[30] and nearly 25 years later Hathaway still characterised them as 'generally sluggish and only occasionally effective'.[31] As Goodwin-Gill and Kumin observe, the test for whether a treaty is effectively implemented domestically depends not on form alone, but on an overall assessment of practice.[32]

It is this that makes reliance on human rights law, either alone or in combination with *non-refoulement* under customary international law,[33] a precarious option. Even though the Refugee Convention repeats many of the same rights as the universal treaties, its retention as a specialist refugee instrument is not redundant. As Hathaway argues, refugee law has its own legitimacy, and co-ordination between refugee and human rights law should not lead to a downgrading of protection for persons in need of international protection.[34] Furthermore, if the substantive rights of beneficiaries of complementary protection were dependent on human rights law alone, the quality of protection would be contingent on the combination of treaties ratified (and implemented) by the State and status would consequently be very inconsistent.[35] For example, while the International

26 Goodwin-Gill and McAdam (n 22 above) 453.

27 UNHCR, 'Note on International Protection' UN Doc A/AC.96/898 (3 July 1998) para 45.

28 JC Hathaway, 'Reconceiving Refugee Law as Human Rights Protection' (1991) 4 *Journal of Refugee Studies* 113 at 113.

29 ECOSOC Commission on Human Rights, 'Prevention of Discrimination: The Rights of Non-Citizens' UN Doc E/CN.4/Sub.2/2003/23 (26 May 2003) para 24; Human Rights Committee, 'General Comment 15' (n 17 above) para 3.

30 P Weis, 'Human Rights and Refugees', Lecture, Yale University Law School (7 November 1967) 13 (Refugee Studies Centre (Oxford) Archive WEIS A21.6 WEI).

31 Hathaway (n 28 above) 113.

32 Goodwin-Gill and Kumin (n 23 above) 4.

33 See n 22 above.

34 Hathaway (n 28 above) 117. States that are not parties to the Convention do not have superior protection regimes: see eg BS Chimni, 'The Legal Condition of Refugees in India' (1994) 7 *Journal of Refugee Studies* 378 at 398; A Helton, 'What is Refugee Protection?' (1990) Spec Issue *International Journal of Refugee Law* 119 at 125.

35 In monist States, international treaties have direct effect, whereas in dualist States, they must be implemented domestically following ratification to be justiciable.

Covenant on Economic, Social and Cultural Rights ('ICESCR')[36] and many of the International Labour Organization conventions cover similar rights to Articles 17 to 24 of the Refugee Convention, certain parties to the Convention have not ratified those instruments and hence they would not apply.[37]

II. THE REFUGEE CONVENTION AS A HUMAN RIGHTS TREATY[38]

Given this state of affairs, it is important to inquire into whether there is a means of extending the protection that States recognise for Convention refugees to others in need of international protection. Accordingly, this part of the chapter considers the historical context in which the Refugee Convention arose, and takes a dynamic approach towards interpreting how that might have a bearing on the expansion of the principle of *non-refoulement* to cover those falling outside the terms of Article 1A(2). It does this in light of the Convention's humanitarian object and purpose[39] to ensure to 'refugees the widest possible exercise of … fundamental rights and freedoms',[40] and by deriving or inferring[41] subsequent agreement between the contracting States and State practice bearing on the Convention's interpretation.[42] Relevant examples include the regional OAU Convention and Cartagena Declaration,[43] the 2005 Executive Committee Conclusion on complementary protection, and the various domestic regimes that States have consistently implemented in response to flows of extra-Convention refugees.

[36] International Covenant on Economic, Social and Cultural Rights (adopted 16 December 1966, entered into force 3 January 1976) 993 UNTS 3.

[37] W Kälin, 'The Legal Condition of Refugees in Switzerland' (1994) 7 *Journal of Refugee Studies* 82 at 95.

[38] IC Jackson, *The Refugee Concept in Group Situations* (The Hague, Martinus Nijhoff Publishers, 1999), and UNHCR, 'Note on International Protection' UN Doc A/AC.96/975 (2 July 2003) paras 49–52 emphasise the relevance of human rights law to refugee issues.

[39] Vienna Convention on the Law of Treaties (adopted 23 May 1969, entered into force 27 January 1980) 1155 UNTS 331, Art 31(1). Even though the Vienna Convention was adopted after the conclusion of the Refugee Convention, this provision is regarded as reflecting customary international law. UNHCR's Executive Committee has noted that refugee law is a dynamic body of law which is 'informed by the object and purpose' of the Convention and Protocol 'and by developments in related areas of international law, such as human rights and international humanitarian law': Executive Committee Conclusion No 103 (n 10 above) para (c).

[40] Refugee Convention (n 1 above) Preamble.

[41] GS Goodwin-Gill, *The Refugee in International Law*, 2nd edn (Oxford, Oxford University Press, 1996) 367, discussing the Vienna Convention rules in relation to interpretation of the Refugee Convention.

[42] Vienna Convention (n 39 above) Art 31(3).

[43] Organization of African Unity Convention Governing the Specific Aspects of Refugee Problems in Africa (adopted 10 September 1969, entered into force 20 June 1974) 1001 UNTS 45; Cartagena Declaration (n 9 above).

The drafting of the 1951 Convention represented a 'profound re-orientation' in refugee organisations, agreements and agendas, but it was '*evolution*, not *revolution*'.[44] In 1947, the Commission on Human Rights adopted a resolution that

> early consideration be given by the United Nations to the legal status of persons who do not enjoy the protection of any Government, in particular the acquisition of nationality, as regards their legal status and social protection and their documentation.[45]

At the request of the UN Economic and Social Council, the Ad Hoc Committee on Statelessness and Related Problems was asked to draft a binding legal instrument to implement Articles 14 and 15 of the Universal Declaration of Human Rights ('UDHR'),[46] firmly cementing the Convention's foundations in human rights law. Its purpose was to

> consolidate existing agreements and conventions and, further, to determine the status of those refugees who had so far enjoyed no protection under any of the existing instruments.[47]

Although the Convention took as its departure point human rights principles contained in the UDHR, it revised, consolidated and substantially extended earlier agreements to create a new protection regime.[48] Many substantive provisions were based on principles of the UDHR[49] and the embryonic ICCPR and ICESCR, known then as the draft Covenant on Human Rights.[50]

[44] GS Goodwin-Gill, 'Editorial: The International Protection of Refugees: What Future?' (2000) 12 *International Journal of Refugee Law* 1 at 2.

[45] Commission on Human Rights Report to ECOSOC on the Second Session of the Commission Held at Geneva from 2 to 17 December 1947, UN Doc E/600 (1948) para 46, in P Weis, 'Human Rights and Refugees' (1971) 1 *Israel Yearbook on Human Rights* 35 at 37.

[46] Universal Declaration of Human Rights (adopted 10 December 1948) UNGA Res 217A (III); Ad Hoc Committee on Statelessness and Related Problems, First Session, 'Summary Record of the 1st Meeting' (New York, 16 January 1950) UN Doc E/AC.32/SR.1 (23 January 1950) para 4 (Secretariat).

[47] Conference of Plenipotentiaries on the Status of Refugees and Stateless Persons, 'Summary Record of the 2nd Meeting' (Geneva, 2 July 1951) UN Doc A/CONF.2/SR.2 (20 July 1951) 9 (High Commissioner).

[48] Refugee Convention (n 1 above) Preamble.

[49] 'Comments on the Draft Convention and Protocol: General Observations' Annex II to Ad Hoc Committee on Statelessness and Related Problems, 'Draft Report of the Ad Hoc Committee on Statelessness and Related Problems' (16 January–February 1950) UN Doc E/AC.32/L.38 (15 February 1950) 36 (Art 3 on non-discrimination), 46 (Art 26 on education); Ad Hoc Committee on Statelessness and Related Problems, 'Refugees and Stateless Persons: Compilation of the Comments of Governments and Specialized Agencies on the Report of the Ad Hoc Committee on Statelessness and Related Problems' (Document E/1618) UN Doc E/AC.32/L.40 (10 August 1950) 31 (France, on the UDHR, Art 29(1)).

[50] 'Comments on the Draft Convention and Protocol: General Observations' (n 49 above) 58; see UN Doc E/1572, 12 (Art 32 (then Art 27) on expulsion).

The Refugee Convention was to establish practical but universal standards[51] for the rights of refugees that went beyond the lowest common denominator, 'since a convention would hardly be useful if it contained only the minimum acceptable to everyone.'[52] Early UN General Assembly resolutions supported its underlying human rights basis, with an emphasis on assisting the most needy,[53] affirming basic principles relating to solutions,[54] and recommending increased protection activities.[55]

The result is a specialist human rights treaty that reflects the tenets of the UDHR, ICCPR and ICESCR in such provisions as the acquisition of property, the right to work, housing, public education, public relief, labour legislation, social security, and freedom of movement.[56] Moreover, it reinforces States' protection of refugees as an international legal duty, arising from Article 14 of the UDHR and embodied in binding form by the principle of *non-refoulement* in Article 33 of the Convention. As one commentator remarks:

> The framers' unambiguous reference in the Preamble of the 1951 Convention to the Universal Declaration of Human Rights indicates a desire for the refugee definition to evolve in tandem with human rights principles.[57]

Lauterpacht and Bethlehem stress that the law on human rights that has emerged since the Convention's conclusion is

> an essential part of [its] framework ... that must, by reference to the ICJ's observations in the *Namibia* case, be taken into account for purposes of interpretation.[58]

The United Nations High Commissioner for Refugees ('UNHCR') has also emphasised that:

> The human rights base of the Convention roots it quite directly in the broader framework of human rights instruments of which it is an integral part, albeit

[51] Conference of Plenipotentiaries on the Status of Refugees and Stateless Persons, 'Summary Record of the 2nd Meeting' (Geneva, 2 July 1951) UN Doc A/CONF.2/SR.2 (20 July 1951) 18 (High Commissioner); Conference of Plenipotentiaries on the Status of Refugees and Stateless Persons, 'Summary Record of the 3rd Meeting' (3 July 1951) UN Doc A/CONF.2/SR.3 (19 November 1951) 10 (France).

[52] Ad Hoc Committee on Statelessness and Related Problems, First Session, 'Summary Record of the 25th Meeting' (New York, 10 February 1950) UN Doc E/AC.32/SR.25 (17 February 1950) para 68.

[53] United Nations General Assembly ('UNGA') Res 639 (VI) of 20 December 1952; UNGA Res 728 (VIII) of 23 October 1953.

[54] UNGA Res 1166 (XII) 26 November 1957; ECOSOC Res 686 (XXVI) B of 21 July 1958.

[55] UNGA Res 1284 (XIII) of 5 December 1958, para 1, in GS Goodwin-Gill, 'The Language of Protection' (1989) 1 *International Journal of Refugee Law* 6 at 14.

[56] J Patrnogic, 'International Protection of Refugees in Armed Conflicts' (reprinted by UNHCR Protection Division from Annales de Droit International Médical, July 1981) s 4.

[57] MR von Sternberg, *The Grounds of Refugee Protection in the Context of International Human Rights and Humanitarian Law: Canadian and United States Case Law Compared* (The Hague, Martinus Nijhoff Publishers, 2002) 314.

[58] Lauterpacht and Bethlehem (n 22 above) para 75.

> with a very particular focus. The various human rights treaty monitoring bodies and the jurisprudence developed by regional bodies such as the European Court of Human Rights and the Inter-American Court of Human Rights are an important complement in this regard, not least since they recognize that refugees and asylum-seekers benefit both from specific Convention-based protection and from the range of general human rights protections as they apply to all people, regardless of status.[59]

While developments in human rights law may shape interpretations of 'persecution',[60] they may also *independently* form grounds for non-removal. Article 3 of the CAT, Article 7 of the ICCPR and Article 3 of the European Convention on Human Rights ('ECHR')[61] are recognised sources of human rights *non-refoulement* (or complementary protection) which prohibit removal in circumstances additional to (and sometimes overlapping with) Article 1A(2). External to and independent of the Refugee Convention,[62] the instruments provide only a trigger for protection and do not elaborate a resultant legal status. The main problem with the EU Qualification Directive, and one which has characterised many ad hoc complementary protection schemes, is that beneficiaries do not receive the same level of rights as Convention refugees. In so far as there is no legal justification for distinguishing between the status granted to Convention or extra-Convention refugees,[63] it makes sense that the Convention, as a 'Magna Carta for the persecuted',[64] applies to both. Since the Convention is itself a specialist human rights instrument, the protection conceptualisation it embodies is necessarily extended by developments in human rights law, rather than via the conventional means of a protocol. It therefore acts as a form of *lex specialis*

[59] UNHCR, 'Note on International Protection' UN Doc A/AC.96/951 (13 September 2001) para 4.

[60] See JC Hathaway, *The Law of Refugee Status* (Toronto, Butterworths, 1991) 112, approved in *Horvath v Secretary of State for the Home Department* [2001] 1 AC 489 (HL) 495 (Lord Hope of Craighead); *Sepet v Secretary of State for the Home Department* [2003] UKHL 15, [2003] 1 WLR 856, para 7 (Lord Bingham); *Ullah v Secretary of State for the Home Department* [2004] UKHL 26, para 32 (Lord Steyn); International Association of Refugee Law Judges Human Rights Nexus Working Party, 'Rapporteur's Report' (1998 Annual Conference, Ottawa, 12–17 October 1998) 8. See, eg gender-related persecution.

[61] Convention for the Protection of Human Rights and Fundamental Freedoms (European Convention on Human Rights, as amended) (4 November 1950) ETS No 5.

[62] Some States may procedurally determine the order in which protection may be invoked, however.

[63] UNHCR's Observations on the European Commission's Proposal for a Council Directive on Minimum Standards for the Qualification and Status of Third Country Nationals and Stateless Persons as Refugees or as Persons Who Otherwise Need International Protection' 14109/01 ASILE 54 (16 November 2001) para 46; UNHCR, 'Note on Key Issues of Concern to UNHCR on the Draft Qualification Directive' (March 2004) 2.

[64] Conference of Plenipotentiaries on the Status of Refugees and Stateless Persons, 'Summary Record of the 19th Meeting' (Geneva, 13 July 1951) UN Doc A/CONF.2/SR.19 (26 November 1951) 27 (International Association of Penal Law).

which applies to persons encompassed by that extended concept of protection.

III. 'HUMANITARIAN REFUGEES': ARTICLE 1A(1)

Analysis of the Convention's conceptualisation of 'protection' invariably focuses on the refugee definition in Article 1A(2), since an individual must satisfy its requirements to trigger Convention status. Article 1A(1), which extends the benefits of the 1951 Convention to any person who

> [h]as been considered a refugee under the Arrangements of 12 May 1926 and 30 June 1928 or under the Conventions of 28 October 1933 and 10 February 1938, the Protocol of 14 September 1939 or the Constitution of the International Refugee Organization

is generally overlooked as an historical remnant. Although eligibility under Article 1A(1) is retrospective, the fact that the Convention recognises all previous refugee definitions as giving rise to Convention status is significant, since they typically protected victims of armed conflict or communal violence. The incorporation of these definitions necessarily broadens the Convention's conceptual basis of protection, making it difficult to sustain the argument that, conceptually, the Convention does not support the grant of its international legal status to persons fleeing situations of armed conflict or communal violence.[65] This has particular significance for persons seeking complementary protection on the basis of civil war, and challenges the EU's current approach of creating a new and separate protection status for such persons.

Furthermore, even though an applicant today cannot invoke an Article 1A(1) instrument as the basis of an asylum claim, the fact that Convention status flows from the definitions contained in those instruments, which embody what Melander has termed the 'humanitarian refugee' concept,[66] makes it more difficult to justify differential treatment for persons seeking complementary protection on similar grounds. Not only has State practice continued to recognise both 'humanitarian' and Convention refugees, but the dominant legal refugee instrument implicitly retains the humanitarian concept of protection within its definitional provision, further illuminating the Convention's object and purpose.[67]

[65] Of course, many of those fleeing such circumstances may qualify for protection under Art 1A(2). For discussion of this, see Mandal (n 9 above) paras 21–4.

[66] G Melander, 'Refugee Policy Options—Protection or Assistance' in G Rystad (ed), *The Uprooted: Forced Migration as an International Problem in the Post-War Era* (Lund, Lund University Press, 1990) 146–7.

[67] Vienna Convention (n 39 above) Art 31(1).

Thus, while the text of Article 1A(1) does not support an argument that the provision itself gives rise to additional grounds for claiming protection under the Convention, its implicit incorporation of earlier legal definitions of 'refugee' (and the concepts of protection which those definitions embody) supports the view that the Convention tolerates a broader protection concept than Article 1A(2) might suggest, and that Convention status is the appropriate status for persons in need of international protection for humanitarian reasons.

IV. RECOMMENDATION 'E' OF THE FINAL ACT

Recommendation E of the Final Act of the Conference of Plenipotentiaries, which is appended to the Refugee Convention, expresses

> the hope that the Convention relating to the Status of Refugees will have value as an example exceeding its contractual scope and that all nations will be guided by it in granting so far as possible to persons in their territory as refugees, and who would not be covered by the terms of the Convention, the treatment for which it provides.

This was an initiative of the UK delegation, prompted by the deletion of a provision which would have allowed the Contracting States to add to the definition of the term 'refugee'.[68] The UK representative explained that his delegation had felt that a general recommendation was called for to cover those classes of refugees who were altogether outside the scope of Article 1A.[69]

Recommendation E reveals that the drafters of the Refugee Convention to some extent 'envisaged a complementary protection system'.[70] This statement needs further explanation to avoid any suggestion that the drafters envisaged a separate, complementary protection system operating outside the Convention's parameters, which is not sustained when

[68] Conference of Plenipotentiaries on the Status of Refugees and Stateless Persons, 'Texts of the Draft Convention and the Draft Protocol to be Considered by the Conference' UN Doc A/CONF.2/1 (12 March 1951) 5 (citations omitted). A Final Act to a treaty provides a formal summary of the conference proceedings, and may also seek to establish political, rather than legal, agreement on particular issues or set out matters for future discussion. It may also provide a useful aid for interpretation of the treaty, and at times the treaty text may even be incorporated into the Final Act: see I Brownlie, *Principles of Public International Law*, 5th edn (Oxford, Oxford University Press, 1998) 610; and A Aust, *Modern Treaty Law and Practice* (Cambridge, Cambridge University Press, 2000) 73–4.

[69] Conference of Plenipotentiaries on the Status of Refugees and Stateless Persons, 'Summary Record of the 35th Meeting' (Geneva, 25 July 1951) UN Doc A/CONF.2/SR.35 (3 December 1951) 44.

[70] H Storey and others, 'Complementary Protection: Should There Be a Common Approach to Providing Protection to Persons Who Are Not Covered by the 1951 Geneva Convention?' (Joint ILPA/IARLJ Symposium, 6 December 1999) (copy with author) 4.

one considers the phrasing of the Recommendation. Certainly, the Recommendation envisages the expansion of the Convention to encompass additional categories of refugees not provided for by the terms of Article 1A(2).[71] Its wording makes clear that what is imagined is not a complementary status for such categories, but rather that the terms of the Convention itself would be extended by the General Assembly.[72] It expressed

> the hope that the Convention relating to the Status of Refugees will have value as an example *exceeding its contractual scope* and that all nations will be guided by it in *granting* so far as possible to persons in their territory *as refugees* and who would not be covered by the terms of the Convention, *the treatment for which it provides* (emphasis added).

Read in this way, the Recommendation is a most useful guiding principle in the complementary protection debate. Though aspirational, rather than articulating a firm legal duty, the Recommendation helps to counter claims that the Convention is too restrictive to absorb the additional groups of refugees covered by complementary protection sources, or that the Convention was not intended to apply to additional groups. This interpretation is reinforced by an earlier version of the text, which was originally proposed as part of the Preamble to the Convention:

> Expressing the hope finally that this Convention will be regarded as having value as an example exceeding its contractual scope, and that without prejudice to any recommendations the General Assembly may be led to make in order to invite the High Contracting Parties to extend to other categories of persons the benefits of this Convention, all nations will be guided by it in granting to persons who might come to be present in their territory in the capacity of refugees and who would not be covered by the following provisions, *treatment affording the same rights and advantages* (emphasis added).[73]

Recommendation E is important in two respects. First, with respect to eligibility, it encourages the extension of protection to individuals not encompassed by the Convention definition of a refugee. Secondly, with respect to substantive rights, it envisages the application of the Convention framework to persons covered by extended eligibility, tacitly

[71] Conference of Plenipotentiaries on the Status of Refugees and Stateless Persons, '35th Meeting' (n 69 above) 44. In 1966, it was observed that Recommendation E of the Final Act had encouraged States to 'frequently accord the treatment provided for in the Convention to persons not falling within its terms': Proposed Measures to Extend the Personal Scope of the Convention relating to the Status of Refugees of 28 July 1951 (Submitted by the High Commissioner in Accordance with para 5(b) of UNGA Res 1166 (XII) of 26 November 1957) (12 October 1966) UN Doc A/AC.96/346 para 2.

[72] 'Comments on the Draft Convention and Protocol: General Observations' (n 49 above) 34.

[73] Conference of Plenipotentiaries on the Status of Refugees and Stateless Persons, 'Texts of the Draft Convention and the Draft Protocol to be Considered by the Conference' UN Doc A/CONF.2/1 (12 March 1951) 2–3.

recognising that the source of the harm causing flight is irrelevant for the purposes of status. This is, in fact, the position adopted in the 1969 OAU Convention, which, as a regional complement to the Refugee Convention, applies Convention rights to persons fleeing external aggression, occupation, foreign domination or events seriously disturbing public order in part or the whole of the country of origin.[74] This is very significant in light of EU developments, where subsidiary protection status instead results in a lower form of rights than Convention status. The Recommendation supports the argument that there is no justification for creating two levels of rights simply by distinguishing between the source of harm (or the legal basis for protection).

The Hungarian refugee crisis of 1956 provided the first real challenge to the Article 1A(2) definition, and reflects the first example of widespread Refugee Convention-related complementary protection.[75] The refugees did not strictly fall within the temporal requirements of the Convention definition, however the High Commissioner determined that since the flight of Hungarian refugees was related to recent events and political changes resulting from the end of the Second World War, they should be considered as falling within the Convention's scope.[76] Austria followed this interpretation when it granted asylum to 180,000 Hungarian refugees.[77] It issued them with normal refugee eligibility certificates as soon as technically possible, unless individual status determination showed that a person was not entitled to the Convention's benefits.

Most other States granted protection on a prima facie basis, at least initially.[78] Norway granted all Hungarian citizens a residence permit for one year that included permission to work, renewed automatically on request. After two years, they could request a permanent residence permit, which was mostly granted. It was only at this point that individual status determination took place.[79] The distinction between Hungarian refugees and Convention refugees in Norway lay in the grant of travel documents. If an individual had not left Hungary for an Article 1A(2) reason, then he or she was not entitled to a Convention travel document but to an alien's passport. In reality, this did not have a substantial impact on the rights received.

[74] OAU Convention (n 43 above) Art 1(2).

[75] Earlier instances of complementary protection can be found in relation to League of Nations instruments on refugee protection. See McAdam (n 5 above) 23–28.

[76] UNHCR, 'The Problem of Hungarian Refugees in Austria' UN Doc A/AC.79/49 (17 January 1957) Annex IV, para 4.

[77] *Ibid*.

[78] *Ibid*, para 5.

[79] Letter from A Fjellbu (Norwegian Refugee Council) to P Weis (1 July 1959), in UNHCR Archives Fonds 11 Sub-fonds 1, 6/1/HUN.

The United Kingdom did not have a special eligibility procedure for Hungarian refugees but granted them the same rights as Convention refugees. As in Norway, the only distinction was with respect to travel documents. In Germany, they were subject to a simplified eligibility procedure for recognition as Convention refugees and received Convention rights, including Convention travel documents.

A 1956 Resolution on Hungarian Refugees of the Consultative Assembly of the Council of Europe requested all Member States

> to accord to all of them who are able to work the facilities available under the system established by the Statute relating to refugees and provided for under the Geneva Convention of 1951.[80]

A memo by Paul Weis the following year revealed that

> [o]n the whole … no Government has, as far as we know, raised any objection to the application of the Convention to Hungarian refugees who otherwise fulfill the conditions of Article 1 of the Convention and it can, therefore, be assumed that the interpretation of the dateline of 1 January 1951 contained in Document A/AC.79/49 Annex IV is accepted by Governments parties to the Convention.[81]

Of course, it cannot be overlooked that the policy of declaring every Hungarian to be a refugee 'suited the ideological and racial preferences of western powers'[82]—Europeans fleeing Communism. Yet, in a sense, Recommendation E reflects an optimal system of complementary protection, operating more as a theoretical concept guiding the expansion of international protection within a broadened refugee law framework, than as a separately defined system of protection (as has been created in the EU). Although from a pragmatic perspective, some form of codified complementary protection would seem necessary for States to acknowledge and fulfil their international obligations,[83] the international law regime in principle already contains sufficient safeguards.[84]

[80] Resolution adopted by the Committee on Population and Refugees (Vienna, 15 October 1956) COE Doc 587, adopted with certain amendments by Permanent Commission (Paris, 19 November 1956) acting for Consultative Assembly between sessions, in Interoffice Memorandum to Mr M Pagès, Director from P Weis, 'Eligibility of Refugees from Hungary' (9 January 1957) 22/1/HUNG, para 3 in UNHCR Archives Fonds 11 Sub-fonds 1, 6/1/HUN.

[81] Memo from P Weis to Mr J Mersch, UNHCR Branch Office in Luxembourg, 'Application of 1951 Convention to Hungarian Refugees' (28 May 1957) Ref.G.XV.7/1/8, 6/1/HUN, para 3, in UNHCR Archives Fonds 11 Sub-fonds 1, 6/1/HUN.

[82] Independent Commission on International Humanitarian Issues, *Refugees: The Dynamics of Displacement* (London, 1986) 33, cited in G Melander, 'The Two Refugee Definitions' Raoul Wallenberg Institute of Human Rights and Humanitarian Law, *Report No 4* (Lund, 1987) 14.

[83] This is the view expressed in Storey and others (n 70 above) 14.

[84] For subsequent State practice, see, eg Perluss and Hartman (n 8 above); and Goodwin-Gill (n 8 above).

V. 'COMPLEMENTARY' VERSUS 'SUBSIDIARY': A FINAL WORD

Though the term 'subsidiary protection' is largely descriptive, it may also have some weak normative significance. UNHCR has criticised States' increasing use of subsidiary forms of protection as a means of restricting asylum 'on their own terms', arguing that subsidiary protection implies less binding obligations on States than their obligations under international law.[85] It can be seen as an attempt to remove the entitlements of protected persons beyond the reach of international scrutiny. There is a danger of soft law edging out hard law obligations by 'diluting principles and fudging standards'.[86]

In December 2001, representatives of the Contracting States to the Convention adopted a Declaration

> [r]ecognizing the enduring importance of the 1951 Convention, as the primary refugee protection instrument which, as amended by its 1967 Protocol, sets out rights, including human rights, and minimum standards of treatment that apply to persons falling within its scope.[87]

UNHCR has repeatedly called for States to respect the primacy of the Convention.[88] In 1994 and 1995, the General Assembly passed two resolutions reiterating

> the importance of ensuring access, for all persons seeking international protection, to fair and efficient procedures for the determination of refugee status *or, as appropriate, to other mechanisms to ensure that persons in need of international protection are identified and granted such protection,* while not diminishing the protection afforded to refugees under the terms of the 1951 Convention, the 1967 Protocol and relevant regional instruments (emphasis added).[89]

Creating a protection hierarchy reflects a very literal interpretation of respect for the Convention's primacy. Simply entrenching the Convention

[85] Executive Committee, 'Summary Record of the 540th Meeting' (Geneva, 7 October 1999) UN Doc A/AC.96/SR.540 (12 October 1999) para 44. The Nordic States' relatively generous complementary protection is counterbalanced by very low recognition rates of Convention refugees. In Denmark, the ratio was approximately one-third Convention refugees to two-thirds de facto refugees: KU Kjær, 'The Abolition of the Danish *De Facto* Concept' (2003) 15 *International Journal of Refugee Law* 254 at 258.

[86] Goodwin-Gill (n 8 above) 914.

[87] Declaration of States Parties to the 1951 Convention and/or its 1967 Protocol relating to the Status of Refugees (Geneva 13 December 2001) UN Doc HCR/MMSP/2001/09 (16 January 2002) preambular paras 2, 4.

[88] Executive Committee, 'Global Consultations on International Protection: Report of the First Meeting in the Third Track (8–9 March 2001) UN Doc A/AC.96/961 (27 June 2002) para 14.

[89] UNGA Res 49/169 (23 December 1994) para 5; UNGA Res 50/152 (21 December 1995) para 5.

as the pinnacle of protection does not engage with the underlying protection principles it reflects, and may in fact undermine its primacy by siphoning refugees into complementary categories. Conceptually, the affirmation of the Convention's primacy is, in effect, a commitment to respect its protection principles and refrain from diluting its scope by developing the law *outside* its boundaries. The Convention's primacy would be better observed if it were recognised as the source of international protection status for all persons protected by *non-refoulement*.

To provide maximum protection, international human rights treaties must not be viewed as discrete, unrelated documents,[90] but as interconnected instruments which together constitute the international obligations to which States have agreed. In effect, therefore, this chapter argues for a reconsideration of international law as a holistic and integrated system. Compartmentalising international law into parallel but autonomous and non-intersecting branches leads not only to stultification, but to ineffectual implementation of the interlocking duties which States have undertaken to respect. Viewing the Convention as a discrete instrument implies that refugee law

> possesse[s] its own special purposes and principles which [are] determined essentially by its own constituent instruments and which [are] thus independent of those of human rights law.[91]

But human rights law contains principles that are explicitly or implicitly applicable to the refugee context,[92] having both influenced and been influenced by it. Human rights law not only provides an additional source of protection for persons with an international protection need, but also strengthens the status accorded to *all* refugees through its universal application. Accordingly, while human rights law widens threshold eligibility for protection, the Convention remains the blueprint for rights and legal status.

If international law already accommodates complementary protection within its existing framework, then why is there no discernable universal system of complementary protection? The problem lies not in international law itself, but rather in States' failure to adequately implement their international legal obligations in a holistic and bona fide manner, combined with a lack of enforcement mechanisms. A benefit of codifying States' complementary protection obligations in a new international instrument would be to clearly elucidate the source and (non-exhaustive) content of those obligations—explicitly drawing the links between States'

[90] On the fragmentation of international law, see, eg the International Law Commission's work (n 4 above), especially on self-contained regimes.

[91] GJL Coles, 'Refugees and Human Rights' (1992) 91 *Bulletin of Human Rights* 63 at 63.

[92] *Ibid*.

general human rights obligations and their specific relevance to the protection context—and to expressly describe the legal status that results from recognition of a protection need on those grounds.

Yet, the dangers of codifying complementary protection have been amply illustrated by the negotiations on the Qualification Directive. They demonstrate that States may seek to dilute their obligations to a minimum level, extrapolating some aspects of existing law but not others, and closing off potential avenues for future protection needs.[93] In the context of setting out fundamental standards of humanity, the Commission on Human Rights has noted that any new instrument may be seen to 'undermine existing international standards ... or pose a risk to existing treaty law',[94] even where such standards are largely a 'repackaging' of existing international law. As such, it is imperative to identify the international legal basis of obligations in any codified complementary protection regime, so that 'soft law' is not used to fudge standards or replace treaty-based obligations.

Although an Executive Committee Conclusion on complementary protection was adopted in October 2005, it does not explicitly address the question of beneficiaries' status. Instead, it contains important but relatively elusive statements calling upon States to

> provide for the highest degree stability and certainty by ensuring the human rights and fundamental freedoms of [beneficiaries of complementary protection] without discrimination,[95]

and affirming that complementary protection should be applied 'in a manner that strengthens, rather than undermines, the existing international refugee protection regime'.[96] Further, it emphasises the importance of applying and developing international protection in a manner that avoids the creation or continuation of protection gaps.[97] However, the Conclusion does not go so far as to expressly call for the equal treatment of Convention refugees and beneficiaries of complementary protection.[98] While this is perhaps not surprising, given the political climate and the results of the EU's recent deliberations about the Qualification Directive,

93 For a comprehensive analysis of the drafting process, see J McAdam, 'The European Union Qualification Directive: The Creation of a Subsidiary Protection Regime' (2005) 17 *International Journal of Refugee Law* 461.

94 'Minimum Humanitarian Standards: Analytical Report of the Secretary-General submitted pursuant to Commission on Human Rights Resolution 1997/21 UN Doc E/CN.4/1998/87' (5 January 1998) para 94.

95 Executive Committee Conclusion No 103 (n 10 above) para (n).

96 *Ibid*, para (k).

97 *Ibid*, para (s).

98 NGO delegations sought to have a statement to this effect included: Draft Conclusion on the Provision of International Protection including through Complementary Forms of Protection' (NGO version, 12 July 2005) OP11 (copy with author).

it perpetuates at the international level an approach tied closely to *domestic* political concerns about asylum seekers, that require national governments to be 'seen' to be distinguishing between 'genuine' (Convention) refugees and 'others'. Yet, as one commentator has poignantly observed:

> In the past forty years the rich first world countries have received so many *de facto* refugees that it would not have made any difference if they had agreed to an expanded international definition … . In fact, it would here have helped clarify and identify those circumstances which were insufficiently clear-cut to merit recognition as refugee-like situations.[99]

By retaining the political discretion to determine to whom, and when, protection will be granted, States have in fact complicated the protection regime. Diverging statuses, different eligibility thresholds and variations between States have created incentives for asylum seekers to forum shop and appeal decisions granting subsidiary status. It is arguably in States' own interests to grant a single legal status based on the Refugee Convention to all persons in need of international protection. In this way, they would acknowledge complementary protection as the natural extra-territorial response to their commitment to uphold and promote respect for human rights. A creative use of human rights law can thus enhance the legal status of refugees and asylum seekers,[100] basing international protection on the individual's *need,* rather than on which treaty provides the legal source of the obligation.

[99] P Nobel, 'Blurred Vision in the Rich World and Violations of Human Rights—A Critical Assessment of the Human Rights and Refugee Linkage' (1992) 91 *Bulletin of Human Rights* 74 at 80.

[100] Goodwin-Gill (n 55 above) 16.

11

The Responsibility to Protect: Closing the Gaps in the International Protection Regime

Closing Address at the *Moving On: Forced Migration and Human Rights* Conference, NSW Parliament House, Sydney, 22 November 2005*

ERIKA FELLER

I UNDERSTAND THERE IS interest at this conference both in complementary forms of protection and the debate on them which took place in October 2005 at UNHCR's Executive Committee meeting, together with the Conclusion it generated.[1] I will cover these issues in my presentation, albeit with a Geneva twist and from a rather different angle. This is because complementary forms of protection do not stand alone. This is not a self-contained issue, but finds its natural home within the broader debate around the notion of the 'responsibility to protect', a key element in the current United Nations reform process. I intend therefore to devote some time also to the broader UN agenda and to protection gaps which this agenda needs to address. It is perhaps a bigger spectrum of issues than those which feature in the Australian debate, but I would certainly recommend that they be given some space in your deliberations, with a view to moving the discussion here forward, in tandem with international thinking.

* Where relevant, examples and figures referred to in this address have been updated to reflect the position as at June 2007.

[1] Executive Committee Conclusion No 103 (LVI), 'The Provision of International Protection including through Complementary Forms of Protection' (2005).

I. ORIGINS OF THE CONCEPT OF THE 'RESPONSIBILITY TO PROTECT'

The origins of the concept of a 'responsibility to protect' are to be found in the debate in the 1990s about humanitarian intervention. At that time, the UN Security Council showed itself willing, in some circumstances at least, to characterise egregious human rights abuses as a threat to international peace and security, thus opening up the possibility of enforcement action under Chapter VII of the UN Charter. The problem was a gap between theory and practice, often with tragic consequences, as the genocidal acts in both Rwanda and Srebrenica showed. In addition, humanitarian intervention was, and remains, a politically charged and divisive concept—a fact which did not contribute to its positive reception or use.

In December 2004, the report of the Secretary-General's High-Level Panel on Threats, Challenges and Change set out its proposals for 'a more secure world'.[2] In it, the panel endorsed what it called 'the emerging norm of a responsibility to protect civilians from large-scale violence'.[3]

In his March 2005 report, *In Larger Freedom*, then UN Secretary-General, Kofi Annan, likewise urged all to 'embrace the responsibility to protect, and, when necessary … act on it'.[4] The concept refers to the responsibilty of States to protect civilians from mass atrocities and crimes against humanity. According to its proponents, it entails reacting in situations where these crimes are occurring or imminent; preventing them from arising; and rebuilding affected societies, with a focus on preventing their recurrence. The challenge is to bridge a widening divide between proponents who emphasise the preventive and capacity-building dimensions, and those who are more interventionist.

It is recognised that this responsibility rests first and foremost with each individual State; however, where a State is unable or unwilling, the international community shares a collective responsibility to act—through, for example, humanitarian operations, monitoring missions, diplomatic pressure and, ultimately, as a last resort, force. In theory, this could go quite some way to redressing root causes of displacement, which from UNHCR's perspective is a positive step. It is also a most useful frame, we believe, within which to promote a more flexible and less discretionary approach to addressing the many protection gaps which, at worst, lead to or manifest themselves in situations involving the sorts of crimes which gave rise to the concept.

[2] Report of the High-Level Panel on Threats, Challenges and Change, *A More Secure World: Our Shared Responsibility*, UN Doc A/59/565 (2 December 2004). See also the earlier report of the International Commission on Intervention and State Sovereignty, *The Responsibility to Protect* (December 2001), and also UNHCR, 'Note on International Protection' UN Doc A/AC.96/1008 (4 July 2005) paras 35, 72.

[3] Report of the High-Level Panel (n 2 above) 'Executive Summary' 7.

[4] Report of the Secretary-General, *In Larger Freedom: Towards Development, Security and Human Rights for All* UN Doc A/59/2005 (21 March 2005) para 135.

II. LINKS TO OTHER ISSUES

Human insecurity and displacement are products of war, other forms of conflict and human rights violations. There are, though, other causes as well. As the UN Summit in September 2005 (and all that preceded it) made patently clear, there can be no real human security (incidentally another concept much in vogue) without there being progress in tackling other interlinked issues—poverty, disparities between rich and poor peoples and nations, migration push-and-pull factors, and environmental issues, among many others.

III. BACKGROUND TO THE 2005 EXECUTIVE COMMITTEE CONCLUSION ON COMPLEMENTARY PROTECTION

Of course, all these broader concerns extend way beyond UNHCR's directly mandated responsibilities. Nevertheless, as the world becomes ever more unequal, as inequalities in political power and resources, such as land, provoke social disintegration or exclusion in many countries, violence, forcible loss of nationality and displacement result. And gaps in protection, along with the need for protection, materialise together.

The significance of the concept of a 'responsibility to protect' is that it does not rest on mandates, or indeed on international treaties. It entails the sovereign responsibility of individual States to protect their own citizens and to help other States to do so, together with international organisations. Furthermore, it comes into play in response to needs. As a mission to tsunami-devastated regions in early 2005 drove home to me, displacement, regardless of its causes, produces protection problems which are quite similar. We are seeing this again in Pakistan. It is beyond doubt that sexual and gender violence concerns, vulnerability of children to abuse, or legal property concerns (to take some random protection issues) are not restricted to refugees and asylum seekers. The protection situation may be equally acute for an earthquake victim in Pakistan, for an internally displaced person ('IDP') in Sudan, or for a victim of trafficking in Eastern Europe.

This being said, there are still rules of engagement to respect, which, as the International Commission on Intervention and State Sovereignty indicated in its 2001 report,[5] give rise to complex questions of eligibility, legitimacy, sovereignty, political will and mandates, all of which need to be reviewed as we move to give this new responsibility concrete operational content.

At this point, you are probably wondering what this has to do with complementary protection and UNHCR's Executive Committee. The short answer to this question is that we decided to see how far the soft

[5] *The Responsibility to Protect* (n 2 above).

side of the notion of '*responsibility* to protect' could be brought into play in relation to groups of concern to us. We wanted to provoke a discussion outside the letter of Refugee Convention responsibilities and the constraints of mandates,[6] but which focused on protection gaps and how they might be bridged. We knew in so doing that we were coming at the question of complementary forms of protection from a rather non-traditional angle. The traditional approach has been a more technical one, centred on identifying the minimum components of this alternative form of protection, how procedurally it might be brought into play, and how to make it compatible with other forms of available protection, notably refugee protection. These have all been well discussed and documented, including during the Global Consultations on International Protection, which we ran with States from 2001–02. At the 2005 meeting of the Executive Committee, we decided to try to encourage States to look beyond technical issues of procedures and status, and examine the adjustments necessary in the global protection regime to ensure that there are no groups which fall through the cracks, that there are no gaps, if you like—in other words, to use only the notion of the 'responsibility to protect' also to further the protection of persons of concern to UNHCR, in the expectation that this would contribute materially to preventing the occurrence of situations more traditionally subsumed wider the notion.

So, where are the gaps necessitating a reinforced international response?

IV. INTERNALLY DISPLACED PERSONS

There are an estimated 25 million IDPs globally, far outnumbering the world's 9.2 million refugees.[7] Their access to protection and assistance has been seriously impeded both by the absence of an agreed and implemented international law framework to guarantee access, and by the fact that no single international organisation has the mandate to intervene on their behalf. This has in fact now been recognised as a serious gap in the international protection system, necessitating a range of activities to fill it. The 1998 Guiding Principles on Internal Displacement, which purport to set out the basic normative framework, were a first step.[8]

At the institutional level, there has also been tentative progress with making the UN response more 'collaborative'. UNHCR sees promise

[6] See the Convention relating to the Status of Refugees (adopted 28 July 1951, entered into force 22 April 1954) 189 UNTS 137; Protocol relating to the Status of Refugees (adopted 31 January 1967, entered into force 4 October 1967) 606 UNTS 267; and the Statute of the Office of the United Nations High Commissioner for Refugees UNGA Res 428 (V) of 14 December 1950.

[7] See generally <http://www.unhcr.org/statistics.html> (accessed 15 June 2007).

[8] *Guiding Principles on Internal Displacement*, UN Doc CN.4/1998/53/Add.2 (11 February 1998). Since late 2005, UNHCR has been the lead agency for the protection and assistance of IDPs, and for co-ordinating and managing any IDP camps that are established.

in the model for collaboration being developed, which is built around so-called 'clusters' of activities, and has indicated its preparedness to co-ordinate the protection, camp management and emergency shelter clusters, albeit in situations of internal displacement caused by conflict (rather than those caused by natural disasters). We have, though, made clear that our co-operation is subject to some caveats, notably that whatever we do cannot be at the expense of the right to seek asylum and our work for refugees.

What all this represents, in the context of my presentation today, is some real progress towards closing the protection gap for IDPs. We are, though, still at the beginning here. There are complex issues still to resolve, one being whether it will always be realistic to build protection around categories of people. More specifically, the question being asked is whether it is artificial, in a complex emergency, to make a distinction between persons actually displaced and the broader population of the country, which may well be just as vulnerable. This is illustrated well, perhaps, by the situation in the eastern provinces of the Democratic Republic of Congo—one of the countries where the new 'cluster' approach has been piloted. It is exceedingly difficult there to distinguish between IDPs and the population at large. Humanitarian access is lacking, the population as a whole faces constant harassment by armed elements, sexual and gender-based violence is rife, there is no rule of law, and corruption is everywhere endemic and rampant. In these circumstances, should international responsibilities begin and end with IDPs only?

V. STATELESS PEOPLE

Amongst the various groups of non-citizens with protection needs that are not being met, stateless people figure significantly. In spite of the fact that the basic human rights as set out in the principle covenants[9] have been recognised as

> not limited to citizens of States Parties but must also be available to all individuals, regardless of nationality or statelessness … who may find themselves in the territory or subject to the jurisdiction of the State Party

the reality is very different from this fine pronouncement of the Human Rights Committee.[10] Stateless people, in particular, are the 'forgotten problem' as far as a responsibility to protect is concerned. This is one

[9] See, eg the International Covenant on Civil and Political Rights (adopted 16 Dec 1966, entered into force 23 March 1976) 999 UNTS 171; and the International Covenant on Economic, Social and Cultural Rights (adopted 16 December 1966, entered into force 3 January 1976) 993 UNTS 3.

[10] Human Rights Committee, 'General Comment 31 on Article 2 of the Covenant: The Nature of the General Legal Obligation Imposed on States Parties to the Covenant' (29 March 2004) UN Doc CCPR/C/21/Rev.1/Add.13 (26 May 2004) para 10.

group which, although covered legally, is seriously victimised as a result of gaps in commitments and response. The size of the problem is not mapped, there are international norms but only limited subscription to them, and UNHCR's mandate for stateless people, albeit of long standing, is still having to confront a climate of scepticism—even non-acceptance—on the part of important States.

For the millions of stateless people around the world, lack of nationality means they face countless problems realising their most basic rights. Imagine that you have no nationality. You cannot obtain the identity documents that are increasingly necessary simply to go about everyday life. You cannot register your children when they are born. You cannot own property or go to school. You cannot travel abroad or sometimes even within the country where you reside. In many ways, you simply do not exist.

Whether the cause is the dismantlement of empires, federations as well as the separation of States, lack of proper registration at birth, gender discrimination or conflicting citizenship laws, the result is that an estimated 9 to 11 million people are trapped in this limbo.

The international legal framework is there in the shape of the 1954 Convention on Statelessness and the 1961 Convention of the Reduction of Statelessness,[11] but there are still only 62 States parties to the former and 33 to the latter.[12] When compared to the number of parties to the Refugee Convention and its Protocol (now at 147—with the recent succession of Montenegro in October 2006[13]) it is clear that wider accession remains an important aspiration. There are so many seemingly simple achievements which remain elusive: birth registration procedures being in place in all States, for example, or ensuring equal access of women, like men, to an effective nationality. Resolving statelessness situations, particularly those which are protracted, requires comprehensive strategies, but also, as importantly, political will which has hitherto been absent.

UNHCR recently launched a handbook in association with the Inter-Parliamentary Union to raise awareness on the issue.[14] We hope it will prove a useful tool to address protracted statelessness situations and encourage States to find ways to end them.

[11] Convention relating to the Status of Stateless Persons (adopted 28 September 1954, entered into force 6 June 1960) 360 UNTS 117; Convention on the Reduction of Statelessness (adopted 30 August 1961, entered into force 13 December 1975) 989 UNTS 175.

[12] United Nations Treaty Collection database <http://untreaty.un.org/English/access.asp> (accessed 28 June 2007).

[13] UNHCR, *States Parties to the 1951 Convention relating to the Status of Refugees and the 1967 Protocol* (as at 1 December 2006) <http://www.unhcr.org/protect/PROTECTION/3b73b0d63.pdf> (accessed 4 June 2007).

[14] UNHCR and Inter-Parliamentary Union, *Nationality and Statelessness: A Handbook for Parliamentarians* (2005).

VI. REFUGEES

With this category of persons, the gaps are, perhaps, at least better known and documented. The protection gap is not really a normative one. Rather, it stems from inadequate adherence to proper practices, and implementation deficits as regards the principles.

At the heart of these problems are misconceptions, deliberate or otherwise, which have come into play not least because refugee and asylum issues are now so deeply mired in the broader issues of international security, irregular migration, transnational law and order, and crime. Today, asylum seekers are repeatedly mischaracterised as criminals, 'possible terrorists' or illegal migrants whose presence is to be managed as a matter of border and crime control, and whose protection needs are a secondary issue. With a taint of illegality, abusive behaviour or criminality hanging increasingly over asylum seekers, perceptions about which are genuine refugees, and what is the nature of the refugee problem, have also started to change.

How a problem is characterised can be very significant to how it is managed. To put it simplistically, to see the refugee problem as an issue of human rights creates protection space. To see it as essentially an immigration issue works often to deny protection to those in need. The mischaracterisation of the issue, particularly in the developed world, has contributed to a serious reduction here in the rights accessible by refugees and the responsibilities to them which States are prepared to acknowledge.

Protection gaps result, which UNHCR has sought to address through initiatives to reinstate the centrality of international refugee law, encourage its flexible interpretation, but also to locate the principles in their modern context so that they cannot be swept so easily aside as somehow outdated or irrelevant. We have also co-operated in efforts to devise new tools to manage problems of a mixed character, so that refugees, who may—indeed do—arrive side-by-side with irregular, would-be migrants, or excludable persons of dubious background, are identified and lifted out of the system of complex barriers to entry. We have also actively promoted the appropriate use of complementary forms of protection, to which I will shortly return. Our participation in the Bali Process and the Asia-Pacific Consultations on Asylum and Migration are regional examples of efforts to work with States to help manage mixed movements of migrants and asylum seekers better in this region.

If I have focused on the protection gaps for refugees who somehow manage to make their way to chosen destination countries, it is because this has particular relevance for today's audience here in Australia. There is also, however, a whole other side to refugee protection where it is undertaken in the developing world—in countries of first asylum. Here, more often than not, we are talking of large-scale arrivals, insecure camp hosting environments, under-funded programmes and protracted stay. The gaps in protection are, as a result, many. UNHCR is currently piloting a new approach to gap-identification, consensus-building and programme delivery, which we sincerely hope will assist us to improve the quality of protection and the accessibility of solutions closer to the point at which the need first arises, and before it becomes acute.

VII. RETURNEES

There are also protection gaps for refugees who return voluntarily to their home countries. These lie very much in inadequate follow-up to ensure that return is sustainable over the longer term. Follow-up of this sort has fallen victim to lack of funding—lower priority being accorded to returnee programmes—and mandate gaps between different agencies. Refugees often return in less than ideal conditions to situations of only partially resolved conflict and to places ill-suited to their reintegration due to a range of political and economic impediments. UNHCR has placed considerable emphasis over recent times on programmes in the area of transitional justice and reconciliation of communities, and on managing the relief-to-development continuum, including through encouraging investment in return through development aid.

We have urged donor countries to spend a share of development aid on durable solutions for returnees and the communities to which they return in post-conflict situations, through a '4Rs' programme focused on Repatriation, Reintegration, Rehabilitation and Reconstruction. And we have urged countries of origin to implement the 4Rs by systematically incorporating measures conducive to the sustainable return of refugees in national development plans and poverty reduction strategies. UNHCR has also been working with the UN system to strengthen links with development agencies.

For us the links are clear, even if, unfortunately, many States and some development agencies remain to be convinced.

VIII. THE EXECUTIVE COMMITTEE CONCLUSION ON COMPLEMENTARY PROTECTION

Up to this point, I have been talking of the bigger picture. Complementary protection regimes are certainly part of it, whether they take the form of visa arrangements (specifically provided for in legislation, which extend protection coverage to defined categories of persons, who, for whatever reason, are held to fall outside the Refugee Convention); whether they derive from human rights treaty responsibilities; or whether they flow from discretionary and time-limited protection arrangements for particular situations.

The issue of complementary protection had not been one that the Executive Committee had been ready to address through a Conclusion in the past. Hence, the approval of the 2005 Conclusion was in itself a step forward. The overall aims of the Conclusion, from our point of view, were twofold:

(a) to conceptualise complementary forms of protection within a multidimensional global regime for international protection—including, importantly, to position complementary protection as part of the 'responsibility to protect'; and
(b) to promote greater harmonisation and complementarity in State practice.

More specifically, we hoped that States would agree with us on four propositions:

(a) that protection needs to be provided and the global system developed in a way that leaves no gaps;
(b) that States make maximum and flexible use of existing instruments, notably the Refugee Convention, before resorting to more discretionary forms of status;
(c) that where status of whatever sort is being considered, protection needs are prioritised as a key consideration, even when there may be others; and
(d) that UNHCR is accepted as a credible and legitimate consultative partner on all forms of international protection.

We were also hopeful that States might see the wisdom of a single procedure to house all the various forms of complementary status.

I cannot say that we were totally successful in achieving our aims, but the Conclusion was at least a good start. The debate generated broad agreement that the international protection system has to be developed in a way which avoids protection gaps, and that complementary protection may be a practical way to address protection needs not covered by existing instruments. The process of negotiation led to some timely reaffirmations, including of the centrality of the Refugee Convention in the international protection regime.[15]

Of course, like outcomes from any multilateral process, Executive Committee Conclusions are the result of negotiation, trade-offs and compromise. No agreement was possible on more detailed issues, such as the criteria for granting or ending complementary protection. The debate revealed very diverse perceptions and practice as to the scope of this

[15] Executive Committee Conclusion No 103 (n 1 above) Preamble.

protection, particularly for people fleeing indiscriminate and generalised violence. Some States clearly preferred to confine their obligations to persons falling within the Refugee Convention, together with those facing return to torture as defined in the 1984 Convention against Torture.[16] As to persons fleeing violence, there was a wide gulf between those States which extend refugee status in a more flexible manner, and those which acknowledge no obligations going beyond those accepted through an exercise of sovereign discretion.

On the content of complementary protection regimes, the diversity of opinion was also marked. States took widely differing positions on the rights to be afforded, ranging from nothing more than protection against *refoulement*, through to enjoyment of all the rights normally afforded to refugees. Areas of particular divergence included legal residence status, identity or travel documents, and/or rights to family reunification. There were also wide differences apparent in procedures followed to accord complementary protection.

In short, there was not sufficient common ground to enable a Conclusion going beyond quite broad generalities. The nature of the debate at the Executive Committee meeting clearly demonstrated that we are some way off translating into action the theory of a responsibility to protect. There is a strong reluctance to give a proper place to needs and gap-filling as important determinants.

IX. CONCLUSION

Finally, let us reflect briefly on how these international developments might relate to the situation in Australia. In recent times we have seen a number of pragmatic steps in the direction of recognising a 'responsibility to protect', together with important instances of gap-filling, even if the government remains wary about referring to them as complementary forms of protection. Here I am referring to the on-going public interest powers of the Minister for Immigration to grant visas (such as the temporary Safe Haven Visas for Kosovars in 1999 and equivalent Safe Haven Visas for East Timorese in the same year); the more recent Return Pending Visa (2004) and Removal Pending Bridging Visa (2005); and even the temporary humanitarian visas given to people recently arrived from Nauru, all of which have a different range of rights and benefits attached.

In Australia, the starting point seems to have been sovereignty and ministerial discretion, exercised in accordance with the demands of

[16] Convention against Torture and Other Cruel, Inhuman or Degrading Treatment or Punishment (adopted 10 December 1984, entered into force 26 June 1987) 1465 UNTS 85, Art 1.

national interest. It remains our hope, as we demonstrated at the 2005 Executive Committee meeting, that States will be able to move beyond the sovereignty/discretion approach, and put in place a system which integrates the various available forms of protection, expedites the process of their consideration, and achieves a situation where people with genuine needs do not fall through the cracks. This is not only important from the protection perspective, but it makes good, cost effective, common sense. We accept—and as the Executive Committee debate brought out—that the challenge is to do this without compromising national interests. We are not suggesting that it is the responsibility of all States to take all people who present themselves as having protection needs. Rather, the challenge is to recognise that addressing these needs is a collective responsibility—flowing from the 'responsibility to protect'—and for States to find innovative ways to do this, of which there are a number of possibilities. Setting up a complementary protection regime for arrivals is just one of these possibilities.

X. POSTSCRIPT

Since this speech was delivered in November 2005, the 'responsibility to protect' theme was chosen for the 2006 Note on International Protection to UNHCR's Executive Committee's 57th session from 2–6 October 2006 in Geneva.[17] This now official General Assembly document provides an update on UNHCR's evolving thinking on this concept. It is available on UNHCR's website at <www.unhcr.org/excom>.

[17] UNHCR, 'Note on International Protection' UN Doc A/AC.96/1024 (12 July 2006).

Index

Introductory Note

References such as '178–9' indicate (not necessarily continuous) discussion of a topic across a range of pages, while '60n195' indicates note 195 on page 60 and '60nn' multiple notes on page 60. Wherever possible in the case of topics with many references, these have either been divided into sub-topics or the most significant discussions of the topic are indicated by page numbers in bold. Because the entire volume is about human rights and refugees, and certain other terms occur constantly throughout the work (notably UNHCR as the key institutional player in this field), the use of these terms as entry points has been minimised. Information will be found under the corresponding detailed topics.